THE SPOKEN CABALA

Tarot Explorations of the One Self

by

JASON C. LOTTERHAND

Edited by Arisa Victor

 Fraternity of the Hidden Light
2009

Copyright © 2010 by Arisa Victor
All Rights Reserved

ISBN 978-0-9818977-4-5

No part of this book may be reproduced in any form without the express written consent of the publisher, except by a reviewer, who may quote brief passages in connection with a review.

Spoken Text by Jason C. Lotterhand
Edited by Arisa Victor
Additional Editings by Ed Buryn and Douglas Menville
Cover/Book Design by Arisa Victor

Grateful acknowledgment is made to Builders of the Adytum, Ltd., 5101-01 North Figueroa Street, Los Angeles, California 90042, for permission to use the following

The twenty-two Major Arcana Tarot Keys
The Pattern on the Trestleboard
The Tarot Tableau
Sound and Color Attributions from Highlights of Tarot by Dr. Paul Foster Case

The permission granted for the use of its materials by Builders of the Adytum, Ltd. In no way endorses anyone's interpretation thereof.

FIRST EDITION
Thursday Night Tarot; The Weekly Talks on the Wisdom of the Major Arcana by Jason C. Lotterhand, who lives as he speaks, simply. Edited by Arisa Victor.
Newcastle Publishing, Inc. 1989.
ISBN 0-87877-147-6

SECOND EDITION
The Spoken Cabala: Tarot Explorations of the One Self
Author: Jason C. Lotterhand. Edited by Arisa Victor
The Editor has asserted the right to be identified as the Editor of this Work
ISBN 978-0-9818977-8-9

Published by the FRATERNITY OF THE HIDDEN LIGHT
First Printing, March 2010
Printed in the United States of America

The Fraternity of the Hidden Light is a world-wide organization working according to the Pattern of the True and Invisible Rosicrucian Order with Lodges, Pronaoi, and Study Groups in major cities around the globe.

Please visit our website at www.lvx.org for a location near you.

Table of Contents
Second Edition

Editor's Notes to the Second Edition	b
Acknowledgements	e
Explanations	g
Reminiscing With An Old Philosopher	l
Photos	aa
The Thursday Night Tarot – First Edition	ix

Editor's Notes to the Second Edition

Jason C. Lotterhand's Tarot class in San Francisco began in 1950, migrated through five different venues, and ended with his retirement in 1992. For fifteen of those years, his words were recorded, compiled, transcribed, and edited in order to create this book. During that collaboration, the working title of Jason's book was *The Spoken Cabala*, a name created by both of us.

The first publisher understandably wanted the word "Tarot" in the title, so he changed the name to *The Thursday Night Tarot*. With restoration of the original title, "Tarot" now appears in the subtitle, *Tarot Explorations of the One Self*. Plus, the whole Tarot Tableau of twenty-two Major Arcana Keys appears on the cover, so nobody can miss the connection between Tarot and Cabala. This second edition comes to you by the kind sponsorship of Paul A. Clark, Steward of the Fraternitas Lux Occulta (FLO), translated as Fraternity of the Hidden Light.

The first edition was published as *The Thursday Night Tarot* in 1989 by Al Saunders of Newcastle Publishing Co. This press offered many Tarot titles, among them *Tarot for Yourself* by Mary K. Greer. Mary was a fan of Jason's teachings. Her endorsement appears on the cover of the first edition of his book: "Words of truth that go to the heart; a must-read for all seekers."

Because of Ms. Greer's recommendation, Newcastle was waiting for the manuscript of Jason's book when it was completed. There was no need to go looking for a publisher. This current edition was honored by a similar occurrence. The FLO contacted me out of the blue shortly before the first edition went out of print, at which time the publishing rights (and naming rights) would legally revert to the editor. The second edition was a blessing waiting to happen.

Back in 1974, when I first asked the modest Mr. Lotterhand if I could create a book of his teachings, he said, "I don't know if anybody would want to read that." Well, as time has proven, "His combination of humor and deep insight is irresistible." - Gary Ross, then editor of *The Tarot Network News*. This volume is exactly the same as the first, with the addition of a 1989 *Tarot Network News* interview with Jason, several photos of Jason and friends, and these notes. And, of course, the new cover and renewed title.

Photographs were culled from the collections of Silma Smith, Buddy Born, Bruce Nevin, and Arisa Victor. They were taken so long ago that dates, or names of photographers and participants, cannot be ascertained. You can see we had a lot of fun together. We all knew we were extremely lucky to have a teacher who was "the real deal." May this new edition of timeless truth reach a new readership, and continue Jason's light-filled legacy.

A note on Jason's choice of the spelling of Cabala: This word is a transliteration from Hebrew characters, so there is no one "right" way to spell it. Different viewpoints hold varying opinions and definitions. Briefly, Jason speaks to the "common person." He does not teach anything strange or secret. In fact, he tries his best to *reveal* occult (hidden) information. The ideas expressed in the Cabala apply to every human being; they are not the property of any school or religion. In ages past these empowering teachings were kept secret to avoid persecution from church and state. Today, with the dawning of the Age of Aquarius, the eternal philosophy of the universal Cabala is available to everyone without exception. This spelling of Cabala is the only one to be found in English dictionaries, making the word accessible to all. Jason equates "Cabala" with "Ageless Wisdom."

As with many sacred mystery traditions, wisdom has always been transmitted "from mouth to ear." Words spoken by the master have great spiritual power. Not really knowing why, except that I just wanted to go, I always went to class every Thursday for twenty years. No matter if I was sick. I would always feel better afterwards, and drive home across the Bay Bridge singing in my car. When he retired, Jason passed his class along to me. Six years later I "got the word" to pass it on to Tanya Joyce. Now, I am thrilled to have this opportunity to pass Jason's spoken magic along to you, the reader.

Our beloved teacher transitioned to the Inner Planes on January 18, 1997, a few days after his 86th birthday. He had not wanted a public memorial, so our group gathered at the restaurant near Fort Mason where we had always gone to socialize after class. It had been raining earlier that day, but the showers had stopped. To our utter amazement, over the building where we had met for class, a gorgeous big rainbow appeared in the clear blue sky. Thank you, Jason!

Truth and Beauty, Love and Joy (Jason's mantra) –

Arisa Victor, editor
DBA Granny Rainbow
San Rafael, California
June 2009

Acknowledgements

The editor wishes to thank all the Taroteers who comprised Jason's spiritual family. A big wreath of special gold stars goes to Tanya Joyce, who teaches the Thursday Night Tarot class in San Francisco to this day. Thanks to Silma Smith, Buddy Born, and Bruce Nevin for contributing photos, and to Bruce for all the expert scanning. Thanks to Don Nicodemus for finding that contract. Thanks to Mike Weiner, who persistently suggested that this book be reprinted with its true name. Thanks to Crista Mercuria Artos for spiritual support, and to Da Vid Raphael for believing in me. For the big check, thanks goes to Anna Ruth Uelsmann Kipping, Richard Jerome Bennett, and Barbara Occhiogrosso, hosts of The Thursday Night Tarot in the twenty-first century.

Deepest gratitude to Paul A. Clark, Steward of the FLO, for publishing this renewed version of Jason's book. And to Shirley Ronkowski and Tony DeLuce for finding me. Extra love to Shirley for masterfully supervising the publishing process. Heartfelt thanks to Rob Calef of the Open Secret Bookstore for sponsoring my Tarot and Astrology readings and classes for the last 10 years.

As always, thanks to my amazing family, Patrick, Sharon, Sarah and Benjamin Jelinsky, for untold hours of moral and computer support. Thanks also to Sarah Shockley and Conner Jensen for our convivial Photoshop tea parties. For legal assistance, thanks to Jerome N. Field and Brenda Cariati. And thanks to Ilona Marshall Braden for sharing the use of her home and computer while I was working on this second edition of Jason's book. Finally, Mother Earth has my complete devotion; I also offer glad appreciation for her Ascension process, which has inspired me since I first heard about the New Age at the time of my first Saturn Return.

The Builders of the Adytum Mystery School of Sacred Tarot and Holy Qabalah is to be commended for carrying on the work of Jason's teacher, Paul Foster Case, for so many years. At one time, Jason was one of the Directors of that worthy organization. The

BOTA disseminates Lessons in spiritual occultism written by Dr. Case, and publishes his books, Tarot deck, and the Tarot Tableau that appears in this book.

Explanations

Using pencils and Photoshop, I colored the Tableau of Major Arcana Tarot Keys that appears on the cover of *The Spoken Cabala: Tarot Explorations of the One Self*. I was tempted to paint the skin tones black, yellow, reddish, and brown as well as pale, but did not for two reasons.

Reason 1) The people's features are still European. In England, in 1910, Pamela Coleman Smith originally created most of these images for the deck authored by Arthur Edward Waite. This was the first Tarot deck to have a different scene on each of the 78 cards; it became the root deck that inspired many other Tarot artists. The Waite/Smith Major Arcana cards were re-drawn (mostly copied) by Jesse Burns Parke for the BOTA in America, thus creating the Case/Parke cards. So the people look English. If it had been created in Africa, the people would look African, and so on. In other words, the skin coloring is ethnically correct AND you may visualize the people however you wish!

Reason 2) From day one, students of these teachings are instructed to *identify* with the characters shown in the Tableau. Each Key illustrates an aspect of the One Self. You are in no way separate from the Self, *your* Self. Each person is a piece of the cosmic puzzle, necessary to the whole. So please see your face on each of the "Gods and Goddesses" in this book.

Now for notes on the other Tableau colors. According to the spiritual science discovered by Paul Foster Case, each Major Key has an astrological correlation to either a planet or a zodiacal sign. I call this the rainbow zodiac because the astrological colors progress through the color wheel, in the same order as colors in a rainbow.

The Zodiac Signs

The Emperor/Aries / red
Hierophant/Taurus/red-orange
Lovers/Gemini/orange
Chariot/Cancer/yellow-orange
Strength/Leo/yellow
Hermit/Virgo/yellow-green

Justice/Libra/green
Death/Scorpio/blue-green
Temperance/Sagittarius/blue
Devil/Capricorn/blue-violet (indigo)
Star/Aquarius/violet (purple)
Moon/Pisces/red-violet

The Planets

Sun/Sun/orange,
High Priestess/Moon/blue,
Magician/Mercury/yellow
Empress/Venus/green
Tower/Mars/red
Wheel of Fortune/Jupiter/violet (purple)

Wheel of Fortune/Jupiter/violet (purple)
World/Saturn/blue-violet (indigo or black)
Fool/Uranus/yellow
Hanged Man/Neptune/blue
Judgment/Pluto/red.

The elements are: fire/red, water/blue, air/yellow, and earth/black – or else, earth is the multi-colored container of the other three elements.

If you have colored pencils and the inclination to color this diagram, your efforts will be rewarded by a deeper grasp of the spiritual science currently under discussion.

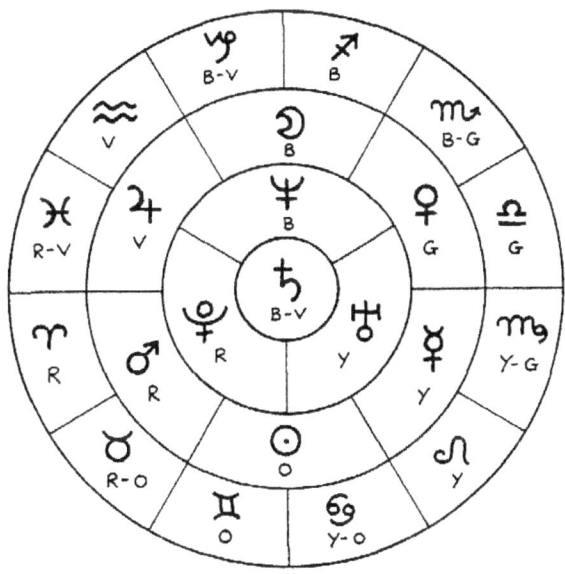

Diagram from page 59 of *High School Astrology: A Textbook of Ageless Wisdom*, by Arisa Victor. This is the companion volume to *The Spoken Cabala*

    The diagram shows how the 12 zodiacal signs form the outer ring, 6 ancient planets form the next inner ring, 3 New Age planets form the innermost ring, and Saturn holds the center. Paul Foster Case teaches that Saturn IS the center, the power that holds any being together, and calls you back to yourself when you stray away. In Tarot, Saturn is The World, Key 21, symbolic of Self-Realization, success at the end of the Fool's journey. On the Tree of Life, Saturn is attributed to the Divine Mother, Binah, colored black. This ancient fact leads me to deduce that Saturn is actually a loving Goddess, not the miserable "bad guy" blamed for our ills in modern astrology. (Patriarchal take-over, anyone?) Dr. Case teaches that Key 21 is androgynous, with female wisdom uppermost. This makes sense because our True Self is three-in-one, diagramed as the Three Supernals on the Tree of Life, One Self with a yang side and a yin side. The Divine Mother has both within her, and so gives birth to both boys and girls.

i

Equally as important as the Creatress is the Creator, the Divine Father, Chokmah, opposite Binah on the Tree of Life. He is in charge of the entire zodiac, which supports and protects his partner's creations. Chokma is colored grey, symbolic of wisdom. Grey is a blend of all the rainbow's colors.

The colors used to Photoshop-paint the Keys, and the borders of the Keys, on the cover of this book are the standard ones given by Paul Foster Case. My apologies if they are not exactly correct. The way colors look on the computer is quite different from how they appear in print. As noted, all these colors are derived from the rainbow zodiac. From studying the diagram, one can see that The Fool/Uranus/air, Hanged Man/Neptune/water, and Judgment/Pluto/fire are in a class by themselves; they embody the three primary colors. These are the three trans-Saturnian, outer planets of astrology. From the diagram, one can easily see that Uranus is the higher octave of Mercury, Neptune is the higher octave of Moon, and Pluto is the higher octave of Mars.

Pluto had not been discovered when PFC was writing, so he called Judgment the Key of fire. Then, Scorpio was ruled by Mars, also a fire planet. Now Pluto is called the Risen Mars, an alchemical phrase that equates with the kundalini process, which is the conscious High Magic transformation of our lower nature into our enlightened True Self. In tropical (western) astrology, Pluto is now the ruler of Scorpio, sign of magic and the occult. The Royal Astronomical Society in England has recently demoted Pluto to the status of "minor planet" but that does not change the fact that Pluto is the most potent force for change known to astrologers. Pluto is very active in our world today, transforming all old and outworn ways of being into new, wiser, more beautiful expressions. The Pluto Key 20 is an image of Ascension, which is humanity's rising out of the three-dimensional coffins of ignorance into a healed, peaceful, four-dimensional Earth.

There are instructions in this book as to how to use the border colors in meditation – all connected to astrology. Tarot and astrology are sister sciences. Like your left and right hand, it is good to use them both.

Between the two companions, *The Spoken Cabala* and *High School Astrology*, I have logged 48 years creating these books. In this time, my life and consciousness have benefited beyond anything words can express. I just want to offer my utmost gratitude to Paul Foster Case, Jason Lotterhand, and the Inner School for the precious teachings you give, and glorious example you set for humanity.

Reminiscing With An Old Philosopher
An Interview With Jason Lotterhand

By Arisa Victor
Published in 1989 by "Tarot Network News," Gary Ross, Editor

In 1923 a twelve-year old boy answered a magazine ad about hypnotism. Thus began Jason Lotterhand's lifelong research into occult science and philosophy. His adventures on The Path led him to an association with Paul Foster Case, a master Cabalist with total commitment to dissemination of the Ageless Wisdom. Many years later, Jason became a Director of the Builders of the Adytum, a mystery school of Tarot and Cabala that was founded by Dr. Case.

In 1958, Jason held the post of Associate Dean in charge of curriculum at the College of Parapsychology of Great Western University in San Francisco. During this time, he wrote a series of Tarot lessons, which was published by the College. He used those lessons to teach a public Tarot class long before most people had ever heard of Tarot. The purpose of his class was "to explore the Self and express the Self." In 1984, the San Francisco Tarot Network honored him with the First Annual Hierophant Award in recognition of his long years of service to the occult community.

Now in 1989, edited transcripts of Jason's public Tarot classes are soon to be published under the title, *The Thursday Night Tarot*. Amazingly, his class in ancient philosophy still continues every Thursday night, as it has for thirty-nine years.

Q: You've been teaching Tarot and Cabala once a week since 1950!

A: It's hard for me to believe that I've been banging away at this for thirty-seven years, but it's true. The early beginnings are all very fresh in my mind.

Q: What kind of developments have you seen over the years?

A: In the beginning there was very little interest. Then there were just a few people. But when the sixties came along, the picture began to change. The Flower Children were very interested in the Tarot and, of course, they plagiarized Paul Case's work like crazy. They got his lessons from the Builders of the Adytum; they'd run a whole printing and spread them all around. I was amazed. There was nothing anyone could do about it. You couldn't sue anybody; there was no one around to sue.

Q: Up until then the B.O.T.A. material was secret?

A: That's right. In the Golden Dawn tradition, Crowley spilled the beans first. He broke his vows and published anything he felt like. Then Regardie, who was a friend of Crowley's, went the whole way.

Q: What was this material, these beans that were spilled?

A: "Secret" information. There are still secret societies like Masonry. You take a vow in Masonry not to divulge the initiations.

Q: Why is that?

A: As an organization, it gives them a certain amount of power and dignity that they wouldn't have otherwise. If the mysteries of Masonry are secret, for example, they exert a very real fascination upon the outsider.

Q: But aside from that, do you think these Flower Children did something wrong?

A: Well, like children, they never heard of ethics, so they didn't do anything wrong except in the sense that ignorance is no excuse as far as the law is concerned.

Q: Where do you stand on this personally?

A: I don't like vows. If I was being initiated and I was told, "This information is for the group only; please don't spread it around," I would either accept that and live up to it or I'd resign.

Q: Your classes are public. You don't teach anything that is secret, is that right?

A: No, I don't teach anything that's secret. Anything that's published in a book is public domain as far as the knowledge is concerned. For instance, scientists meet together and talk and exchange ideas. That's the difference between science and institutional religion. Science is wide open and I'm very much in favor of that.

In the Tarot and the Cabala, ninety percent of the study material is psychological. Anything that's psychological in nature is of interest to science. For example, Saint Paul didn't think he was having a "psychological" experience nor did Joan of Arc, but to the scientist it's another story. These happenings are worth looking at – without any religious explanations. They exemplify innate capabilities of people.

There is much to learn in the Tarot and the Cabala. The principles are not secret and have never been, but in order to understand the ideas you have to put a lot of time into study and practice. You don't just take a look at it and say, "Oh, I know it all." You don't know it all. The effort that you make or I make is precisely what opens the door of understanding. You don't have to worry about secrets because the secrets are locked up in effort. If you don't make the effort, you won't know the secrets. It's the same in any field. If you want to be a master chemist, you've got to beat your brains out for a long time. There are no short cuts and no golden pill that you can take.

Q: If you apply this effort, won't the secrets be unveiled to you privately?

A: That's correct because the doctrine of the Self has validity based on one's own experiences. If one has the wit to understand, one will be able to see that key people in history have created everything new in culture, including historical change, out of their Inner Self. Gandhi, for example, illustrates what can come from within. He wasn't acting on what somebody told him to do; he was *inspired*.

What does this indicate? It simply means that the Superconscious Self in the person knows a great deal more than the average person in ordinary waking consciousness. Obviously, that Self can communicate at times with you and me.

Q: How does the Tarot plug you into that Superconscious Self?

A: It's not really the Tarot; it's the principles and instruction that go with it. The principles are the eternal verities that you've heard about. People play bridge all their lives and the cares have no inner meaning for them. Those familiar playing-cards come from the Tarot. The pip cards are the ten Sephiroth on the Tree of Life, and so forth. So it's kind of comical, isn't it? The Secret Doctrine has been transmitted for eight hundred years, more or less, in playing cards, but if you don't have any curiosity it's just a sealed book for you.

Q: The alchemists used to say that secret was hidden in plain sight.

A: Yes, and such statements by the alchemists are very tricky. What is plain sight? It is direct perception, where you see what is going on without having to read a book. This is the plain sight of people like Einstein. It's an <u>insight</u>, an intuition, which is a gift from your innermost Self. There's no way that you can just go and kick down the doors to understanding and insight. Chemistry is an outgrowth of Alchemy. There were two kinds of alchemists. The good alchemists believe in God and, since they were men and women of imagination, they could see the handiwork the Creator in all that was going on around them. God was the source of their success, if they had any. The good scientists are the same. They have a conscience and that's good for everyone. George Washington Carver would be a good example.

Q: This instruction that goes with the Tarot, is that was the Cabala is?

A: Absolutely! You have to have instruction if you want to understand your Self. Say for instance that you want to drive a car; you have to <u>learn how</u> first. When you understand the controls, you can move into the fast lane.

Q: If a reader of this book wanted to get some instruction, what would you suggest?

A: There is a solid body of literature that's available to study. For the average person, I think a good introduction is *The Mystical Qabalah* by Dion Fortune. I personally have a lot of feeling for Christian Ginsberg's book on the Cabala which is sometimes in print and sometimes not. Another source is *The Kabbala Unveiled* by Mathers. There's a lot of basic information in these books.

If you want to spend a lot of time studying the Tarot and the Cabala, you could join the Builders of the Adytum in Los Angeles. They have all the information, which they'll mail to you at a reasonable price. The course lasts about seven years and covers all the Hermetic sciences.

Paul Case wrote a book called *The Tarot* and a booklet called *Highlights of the Tarot* that are available in any metaphysical bookshop. These present very briefly the principles behind the symbolism of the Tarot and they raise very deep questions for you to consider. The first question is, "What's going on here?" or, "What's all this about, anyway?" If you want to learn something about yourself, you will not be able to go to the university and sign up for a course called "The Nature of Me." Paul's writings are basically trying to explain yourself to yourself so that you will have a well-established idea of what's going on in yourself. His work isn't any easier than learning depth psychology or trying to unscramble everything that Jung ever wrote.

Q: You mentioned that psychology was perhaps ninety percent of Tarot experience. What would be the other ten percent?

A: I would say… mysticism. A mystic believes that there is a connection between the average person and God. The goal is to bring a person consciously to God. This leaves some burning questions: What is God and where is God? In the East they say God is within yourself, so you have to turn to the God within yourself in order to understand and experience mysticism. If you don't believe in any God at all then you can't be a mystic. This extra ten percent that you asked about is quite different from the psychological investigation that gets you started on the Path.

Q: Are the Tarot and Cabala parallel to the Eastern approach?

A: The method of Cabala is very close to some of the yoga systems. Meditation, for instance, is a prolonged dwelling on the material that the Cabala presents to the student. Under ideal conditions this will bring you into contact with the "inner side of life."

Say for instance that you like rock music and you can't stand classical. Now, there happens to be some classical music that is very much inspired. It can lead you to a very interesting realm of experience. Rock is very entertaining and I think it's physically very good for you to rock around, but there's a difference. The subtleties that are open to a serious student of music are not something that just any buff can grasp.

Jung was very much aware of the difference between ordinary notions and all the special ideas that are of no interest to the average person. In the first place, the average person is extremely busy, especially in America. From the cradle to the grave, there's "every reason" why they should be busy. Everybody says you should *do* something, make a mark for yourself, be a success, until it's go, go, go all the time. There is just no opportunity for reviewing what's going on inside yourself. It's interesting that some people have an inclination or curiosity about inner matters and other people don't. The inner life is *terra incognita* for somebody who doesn't have the inclination.

Q: Some people equate the Cabala with the patriarchal Judeo-Christian tradition.

A: The Cabala is not of much interest to average Jews or Christians. It is certainly as much philosophical as it is theological, and it is the philosophical aptness of the ideas that has always appealed to me. Of course, it has a very practical side, too, because it deals with everyday existence.

The Cabalists say that there are four stages of understanding the Bible. First, it is a story like a fairytale. Secondly, it is an allegory in which the imagery speaks of inner matters. Next the Bible speaks to the Law of Life. Finally, it is a mystical gateway to the experience of God, and as such is inspirational.
In the Cabala, inspiration comes from God. There is nothing in the Cabala or any of Paul Case's writings that is anti-religion. As a matter of fact, Paul Case was a priest in the Liberal Catholic Church, which is a part of the Episcopalian Church.

Q: Just who was Paul Foster Case?

A: He was one of those inquiring souls we were talking about. Initially he was an orchestra leader but he had a powerful leaning toward the occult. He was also a great prestidigitator – a master of card tricks. Being a very analytical person, he explored all the current literature on New Thought. He knew a lot people in the New Thought movement. Among his friends were William Walker Atkinson, known as Rama Charaka, and Claude Bragdon. It was Bragdon who asked Paul, "Where do you think playing cards came from?" thereby precipitating Paul into the study of Tarot. He started to investigate the history of playing cards and before long he knew more about the Tarot than anybody around.

By 1915, Paul had a school in Boston called The School of Ageless Wisdom. By 1920 he was the editor of New York City's great occult magazine known as *Azoth*. He founded the Builders of the Adytum in 1922 and made all the information he had acquired available in lesson form. Originally the B.O.T.A. was strictly an educational institution. After Paul's demise, his successor Ann Davies made it a church.

Q: Paul Case was such a great occultists; why is it that so few people know about him?

A: Well, nobody ever heard of Gregory Mendel until a hundred and fifty years after he died; yet he had a very far-reaching effect on biological science. Perhaps it will be the same with Paul and occult science.

Q: How did you meet Paul?

A: In 1933, my first Tarot teacher, Algernon Tassin – who was a very able person and a professor of English at Columbia – had an enthusiasm for Paul that was catching. I had a chance to meet Paul in 1937. He was living in East Pasadena, California. I had always has a yen for the west so when the opportunity arose in 1940, I moved to Los Angeles. I saw a great deal of Paul until he passed away in 1954.

Q: What sort of person was he?

A: Paul was a very attractive person with a good sense of humor. He was very quiet and very modest. I never heard him toot his own horn, never! Of course, as far as the Secret Doctrine was concerned, he was pretty hard-headed. As editor of *Azoth* he was the boss as to what was going to be in the magazine and what wasn't. He applied criteria to everything in the light of the information that he'd acquired over the years. He was no wimp when it came to criticizing someone. If someone got out of line, he would comment on it in the magazine. He had a great critical ability and was not afraid to use it. So respected was he that he served as American Prolocutor General of the famous (and infamous) Golden Dawn organization.

Paul was not ambitious for money or notoriety. The people who knew and loved him helped him to keep going because he was giving himself totally to the work of writing down all the information about the Tarot and the Cabala and other occult sciences. He devoted all of his time to that work. I was fortunate to attend his last private Tarot talks after he had retired from public speaking. However, he did give a final series of public lectures in the Masonic Auditorium in Los Angles that were very well attended.

Q: You mentioned that people don't often get the message. Do you ever feel lonely that your message isn't getting through?

A: I don't feel lonely. I got the message; at least, I think I got a message. The fact that I devote time to preaching the gospel of the Tarot is because I have been the fortunate recipient of what I would call favors in connection with my studies. Whatever insights or understanding I have are like gifts and I appreciate them very much.

Like everybody else who has led a fairly normal life, I've married and I have a couple of grandchildren and even a great-grandchild. I've had my share of experiences on an ordinary level and I'm very grateful for them. But perhaps I'm even more grateful that I've been blessed with the inclination to pursue my occult studies from the time I was very young. It's been my avocation since I was twelve years old. No special revelations on such and such a day or anything like that. But from time to time, I've been able to grasp ideas I couldn't understand before.

The reason I started teaching the Tarot in the first place was because I had found it extremely valuable in terms of understanding, and of great practical use in offering guiding principles for my life. In 1950, I asked Paul what he though about my starting a Tarot class. He thought it was a very good idea. He was a friend of Fritzi Armstrong, owner of the Metaphysical Townhall Bookshop in San Francisco. He introduced me to her and she gave me a roof over my head to start my experiment. Our relationship lasted until 1987, when Mrs. Armstrong retired. Now my friends and I meet in Fort Mason Center, a most agreeable place.

Q: What's it like to look back on thirty-seven years of teaching?

A: It feels good. I've enjoyed some very rewarding correspondence from people who have studied the Tarot with me. This has been a real satisfaction. I don't feel like I've been just batting the air all this time.

Q: You've seen people flower around you?

A: It's just a question of whether or not they've gotten anything out of it. If they've gotten something out of the information I've dispensed over the years, that's all I expect. If they're kind enough to tell me, then that's reward enough for me because I'm not in this work professionally.

The Tarot has a real message for people who have the inclination. To simply convey that message is all I expect to do in this particular life time. You can't convey the message to everybody; that's why I'm not interested in having a great many people around. If a person lacks the necessary inclination then there's no possibility of my being able to convey the meaning that I'd like to convey.

Q: And yet you keep your classes very open to all kinds of people.

A: Yes. I have a bird feeder outside my house because I don't want to put the birds in a cage. It's much more fun to put the food out there and let them take it or leave it. Most of the time they want to take it.

Q: You don't say "Sparrows only" or something like that?

A: No, I don't, and I think this is the way it should be. It doesn't bother me a bit if someone walks into class then turns right around and walks out. That's been going on for years and I'm used to it. In fact, I'm pleased and the visitor is pleased. It would be a waste of time for both of us if the Tarot is not their cup of tea.

Q: For the person who sticks around, what do they get out of it?

A: I recently wrote a letter in which I said that for thirty-seven years I ran a study group directed to the Self, with a capital S, which is now a common term in psychology – Jung was responsible for that. Everybody knows the expression, "Know Thyself," but very few are sufficiently motivated to do anything about it. Most people go to a psychologist or the parish priest.

Q: Would these studies replace the need for psychotherapy?

Tarot is a sort of do-it-yourself psychotherapy, based on the principle that your salvation lies within yourself. In therapy, you want someone to save you from a ghastly situation. On the other hand, the Secret Tradition in the West clearly states that if you want to be saved, you'd better look inside yourself. The symbolic representation of salvation in the Tarot is Key 20, Judgment.

Q: Do you have a favorite Tarot card?

A: I find that the Fool key epitomizes the Tarot; it has more subtleties than any other card. The *spirit* of Tarot is the Fool. It goes contrary to popular opinion about the nature of things. Since it represents a different point of view, it can be very upsetting. Suppose some character comes along and says, like

Little Jack Horner, "What a big boy am I!" The Fool would say, in a loud voice, "You must be kidding!"

Q: You are indicating that the Tarot doesn't take the ego very seriously?

A: We are spirits; we are not just intellects. The spirit in humanity is a Being, which is *superior* to intellect. We should thank God for the gift of intellect but also remember who's boss. The average person is not aware of the nature of his Inner Self. It's like your self being in an automobile. *You* are the driver. The car will take you anywhere, but without *you* it's just a piece of junk. The body without the spirit is a piece of junk too.

The body is the *means of expression* for your spirit, the physical instrument for living on this planet. The structure of the body and all the capabilities of the brain are fantastic – well worth being included in your life-long studies. If you've ever seen a corpse, you know how dull and uninteresting it is. The animating spirit is gone. *Meaning* is also gone.

It's very hard for people to understand that their bodies are instruments like an automobile. The person is the boss of the body and the body is stuck with the boss. If the boss is at a certain stage of evolution, the body can suffer because of that. If the boss is more advanced then the body is lucky.
Even though you may not be able to follow all the intricacies of the physical vehicle, you can still understand what the situation is without getting off into some fantasy. If you're serious about the Tarot, you're going to find out that it's not dealing with fantasy. What's going on in the universe is far more interesting than any fantasy that anyone could possibly dream of. The minute you can *see* that, you don't need fantasies. You're staring at something that's fantastic all the time, looking straight at it. It takes awhile before you can understand this and see it with your own inner vision.

Q: It seems like people have to get back in touch with nature and natural processes.

A: In the Tarot and the Cabala, there's no difference between Reality and Nature. There's only One Thing in the universe. You can call it anything you want – God, Nature, Reality – but there are not two things; there's only One Thing. You can approach it though the gate of Nature or through intellectual insights. If you approach it with the right spirit, it all leads in the direction of unity.

From a practical point of view you're not being very helpful to somebody who needs answers when you say, "God is All." Of course God is all but, if you've broken your arm, this is not going to put it right for you. You need a being who can fix it. Then you can be grateful to the Powers That Be that there are such people

Education is critically important for everybody; it is the way we advance. Paul Case's school was a place where you *learned something*. He was trying to teach you the best way he knew. He didn't want to get you into trouble so he didn't give you a lot of goofy exercises that might put you on the wrong track. He wanted to keep you well and reasonably happy so you could *continue* to learn something.

Q: What's the connection between the Self and God?

A: If you're a mystic, they're the same thing. If you believe God is All, then you can figure out your own theology quite easily. Some people who are not quite logical say, "God is All, therefore I am God." This is not exactly a smart thing to do because the limitations of a human being are very real and the limitations of God are non-existent.

Q: What do you see down the road for the human race?

A: If you're referring to the physical beings on planet Earth, then I would answer that they're going to outer space. That drive is already manifesting.

Q: So you think we'll be around to do that? You don't think we'll blow it?

A: It isn't my movie, but after reading history, since we're still here I'm very hopeful. Talk about a bunch of devils, we've been a bloodthirsty lot throughout our history.

Q: What do you foresee in the future for the Tarot?

A: The pictures in the Tarot are just fine for now, but I think the imagery will become more explicit. By comparison with the present cards it should become more sensational. It may not even be called the Tarot, but it will be imagery that is systematically arranged so that you can grasp a lot of very interesting ideas and relationships. For example, it might present what's going on in the body, the interplay of all the forces that are operating. Another possibility might be to show the organization of Life Itself, with its mysterious Powers That Be controlling all the departments of Nature.

Q: You have a book soon to be published. Do you have any comment about this?

A: It's very pleasurable to know that my point of view will be expressed and that other people can look at it and decide for themselves what it means to them. I couldn't ask for any more than that. In a book like *The Spoken Cabala*, there's more going on than just the words on the pages. It could seem like a will-of-the-whisp until you realize that there is a really big body of literature backing it up.

If someone were to ask, "What's the purpose of the book?" I would say that it's mainly to remind you that there's still a whole lot about yourself that you can discover. I think this information is the best medicine there is – knowledge about the Self.

Dr. Paul Foster Case,
Jason's teacher

Jason C. Lotterhand in the
mid 1970's

After class, chatting at Lefty
O'Doul's Hoffbrau on Sutter St.
in San Francisco.

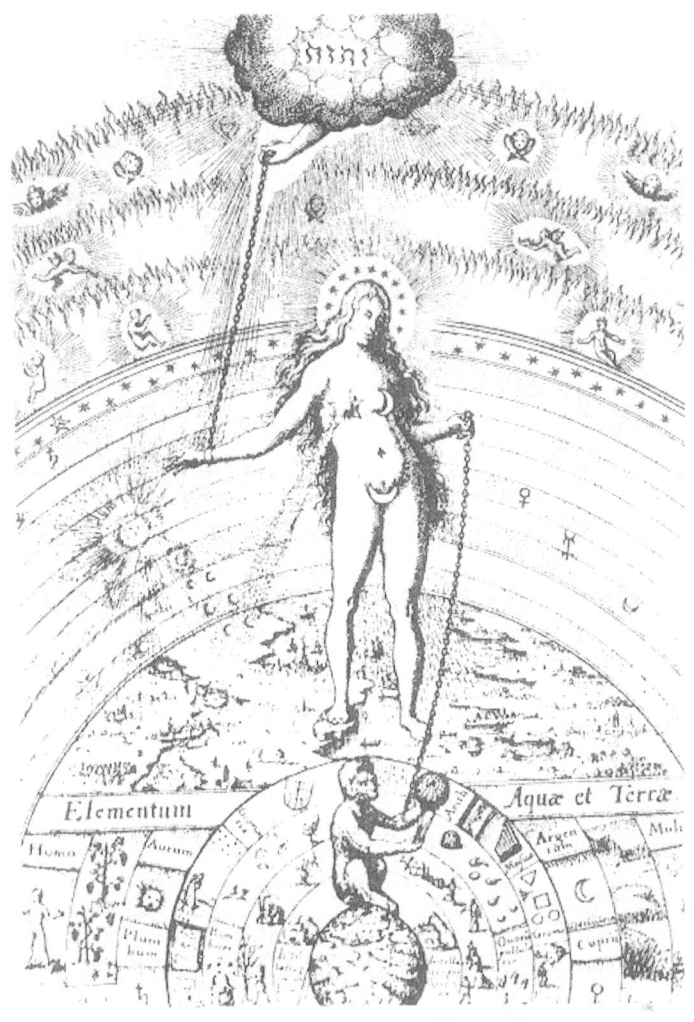

Fig. 21. The Soul of the World

Jason often gave handouts to class participants. "The Soul of the World" was a favorite; another was a Roman Isis, dressed in majesty and loaded with symbols.

Jason was very community-minded, a perspective that inspired a yearly gathering called the Taroteers Picnic. We always had a sacred ceremony honoring whatever Key we were studying that week. Costumes were part of the fun. There was sure to be lots of good food and fellowship.

Jason in his beloved Admiral Hat with our bright orange Taroteers banner in the background.

Everyone got crowned when we celebrated Key 14.

Our picnic site was Baker Beach in San Francisco. Views of the Golden Gate Bridge, the Marin Headlands, and the magnificent Pacific Ocean were a never-ending source of inspiration. We had twenty-four picnics in all (a few after Jason crossed over). This is a typical snapshot of a typical Taroteers Picnic.

This was the only time Jason consented to play a part in one of the ceremonies. That week we were studying Key 1, The Magician. Our teacher is wearing a red robe and a stuffed toy snake. He is surrounded by the elements (from left to right: Earth, Air, Water, and Fire).

At picnics, Jason would usually stand in one spot for a couple of hours, surrounded by friends, all avidly engaged in conversation. He was always making us laugh.

This was a book signing for *The Thursday Night Tarot* at the Sunrise Bookshop in Berkeley in the fall of 1989.

At Fritzy Armstrong's Metaphysical Townhall Bookstore

At Fort Mason's Center

On Mt. Tamalpais

Ft. Mason Center — Jason's last class, Key 21, The World, July 30, 1992.

ACKNOWLEDGMENTS

Heartfelt appreciation for the help of these friends:

David Victor Burrill
Michael Bonnifield
Judith Early
Della Ruth Farmer
Mary K. Greer
Carl Hunt
David Miller
Ann Mine
Bruce Nevin
Don Nicodemus
Silma Smith
Mort Tolson
Linda Verdugo

Special thanks to
Fritzi Armstrong and Mickey Goodspeed
of the Metaphysical Townhall Bookstore,
where *Thursday Night Tarot* began in 1950.

*To the memory of
Dr. Paul Foster Case
with deep love and respect.*

CONTENTS

Introduction by Arisa Victor	xi
Author's Preface	xv
Editor's Preface	xvii
The Pattern on the Trestleboard	xix
The Tarot Tableau	xx
The Tree of Life	xxi
Sound and Color Attributions	xxiii
Key Concepts, Intelligences, and Astrological Attributions	xxv
Chapter 0: The Fool	1
Chapter 1: The Magician	17
Chapter 2: The High Priestess	35
Chapter 3: The Empress	53
Chapter 4: The Emperor	71
Chapter 5: The Hierophant	87
Chapter 6: The Lovers	103
Chapter 7: The Chariot	119
Chapter 8: Strength	133
Chapter 9: The Hermit	149
Chapter 10: The Wheel of Fortune	165
Chapter 11: Justice	181
Chapter 12: The Hanged Man	197
Chapter 13: Death	213
Chapter 14: Temperance	229
Chapter 15: The Devil	245
Chapter 16: The Tower	263
Chapter 17: The Star	279
Chapter 18: The Moon	293
Chapter 19: The Sun	307
Chapter 20: Judgement	321
Chapter 21: The World	335
The Taroteers' Picnic	351
Glossary	353

INTRODUCTION

Born to tread the occult Path of Return . . . no doubt many readers feel this is their destiny. But how many of us have been on that Path almost eighty years? Jason Lotterhand is an inspiring example of someone who has devoted a lifetime to the study and practice of the AGELESS WISDOM.* He became interested in hypnotism at age twelve and his ensuing explorations into occultism awakened his soul to the Way of Liberation when he was fifteen. Today, Jason is a healthy, happy seventy-eight-year-old, sharing the wisdom and understanding of a fulfilled maturity.

True to his belief that one's inner spiritual life is independent of outer activities, Jason worked professionally as a consultant in the textile business. Now retired, he lives in Mill Valley, California, with his wife of more than fifty years. The Lotterhands are great-grandparents.

On Thursday evenings Jason becomes the beloved teacher of a loosely knit group that studies Tarot and CABALA at the Fort Mason Cultural Center in San Francisco. The purpose of our meetings is to explore and to express the SELF. It has been my privilege to attend these classes for the past sixteen years. I've never ceased to be amazed at our mentor's grace and modesty—and good humor—while discussing profound concepts in simple terms. Accurate teachings about spiritual Selfhood are as beautiful as they are rare.

Jason Christopher Lotterhand was born on New Year's Day in 1911 (1/1/11) to a Roman Catholic family in New York City. His father was a successful inventor. His mother, employed by the Hammersteins, sang in the vaudeville Keith Circuit. Jason recounts how, as a boy of six, he was taken out of the city to spend a summer by the seashore. With this sudden, totally delightful introduction to wildness, Jason began a love affair with Nature that is still going strong.

His introduction to the Tarot was a somewhat similar experience. In 1933, at the urging of a fellow student from Columbia University, he was dragged off unsuspectingly to a class about The Fool Key in a Green-

---

*Words explained in the Glossary are emphasized by small capitals on their first reference. (A few words are emphasized several times.)

wich Village bookstore. Both of these young men were astounded by the mystery teachings presented in the Tarot symbolism. They went home with the teacher and stayed up far into the night, excitedly asking questions about this spiritual treasure trove. Needless to say, they returned for the complete course of twenty-two lectures.

The man who so fired the minds of those youngsters was Algernon Tassin, an intelligent and popular professor of English at Columbia University. He had personally studied with Paul Foster Case, the Tarot master who expressed the Ageless Wisdom in psychological terms comprehensible to the Western intellect. Thereafter, Professor Tassin conducted Tarot classes in the New York metropolitan area for the rest of his life.

Moving to California in 1940, Jason himself became a friend and student of Paul Foster Case. In 1944 Jason became a Director of Dr. Case's educational organization, the Builders of the ADYTUM (B.O.T.A.). He is now a Director Emeritus of that venerable Mystery School of the Sacred Tarot and Holy Qabalah, and a true successor to the Wisdom Tradition. In 1950 his own classes in Ancient Philosophy began in San Francisco. Paul Case's book *The Tarot: A Key to the Wisdom of the Ages* is the text for these explorations, which cycle through the Major Arcana.

In 1958, while Jason was Associate Dean in charge of curriculum at the College of Parapsychology at Great Western University in San Francisco, he wrote and published a series of Tarot lessons.

"As they say about chicken soup, it wouldn't hurt you," is now a favorite comment from Jason about the Tarot. His approach to occult science is very practical, which might have something to do with his being a triple Capricorn. The public is welcome at his classes, which are attended by a wide variety of people. Jason gives an introductory talk focusing on one of the Major ARCANA; then the rest of the evening is given over to discussion. Cabalistic philosophy and the process of Self-transmutation provide the basic ideas around which questions and answers revolve.

His classes are free, but most people contribute some donation. This is definitely the best Tarot "deal" in the Bay Area. Afterwards, most of the group accompanies Jason to a nearby cafe for drinks and friendship. One goes home feeling glad to have spent time with a genuine philosopher, a true lover of wisdom.

Arisa Victor
Oakland, California
1989

An earlier version of this introduction appeared in the Spring 1984 issue of the Tarot Network News *as an article entitled, "Jason Lotterhand, Lover of Wisdom," by Arisa Victor (then known as Maud Reinertsen). In the fall of that same year, the International Tarot Symposium honored Mr. Lotterhand with the First Annual Hierophant Award.*

AUTHOR'S PREFACE

An ancient legend tells us that the doctrine of the Cabala was sent from on high to restore humankind to its former felicity.

Before the time of Isaac the Blind, who taught from 1190 to 1210 A.D., the Secret Wisdom was transmitted exclusively from one generation to the next in the form of dialogues between masters and their pupils. Isaac is credited with coining the word "Cabala."* His pupil Azariel compiled and published the doctrine.

By the end of the thirteenth century the literature on the Cabala had become extensive. *The Zohar*, called the pillar of Cabalistic wisdom, was published by Moses de Leon (1250–1305). It collected and elaborated upon the commentaries of previous authors. In 1677 Knorr von Rosenroth published *Kabbala Denudata* in Latin, which was translated in 1900 into English by S. L. MacGregor Mathers as *The Kabbalah Unveiled*. More recent (1972) is Arthur Edward Waite's encyclopedic study, *The Holy Kabbalah*.

The major symbol of the Cabala is THE TREE OF LIFE, which sets forth the SECRET DOCTRINE in diagrammatic form. The ten centers on THE TREE, called SEPHIROTH (or Spheres, Centers, Seats), express the observable characteristics of THE ONE DIVINE BEING. The doctrine states that MAN is made in the image of that BEING. It therefore follows that Man's nature contains, to a degree, all the powers of the Sephiroth. Consequently, to know oneself requires a thorough mental grasp of these divine elements.

The Sephiroth are named:

(1) Crown
(2) Wisdom
(3) Understanding
(4) Mercy
(5) Severity
(6) Beauty
(7) Victory
(8) Splendor
(9) Foundation
(10) Kingdom.

---

*Also spelled Qabalah, Kabala, Caballa, etc. "Cabala" was chosen because that is how it appears in Webster's Dictionary.

The meanings of some of these names are familiar. Others are obscure, purposely veiled to invite closer study.

In addition to the ten Sephiroth, the twenty-two Hebrew letters appear on THE TREE OF LIFE as the paths among the Sephiroth. For example, the letter ALEPH is placed on the path between (1) Crown and (2) Wisdom; BETH is placed between (1) Crown and (3) Understanding, and so forth.

The ten Sephiroth and the twenty-two letters are the Lights of the Divine INTELLIGENCES shining on THE TREE OF LIFE. They represent the thirty-two degrees of contemplation by which one's mind is raised to the vision of the DIVINE SELF, the Crown of THE TREE OF LIFE.

The Cabala states that nothing exists outside THE ONE DIVINE BEING, THE ONE SELF of the universe. We are part of THAT even if we are totally ignorant of our relationship with IT.

Insofar as we become acquainted with this truth about ourselves, we come to realize the Divine Presence in our lives. When this happens, we can rest on the bosom of THE ETERNAL BEING. All our studies and all our meditations bring us to a clearer vision of the DIVINE SELF whose creations we are.

Once we are established in this awareness, we can proceed along our own individual paths of purpose and expression. Freed from delusions concerning what life is about, we can concentrate our efforts on being our own true selves—successful members of the Divine Plan.

Jason Lotterhand
Mill Valley, California
1989

EDITOR'S PREFACE

Spiritual occultism saved my life. At age twenty-nine all I knew was what I didn't want and didn't like about living on this planet. Angry, frustrated, deeply unhappy and disillusioned with the beliefs and practices of my Middle American culture, there was nowhere to turn for any truth or beauty—or so I thought. I'd never heard of the Path of Return. Occultism as a valid foundation for living never occurred to me. I thought it was evil.

Subtle are the threads in the tapestry of destiny. Unknown to me, my astrological Saturn Return was in progress. On my thirtieth birthday, a new friend surprised me with a gift enrollment in the Builders of the Adytum Tarot study curriculum. Occult correspondence lessons? "I just thought you'd like it," said my friend. And he was right. Paul Case's completely sane, intelligent approach struck me as anything but evil. I read on . . . and on and on . . . for ten years. I was taught to know and express my Self. My life opened and blossomed in undreamed-of happiness. What happened for me can happen for anyone. My greatest wish is to offer the Ageless Wisdom to others like myself who may also benefit from Self-discovery through real occultism.

I met Jason Lotterhand in 1972. The High Priestess was the topic of discussion on the night I first arrived in his class. Jason exemplified the principles and philosophy I had been studying. I've missed very few Thursday-night sessions from that time to this. Work on *The Spoken Cabala: A Living Philosophy of the Tarot* (as this book was called then) began in 1974. Bruce Nevin transcribed a class session, and as I read it, I knew a book should grow from this. The text was compiled by editing and sifting through transcripts of approximately ten classes for each Major Arcana card, or 220 classes—tracking down themes, organizing information, and capturing some of those special moments of breakthrough, of laughter, of deep love and joy.

Some of the comments and questions from the participants have been included in the text. You will find them in boldface, introduced by a black triangle (►).

Of course, Jason has reviewed all the contents of this book. May his shining spirit live on and continue to inspire from mouth to ear, in the grand tradition of the Ageless Wisdom.

Arisa Victor
Oakland, California
1989

THE PATTERN ON THE TRESTLEBOARD

This is truth about the Self:

0. All the power that ever was or will be is here now.

1. I am a center of expression for the Primal Will-to-Good which eternally creates and sustains the universe.

2. Through me its unfailing Wisdom takes form in thought and word.

3. Filled with Understanding of its perfect law, I am guided, moment by moment, along the Path of Liberation.

4. From the exhaustless riches of its Limitless Substance, I draw all things needful, both spiritual and material.

5. I recognize the manifestation of the undeviating Justice in all the circumstances of my life.

6. In all things, great and small, I see the Beauty of the divine expression.

7. Living from that Will, supported by its unfailing Wisdom and Understanding, mine is the Victorious Life.

8. I look forward with confidence to the perfect realization of the Eternal Splendor of the Limitless Light.

9. In thought and word and deed, I rest my life, from day to day, upon the sure Foundation of Eternal Being.

10. The Kingdom of Spirit is embodied in my flesh.

THE TAROT TABLEAU

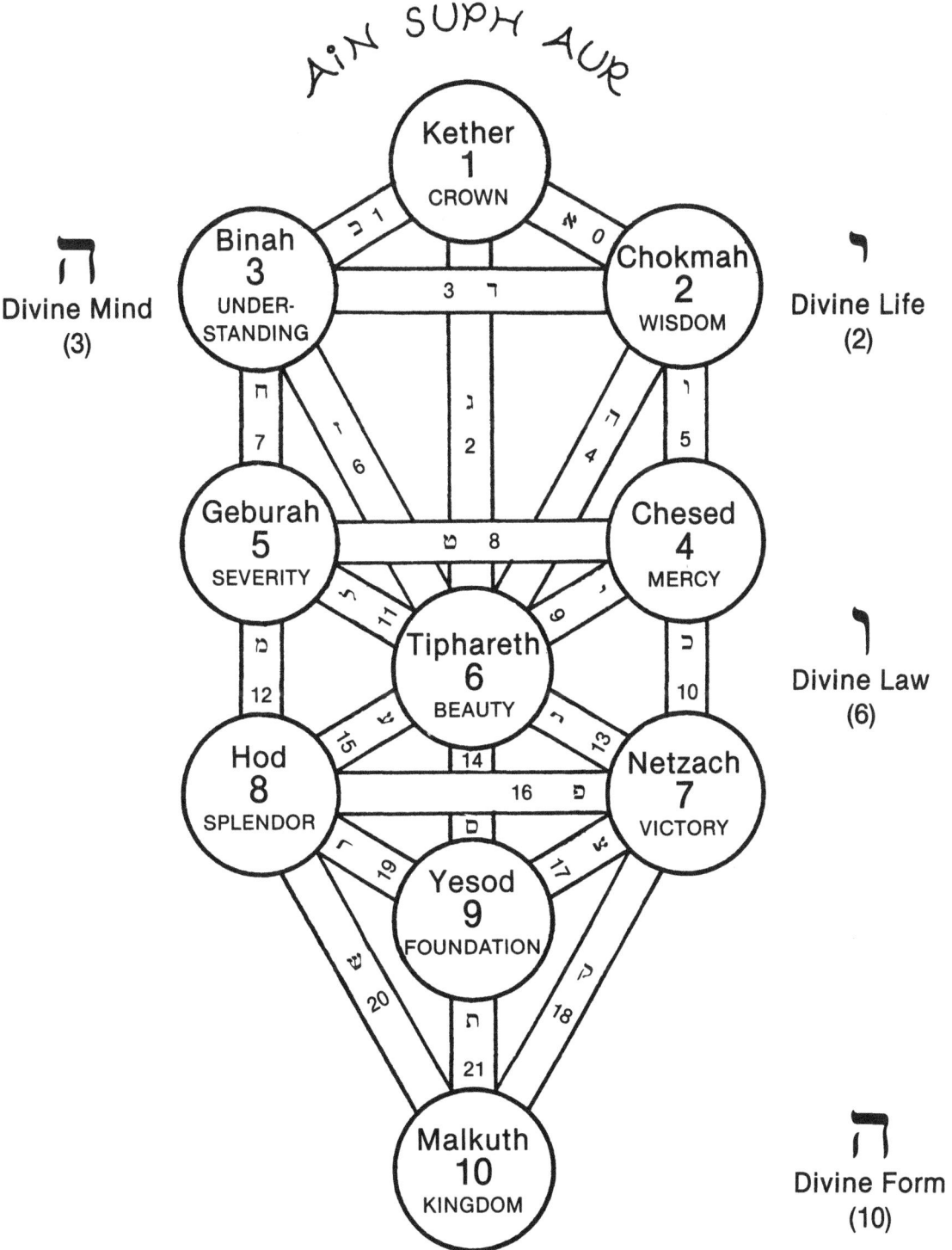

THE TREE OF LIFE
Hebrew and English names of the ten Sephiroth.
Hebrew letters and corresponding Tarot Keys on the twenty-two paths.
The Tetragrammaton, or "Name of Four Letters," located on the Tree.

SOUND AND COLOR ATTRIBUTIONS

This information is from a class handout sheet.

Welcome to another round of Tarot practice! You will need:

The Tarot: A Key to the Wisdom of the Ages by Paul Foster Case. This is our textbook.

The Highlights of Tarot by Paul Foster Case. Includes detailed instructions for coloring the cards.

A set of uncolored B.O.T.A. Major Arcana Tarot cards.

Water colors, acrylics, or colored pencils.

A pitch pipe (available at retail musical instrument stores).

A color wheel (available at retail art supply stores).

Construction paper in the colors listed below, or you can hand-paint the colors on lightweight cardboard. These color sheets make a background on which you may lay your cards for study.

These are the colors for each card and the notes to be intoned for each card, per instructions in Chapter 26 of *The Tarot*:

Card	Color	Note
The Fool	Yellow	E Natural
The Magician	Yellow	E Natural
The High Priestess	Blue	G Sharp
The Empress	Green	F Sharp
The Emperor	Red	C Natural
The Hierophant	Red Orange	C Sharp
The Lovers	Orange	D Natural
The Chariot	Yellow-Orange	E Flat
Strength	Yellow	E Natural
The Hermit	Yellow-Green	F Natural
The Wheel of Fortune	Violet	B Flat
Justice	Green	F Sharp
The Hanged Man	Blue	G Sharp
Death	Blue-Green	G Natural

Temperance	Blue	G Sharp
The Devil	Blue-Violet	A Natural
The Tower	Red	C Natural
The Star	Violet	B Flat
The Moon	Red-Violet	B Natural
The Sun	Orange	D Natural
Judgement	Red	C Natural
The World	Blue-Violet	A Natural

Intone either I–A–O or A–U–M.

Key Concepts, Intelligences, and Astrological Attributions

Key	Concept	Intelligence	Astrol.
0	Superconsciousness	The Scintillating Intelligence	Uranus
1	Self-consciousness	The Transparent Intelligence	Mercury
2	Subconsciousness	The Uniting Intelligence	Moon
3	Creative Imagination	The Luminous Intelligence	Venus
4	Reason	The Constituting Intelligence	Aries
5	Intuition	The Triumphant and Eternal Intelligence	Taurus
6	Discrimination	The Disposing Intelligence	Gemini
7	Receptivity-Will	The Intelligence of the House of Influence	Cancer
8	Suggestion	The Intelligence of the Secret of All Spiritual Activities	Leo
9	Response	The Intelligence of Will	Virgo
10	Rotation	The Rewarding Intelligence of Those Who Seek	Jupiter
11	Work, Action	The Faithful Intelligence	Libra
12	Reversal	The Stable Intelligence	Neptune
13	Transformation	The Imaginative Intelligence	Scorpio
14	Verification	The Intelligence of Probation or Trial	Sagittarius
15	Bondage	The Renewing Intelligence	Capricorn
16	Awakening	The Exciting Intelligence	Mars
17	Revelation	The Natural Intelligence	Aquarius
18	Organization	The Corporeal Intelligence	Pisces
19	Regeneration	The Collecting or Collective Intelligence	Sun
20	Realization	The Perpetual Intelligence	Pluto
21	Cosmic Consciousness	The Administrative Intelligence	Saturn

KEY 0

CHAPTER 0

THE FOOL

In 1933, while attending Columbia University in New York, I had my first opportunity to become acquainted with Tarot and Cabala. A college friend insisted that I accompany him to a Tarot class in Greenwich Village given by one of our English professors, Algernon Tassin. After much persuasion I grudgingly agreed to go.

We arrived at the beginning of the course. The Fool card was on view. When I looked at it my first thought was, "What has this got to do with me?" The symbolism was totally unfamiliar. It had a sort of fairy-tale aspect. I had grave doubts that I could handle this sort of stuff. However, our professor did such a good job that my friend and I followed him home after class. We listened to him expound further on the Tarot until three o'clock in the morning. Needless to say, we were hooked!

From the start we learned that The Fool is our Inner Self about to engage in another adventure. The immortal part of ourselves is adventurous, to say the least. It has been on many, many adventures in the course of cosmic history. Here *we* are tonight, about to embark on another voyage, quite unafraid of the consequences.

The Fool is a Being, which is not the same thing as a person or a personality. In the scheme of the Cabala, a Being is eternal. *Your immortal Self* is the Being pictured here. This Tarot Key represents the total freedom of your innermost spirit. Once launched into your adventure, you become *embroiled* with all sorts of forces and intelligences. You enter the mythical kingdom of what is called "forms." In fairy tales there are always a dragon and a villain testing you as you proceed on your path.

The Being is willing and even eager to go through all the experiences. But once your spirit becomes taken up with the "ten thousand things," as they say in the East, it becomes easy to forget who you really are. One of the advantages of pursuing the study of Tarot and Cabala is that it brings you back to remembering your Self. You cannot be free until you have *freed yourself*. This effort is an act of devotion to the truth about your Self. Our main problem in this course is to find out what we are, to define ourselves in accurate terms. Our purpose is twofold: to explore ourselves, and to express ourselves in the light of what we have learned.

The Secret Doctrine is like a well-constructed ship that can take us wherever we want to go. It is not a religion and it has no denominations. Each presentation of the Secret Doctrine is geared to a certain culture, a time and a place. The Cabala is designed for the West.

The innermost spirit of humanity has nothing to do with time and place, or with name and form. All these are the *playground* of the spirit. The Being writes its own script and creates its own play. That's why The Fool is so joyous. His very buoyant mood shows that he must have something going for him besides what he reads in the daily newspaper.

His secret of happiness is symbolized by the white sun in the upper right corner. This is the white light of KETHER, first center of the Cabalistic Tree of Life. White represents the unity of the Limitless Light from which all colors are derived. Kether is a Hebrew word that translates as *Crown*. It is like the Chinese TAO, which is non-conceptual and free of phenomenal aspects. It is That which was, and is, and will be. The first aspect of That which we can contact is Being. We turn to this Being to be lifted out of the ordinary viewpoint into SUPERCONSCIOUSNESS, a key concept in connection with The Fool card.

This Key is above the other twenty-one Keys in the Tarot Tableau. It is also between all the others. In effect, it is the most important Key in the pack. The superconscious Self lives in the Land of the No-Thing. Key 0 enjoys the universe of things, but is not a thing itself. The contrast between *nothing* and *something* creates the freedom that makes life so enjoyable.

AIN SUPH AUR is the Hebrew name of the Limitless Light. It means the *boundless*. It is negative existence, as far as we're concerned. We can't describe it. We can't say, "It's this way, that way, or the other way. It's powerful. It isn't powerful. It's right. It's wrong. It's good. It's bad." It is *none* of these things. To us it is a complete *blank* because it totally transcends our minds. All of us who are, we'll say, aspiring philosophers, know that behind the facade of the universe is some sort of agency, power, or what-you-will. You are perfectly welcome to call it God. You may call it the Life Power, or Reality, or the Big Whatsis. The main thing is to remember that the whole phenomenal universe hangs on something indescribably great and impossible to penetrate.

Sir Edward Arnold wrote, "Sink not the string of thought into the fathomless." This is a good piece of advice. Notice that he didn't say, "Forget the fathomless," or, "Overlook the fathomless." On the contrary, it's the very thing that is most important in the whole affair. The Buddhists have pointed out masterfully the supreme importance of the Void—and the Void is precisely one of the names of the Ain Suph Aur.

You and I have to understand somehow or other that we live in a universe in which *every point* contains the *entire potential* of the divine, the Life Power. In other words, it isn't over there or over here. It isn't up; it isn't down or any way that we can point. It's everywhere. Mystic teachings all over the world agree on this particular idea: Every one of us is an expression of this Void, and the root of our Being is in this simply remarkable basis that stretches throughout the entire universe.

The root of the Tree of Life is in Kether, also called YEKHIDAH, the Indivisible Self. This is your Self and my Self, rooted in *the* Self. The Self is not something that is capable of description; neither is your Self or my Self. We are beyond mind and we are beyond matter. We are beyond motion. We are above what we normally think of as the universe. The Fool in Tarot expresses *our essential freedom*. He is on a mountain peak, way, way up there, miles above ordinary considerations.

▶ Is this what is meant by the term, "The Fool of God?"

You've heard that the wisdom of God is foolishness unto men. The Fool of God is the only one who can hear the Tao and pay attention to it and follow it. In fact, he doesn't pay attention to anything else. It involves a complete submission to Life. This means not being bound by anything at all, which is perfect freedom. The Fool is not burdened by attachments to what is considered good form. As far as he is concerned, the only good form is what pleases the essential Self.

The Cabalists and the wise of every culture have pointed out for a long time that you and I are simply *super*. Since birth, however, we've been sold the idea that we are not so great. This Key is a statement that we *are* super, that we are *magnificent*. I only present this to you as something to explore. I'm not giving it to you as gospel, but I am telling you that you will find it in the books of the wise. I hope you will want to explore this particular area, because the Self is our foundation. It's not a teacher. It's not a school. It's not a group of loving beings who are looking over you for your salvation. Your salvation is going to be the Self in you that is rooted in the Self of all. Without understanding this relationship you can hardly be very buoyant.

If you look into your mind, you can see many negative characteristics that detract from the natural buoyancy that is yours as a free Self. If you look around with your mind, you will see both good and evil. But if you attach your mind to the Self, you will see something else. Life is not the qualities that we observe around us. It is not the interrelationships that we see with the mind's eye. It is our essential Being, and by the grace of God or by the grace of our Self, we have to get into this area within ourselves so that we are free of appearances. This is liberation.

▶ **This sounds like running after ourselves, like a cat chasing its tail.**

Ideally we are able to go to the heights, which is going to the center of ourselves, and then return to the outer world, gracefully making the transition from the innermost to the outermost. It's like a modest artist (there are such people!) who performs with amazing skill, yet inwardly maintains a sense of Self that keeps him or her from falling into an ego trap. The true artist simply enjoys doing the art, the creative act.

For all of us, it doesn't mean that we are geniuses or anything of that sort, but in our own sphere, in our own way, we can be creative. We get the energy from a certain place within ourselves and that's about the size of it. The Fool represents cultural power and creative energy. Insofar as we exercise that energy, we have a lot of it. If we don't *use* our powers they just remain latent.

▶ **Why are we so reluctant to use our powers?**

It's because of the ego. Nobody who lacks success wants anyone else to be bigger or better than himself. If somebody emerges from the pile of worms or whatever they happen to be in, well, there's an outcry. People are jealous of success. They have some of the craziest notions about themselves that you could ever imagine. Inferiority complexes, superiority complexes ... Most people are not interested in being themselves. They want to be "important."

As the Buddha said, it's better to take one step in the right direction than ten thousand in the wrong direction. In order to disabuse our minds of all the bunk, the obstacles that obscure the truth about ourselves, it's worthwhile to exercise ourselves in the direction of the Tarot and Cabala. A little of this *fresh air* in the psyche goes a long way and makes you feel better.

If nobody had ever told you that there is a superconscious side to nature, it might not occur to you. But if somebody tells you that there is such a thing and it interests you, then you can go ahead and explore this aspect of life. There's no use in me going out and waving my hands frantically and saying that this is great, but if you have the inclination, then the Tarot can supply the map. It will lead you in the direction of intuition, inspiration, and direct firsthand experience of extraordinary things. You will have some very remarkable experiences in connection with the superconscious side of life. Period. Amen. Hallelujah.

▶ It seems there is a mystery that we must penetrate.

We are fortunate today in that we have the eye of science, which looks at you and me and says, "Do you know what you're made of? You're made of radiant energy. And do you know something else? You're full of holes. You're just a series of little dots. They're organized, to be sure, but you're mostly space. You're nothing." Well, when you start talking like this, you are getting close to a dream. And then you know that everything flows; everything is moving and changing. That's the way dreams are. You say, "I thought it was that way," but it wasn't that way. You were mistaken. How can you see what is true? Where is Reality? What is it as far as you're concerned? Doesn't it change? Aren't you in one reality when you are ten years old, another reality when you are twenty, and another reality when you're an old guy like me? Who are you to say what is real? But there is a way. The way is in the Self, because the Self knows itself. It knows what's going on.

We don't know what's going on until we apply to the Self and then by inner instruction find out what's going on. We find that we have been living in a world of illusion. Our Buddhist masters tell us, "Be careful. What you *think* is so, and what *seems* to be so, may *not* be so." They don't categorically say it isn't so because maybe it is. But they urge caution because you might be chasing a will-o'-the-wisp. As far as *freedom* is concerned—from KARMA, from everything, from the entire illusion that is possible in life—they say, "Look very hard." When you look very hard you come to know the Self. You have to see with the eye of the Self. This is the only way that you can be free. There is no other way.

Otherwise, it's the carrot before the horse that motivates you and makes you move every time, or the mechanical rabbit in front of the greyhounds at the dog races. This can be very subtle. It's a live human being that's the mechanical rabbit, or it's the voice of the orator, or it's an idea. Fortunately, you have in yourself the power to discriminate among these things, and to arrive at the freedom that comes from discrimination. When you get to that point you are in The Fool's state of mind. The Fool says to the world, "I listen to you, I hear you, I see you. I know what you think . . . and I don't believe a word of it!"

▶ **Through the process of discrimination you might eliminate everything and look at nothing.**

It's a good spiritual exercise to discard everything, to just say, "Forget everything." If you can maintain your composure in this practice you will find that, like migrating birds, some things come back. If you've fed the birds in the past, they will return to be fed again. You will find that things have a way of reintegrating in new patterns after you have abandoned the old ones.

Just as the Tarot teaches, you have to depend on inner instruction to find out what is real because the outside world cannot supply this very important information. It's not capable of doing it. It can give you a lot of information that will keep bread on your table. It knows how to get along in the world, to be sure. But it can't do much for your heart—and that's where you live. You don't live in your head, you know; nobody does. Nor does Man live "by bread alone," as Jesus said. In fact, we need very little bread to live well.

The Fool is wearing garments which represent worldly trappings. These may be removed at any time. As long as we identify with our clothes, which is to say our personality, then we are subject to the *illusions* of this identification. If we return to our pristine nakedness, which is always a good idea—in Zen it's called beginner's mind—then we are *inside* and we have a vantage point from which to make certain judgments that are critical to our well-being.

The garments are colored white, red, and black. These are the three qualities, or GUNAS, of the Hindu philosophy. The white undergarment represents the quality of SATTVA typified by light and consciousness. The red lining of the outer garment stands for the quality of RAJAS, or desire and passion. The black outer garment represents TAMAS, the inertia that is typical of the physical world. All of these clothes are just a costume and the spirit inside is much like an actor.

The whole Tree of Life, which is to say the universe, decorates The Fool's outer robe. If you bought this outfit here in downtown San Francisco it would cost you thousands of dollars. This personage is richly garbed, like a prince or princess; we will never know which. I've looked on the back of the card and I've held it up to the light. There's no way you can tell for sure whether it's a boy or a girl. It's been described variously. But *rich it is*, and this is the *richness of ourselves* before all the nonsense comes along and happens to us. The fact that we can return to ourselves in the midst of the outer nonsense is the greatest boon we have. We should hang on to it at all costs.

The first function of a garment is protection. The symbols of the Tree of Life, the Sun and Moon, and the Triple Flame of Consciousness are saying that *we have the protection of the cosmos*. It is obvious to any thinking person that if we didn't have this support we wouldn't be here. Humanity has been assisted through all sorts of vicissitudes, so somebody is interested in humanity in general, and you and me in particular.

On The Fool's white undergarment is written YOD-HEH-VAV-HEH יהוה, the TETRAGRAMMATON, which is the Cabalistic Name of Names for God. This stands for Reality; that's THE REALITY. The Cabalists think of Reality as something far beyond the average person's notion of God. In fact, it's anything but such a notion. It's quite abstract.

Our relationship to that Reality is magical. The difference between science and MAGIC is this: The scientist, through persistent investigations, and only with Nature's permission, discovers what is possible providing he or she follows the laws of Nature. Whereas, as far as Reality is concerned, *everything* is possible. That's magic. Magic is not popular with science, but that's neither here nor there. Magic has always existed and still exists, for the simple reason that it represents the direct relationship between you and me and Reality.

Do not confound this with low magic, where you call on various forces because your man or your woman or your tea isn't hot enough. These things are possible, but I'm not talking about low magic. I'm talking about High Magic, wherein you *expect the impossible*. You don't define it. Your ego is not involved. You say, "The outer aspect of everything seems negative, but I still have my expectation of a result that would normally be an impossibility." Then you are beginning to touch the nature of this Reality, which is suggested by the Yod-Heh-Vav-Heh. It is a power that is transcendent. This Key reminds you that there is such a thing as magic, and that you're part of it. The letters embroidered on the undergarment are not far away. They are part of your innate properties that you discover as you go along. They are yours in the sense that *you can use them.*

▶ **How would you define infinity?**

The Infinite is that from which you can draw forth anything without depleting it in any way. It is like the old fairy tales of endlessly productive pots and purses. As it says in statement zero in the Pattern on the Trestleboard, "All the power that ever was or will be is here now."

▶ **Why is there a Hebrew letter in the lower right-hand corner of the Key?**

In ancient Cabalistic lore, God created the world with numbers, letters, and symbols—which is to say, with various kinds of powers. The letters represent *conscious powers*, sometimes called *Intelligences*. The old masters of wisdom placed the letters as paths on the Tree of Life. Paul Foster Case, a twentieth-century master, placed the Tarot Keys in association with specific letters because of their esoteric correspondences. Thus, the Intelligence attributed to the letter is pictured in the Key. The Fool represents the Scintillating Intelligence.

The letter Aleph א, attributed to Key 0, stands for the *Divine Breath* that is the spirit within the entire universe. We directly communicate with this spirit every time we breathe. The Life Breath is so subtle that we forget how powerful it is and how it supports everything. Aleph reminds us, because as a noun it means the *ox*, a mighty powerful beast, "strong to carry the heavy load of the manifest," as it says in *The Book of Tokens* by Paul Case.

There once was a man who always worried about the problems of the world. He would get all worked up and lose sleep over it. Finally, as he was going to bed one night, God came to him and said, "Hey look, George, why not just let me handle it until tomorrow morning? You get a good night's sleep and I'll take care of the universe." We are supposed to do our share—wash the dishes, water the lawn, feed the canary—but with the major operations, we can let the Life Power handle it, and chances are the Life Power will pull it off somehow.

According to Cabalistic philosophy, which you are at liberty to discuss, reject, regurgitate, or do whatever you want to with it, the universe is self-fulfilling. It's unthinkable that anything as powerful as the Life Force that drives the universe couldn't find what it wanted, that it couldn't find a satisfactory expression of itself. There is nothing to oppose the Life Power. It doesn't have any enemies. It is what it is and it does what it pleases. Opposition comes in when you get to the level of polarity. The Life Power creates polarities but it does not reside there. It resides in unity.

▶ **What do you think keeps The Fool from stepping off the cliff?**

Why don't you ask him? That's a Tarot technique. If you have a question about a Key, you contemplate the Key itself.

▶ **Maybe the dog is warning him.**

In many myths an animal is the secret of the hero's success. However, when you understand what The Fool really is, you know that nothing can happen to him. He can't fall off the cliff because he is actually going around in a circle. As far as your Self is concerned, you never go anywhere. You have a lot of experiences; there is all this stuff going on around you. As the Chinese sages say, these are the *conditions* and you remain in the center of the conditions at all times. You never *go* anywhere or *get* anywhere, because there isn't anywhere to get. You're already where everything is, you see, so there's no reason to try and get anywhere. You are where it's all at. *Right now!*

The little white dog represents the spiritualized ego, your friend and fellow traveler. It is also referred to as the spiritualized intellect. Those of us who are touchy about our intellects might feel somewhat hurt to see it shown in the form of a dog, but the dog is really a nice kind of beast. Its faithfulness and the joy it takes in your company are something remarkable. In this case the intellect is happily associated with the superconscious Self, an excellent situation for us to emulate. The more we can build up this association, the better it is for us. A dog needs a master. When we are on an ego trip, we make the intellect number one. Actually it is supposed to be an executive function that simply carries out the inspiration that comes from above it. The real master is the Innermost Self.

▶ Besides the sun and the dog and the underwear, there is another white thing in this picture: the rose.

Roses in the Tarot represent the DESIRE-NATURE, and the single white rose is purified desire. This means a *focusing* of desire in a fruitful area. You understand that the highest goal in the Cabalistic system is to be oneself. The white rose symbolizes the ideal of finding within yourself the desire that *most represents yourself*, and cultivating it at the expense of everything else. This is *all* that is meant by the purification of desire. It has nothing to do with morality. It has to do with singleness of purpose.

Desire usually pulls us unconsciously all over the place. This is our weakness until we overcome it. When we finally meet ourselves and know what it is we want, then we get *intense* about what we want. We become polarized in one area; this is very protective. The desire-nature has been transformed into a very powerful purpose that we have for ourselves. This is the purification of the rose.

Desire also appears in the red feather on The Fool's head. Red is the color of what Cabalists call the Mars force, which is the reproductive power we share with the animals. Here it is raised to energize the highest level of consciousness.

▶ What about the other things that The Fool is carrying?

The wallet and the wand form a sexual symbol. The wallet is feminine and the wand is masculine. The wand is his power stick, his *Star Wars* light saber. It's also convenient for carrying the purse, which contains a whole string of special powers to be used as needed. For one thing, the purse or wallet is said to contain the cosmic memory of all The Fool's adventures in other rounds of existence. The eye on the purse is the All-Seeing Eye, which actually creates the future, much like the Dream of Brahma in Hindu symbolism.

▶ What is The Fool looking at?

He is looking in the direction of the unknown. That's where all the excitement is. We are so constructed that we *insist* on having adventures. This part of us is like the knight who gets on his horse and rides off into the forest, expecting something to turn up. It will.

Astrologically, Key 0 is connected to the planet Uranus, which symbolizes the spirit of adventure. An erratic and eccentric planet, it causes change on a major level. It can change you from an ordinary person into someone who is "crazy." The Fool is in the act of being ridiculous. There is no logic in his relationship with the Big Whatsis.

Reality is impossible to describe, but it's a good idea to depend on it. It's possible to get a good intellectual grasp of how big it is, which makes it easier for us to rely on it and be full of expectation. This is the *creative attitude*, which makes it possible for the unusual to happen. The negative aspect in our mind says, "Oh, it will never work," so we have to keep looking.

▶ **What if you don't know what you are looking for?**

It will come to you. For instance, I never dreamed I'd get married. I had envisioned living my whole life as a bachelor. Now I'm glad that I did get married. Good things happened to me because of it. It was a big surprise, though.

▶ **What if there was a situation that didn't exist but we wanted it to? We might have to lie at first.**

You don't have to lie. There's nothing to lie about. There's only one thing going on, so there's no *reason* to lie about anything.

What you are really talking about is using your creative imagination. Perhaps you want to create something pleasurable for yourself and others. This is perfectly all right. Why shouldn't you? Why shouldn't you be an artist if you want to be? To be creative is part of life. I might or might not like what you create, but the important thing is that you create it if you want to.

For example, you might think Bartók is tremendous. Personally, I don't like his music, but for Bartók it was very important that he wrote Bartók. So I accept that, but I don't have to listen to him if I don't like it, see? I've had critics point to me and say, "The trouble with you is that you don't like Bartók." You can guess what I told them.

The ultimate purpose of life is our own Self-fulfillment. This might seem selfish until you know what the Self is. Self-fulfillment means that you satisfy your deep inner Self, not something you might think you are, or that some character said you are.

▶ **The information you get from your insides, from your heart—how do you know that isn't just an illusion?**

There are very few rules of thumb in the Tarot and the Cabala that I've ever come across, but one of them is: If you feel better and everything works better, then what you are doing is right.

▶ But it could still be an illusion. I mean, isn't it as much an illusion as everything else?

The best information I have is that Reality is not an illusion on any level whatsoever, including the physical level. I never said that bananas weren't bananas or anything like that. Everything that's going on is real, but the interpretation of it is likely to be an illusion.

▶ What do you mean?

The interpretation that people put on what is happening is likely to be based on a misconception. For example, right now everyone is chest-pounding and screaming, "Recession—everything is going to hell!" What is overlooked is that we have a country of two-hundred-odd-million people whose economy goes on every day, no matter what the politicians say. It's as though someone said, "The economy of the sea is no more. It's over," as a piece of oratory. Yet despite that, there are still literally billions of fish in the sea. They go on about their business of living just as they've been doing for quite some time.

It's the same with us. We can have any silly idea that we please, but the necessity of ourselves continues and will lead us out of the desert of nonsense into the truth. Necessity is not against us; it's for us, you know. Once we get our heads in the right place, we're on our way. This doesn't mean knowing a certain doctrine or something of that sort. It means mostly getting your head *clear* so that you can see straight, so that you are not filled with illusory notions, or deluded, as the saying goes. You've got wonderful eyes, wonderful ears, a marvelous brain, a marvelous power of discrimination, and everything else. These are *gifts*. All you have to do is keep these faculties from becoming beclouded, and you'll stand in the high country that is pictured in The Fool Key.

If you "feel out" your own personal values about what is important to you, and if you persist at it whether school keeps or not, you are going to become a philosopher. You will become philosophical simply by developing your power of discrimination. Your value system becomes a world-idea for you. It's very much a part of your everyday experience. You might call it the stage on which you enact your life. This is a different approach to life from the ordinary one. The meanings you attach to things, and what you see when you look around—these are different when you have your own world-idea.

In a lot of instances we just have things shoved at us—*bleh*—and there it is. You are stuck with a happening. You didn't choose it. That's karma in the old-fashioned sense of the word. Eventually we expect to get rid of karma because a karmic existence is a very disorderly affair to the poor guy who's trying to live with it.

▶ Isn't everybody's life karmic, though?

No. I would say that most people's lives are karmic, but not everybody's. There is a minority who have gotten out of it. They have learned to create their own world. That is literally the world they live in. Karma works through our desire-nature. If we don't have anything in us that reacts to the world at large, there's no karma. You might say, "Well, then you're dead," but that's not so because if you want to use your desire-nature, it becomes like your automobile. You can get in it and go anywhere you please. You decide to create something with the strength of your desire and then you channel all that energy into an expression of yourself.

The energy has to be used because it never goes away. That's the doctrine; I'm only reporting. The desire-nature is your engine, the Life Force itself, and you *are* dead if *that* goes away. If you eat candy bars all the time, then your desire-nature is using you, but you can say, "I think I've eaten enough candy bars. Now I'm going to do something more creative with my energy."

This is evolution. As we proceed on our path, we become less and less unconscious and more and more conscious. The more conscious we become, the more positive and *directed* we become. Then we are on our own trajectory, safe from interference because it's part of the *plan for us*. There is an infinite number of trajectories. Each of us has one of our own, which is our unique path.

▶ Jason, what is the Cabala?

The Cabala is the attempt of Western sages, Hebrew and otherwise, to tie everything together in terms of meaning. That's a large order. They have attempted in their philosophy to develop a method whereby you can approach any aspect of life in a systematic way. This is one of the important uses of the Cabala. It is very helpful for getting our own heads and houses in order, symbolically and literally.

The Tree of Life exemplifies the structure of the Cabala. It doesn't leave out anything. There are hooks on the Tree for hanging everything you could possibly think of. The Tarot is very much part and parcel of the Tree of Life. All the colors on the Tree are expressions of the white sun in The Fool Key. The general idea is that the Life Power is broken down into special powers, represented by the different colors and centers of expression. White, gray, and black are found in the THREE SUPERNALS at the top. The colors of the spectrum are assigned to the lower seven centers. The Tarot colors are keyed to the Tree and have the same meanings.

Of course, as with all systems, there's a certain amount of technique in the Tarot approach to life. If there were no other reasons for taking up the arduous task of occultism, the fact that you can never become bored with it is reason enough. I don't know why, but it has an inspirational side that works twenty-four hours a day and seven days a week, unceasingly. This is something I cannot explain but must testify to. In all the years I've been involved with occultism, I can't say that I've *ever* been bored with the thing because it is so immense and has so many different angles to it. It's been completely fascinating for me as an experience. I hope it will be for you too.

This adventure we are about to go on is like a world tour. A world tour doesn't go just once. The vessel will continue to circumnavigate the globe as long as people want to go on the tour. That's why I've been here for so many years. I'm hoping that you will enjoy this particular round, which officially starts next week, because The Magician Key is actually number one, the beginning. Key 1 is the foundation for everything that comes after. The manipulations of The Magician underly all ensuing operations in the Tarot.

The word *magic* in itself is stimulating. We are dealing all the way through with what is magical; this is quite true. The whole idea of the Cabala is a magical idea. And like all magic, it has a high emotional content. It's exciting!

Next week we will receive our magical implements and get out our bankbooks, ready to put all the money we make into the bank as soon as possible. The kind of money that we shall accumulate is not the dream money that can disappear in a bad stock investment. It is something we can never lose. The coin of the Tarot is something that, once acquired, you own forever. It's the progress you make. So you will amass a great fortune in Cabalistic money as we proceed on the voyage.

The Magician is the exact opposite of the transcendent Fool. Among other things, The Magician represents concentration, will, and technique. There are certain practices we can do to advance in the magical art. But don't concentrate too hard because that makes for congestion. I want you to have a nice week. Remember, *you are The Magician.*

Thank you for coming. I appreciate it.

KEY 1

CHAPTER 1

THE MAGICIAN

Key 1 is the specific beginning of the Tarot, since Key 0 is said to be dancing everywhere throughout the deck. The mysterious Magician may seem rather shocking, because today we live in a scientific world that is not magical at all. Babies are produced scientifically; grain and all other natural support systems are produced scientifically—and if you believe that, better think again.

Let's say that in your imagination you could suddenly be Life Itself. You would be greater than the greatest conceivable super master, because Life is the most powerful force we know anything about. It is *The Force*. Just look into the area of biology. Look at the incredible magic and mystery in an embryo. Biologically, things are done that would astound us if they were done by legerdemain, but because they are done invisibly, we watch and take them for granted. We are watching *magic* and we don't realize it.

This primary Key illustrates the fundamental task we have to do in order to achieve the amazing success we are aiming for in this work. First of all, The Magician shows us how to contact the Life Force. The most important symbol in the first Key is the gesture of the upraised wand. This means that The Magician, which is your SELF-CONSCIOUSNESS, recognizes that all the powers he uses are derived from the basic Reality in the universe. He is saluting the superior power and plugging into it. By this gesture we are shown the technique of concentration and dedication accepted by Cabalists and Taroists and all those who are seriously involved in the Path of the West. If you can remember this gesture you will never fall into the trap of egotism.

You could get into an ego-inflationary spiral if you thought, "These powers are really mine! I can feel them! I'm using them! Wow, I've got it made!" Such affirmations are fine, provided you come back to the original understanding that your power isn't coming from your cornflakes.

It's coming directly from the universe. So please don't make this enormous error in your calculations. It would put you into the sorcerer's apprentice class and that's the last thing the Cabala wants to happen to you.

Tarot deals primarily with liberation through mental methods. Key 1 corresponds astrologically to Mercury, the intellect, which energizes things within the mind. We can see that we all have beautiful bodies, so perhaps it's our minds we really need to work on. This is where the Tarot is extremely useful to us. It provides practical information about ourselves that we can apply. That's what we want to do—apply it.

The Magician's *main magic* consists of what he can do—what you and I can do—just by *wanting* to do it! This is symbolized by his red robe, which represents his desire-nature. The Being inside can take the robe off and walk around in the white undergarment, but when he is doing magic he must wear his red robe. It activates his particular universe, represented by the implements on the table.

Whereas most people hold a low view of Man (speaking generically), the Cabalists take a high view. They say the energies that come through Man literally affect the universe. In the Cabalistic definition Man is a mediator between the inner and outer aspects of life, exercising this power primarily through his desire-nature. Desire is the motivating force in the magic that we perform on ourselves. This is true of any human being, regardless of the person's secondary sexual characterisitcs.

True magic is the magic of the Self. You and I know that we are extremely complicated. We are always mystified about ourselves. We can look outward and classify everything and say, "That's a horse; that's a cow; that's the President; that's the Pope." We're smart that way, but when it comes to little old us, we're not so sure. It appears that whoever created us decided to make us the most baffling puzzle in the universe, which we are. This course is presented as an attempt to introduce you to some hidden parts of yourself, which when understood will ensure a much better life for you.

The Cabalistic teaching is that Man is made in God's image. As a microcosm, Man can know himself. This is extremely important because if he didn't know himself he would be on the level of the animal kingdom. He is fortunate when somebody comes along and tells him a few things about himself that help to wake him up. Then the burden is on the lucky person to go ahead and finish the work of Self-knowledge. This is called the GREAT WORK. When the person gets the whole job done he is the master of his own universe, which is himself.

This person is the master of what we call matter. He learns how to manipulate matter by practicing on himself. Once he learns how to handle matter in himself, he can manipulate all matter because matter is plastic, not fixed. Then he's a real master.

▶ **Is that what Jesus meant when he said you could move mountains if you had the faith of a grain of mustard seed?**

Well, he probably said, "in time." In time you can move mountains.

▶ **So the ability to manipulate matter within yourself does not mean pointing your finger at a mountain and having it do whatever you wish?**

No.

▶ **Then what does mastery over matter entail?**

Everything that happens in outer nature—the earth, the plants, and everything else—all of physics, chemistry and biology, all of mechanics, all the subtleties—these are all going on within yourself. Everything we know about is happening in the body itself. The teaching is that you are the same as the universe. If you knew everything about yourself, you would know everything about the universe. That's the whole story.

However, there are two aspects: the soma and the psyche. The soma is the physical part, where we take the scientific approach. We must also know the psyche, where we become involved in art. And of course, we must know the relationship between the two.

In the meantime, there are many things about ourselves that the wise can tell us. If we have the wit to listen, we can learn from what they have to say.

▶ **We would probably learn that we very seldom need to move a mountain.**

Well, we do move mountains, but not by pointing our fingers at them. Neither do we drive nails with feathers, as they saying goes. We must use the proper means to accomplish whatever we want to do. In working with the psyche, we have to make an image. This is an art. If we can't make a specific image, we won't succeed.

The Tarot is all about images. All these symbols go to work on our mind and get it moving. Our teachers ask us to make an identification with each one of the Keys. Get into the Key and be like it, feel like it. Try on The Fool, The Magician, The High Priestess. Imagine yourselves as these beings, as a way of knowing them.

▶ Jason, what is black magic?

That's what most people are doing every day, all the time. We do what we damn well please. The individual says, "I'll do what I want, any way I can." He's not concerned with whether there is a God or whether his actions will affect other people. He's only concerned with himself. That's black magic.

▶ And does it work?

Sure it works. Look around. Ambitious people who are not, shall we say, enlightened philosophers, have specific goals and they stop at nothing to achieve those goals. But it's a short-term proposition because coercion is always used in black magic. You *force* all the powers around you, whether they are people, elements, or inner powers. You make them obey you and when you do that, when you exert force, there is going to be a reaction. The egotism of the black magician is so great that he overlooks this well-known feature of the law. He can't imagine that there could be a reaction, but there always is and it can be fatal for him.

▶ How can I protect myself from black magic?

The head of the Tree of Life is Goodwill. That's the greatest protection you can have. It is impersonal and has no object. This includes *harmlessness to all*. The truth has always come through goodness. It has never come through someone who was ambitious. All great teachers have been people of goodwill.

Life is not destructive nor does it put itself down. Life supports itself. Ultimately, the Will-to-Good is Life's own *pleasure*. Therefore, *your own pleasure is your greatest goodness*. Your true heart's desire is always beneficial to others. This is why we affirm, in statement number one in the Pattern on the Trestleboard, "I am a center of expression for the Primal Will-to-Good, which eternally creates and sustains the universe." When you say that and know it's true, that's the end of all your worries.

▶ What do you think of the alchemists who wanted to make gold?

Outwardly, the alchemists were some of the most ambitious people the world has ever seen. Inwardly, however, ALCHEMY is a search for spiritual experience. *God is included* in the basic premise. For instance, pictured in Jung's book *Psychology and Alchemy*, God is shown as being right there in the alchemist's laboratory. This means that if the alchemist can get God to work in what he's doing, then all things become possible, including physical transformation. This is the spiritual approach to alchemy.

The average chemist believes that many things are impossible. When God is involved, that changes everything. The alchemist says, "If God can do it (and God can do anything), then by God's grace, if I'm *mindful* of God, I can do it." This is different from trial and error or manipulations. Like George Washington Carver, the alchemist is continually praying to God to tell him how to do it. We're not smart enough to know what to do next. We have to be guided.

It's just good sense to be humble about our capabilities and to ask for a little light. Within ourselves (that's where to find the God we've been talking about), we have a lot of guidance, but not much on the personality level. If it were easy on the level of the personality, everybody would be fulfilled.

▶ A real scientist has no prior opinion about what he's going to find.

That's pure science. Truth is the only goal. That's how an obscure monk like Gregor Mendel came up with an earth-shaking proposition about genetics. You don't have to be a big shot to be a scientist or to perform some useful service for people.

It's interesting historically that the ancients weren't involved in science the way we are today. The Greeks had a tremendous interest in the humanities and psychology, and in the improvement and enhancement of life. Their major concern was in working out a system of values applicable to life almost anywhere. We tend to think of the ancients as being a bit on the primitive side, but this is not so. They were just as smart as we are but they were not interested in the same things.

Today we have an advanced state of science because that's what we care about. It's a fun game and usually someone else is paying for it. In fact, it might be you and me who are footing the bill, as taxpayers.

▶ **Science limits itself to what can be observed, measured, and tested.**

Science has no way of measuring feeling. There is no exoteric scientific instrument for observing the psyche. The closest thing to such an instrument is another human being. If you perspire, turn pale, and have heart palpitations, science can infer that you are experiencing an emotion. However, that's not the feeling. It's simply their scientific reaction to your feeling.

▶ **In ancient Egypt the word "magic" meant what we mean by "science."**

You know that in the old days the magicians were also the priests. They had all the learning, whatever magic and whatever science there was. They preserved and taught their knowledge. That was part of the priesthood. Key 1 is HERMES TRISMEGISTUS, magician and priest. In the old days Hermes symbolized the principle that actually liberates the soul. The problem of liberating the soul hasn't changed any, and Hermes still represents the enlightened intellect. The higher mind actually leads the lower mind toward the light. If we didn't have some light we wouldn't know where to go and we could wander around indefinitely. Once we get the Divine Idea, we hold on to it by repetition.

▶ **It takes discipline to remain attentive to the higher power.**

This Key represents the ideal, not the everyday. When people who have never seen the Tarot come upon this Key, it strikes them as an ideal because they realize immediately that they are a long way from what it represents. Therefore, in order to make a success of your life, you have to assume the role of The Magician. You must *exercise* your capability.

You must proceed in an orderly fashion, as suggested by the implements on the table. In the Cabalistic tradition there is no other way. This is the Saturn aspect of the work. Discipline is part of the message of Key 1, indicated on the Tree of Life by placement of this Key on the path that leads directly from Kether to the Saturn principle in BINAH. This path begins the side of the Tree called *rigor*. If we don't embrace discipline, we can expect very few results.

In order to get the results you want, you have to limit your material. If your attention is all over the place, your life goes sort of like this: "Oh, dahling, I just found the most marvelous book and it says blah blah." Next week it's, "Oh, dahling, did you see the new Swami So-and-so? He's just absolutely divine." Then next week it's something else. This can go on year after year. Well, it doesn't work. You have to put away your diversions to get into the concentration that's spoken of in Key 1.

If you don't have a taste for this challenge, for heaven's sake don't think there's any morality involved in your choice. If you *like* the Tarot and Cabala and have a feeling for it, then that's lovely. If you don't like it but think there is some moral reason why you should go into it, that's ridiculous. There are other perfectly good disciplines you can get into that might be exactly right for you. There's no forcing it.

▶ **Do you have to know Hebrew to study the Cabala?**

No. The minimal requirement is that you learn the letters and their meanings. It's a good exercise to learn to construct the letters, too. Other than that, it's up to you. You can analyze the Hebrew letters from an occult point of view, and if you have a taste for that, then you can go into the thing as deeply as you please. You can interpret the Bible in terms of Tarot and Cabala. This kind of analysis is a realm of its own if you want it. *The Book of Tokens* gives you a taste of it.

If you *do* get into the discipline of Tarot and Cabala, you have the real satisfaction of acquiring skill in the expression of your creative capabilities. This system wants to bring you to your happiest life expression. One of the irksome things about the Path of the West is that it will never let you alone until you become yourself. It will *bother* you until you finally reach the place where you are happily yourself. That's the greatest boon Life can bring to you. There's nothing higher. Of course this means that you have to be a bit on the brave side, because everybody has some idea of what you should be. You have to be willing to tell them to go soak their heads, as we say in the vernacular.

Our late lamented brother, Paul Foster Case, produced an enormous amount of written instruction which is published and distributed by the Builders of the Adytum in Los Angeles. His opening page gets right down to the basics of *what you really want*. It seems easy in the beginning to find out what you want, but it isn't. You want many things and you want them all as soon as possible. Over a period of time you find out through experience that there are some things you want much more than anything else. Part of this training is to get you to make the choices that represent your desires—not mine, not somebody else's—*your own* desires. Insofar as you can *muster the inner forces* in yourself, you will be able to transform yourself.

It is hoped that you will flower into being your Self, which is the goal of this work. In the Tree of Life it is represented by Kether at the top, entitled IPSISSIMUS, which means the person who is most himself or herself. The goal is not easy. It's very difficult to make the proper identification of who and what you really are. If you succeed in this, you can really perform magic as far as your life is concerned. You can transform yourself into your True Self. Then your life goes along swimmingly. That's precisely the real magic that's involved in this Key.

▶ **You must *want* to transform.**

That's why The Magician lives in the house of desire. The red roses in this Key represent desires. The Hebrew letter Beth ב means *house*. His desires form an arbor around him, providing privacy for his magic.

In our textbook, Paul Case makes the statement that there's no magic higher than the will, and he also tells you that behind will stands desire. When you get down to the practical part of this endeavor, you'll find that the biggest study you have to embark on initially is your own desire-nature. All you have to do is become introspective about your desire-nature and be honest with yourself. You'll begin to learn the Secret Doctrine first hand.

The desire-nature is rooted in CHOKMAH, the Wisdom center on the Tree of Life. Chokmah includes the idea, as well as the desire to realize the idea. On the other side of the Tree, Binah becomes *activated* by desire. Chokmah fulfills itself in Binah, the center of Understanding on the opposite side of the Tree.

According to this psychology, the desire-nature is always a reflection of experience that has gone before, so your memory bank is the source of your desires. As you progress in this study you become more and more free from habitual attitudes about what's important to you. Much of the time you and I *think* we want something, but we don't *really* want it. The proof of this is that when we get it, we usually don't like it.

▶ **How do I know what I really want?**

You just have to wait until Christmas morning! No one can tell you the answer to what you really want because if you are getting everything you want, then you are already where you should be. If you're not getting everything you want and it's not satisfying for you, then you have not arrived at the proper point. That's the way you can tell. Nobody can say, "If you just had this, or did this, you would be perfectly contented." I'm being heretical, but I don't mind. No doubt I've been burned at the stake many times.

Let's say you want money, which is perfectly okay. You decide that's what is important. If you devote all your attention to it, you won't get anything else but you'll get all the money you want. After you get it, you might wake up some morning and say, "What's going on here? This isn't satisfying. I guess what I really want is sex." So you start cultivating that, and so on. Finally, when you've had it *all*, you say, "Money is okay. Sex is okay. But there must be something else because I still don't feel as if I've hit the mark." In India they call this NETI, NETI (not this, not that) as a description of the Path.

The Cabala states quite clearly that until you begin to *create* what you want, you will never be satisfied because your essential nature is to be creative. This is the last thing you will think of if you want some *thing*, if you are trying to settle on an *object* for your desire-nature. When you finally reach the point in your life experience where you decide, "I've got to try a different tack," then you become open to the suggestion that it would be worthwhile to create something for yourself with your own tremendous powers.

▶ **After all the searching, it might be something quite close by.**

From the *very beginning* your desire-nature is concerned with a life of fulfillment. Going for what feels good will lead you to your *highest* good. Your efforts with the Tarot or any spiritual path are simply a *refinement* of your desire-nature, as symbolized by The Fool's white rose.

▶ **I have been taught that desire is sinful.**

The fact that we can and do desire makes us feel alive. Desire is normally something that we think of as being our own, but in the dogma of the Cabala there is no such thing about us as a personal quality. *Every* quality, every faculty, is a *cosmic principle*. This helpful thought reminds us that our desire-nature is also the driving force of the universe. It's driving in the direction of fulfillment. The desire-nature that we exercise within ourselves is our birthright, from being a part of life, particularly human life. We get our motivation and power from the great big push that's going on everywhere all the time. It's leading God knows where, and that's all you can say about it.

In each individual case, we do have the possibility of some control, so that in our own small way we can be like God too. We can use these energies to get to a certain place, condition, or whatever, that pleases us. That's what the Universe is doing itself. Why not? Who's going to stop it? The Boss does what He wants. He says, "Here, you've got all this stuff, the same as I do. Now all you have to do is get it organized. Just remember where it came from. It would be nice if you would remember Mama and Papa. But you're on your own."

▶ Is that what is meant by following your true will?

Well, your true will is the same as The Will. It's as though somebody gave you a gift of a million dollars. Now you have the responsibility for it. You're stuck with it, in other words. You might knock yourself out trying to decide what to do with it. It might make you happy or it might make you miserable. Anything could happen. The same thing goes for our responsibility for ourselves. It can make us deliriously happy or it can make us quite sad, depending on our understanding.

▶ Sometimes I feel as though I just can't handle myself.

You must remember that in the scheme of things as taught by the wise, we are in a very high place. We are above nature in the sense that we can control it. Nature is willing to respond to us, making our position quite different from that of the animals. You and I are not responsible for the basic scheme of things; that's just the way it is. As the director of *our part* in the scheme, we have a real responsibility concerning what we want. Our desire-nature is the aspect of ourselves that is of the most concern to us. In every moment of our lives, this is what counts, what makes the difference between being and not being, in terms of experience—not in terms of ultimate consciousness, but in terms of *living*.

The Magician's table represents the field of attention in which he is working. It is a workshop. Whether you want to make a cake or a spaceship, the intellectual faculty is indispensable for accomplishing your aim. This self-conscious, waking aspect acknowledges superconsciousness by the raising of the wand. In the Tarot, "up" means "within." It means "in" instead of "out." So our inspiration comes from the innermost Reality, the Ain Suph Aur.

The Ain Suph Aur isn't in any one particular place. It's *anywhere you happen to be*. The point of the wand is what connects us with this remarkable Reality, because the point of the wand is Kether in you and me. The Reality is big enough so you don't have to worry about running out of steam as long as you're holding this point in the right place. And that's anywhere you happen to put it, you see, which makes it most convenient.

The head of the wand is a crystal in rhombus form. There is a four-fold expression in the upper part that is reflected in the lower part: "As above, so below." Crystals transmit light; Key 1 is the Transparent Intelligence.

The wand itself is a phallic symbol. The most powerful force we know is biological, the Life Force. The Magician holds the "strong force of all forces" described in the Emerald Tablet of Hermes Trismegistus. He draws down this power and directs it to the table. He is an artist, a *creator*. Beth, the Hebrew letter connected with Key 1, is associated with the powers of Life and Death. This is a picture of the divine creative act, which we're supposed to be doing.

Sometimes we get involved in reacting rather than acting. This is not the greatest as far as the Tarot and Cabala are concerned, but since everybody suffers from this particular disability, we don't have to become too exercised about being naughty. If we're all in the same boat, the problem is to improve our situation. More particularly, our problem is to improve our own life situation.

The tools on the table represent the Four Worlds of Cabala. There is a certain *natural order* to their use that The Magician must learn. This pattern is said to be an angelic revelation. Regardless of what you set forth to do, you need not do it haphazardly. Energy moves in a path through these Worlds. The wand is the Archetypal World of ideas. The cup is the Creative World of forms. The sword is the Formative World of mechanics. The coin is the World of Result, which would correspond to all the objects in this room, including ourselves.

The tools also symbolize the four elements. The wand represents the fire that is making everything go. When we are ignorant, we think *we* make it happen. We have to be educated about the archetypal plane, the Land of Superior Powers. The special sacred fire becomes known to us through water, the cup, which is mind. Mind translates the ineffable idea into concrete thought, but it is undifferentiated until the sword of air comes into play. The sword achieves planned accomplishments. Results are symbolized by the coin, the element of earth.

▶ **If I get some implements like this, will I be able to do magic?**

The implements are *symbolic only*. You could have a craftsperson make these articles and you could put them on a table and stand there until your head falls off. Always remember that the Tarot is symbolism, purely and entirely.

▶ **I notice that the cup is more dimensional than the other implements. It reaches above them.**

The cup is uppermost because our receptivity reaches to our intuitive powers. It takes us out of the ordinary three-dimensional mentality into spiritual realms. This could be quite a jolt for somebody—the discovery that the *Wall Street Journal* and the Bank of America are not the "be-all and end-all" of existence. The limiting thought doesn't have to be business. It could be—unfortunately—religion. Amen.

To be like the cup is to be successful in this work. The Holy Grail is our ability to receive inspiration. The word "Cabala" literally means *The Reception*, and that tells us that receptivity is the most important thing in this philosophy. This is exactly like the Chinese Taoist who feels that the Tao is moving in a certain direction and leading him or her in the best way. In practical matters, the cup represents receptivity to *guidance*, which is essential. This is the feminine, receptive power in ourselves, corresponding to Binah on the Tree of Life.

▶ **What is the meaning of the five-pointed star on the coin?**

The pentagram is the figure of generic Man. It symbolizes Man's dominion over all the powers of nature. It's quite true that humanity can command the spirits of air and so forth, as they say in occult terminology. But thank God you can only produce just so much of a bang, because people being what they are, they simply should not be entrusted with any more power than they have right now. We must learn the proper use of our powers. Just as coins represent success in the world, the pentacle represents spiritual success.

There are four occult admonitions: to will, to know, to dare, and to be silent. They correspond to fire, water, air, and earth. The admonitions are something to think about and practice. You should cultivate will and accumulate knowledge. The daring refers to action, which is fundamental on this level where we live. As for silence, that's obvious. It's a serious mistake to run off at the mouth about what you're going to accomplish.

We are told by the authors of the piece that the lilies in The Magician Key correspond to knowledge. The particular kind of knowledge we're interested in is going to be a means of liberation for us. It doesn't mean just knowing a lot of things. It means knowing Reality Itself. There are so many interesting bits of facts around that you could collect them horizontally throughout eternity and not be a whit wiser than you were in the first place. All of us would like to be wiser than we are now, I'm sure.

▶ **Isn't there something called the quintessence, in which the four elements together equal a fifth thing?**

The four lower points of the star represent the elements and the upper point represents the spirit, which is the spirit of Man. The quintessence means that the spirit is actually in all the points. It has infused everything.

▶ **Why does The Magician have his right hand up and his left hand down?**

He is collecting cosmic forces in his heart. The heart is like a sun. Our sun, our solar friend in the sky, collects all the cosmic forces that come into our planetary system and disburses them to its satellites. The same is true of us. The entire universe is pouring influences into our hearts.

The position of the Magician's arms forms a YOD י, the Hebrew letter that signifies the Creator. Yod is the first stroke of the first letter and is said to occur in all the letters. This is a godlike gesture. The person is actively soliciting the creative power with his right hand and letting it run through him and out the other end. The left hand acts as the passive transmitter of the power. The Magician is practicing a technique known as concentrating in receptivity.

There is a theoretical foundation involved in this kind of receptivity. Confident expectancy can only be *real* for a person who has some philosophical background. He understands *why* he should be expectant. Otherwise it's a case of, "Everything is going to hell around me, so why should I be confident?" There has to be something else, and that something else is the philosophy of the Cabala, which expands your mental view of Reality. You have to push the sides of your head out—and out and out and out—to get some conception of That. When you get a big, husky definition of Reality, and you realize that this is your foundation, then you can see why you should be confidently expectant.

▶ **In Cabalistic terms, what is concentration?**

Those of you who have read some Eastern books know that the mind has a tendency to jump about. It follows the laws of association. You think of one thing that leads to another and then to another. For the average person, this isn't easily controlled; the mind just slides around. So, from a technical point of view, concentration is learning to keep your mind in a certain given area for as long as you please.

Again, I think you'll find that, in practice, unless you're interested in the area, you'll never be able to keep your mind on it. You might try to say, "I'm going to put my mind on this whether I'm interested in it or not," but that won't work. You can't kid yourself that way.

▶ **When you say, "Put your mind on it," do you mean associate one thing after another as long as it's on the subject? You're not thinking of just one thing?**

I'm not talking about one-pointedness. I'm talking about The Magician drawing his magic circle and saying, "There are certain things in this circle that I'm going to work on." To try to make your mind completely one-pointed is forcing the issue, which isn't a good idea. If you start inside a reasonable circle, gradually, like a June bug, your mind will come to rest.

▶ **His white robe is his pure nature, his real insides, right? Is the snake a limit between that and the desireful red robe?**

Yes. If you want to express yourself in the world of creation, you have to go through a boundary. You go from one level to another, and on the other side is the robe. In other words, you go into the land of desire that's directly tied to the world of creation.

▶ **We create everything by desiring it.**

That's right. And inside the boundary of the snake, there isn't any desiring, because this is where everything is fulfilled by itself. It's hard to conceive of a situation that exists for eternity in which there is a state of fulfillment. How shall I put it? It's not a state of mind, exactly ... it's a kind of consciousness that's always satisfied, so it doesn't have to go into the mechanics of desiring something as an object, and then getting it, and then desiring something else. It always has this sense of peace because it is Self-sufficient.

This is the condition of the spirit in Man, as opposed to man the poor, struggling beastie. The spirit doesn't need anything. It already has knowledge, existence, and bliss, as they say in the Hindu tradition. What more could you want? That's what it's all about, isn't it? The rest of it, the ordinary fun and games, is played in another theater outside the serpent boundary.

The serpent also symbolizes our continuing transformations. Old selves drop off just like old skin. In this case, we are the snake ourselves, because snakes are known to shed their skins and grow new ones.

In the highest interpretation, the snake swallowing its own tail is Life Itself. Being Self-fed, it doesn't need anything outside itself. This is the ancient concept of the OUROBOROS, the eternal cyclicity. One change devours another and the whole thing keeps going around. For example, in the water cycle, the same substance falls from clouds, runs in rivers, becomes the sea, and evaporates back into the clouds. It is all One Thing.

▶ **The infinity sign over The Magician's head looks like a circle that has been twisted in the middle.**

The center of the LEMNISCATE ∞ or infinity sign is a balance point that harmonizes the opposite sides of the Tree of Life. The two sides, the Pillar of Mercy and the Pillar of Severity, seem to be warring forces. If we identify with one side or the other, we immediately assume a warlike stance. The lemniscate shows that the two sides are actually in reciprocal action with each other. Thus the problem is successfully overcome. Forces are continually flowing from one side to the other on the Tree, very much like YANG and YIN in the Chinese scheme. They are not really in opposition. The masculine and feminine principles are working together to produce the entire universe. In spite of the fact that we can mess it up pretty well, harmony is basically possible—the harmony that we see in the heavens, as contrasted to the lack of harmony that we see in our politics.

▶ **Was Paul Foster Case a magician?**

Paul was an excellent prestidigitator and he enjoyed ritual magic, but it was on the inner planes that he was recognized as an accomplished high magician. The classical definition of High Magic is the transmutation of the personality from its lower forms of expression into a conscious temple of the Holy Spirit. The letter Beth, the house, is a dwelling place for the Self.

▶ **What about ritual magic?**

I don't know anything about it. I'm not a magician, except in the Tarot sense that we all are. I guarantee that you'll never be able to levitate by taking my course. For those of you who don't want to float away on the first breeze that comes along, this guarantee should be meaningful to you.

Now let's take a look at next week's Key. Our Lady, The High Priestess, is the cup, the container of everything. Whereas most systems in the West don't include the feminine, you'll find that the Cabala very much includes it and ascribes many wonderful qualities to the feminine aspect. Key 2 possesses powers of *mind* and *memory* that integrate everything that is going on. The TORA on her lap is the total law of all the energies operating in the universe.

So if you will, during the coming week, become introspective about mind and memory. For starters, think of them as universal principles rather than something we just have as individuals. This viewpoint opens new doors, so let yourself go a little bit. Our teachers tell us that when we get full of smarts, we'll be able to tap the cosmic memory and see all sorts of fascinating things. Who knows?

Thank you so much for joining me.

KEY 2

CHAPTER 2

THE HIGH PRIESTESS

THE HIGH PRIESTESS is one of the most fascinating and powerful figures in the entire Tarot. She is the Divine Mother on the Tree of Life, enthroned in Binah, Root of Water. As the chief feminine principle in the Cabala, she is the substantiality and the responsiveness in life that make magic possible. Our teachers call her Universal Mind, the Great Sea within which we live and move and have our being.

In the doctrine of the Cabala the universe is mind-conceived, mind-constructed, and mind-supported. This nurturing principle affects us immediately. In exactly the same way that a fish is supported by the sea, your mind and my mind are duly sustained by the Great Mind.

In psychological terms all the powers of Key 2 represent SUBCONSCIOUSNESS, the feminine element in the psyche that responds to the masculine, self-conscious element typified by The Magician Key. The relationship between these two principles is crucial. There must be an exchange between male and female in order for anything to happen. Motherhood won't work unless there is instigation and activation, and the animating principle won't work unless there is a body to animate. It takes two to tango, as they say, and so Binah, the *form-maker*, balances Chokmah, the *ineffable spirit*.

The use of the word "*sub*consciousness" does not mean that the Father aspect is in any way superior to that of the Mother. They are equal. On the Tree of Life they both come from the single point of Unity and they exist together on the same level. The Tree of Life is an expression of Reality as it exists in the universe and in ourselves. In other words, we are made in the image of God. Like the Tree of Life, we have both masculine and feminine aspects within ourselves. The whole Tree—our life —results from the relationship between the spheres of Wisdom and Understanding, the fire and water that are the Big Two of occult philosophy.

The prefix "sub" means that The High Priestess is totally responsive to and reflective of self-consciousness. Modern psychology uses the phrase "the unconscious" in reference to this principle. It's a shame to call the Universal Mind unconscious, but we don't have better terminology at the present time. The whole point of our effort here is to involve ourselves consciously with the unconscious. The unconscious is not just a bunch of nothing. It happens to be *the law of the universe.* That's the Tora rolled up on the lap of The High Priestess. We are trying to learn how to manipulate this law from the level of The Magician.

The High Priestess is very tender-hearted. She protects you because you are her own. She explains to you as her child that you are born of mind, that you *are* mind. We always say, "I have a mind," but we don't realize that we can say, "I am mind." Mind is not like a muscle in the body; it is not a thing. We are not a thing. We are spirits. The nature of mind is the nature of spirit.

Water is the main symbol of Key 2. It flows from the robe of The High Priestess and continues flowing through the whole Tarot. Water is a mysterious element that contains everything in solution and can precipitate anything out of itself. In like manner, mind holds all possibilities. Chemistry would call mind a supersaturated solution. Things precipitate or jell out of it. The solution itself does not change; mind does not change. It is said to be forever virginal. The essential virginity of Key 2 holds all things *in potential.* (The worship of the Virgin Mary in the West is the adoration of the same archetype as that represented by The High Priestess.)

According to our teachers, there is a logical sequence to creation. Before the feminine aspect in Binah is inseminated by the masculine aspect from Chokmah, nothing happens. If you were a chemist in a laboratory, you would have many bottles of substances that react variously. However, *you* are the one who puts them together and decides what you want to happen. The different qualities of all the bottles are what Key 2 represents. The High Priestess is the total fecundity of life *before* the whole process gets going. The pregnant Empress in the next Key illustrates that something has *happened.*

The mind is endlessly fruitful, but unless we know how to use this aspect of our equipment, nothing happens. When we learn how to operate in the mind, then we become creative. Being creative is a great accomplishment as far as the Tarot and Cabala are concerned.

If you study history you will notice that, without exception, any advance in the history of humanity has come about by a certain person finding out something extraordinary *from within that person's self*. Probably the easiest example to look at is the great religious teachers in the world. As you know, *they wrote the book*. They did not read the book or get the information from any outside source.

There has also been another type of person interested in knowing the nature of Reality. At first these people were called alchemists. They gained respectability as the centuries rolled on and became known as scientists. Inside every scientist there's a bit of the alchemist—the mark of a person who wants to learn something about nature without reference to a book. The books in science are records of discoveries. The discovery itself is the *spirit* of science. If you take a close look at what has happened in science, in every case these people have *intuited* something about Nature and they've had the patience to express it to their fellow beings in words, formulae, or whatever. In Tarot terms, they have received their information from The High Priestess.

This rule has *no exceptions*, which means that you and I (who are just as good as anybody else) are connected to the Divine Mind and perfectly capable of receiving information and guidance from within. You may ask, "If I'm connected to this wonderful Divine Mind, if I'm so magical, how come my life doesn't work?" The sages say that you have to get rid of distractions and *still* your mind in order to pick up the information that comes from The High Priestess. The Magician Key teaches us that we must concentrate and be dedicated to make real progress. Sir Isaac Newton lived in a particularly wild time in England when there were plenty of distractions. He put these aside, stuck to business, and came up with some remarkable results.

You don't have to be a scientist to read the Reality that is hidden in the Universal Mind. You could be an artist, or any kind of creative person. If you would like to apply the technique of using this power—whose immensity is really quite beyond our intellectual grasp—The High Priestess will initiate you into how to go about it.

As you would expect, you don't go into her holy temple and yell, "TA-DA! I'm here!" You can go in this way, but you probably will be escorted off the premises in a hurry. There have always been temple guardians whose job it is to take the overexuberant by the ear. There's something about the Holy of Holies that needs peace and quiet to be appreciated. It's a Presence, not a thing. The High Priestess represents the element of transcendence *par excellence* in the Tarot. What's more, she is the receptacle of all the information we would dearly love to get our greedy little hands on.

In this philosophy there is no difference between yourself and myself and the Divine Life. There are not two realities, there is only one. There is only one mind. The illusion is that our mind is different from that mind, but this is not so, according to the Cabala. I am here to suggest to you in the strongest possible words that you have a *direct* connection with a power that has been responsible for all the progress that the human race has ever experienced. This connection is demonstrable in history and in your own life. It is more than sufficient to keep you going.

▶ **Doesn't the Divine Mind remember everything, including us?**

Absolutely. In the occult teaching, the scroll of The High Priestess contains a perfect record of everything that has ever happened. Our personal memory is part and parcel of the cosmic memory and that's the reason we *can* remember. This is part of our heritage. We can accept this doctrine or leave it or analyze it at our leisure. In any case, it's a stimulating idea: the cosmos remembers everything, and out of this storehouse you draw forth anything you wish.

We can see that the cosmos has a powerful intellectual basis. You may be sure that there is a memory bank that underlies the Cosmic Logos. That memory bank is always functioning perfectly. We are in the middle of a grand operation. We don't need anybody to explain it to us because we experience it with our own eyes, ears, and so forth. It's just a matter of *looking*, and we can see lots of *magnificent* things going on. Our Lady holds the law of all this.

On the scroll, the word "Tora" reveals that Tarot speaks the Law of Nature, or Isis. The High Priestess is Isis Veiled in this picture, and Isis Unveiled in The Star card (Key 17). Isis is very much like Alma Mater, as we call our universities. Alma Mater, the all-embracing Mother, integrates all of life's different departments and brings them into unity. She never loses track of what's happening, or how it's done and how it's all interrelated. Key 2 is the Uniting Intelligence.

▶ **Isn't Kether the unifying principle?**

Technically, The High Priestess is the mechanical aspect of continuity. She's the telemetry that ties everything together. Kether ties everything together in another way, by way of the All. It's the underlying Idea of Creation on the level that defies description.

▶ In its pure state.

Yes, exactly. To us it is negative existence, but it's the *positive cause* of everything, according to the Cabalists. I'm only quoting, giving you their explanation. Kether is Being on the very deepest level. Everything that can be seen, measured, or thought about—everything in the domain of The High Priestess—has this substratum.

▶ I don't get the connection between mind and matter. I always thought they were opposites.

That's how it looks from the outside. A thought doesn't *seem* like a thing, any more than your shoe seems like radiant energy.

Looking from the inside, Key 2 represents the PRIMA MATERIA, the First Matter spoken of by the alchemists. The First Matter is the mind itself, which has substance, not only in a philosophical sense but in a real sense. A city that you imagine in your mind is just as real as a city you see through your outer eyes. The nature of mind is particular; it has particles. These can be arranged in patterns. When you envision a city in your mind, you have actually taken these particles and arranged them in a certain pattern. An electrical image is created, exactly like the signal in a TV set. In our ignorance we say, "But that's just something I imagined. That cathedral I saw in my mind is nothing." Well, it *isn't* nothing. It's the same as a cathedral in physical terms, but on another level of expression. In the Cabala it's on level two, the level of mind and of the Divine Mother.

The idea comes from level one: "I would like to go to the moon." You would never actually *get* to the moon without going through the next stage. There you take particulate matter and arrange it in patterns, giving form to the idea. That's the role of mind.

▶ Is the alchemical discovery of the First Matter simply recognizing that you can do that?

Of course. It's not that difficult. There's a lot of obscurity about the First Matter because nobody wants to *believe* what you can do with your mind.

Important in Key 2 is the concept of the stream of consciousness, symbolized by the flowing robe. The entire display of all the mental activities in the universe is like a great river without any limits. We are immersed in this enormous stream of phenomena. Now, one of our problems is to understand that we are not the river, that we are something else again. Our spirit is not what it sees. It is able to look and keep itself dry while it's in the water—which is a paradox, but that's the way it is.

▶ When I look at the world of things around me, am I actually looking at memory?

I think that if you just change the word "memory" to "mind," that would be true. You're looking at a mental creation. The reason you can grasp it at all is that you understand mental creation. You have a kinship with this kind of magic; otherwise it would be totally meaningless to you.

▶ What seems to be outside is actually inside?

Most people have the idea that they are living on the physical plane, which is a gross error. You get input *from* the physical plane but your tidy little quarters are in the mind. This matrix is the only place you'll ever live. In India they use the word MANAS, from which we derive the word "Man." Manas means "mind."

Binah is the seat of Saturn, the principle of resistance. In the Cabala the feminine aspect is the *medium of expression*. Like clay, it can receive impressions. That's why it's able to produce everything. Think of this analogy in terms of mind. Mind is totally impressionable. By its very resistance it holds an impression of whatever is put there. The mind is not clay, not at all, but it's helpful to think of it as being *like* clay. Actually, it's very weirdo stuff.

Thoughts have weight and value. They mirror the other side of the Tree of Life. In fact, looking in the mirror of Binah is the only way to know what's happening in Chokmah. Just as the moon reflects the sun, Key 2 reflects the spirit of life. When the mind is still, it is the perfect reflector.

The High Priestess is crowned with the phases of the moon, referring to cyclicity. She signifies the principle of duplication that is the basis for all reproduction. Her law insures continuity of life. You might say the universe remembers itself in reproduction. Cosmic memory is a vast treasure trove that we utilize when we create.

There is *always resistance from the medium* when we create. This is the necessary meeting of fire and water. The equal-armed cross on the breast of The High Priestess symbolizes the balance of these forces. The balance of forces goes like this: In a restaurant you order (that's the idea) and you pay (that's the energy). This is the yang or fire phase. When the food comes out, that's the substantiality, the yin or water phase. Note that you don't need to tell the cook how to prepare the meal. The High Priestess already has the cookbook on her lap. In other words, we don't have to worry about the mechanics of response. The universe always responds to our initiative, to our Magician aspect.

▶ **The equal-armed cross reminds me of Hecate, Greek goddess of crossroads.**

This cross in Key 2 is exactly the same as Hecate's crossroads. She was a patroness of magic—definitely an aspect of The High Priestess. The Uniting Intelligence encompasses all polarities. Her throne is right in the middle, between the white and black pillars. I won't burden you with enumerating all of the polarities, but you can start with male and female, positive and negative, day and night, yang and yin, the artist and the clay, and exhaust yourself with all the opposites any time you want. They are *legion*.

A veil stretches between the two pillars. Behind the veil is that lively abstraction we call the Ain Suph Aur. The whole Tree of Life is embroidered on the veil itself, reminding us of the pattern in things.

▶ **Another way that The High Priestess connects things: The horns of her headgear touch the two embroidered pomegranates of Chokmah and Binah.**

That's very good. I hope the artist did that on purpose, because it's an accurate rendition of what's going on. Yet another connecting symbol is the Hebrew letter associated with the second Key, GIMEL ג, the *camel*. This highlights the associative powers of the mind. You can travel anywhere in the subconscious.

A particular pair of opposites is given to each of the seven double letters in Hebrew. Gimel is said to rule Peace and Strife. Of course, it never gets involved in peace *or* strife. *We* have peace when we remember ourselves. When we forget, we have strife. The way to know oneself is to *remember*.

In the Tree of Life, the power descending from each center impresses itself on the one below. When the flow reaches the bottom, it reverses itself. At the turning point, the person digests what has happened —remembers—and then finds himself or herself on the Path, starting with MALKUTH. All the powers of the Self are added as the aspirant goes up the Tree.

▶ Is there a Cabalistic method of Tree climbing?

The method for progressing upward is that you *use desire* to stay with the thing you like, rather than bounce around and repeat cycles. The reason this method works so well is that the desire to experience the Self is the root of all desires, and the Self is the top of the Tree.

The Tree of Life is designed to be a useful working model of the cosmos. Whoever devised this, or whatever group was responsible for it, did everyone a service. They thought very deeply about what was going on, took into account all the ideas that were floating around at the time, and organized them into the Great Glyph.

The different aspects of the Tree of Life have the quality of the Infinite about them. They're not limited as far as having a beginning or end. They are *there* and they *stay* there. Other aspects that cannot be penetrated are indicated simply by the background.

▶ Does each center retain a positive or a negative charge?

We only see the polarities from the standpoint of analysis. The High Priestess views the Tree—which is an expression of herself—from the standpoint of synthesis. She sees everything going from one level to another like waterfalls. All of the elements are in each one of the centers in a very *real way*, so that you have an accretion of qualities. When you get to the bottom, that's the whole works. Everything is there. Your physical body is an expression of this bottom level.

The difference in each of these centers is one of emphasis. You're looking at One Thing, yet each center has its own note, color, and quality. All are in each and each is supported by all the others within itself.

▶ Jason, is disease of the body due to misuse of the mind?

I'm not trained in this area, so I can't say what equals what. But I will say that if your spirit is at peace with itself, this is the healthiest situation. If your psyche is disturbed, which is a commonplace today, then the harmony of your body is upset. Not just in typical ways, such as turning pale or becoming flushed; this is obvious. It can happen in subtle ways. Science can't measure what mental anguish can do to the physical body, but it's true that a prolonged agony of spirit has a deranging effect on the soma.

▶ **What we believe to be true manifests itself in our bodies. To be able to change, we must remember the original decisions that created our belief structure.**

You can get around this by having a pattern for yourself that you can repeat as needed. We have the Tree and the Pattern on the Trestleboard, and we are also advised by our superiors that we should have a personal pattern. That subject is coming up in The Emperor Key. It's called your "constitution."

There's a danger in being wrapped up in memory. We've all experienced seeing someone who is caught in memory, not moving ahead into more exciting realms. Since you can remember everything, you don't have to worry. You can go on to the real excitement of life, which is, you might say, enjoying the meal for the day—not an exercise in memory.

▶ **You can use memory to look into your mind and see what is going on behind the scenes that you may not be consciously aware of.**

If you have the guts to do this, it's a perfectly elegant way to advance yourself. Most people never look at themselves and that's a pity. Actually, there is nothing the matter with us in the first place, but lots of times we have guilt feelings. That is simply a lack of sophistication on our part, because nobody has done anything right, ever! Once you understand this, you'll simply say, "Oh, what the heck. I'm just like everybody else as far as my mistakes are concerned."

I've made a couple of good ones in my lifetime. I expected that people were going to react in a negative way to my mistakes. On the contrary, they didn't react negatively at all. At first I didn't understand the reason. Later on I understood that their mistakes were bigger than mine!

▶ **What if you are stuck in your memory, as you mentioned?**

Fortunately, you have the ability to ignore it. You simply focus your attention on a completely different area and concentrate on that. That's the technical answer.

▶ Say your mind was in some memory that depressed you. You wouldn't concentrate on some happier moment; you would concentrate on . . . ?

You would concentrate on something *new*, something *different*. Otherwise you would simply be energizing one side or the other, and you'd bounce from side to side. "Tennis, anyone?" That you don't need.

Let's say you decide to take a boat trip and it happens to be on the *Titanic*. Everybody on the *Titanic* gets clobbered one way or another so that's the way it *is*. If you're on planet Earth—which is a kind of *Titanic*, too—you partake of the entire destiny of the planet in spite of anything that you can do. As long as you are here, you are an earthly critter. But as an individual, you can avert disaster through the process that's recommended by Krishna in the BHAGAVAD-GITA, which is to put your mind in a completely different direction from what bugs you or what pleases you. Krishna proposes to get poor old Arjuna out of his karma by the simple process of having Arjuna concentrate on Krishna. That cuts the karmic string right there.

▶ Sometimes I hold on to good feelings in my love life. Then my desire-nature, which is basically good and can motivate me to go forward, gets possessive and becomes perverted.

The things you desire are all based on memory. It was good, so you want it again. If you can't get it, you raise a ruckus. You're frustrated and you kick and scream and everything else. The way out of this is to find your own path. As you just pointed out, you can use your desire-nature in *that* development. Your desire-nature can be aspiration, your *own* aspiration. This is not "sublimating your lower nature," making it into some exquisite thing. This is just doing what comes naturally.

▶ Based on memory and your desire-nature?

Well, there's a little more to it than that, because your Inner Self is urging you in this direction. It's not a case of somebody saying, "Now, young lady, don't you think this is a fine thing, and don't you think you should do this?" Your own aspirations have nothing to do with somebody pushing you along the path of light, or the path of glory, or the path that leads "straight to God." Sometimes it doesn't *seem* as though your aspirations are leading straight to God, but they *are*.

What you said is true, about setting your desire *free* of the memory bank. In other words, you pioneer with your desire. It's as though you had a boat and you said, just like Columbus, "I don't know what's out there, but I like to sail and I want to see what's going on," so out you go! The desire-nature is the wind or the engine or whatever, the thing that makes your vehicle go. And you're in it. This is the faring forth of The Fool.

▶ I can feel what we're talking about, but I'm . . . confused.

You're *supposed* to feel it. It's not an intellectual thing. You can have a clear *sensation* that something important is going to happen. You don't know what it is but it gives you a certain direction anyway. Now if you're not the type of person who can be led, you won't go, and that's the end of the story. You say, "No, I think I'll stay here with my things," which means everything in the memory bank, your pet ideas and all your glorious notions. "Don't take my teddy bear away from me!"

Fortunately, we intuit what's really going on. We're ignorant of the details, but we know what's essentially true about life. We put up with all the foolishness because in our hearts we know there's something tremendous going on. Inside, we never lose sight of this and it supports us. The problem, of course, is to get the ordinary self-consciousness aware of what the inside knows. And the only way to do that is to try.

▶ Can't we sort of develop our intuition?

If you want to develop your intuitive faculties, you most certainly can. No question about it, you can always court the Muses. The High Priestess is Queen of the Muses and she can give you all the inspiration and guidance you could ever hope for, and more. It has to be *given*. You can't demand it. If you knew everything there is to know about the universe, if you had all knowledge without any exceptions, if you were the super wonder of the universe because you knew it all, *inspiration* would still elude you.

Einstein called it intuition; that was his name for it. He said that no matter how smart you are, you don't sit down in a chair and say, "Now I'm gonna think a great thought," or, "Now I'm inspired (grunt)." No way! The inspiration is available but it works in mysterious ways. It has its own times and places. Anyone in the arts knows that this is true. Sometimes you're a real whiz kid and other times it's heavy going.

▶ The Fool carries his memories in his wallet but he's not wrapped up in them.

That's The Fool of God, who isn't concerned with knowledge. If he wants it, it's there, like the folding donkey of one of the Chinese sages. Anytime he needed it, he just took it out and unfolded it and rode it, which is an absolutely delightful idea. There's something similar in the nature of the Tarot. You don't go around mumbling Tarot all day long, but it's there if you want to get into it at any time. Ageless Wisdom isn't going to run away.

I remember one time when I was bearing down pretty heavily in the area of Hermes. I discovered, to my youthful amazement, that the whole spectral band of occult knowledge is there just like a planet in the sky is there. Any time you want to explore it, it's waiting for you. It's all solid stuff, just like mathematics, chemistry, or physics, so that a couple of million years or even a billion years doesn't make any difference. Occult knowledge has always been a solid stratum that never changes. It doesn't make any difference where you are in the cosmos, or what planet or plane you're on. The Path has always existed.

▶ When I was in school, I was really excited about astronomy and physics and various things I was learning about life. Now in the Tarot and Cabala I can see all the same truth, the same knowledge.
▶ Yes, yes! It's all the same search!

That's right. Any real education has this kind of excitement. I'm reminded of my recent experience as a beginner in art. When I started painting, I discovered the ability to see. Of course it was potentially there but I had never used this ability. It was only through messing about with art—and in my case it really is messing about—that this sense developed. Then I found out that you never exhaust the possibilities of seeing into things more deeply. The more you pursue it, the more you see. It's a limitless subject.

You know that in the old days one of the terms for a wise person was the seer, the one who could see. What most people don't realize is that this path is open to everyone. Anybody who wants to see is welcome to develop their natural ability. "Seek and ye shall find" is one way of putting it, but you can put it even more simply: If you want to see, *look*! Just keep looking and it keeps coming.

▶ It doesn't really matter what you look at.

That's true. The moralistic tone of the nineteenth century has become outworn and has been replaced by beauty. In other words, the beauty of Reality is so overpowering to the beholder that it's simply a case of wonderment. Beauty is the central feature of the Tree of Life. As long as somebody or something is beautiful, why bother about morality?

I'm sure these statements about beauty supplanting morality could be thoroughly misunderstood, but I don't think anybody here misunderstands. It is simply a propriety that is cosmic rather than local. An inner concern with beauty would be sufficient to take care of the law. If you are animated by a spirit of goodwill, that's your law right there. The High Priestess typifies the Higher Law of Reality, which is a *living force* rather than a set of mechanical rules and regulations.

▶ Some people believe that humankind is going to develop the power of mind to such a degree that we won't need technology any longer. What do you think?

You must have support systems if you're going to live on the physical plane. I think it's going to boil down to our choice of expression. We have to decide what kind of life we want to live and how much technology we will need for that. We'll probably strike some kind of balance between technology and a completely different life from the one we have now. This way of life that we're in now is going to look strange when we get out of it, very hard to believe. It will look something like the movie *Planet of the Apes,* which is a fascinating satire on our present condition.

What the human race is giong to do, only God knows. For the individual, there are open doors much more within reach. If enough individuals make the proper choice of values, changes will happen almost by themselves. For instance, I don't eat candy. If the candy industry depended on me, there wouldn't be any. By the same token, if the war machine depended on me, there wouldn't be any war machine either. We live in a time when many anachronisms are still around. The most difficult of all to get rid of are the ones in people's heads. You've got to have something in your head, so until you start feeding in new material, the old junk is just going to hang in there.

▶ There are techniques in various disciplines for emptying your mind.

Yes, and you do it in order to put something else in there. You *must* have *something* in your head. There are techniques in psychoanalysis for emptying a person, in the sense that his mind is disabused of everything. But if you can't give him some sort of foundation, you might leave him in a despairing state.

This is one of the good reasons for having a philosophy. When you're in the soup all the time and you can't see yourself in the general context, you're vulnerable. If you see yourself in relation to everything else that's going on, you are much better off.

▶ **It can be depressing just to see yourself with all your hangups.**

As far as your faults and feelings are concerned, the only reason you might think you're alone is that nobody communicates with you. If everyone communicated all their guilt feelings, it would be a happy time for all. But most people conceal everything, so all you know is what's going on in your own life. You don't know about all the slobbing around that's going on elsewhere.

Since we live in a world of persona—masks and concealment—we can get some strange notions about ourselves. If we make analytical studies about what's going on, then we see ourselves in perspective and we can't possibly take ourselves so seriously. They have a saying in England about the Queen, that she has to "go" too. This is a great leveler. If we see that our so-called sins are more widespread than is generally acknowledged, then that makes it not so dark.

▶ **Would you tell us more about your experiences with making mistakes, which you mentioned earlier?**

At first I suffered guilt feelings and embarrassment about my mistakes. I decided that I'd better do something about them, so I began to study human behavior. Questions arose in my mind such as, "Is this something I did alone or has anyone else ever gotten into the same situation? What happens to other people when they make mistakes?" I had to do a lot of studying of what was going on. I found that the key to the whole thing was in my mind. In other words, it was my attitude that was making me suffer. When I changed my attitude, my suffering disappeared.

▶ **So you changed yourself.**

Well, I changed my mind, which is the same thing. I changed my relationship to my past experience. My new interpretation of the experience was completely different.

▶ **I see our apprehension of the physical world as a kind of telepathically maintained hypnosis. It's a continuum that can be transcended in some way.**

Yes, but it's possible to understand this more deeply. If you want to get to the fundamentals, the teaching is that any particular center of human expression is completely in bondage until it is free. There are just two conditions: freedom and bondage. Bondage goes all the way through all the planes of existence. It can get very extensive indeed, with countless marvelous things going on that are part of the illusory character of the universe. The spiritual nature of Man is not part of the illusion. But when the spirit of Man *identifies* with it, that's the problem right there.

Both the Cabala and Eastern philosophy speak of crossing to the other side. It's only on the other side, the creative side, that we're free. The creative side has nothing to do with the illusion, any more than if I create a play, I am that play. I'm not. But if I identify with it, then whatever happens in that play happens to me.

The world of illusion is the entire complex of the universe, nothing less than that. Considering all the possibilities for interplay among the parts of the universe, reflections and reactions from one part to another, it's a tremendous play. But that's *all* it is. Insofar as we identify ourselves in any way, shape, or fashion with it, we hook ourselves up with it. We put our nerves into it, so to speak.

▶ **When you drive, the car is like an extension of yourself.**

And if you've driven as long as I have, you have to be careful that you don't fall asleep, because it all becomes subconscious. As the Buddha said, "Stay awake."

Mystics through the ages have indicated that when you reach a certain stage of your development, you recreate the universe. You create one that you enjoy much more because it's your own. This active, satisfying process takes the place of reacting to the illusion.

▶ **You are not created by the illusion. You're creating it.**

That's right. You're creating it. This is exactly what Life does, according to the experts. It creates the illusion for its own pleasure. That's the only reason for such a RAMAYANA. Naturally, we wouldn't be satisfied with somebody else's creation. We want it after our own heart's desire, as you know. This possibility is open to all of us.

Meditation, listening to your inner High Priestess, allows you to see the whole picture of yourself and to arrive at a sensible response to the great question, "What is it that I really want?" Do you want to be happy? Or do you have some ambition in your mind? Happiness is not the path of ambition. Happiness is your natural condition if you're not bugging yourself. You don't have to be smart to tell the difference between bliss and pain; this is a simple arrangement we have in ourselves. But if you achieve bliss, don't tell anyone, because they may hang you or stone you to death out of jealousy.

The trouble with ambition is that you can never become satisfied. You never reach any final goal. You'll simply wear yourself out, much like the old Greek myth of Sisyphus. You roll the stone up the mountain and as soon as you get it there it rolls down, and you have to roll it back up again.

There is a great difference between ambition and achievement. Our creative potential lies in achieving co-creatorship with Life Itself, and experiencing the *joy* that is typical of the Self. Life is a very big proposition, and in our personalities we are really tiny tots.

Fortunately, the Divine Mother loves us all, great and small. In the next Key she appears to us as The Empress, who represents the entire natural support system that keeps us going on a day-to-day basis. The whole idea of fertility and growth is almost the polar opposite of The High Priestess and yet they are two aspects of the same thing. The High Priestess represents mind in its most abstract aspect, while The Empress represents mind in its active aspect. The High Priestess *knows* everything; the Empress *does* everything. Key 3 is in the production business. Fruitfulness and plenty, peace and prosperity are the nature of this Key. It's a bringing-forth of everything that's needful. The Earth Mother is the aspect of Nature that supports us in the most direct way.

If you ever should have a good week, this ought to be it!

KEY 3

CHAPTER 3

THE EMPRESS

About two thousand years ago, the Christian Fathers decided to get rid of Isis. This is like waving your hand and saying you're going to do away with the sun, moon, and stars; their decision was just about as effective. Since the human mind is constituted in such a way that people will believe almost anything, and by the same token will disbelieve almost anything, the concept of Isis was completely sidetracked. However, it has never really gone away. *Isis is not dead,* not by any stretch of the imagination. The Divine Mother exists, much to the amazement of everybody, despite being put down for centuries in the Western world, although not in the East.

Isis is a force that can't really be downed. She simply went underground with the greatest of ease. She has stayed in her crystalline, subterranean cave and awaited her time. The rediscovery of this principle is a delightful surprise for many people. We are in a time when the feminine aspect is being recognized for what it really is. The Divine Mother is becoming part and parcel of our religion and that is a good thing for everybody. It used to be that way in the old days and it will be that way again. In terms of a worshipful being, if anybody deserves our appreciation, it is the spirit that Key 3 represents.

The Church tried to turn Isis into the Virgin Mary because there was an outcry about the ancient Divine Mother getting swept under the rug, but the concept of the Blessed Virgin omits the tremendous natural support we receive every moment of our lives from the feminine principle. Isis represents the entire life support system that makes it possible for us to exist on this planet.

There is *absolutely no way* that there can be any substitute for women as far as motherhood and the propagation of the race is concerned. Although some people don't care whether the race continues or not, apparently Mother Nature is seeing to it that the race *does* continue. The handmaidens in this activity are women, not men.

Using the feminine principle, we recreate *ourselves* in occult work. The *woman within* each of us is our CREATIVE IMAGINATION. That is the area of our psyche where we receive inspiration and nurture ourselves and our creations.

If you want information you go to the university, to Alma Mater, the all-inclusive receptacle of wisdom and knowledge. The ultimate place to apply for knowledge and information is Nature herself—Isis, in other words. There's an old saying, "If you want to know what's cooking, ask Mother."

If you exclude Mother from your assessment of what you think is going on, you are making a sad mistake as far as the Cabalists are concerned. The Cabala goes back a long time to the days when Isis was venerated in the Middle East. Everyone was aware of her as the source of all nurturing and all inner and outer knowledge. Key 3 is ample evidence of the existence of Isis. She was the same mother who cooks your breakfast and gives you lunch and dinner. She was a *good mother*. That's the way Isis was, very *close*, not far away, not abstract. Consequently, everybody in every conceivable walk of life could understand and love Isis as God.

Today we have to remember that Isis is alive and well. We love her because she is our mother. If you don't love her, the consequences are serious. For one thing you may find that your bones . . . are . . . getting . . . drier.

In astrology, Key 3 represents Venus, the aspect of Isis as the *desirable one*. Of course, there is a male principle that balances the female. The male is equally desirable—in her eyes. Her love is none other than The Emperor, who is about as opposite a character as you could find anywhere. She is the part of life that we can touch and are close to. The abstract, masculine aspect is difficult to approach. That's Wisdom on the Tree of Life, Chokmah the Father. The only way we can get any inkling of what that is like is through the agency of Understanding, Binah the Mother.

Binah's symbol is the cup, the Holy Grail, which is able to receive the message that's transmitted from the other side of the Tree. Insofar as we have associated ourselves with that cup, we too can catch the inspiration that comes from Chokmah. Of course we mustn't divide everything in two's. That would be a mistake because everything is one, not two. This is simply the description of a process.

As I've said before, the ultimate adventure is to reach the Holy Grail.

We can't go any farther than that because we become as one with the principle of Binah, who contains all within herself. The root of the Cabala is receptivity. As long as we are willing, we *can* and *will* receive our heart's desire. There are sayings like, "Greater things than these are laid up for you." These sayings are true but they don't become real for you until you've experienced them. The machinery of the Tarot and Cabala can get you to the point where you can experience all these spiritual verities you've heard about.

The main symbol in Key 3 is the heart. In Tarot symbolism, the right hand is the active hand. Venus embraces the heart with her right hand, indicating that love is her primary concern. The law of the Mother is love. If you want to connect with her, you have to practice love. We can approach nature through science, of course, but the direct approach is through the heart, through feelings. The dove that represents the Holy Spirit is seen moving in the heart, not in the head. After doing "neti, neti" with the head, we finally grind it off and realize that *meaning is found in the heart*.

The Holy Spirit is none other than Chokmah, the Life Force. In the Cabala there is no such thing as force without consciousness. This force —the spirit moving in matter—consists of life, intelligence, and energy. Alchemy calls it fire. The fancy Cabalistic talk that you hear about the fire in the water speaks of the *fire of love* in The Empress's heart.

The dove is colored white, the heraldic color of the Crown on the Tree of Life. We remember that white is the highest vibration in this particular system of coloration and discover that the dove in the heart is an exact parallel to grace in the Holy Grail. If you are looking for your spirit, this Key shows you where it is. It's almost a silly way of telling, because it's so simple, but it's a very important symbol.

▶ **In astrology, Venus is patroness of the arts as well as the realms of love.**

The Empress rules the whole universe in the sense that she knows all the laws and is capable of producing all the transformations. She rules all the arts *and* sciences. This doesn't mean that she is strictly a mathematician or an astrologer or a musician or a thespian, but rather that she contains all these different expressions of life. When we meditate, we contact this Source.

On the Tree of Life Venus rules NETZACH, the seat of Victory.

When you are studying this Key you are looking at an aspect of life that is *always victorious*—not some of the time, but *all of the time*. This is the power that brings forth all things. You and I aren't going to achieve much of a victory in our efforts unless we fully appreciate the role of The Empress. For us, the most important aspect of her birthing powers is that she is pregnant with *us*. She is carrying our regenerated Self.

In our case it is not a nine-month pregnancy. It takes years, but the child finally does appear. The regenerated Self is the child in Key 20, the Judgement card. A mother fox can arrest her pregnancy if conditions are poor, then commence it again when things get better. Fascinating but true. So you may be sure that your Divine Mother, who is carrying you, will be patient with you. If you get sidetracked from the Path, she can wait. She is "smart as a fox," as the saying goes. On the other hand, don't worry about a premature arrival at the stage of Key 20, either. It will take as long as it takes. Our unfoldment is a natural process. We *don't* have to *make* it happen.

There is no time but there *is* process. Self-consciousness initiates the process. Just hold on to your idea, and subconsciousness will take care of the rest. There is nothing standing between you and success.

▶ **I get confused about all the types of consciousness.**

We have just three kinds of consciousness that we're selling around here. One is self-consciousness, which is something we are all familiar with, although I must say that most people haven't the foggiest notion of what it really is. Then we have subconsciousness, which covers everything that we think of as being automatic. It has an immense area of control, including all the bodily functions. It doesn't just nurture us physically; it also nurtures us spiritually. Without the riches that we have in subconsciousness, our lives would be dull indeed.

Superconsciousness joins the other two and makes sense out of their interworkings. The universe is a complex place, as we all know, and the polarities that exist between self-conscious and subconscious, male and female, stimulus and response, are so vast that it's staggering. Superconsciousness has the ability to look at both sides and reconcile them.

Now where do *we* come in; where does self-consciousness come in? Well, of course, it isn't ours anyway. Self-consciousness is also an extremely powerful aspect of Life Itself. As we grow up and become responsible, we are given information about how to use this principle together with subconsciousness to get new results. That's what creativity is all about. But we're not going to get this information until we're ready for it. The wisdom of that is obvious. We're always on the edge of blowing ourselves up anyway.

As you progress on the Path, you will find out more and more about the practical aspects of consciousness. It is basic occult teaching that you have a critical role in determining what's going on in your subconscious. What you think is what you get. There's no way out of this arrangement, so it's best to discriminate and be responsible for yourself. Life knows what it wants (Chokmah) and therefore it can be fulfilled (Binah). We can look forward to an endless horizon of growth in this area. There aren't any real limits as to where you and I are going to end up. The creative imagination is capable of *anything*.

▶ **What's the difference between The High Priestess and The Empress? Aren't they both subconsciousness?**

There is no difference in person between Key 2 and Key 3. There is a difference in *activity*. The Empress comes into being as a result of intercourse between the spirit and The High Priestess. Another way the Cabala expresses this difference is to say that there is a dark mother and a bright mother. They are spelled with the same letters except that the bright one has an extra letter inserted within—a Yod, which stands for the masculine essence. Yod turns AMA אמא into AIMA אימא.

We forewarned you that in the Cabala the position of Binah is very powerful indeed. Both The High Priestess and The Empress have their seats there. The High Priestess represents the abstract aspect of substance. The Empress represents everything that goes on in nature. Every manifestation of substance is taken care of by law. It's not a haphazard affair. This law is thoroughly understood by what we call the subconscious.

In the marvelous lore of occultism, one of the major statements is that we are small cosmoses intimately and immediately related to the great cosmos. In practical terms this means that what we call our subconscious is virtually the same as the great subconscious of the universe. Beyond the level of the everyday, the *deeper* part of the subconscious literally contains all things. It is an incredible array of powers and potencies.

▶ **How is it that Keys 2 and 3 are paths on the Tree of Life, as well as powers residing in Binah?**

Since antiquity the feminine principle has always been located in Binah. The Tarot Keys were placed on the Tree in modern times, according to their connection with the Hebrew letters that form the twenty-two paths among the ten centers. The path of Gimel (Key 2) links the Crown to Beauty, straight down the middle. It is crossed by the path of DALETH (Key 3), which is one of the three reciprocal paths joining opposite sides of the Tree. In this case Daleth links Chokmah and Binah. So The High Priestess and The Empress are close friends on the Tree of Life as well as being together in the Tarot.

The point where the lines of The High Priestess and The Empress cross is called the point of Knowledge, DA'ATH in Hebrew. It is the invisible center or Sephirah where Chokmah and Binah meet. Knowledge is related to love because that's what happens when opposites come together.

▶ **You have knowledge when you're aware of both sides?**

Knowledge is what happens when both sides *meet*. There isn't any knowledge until something happens, and what happens is that opposites come together in conscious love, conscious awareness.

▶ **The Bible uses the word "knowledge" to mean the coming together of opposites.**

It's sexual terminology in the Bible, but it has a general significance beyond just human sex. The union of opposites has significance in everything.

▶ **The phrase "*yang* and *yin*" has less sexual connotation than "male and female."**

Yes, and again, the yin and yang of Eastern philosophy is a *unity*. This One Thing is emphasized in alchemy because "The Lord our God is One." In other words, Reality is all there is. It has certain ways of working, and the goal of the seeker is to find out what its ways are.

If you take a broad view and don't make a distinction between God and nature, or between spirit and matter—if you can see nature as all-inclusive—then you can understand why the alchemists thought of it as God. They didn't divide up the universe; they didn't divide up Reality. They accepted everything as being *the* Nature.

That's where Isis comes in. Mother Nature is not just the feminine aspect, but the whole creation, everything in time and space. Her character is feminine because she represents the fruitful aspect of life. She makes both boys and girls. The inspiration for what she produces comes from within herself. The Cabala indicates this by saying that Chokmah is *inside* Binah. When we wish to thank God for our daily bread, we might as well say, "Praise Mother, from whom all blessings flow."

▶ **You certainly are enthusiastic about the Divine Mother!**

I *am* fond of certain aspects of the Goddess and make no bones about it. Why did the Tarot choose a woman to symbolize the qualities of reproduction, fruitfulness, and nurture? Why not a list of words that we could read? That would be ever so exciting, rather like reading the phone book for entertainment.

While driving here tonight I was thinking: First you see a picture of The Empress on a piece of cardboard. Then after awhile, if you like the picture, you get it *in your head*. Then finally, if you maintain the picture of Isis in your head, she becomes a *presence* in your *life*—which isn't bad, believe me. I'm here to testify to that.

Consider the wheat field in Key 3. It represents nourishment. It's always a good idea to *think* of this aspect of nature. Nature has many different faces, not the least of which is the immediate and exact cause for our existence, everything that keeps us alive. This is something that we can literally *touch*. There are all sorts of abstractions in the Tarot and the Cabala that have to be reached through the intellect, but as for the aspect of life that SHE is running, it's as near as *that*.

Her scepter means she is queen of the world. The world is her house and there is nothing in the world that she is not lord of. Her power is awesome. You must expect to be overwhelmed when you are admitted to the court of The Empress. If you're not, then you have something to look forward to.

▶ **What's The Emperor doing?**

Oh, he comes in for dinner. He makes all the big decisions, like going to war. The Empress rules The Emperor. This is indicated in the Tarot by the fact that she comes first and that The Emperor is looking at her. In The Lovers Key, the man also looks to the woman.

▶ **Who rules The Empress?**

Nobody rules The Empress except Life Itself, which rules altogether. This is the inscrutable aspect we don't know much about. The Cabalists know a lot about some important things that are happening in you and me, yet they make no attempt to describe the Great Unknown. You may say, "Intuitively I feel there is a God." This is what most sensible people think, but it's impossible to describe it. It *just is*. Our ignorance is much greater than our understanding. We know how to use electricity but we don't know what it is. I asked a master electrician, "What is electricity?" and he said, "Some kind of light." That's the best we can do.

▶ **How about Mother Nature's helpers, the elementals? Where do they fit in?**

The idea of the elementals is a projection that we've made as to how the inside is run. The intelligences that oversee the vegetable world can be called elementals, angels, nature spirits, or whatever. They are a highly organized group over which the Life Power is the guiding principle. The organization of nature is similar to a large corporation. It's likely that, without even realizing it, we've patterned our administration after this inner pattern. *Something* is running the vegetable kingdom. There is a balance in nature; when we upset it, we suffer accordingly. To say that unintelligence rules nature is kind of asinine, I think. Although I'm not personally acquainted with these elementals, still it wouldn't surprise me that someone was looking after the vegetables. The notion that nothing is looking after the vegetables would distress me.

Vegetation in general is sacred to Venus, who wears green for this reason. One of her special favorites is the cypress tree, several of which are in the background of Key 3. Cypress is characteristicly tenacious of life. The oldest trees on earth are in that same genus. They love a rocky environment and extreme weather conditions. Some bristlecone pines have lived at the timberline through *over four thousand years* of lightning storms, wild wintry blasts, and blazing summer sun.

The life in all plants is very strong. In my Bohemian days I lived in Sausalito, California. Right outside my house was some asphalt pavement at least four inches thick. I know because one time I had to drill through it, and it was tough. I went out one morning and the road had just sort of opened up. I was amazed, thinking there must be pressure from a burst water main that had pushed up the road. And what it was, was a mushroom. A mushroom!

▶ **I wonder if we could harness vegetable power to push turbines around.**

You eat vegetables and for the amount of food intake that you have, the energy you put out is extraordinary. So you are turning the turbines in *yourself* with vegetables, and you already have your wish.

Roses are another form of plant life in Key 3. The five roses represent the five senses in The Empress Key, and in The Lovers Key you will see the senses as the five fruits of Eve. You would expect Venus to be in cahoots with the senses. All the movements of living creatures on the physical plane are tied to the senses and the desire-nature. You remember that The Magician can remove his red robe of desire when he wants to withdraw into the world of contemplation, but in order to accomplish anything physical he has to leave the robe on. If he's going to act, he's going to act in terms of desire.

Venus represents that which is desirable. That which is desirable is beautiful and pleasurable. Everything that lives seeks pleasure and tries to avoid pain. This area is controlled by the Venus principle in ourselves. Victory lies in understanding our desire-nature and learning how to handle it.

▶ **Do you think that the victory has to do with transmuting desire?**

Even though my hygiene book at Columbia said we should transmute desire, I never bought the idea. It's sort of un-Cabalistic to speak of transmuting desire. You may think the Cabala is a bunch of you-know-what; that's your privilege. However, Cabalists believe there is nothing wrong with desire and that nothing has to be done with it. It's just like the electricity that's running through the wires in this building.

In Reality, anything that *is* has its own use and its own place. It is always in harmonious relationship with everything else, much like the spectrum. All the colors are different, yet together they make a beautiful pattern in the rainbow. And that rosy red desire, the hot spot, is essential because that's the Life Force.

You can do an immense amount of psychological and even physical damage to yourself unwittingly by misunderstanding the desire-nature as something you have to root out or plow up or transmute. The Tarot and the Cabala are going to leave all your guts in. All your brains and organs will be there at the end of the trail. There's no gouging out whatever seems to be in the way. We're economical—we save everything and recycle it.

The Empress is the one who is capable of handlng the red lion of desire, the beast pictured in the Strength Key. In other words, if you know what you're doing, if you're instructed, there's no problem. You simply connect the wires in the right way. Electricity is our servant; it does all kinds of things for us. That's an analogous situation.

▶ **The red triangle on her dress must be associated with desire.**

Yes, indeed. This is the fire of Chokmah that is hidden within the body of Binah, which is why The Empress is always pregnant. Our evolution proceeds from this inner fire. There's a cosmic one-to-one relationship between the master within ourselves and the Master of the Cosmos. We are not mechanical. We are *alive*. The fire triangle on the breast of The Empress symbolizes this most sacred inner life. It represents her greatest pleasure.

Women tend to project this love on a man. This projection is accompanied by the psychological compulsion for reproduction, which is a decree from Mother Nature. When we ask the question, "What's going on with love and sex?" we start to understand the mechanics of projection and reproduction. You must step aside from the projection and see the person as he or she really is. Eventually you are able to make conscious choices and are no longer taken in by the mechanics. Then you are released from the decree.

▶ **Physics uses the triangle, the delta symbol, to indicate change and heat due to chemical reaction.**

That's interesting, and applicable to this Key. Change happens because the creative imagination uses the old to form the new. We've all been through the status quo in school, and we know that anything that disturbs the status quo is destructive, in a manner of speaking. Some people say that if you want to be an inventor, then don't go to engineering school because your imagination will become too disciplined. You would keep seeing in terms of what you've learned.

Binah is associated with creative imagination, yet she is also the conservative element in the Cabala. She rules the left side of the Tree of Life, the stable pillar. As Creatrix, the Great Mother follows her own inspiration, which is the divine inspiration. Once that fire has been developed into forms, she's very conservative about those forms. She's like a mother cat with her kittens. That's where the stability comes in. It's to *protect* the forms she has developed.

You see this in artistry. Once you've created something, it's like a child. My first Tarot teacher was a professional playwright. He used to call the plays that flopped his dead babies. This was an accurate portrayal of his feelings.

The whole idea of pregnancy is enormously important because the Tarot and Cabala deal with living things—primarily what we call the organic, although of course the scope of the Cabala includes the mineral kingdom as well.

► **I have feelings for these different levels of the Tree and levels of nature, but when it comes to putting labels and names on them, I get lost.**

Hanging ID tags on these things makes them something you can *think* about in a *concrete way*. Cabalistic analysis has real value for us today. It fits in very well with modern psychological analysis.

I think it's always a good idea to read as widely as you can. A scheme like the Cabala is helpful for integrating whatever you are reading. It was designed as a sort of hatrack. Whatever ideas you get, you can classify them and hang them on the Tree of Life somewhere. In the East they have a minutely detailed scheme, but this one is detailed enough for the average person—and by that I mean the average occultist.

If you recall, in our textbook all the Keys are associated with Intelligences, which is a very old tradition. This is something that Paul Case learned like every other student of Cabala. (He did a vast amount of work in compiling and sifting information and doing some tremendous writing, but he didn't invent the Cabala.) Key 3 is associated with the Luminous Intelligence through the letter Daleth ד, which means a *door*. And Daleth is given to the direction east, which is the door where the light of the sun arrives. The Empress makes the light visible. So when you give each one of these powers a name—Joe, Betty, Jill, Morton—you're beginning to give them a concrete form.

► **On the Tree of Life, Daleth is a *swinging* door because the energy passes back and forth between Chokmah and Binah.**

That's very good. We could also think of the path of The Empress as a copper wire, a conductor of energy, because copper is the metal of Venus in alchemy. That's why her shield is made of copper.

► **There is an obvious connection between the door and the birthing powers of The Empress.**

Yes indeed. She is the door to life, the way we arrived here. We are all hungry children. We always want more and more and *more*. All the goodies are part of her domain. The door in this case leads to all the wonders that are waiting in subconsciousness for those who have the patience to investigate this area. It is literally the Gate of Paradise. The outer world is *mas o menos*—more or less okay—but the door to your inner world enters into Light.

It's a challenge to open the door to understanding. Paul Case's brochure for his study program was called *The Open Door*. Almost jokingly, he used to say, "You know all about the Tarot. You know all about the Cabala." You *do* know all about it. He didn't tell you a lie! But on the physical level you don't know all about it; neither do I and neither does anybody else. It's only on the inner levels that we know these things. The purpose of the Tarot is to evoke thought. If you continually think about these matters, eventually you will understand them and then you will have mastered the situation.

Daleth as a double letter rules the pair of opposites Wisdom and Folly. Wisdom is the creative imagination used in a constructive way. Folly uses it in a destructive way. This power to destroy makes the subconscious the source of our fears. If we don't understand it, we will be its victim. Cabalists impose light and will on this raw material—but always respecting the powers of the subconscious. We must be subtle and use suggestion.

▶ **Now you are talking about the scary unconscious that I learned about in Freudian psychology.**

The subconscious is the captive of self-consciousness. Self-consciousness is like the nasty magician in the fairy tales who has the princess in a deep spell. The trouble is that in the average case, the person doesn't *realize* that he's the nasty magician. He blames somebody else, the President or the Devil or God-knows-who.

▶ **You said that it's always good to read widely. Just what does that do?**

First of all, you can't help but see yourself in perspective if you look around. Learning about other people's difficulties minimizes your own.

Philosophically, the student of the Cabala will find the same intricacies treated in Hinduism or Buddhism, for example. You begin to see that the Cabala is not presenting a local idea, but rather a world idea. It's reassuring, in fact it's remarkable, that the sages in other times and other countries have so much that they agree upon.

▶ **When you find the same concepts coming from every age and continent, you figure there must be something to them.**

It never did anybody harm to learn what the other fellow thinks. The Cabala is just one approach. You could get your head into Taoism or Sufism or whatever, and you'd find a lot that is similar. This particular approach was designed for the West. We have a certain karma. We're extremely active people. Rather than sitting around and listening to someone tell you over and over that life is beautiful, in the fond hope that you may come to believe it, this is much more of an active affair. The Tarot says, "Sure you're beautiful, but what are you going to *do* about it?" If all this material is true, then you can *use* it.

▶ **I'm new to the Tarot and the Cabala. Can I assume that how to use it will become clear?**

You have to become acquainted with it before you can use it, just as with chemistry or anything else. And yet, some of the most important applications are extremely simple. Number one is: It's very important what you put into your subconscious. If you listen to the poppycock that's all over the place, then your subconscious is going to be like the newspaper, and God help you! So the Tarot starts off by telling you, "Look, this is your subconscious. It's not a garbage can. It's a living thing and it's yourself, so be careful."

Our teachers tell us right at the beginning that our conscious mind is supposed to be *awake* and that we are supposed to use it in a positive way. And of course, the whole idea is to use it *your* way. They don't say what you should do. They just say that you should do your thing in your own special way, with no admixture coming from the outside. What you put into your subconscious is your own private business, and it's the first order of business. If you dump *anything* into it, don't be surprised when anything comes *out* of it, because it will.

▶ **Computer people have a saying: "Garbage in, garbage out."**

That's funny, and very true.

▶ **It seems that more people are waking up all the time.**

If you proceed with this work, you get to the point where you are wide awake, which means being in a constant state of meditation. This may not *sound* exciting, but it *is* exciting because it's a very creative state to be in. The general condition, far from being one of meditation, is one of distraction. Distraction is not comfortable; it's an irritated state of mind.

Here we are reminded of Goethe's remark that if everybody swept up the street in front of his own house, then all the streets would be swept. This is precisely the approach of this particular school of thought that you and I are involved in. If everybody does it correctly, insofar as they are capable, the total result will be like a spiritual A-bomb. The reaction in an A-bomb is miniscule, but when you multiply it by the speed of light squared, you are talking about a great big *boom*. You and I and everyone in this forthcoming age don't amount to a hill of beans individually, but together we are an explosive force.

It's already been felt as far as its effect on the history of people like ourselves. Just a few years ago, the power-mongers were ready to strip the whole Pacific coast of every tree. Now in our time we have the magical concept of ecology. As far as I'm concerned, this is one of the strongest indicators of a new age. People are beginning to think not just in terms of themselves, but in terms of the state of the whole planet. This coming age belongs to The Empress, our Earth Mother.

All that we have discovered in the last 500,000 years has been an exploration of nature. There was as much nature in the time of ancient Egypt as there is now. We are finding out more every day, but what we know is nothing compared to what remains to be known. The entire cosmic panorama is not something you can just go out and master. Ahead of us lies a beautiful horizon of endless poking around in the universe. Sir Isaac Newton said at the end of his life that he had been like a boy playing with pebbles on the beach, while the great ocean of truth stretched infinitely before him.

The Empress's crown of stars represents the zodiac. Since each sign of the zodiac is an eloquent expression of Life, these twelve stars symbolize the multitude of possible life expressions. Her string of pearls suggests the seven original planets of astrology, which correspond to the metals of alchemy and the chakra system. The crown and the necklace are equated with all the powers of nature. They are archetypal patterns that are really *relationships*.

KEY 3: THE EMPRESS • 67

▶ **Why is her foot on the moon?**

The foot represents understanding and its yellow color signifies intellect. So here we have the conscious understanding of the cyclicity that underlies all life expression.

There's an interesting piece of symbolism in the waterfall. It represents the way that power descends from within. "Descends from within" sounds strange until you remember that in our symbolism *within* means *above*. In the Tree of Life, power descends in an orderly fashion from one center to another. Power goes over the falls from Kether to Chokmah, then over the falls to Binah, and so on all through the Tree. Consequently, every center is energized by the preceding one. The smaller the number, the more powerful it is. The lower Sephirah is always negative, or receptive, to the one above. When the flow reaches the limit of the world of sensation in Malkuth, it reverses itself and goes upward and inward. Power goes out and then it goes in, very much like breathing.

▶ **This God-power seems so present and yet so elusive.**

There is a legend in Cabalistic lore about the person who is zealous in the pursuit of Wisdom. Sometimes the story refers to the study of the Bible, as well.

Picture an exotic Middle Eastern street and a handsome young man on fire with the love of Wisdom. Wisdom is a beautiful woman who lives on this street. Her private quarters are on the second story. He walks by her house several times a day and looks yearningly up at her window. She notices him from behind closed shutters. This is the literal, obvious approach to the Bible, the outer book that anyone can read.

The young man continues and intensifies his courtship. Wisdom likes this attention, so she opens the shutters a little. Each day she opens them a little more. This is the level of allegory.

As the man feels the woman's response, he comes even more often to her house. One day she smiles at him and the next day she comes out on the balcony. This is the level of the law.

Finally, when his ardor knows no bounds, Wisdom invites him up into her chamber and imparts to him the Secret of Life. This level is called the Secret Wisdom.

▶ **Jason, you make the Cabala so racy!**

It *is* racy. It's a love affair. I don't want to bore you by going on and on about the beauties of Wisdom, but it's super stuff.

▶ **Do we actually merge our self-consciousness with our subconscious, making them one?**

They are already merged. We only go through the analysis in order to realize the synthesis. In the Hindu system, Shiva and Shakti are forever joined in ecstatic embrace. Nothing happens without the Divine Pair. They coexist and are essential to each other's performance. The only way one *means* anything is in terms of the other. This continual insistence on the pair is the same in the Cabala.

Since The Empress is the ultimate female, you would expect her to have a fiery boyfriend. So the next Key is Aries the Fire Lord, known in Tarot as The Emperor. Key 4 represents the intellectual power that destroys as easily as it creates. This is the side of our nature that is involved in the mathematical and structural aspects of life.

It is quite obvious that there is a superior intelligence in the universe. Sometimes it is called the Author or the Architect of the Universe. Since we are a microcosm, we have this intelligence like a seed in ourselves. It can be developed. In time we will become more intelligent about ourselves and our relationships, and so on into a glorious future.

The Emperor is a good, kind father. He handles the responsibilities of authorship well and he doesn't have to worry about the critics, because where he is, there aren't any. He exists in the Archetypal World as the creative impulse.

Thank you for joining me and making my Thursday a happy one. Without your company it wouldn't be Thursday at all. You should have a good week because The Emperor isn't a bad fellow. He doesn't have any offensive weapons and if he's not offensive, then he must be okay.

KEY 4

CHAPTER 4

THE EMPEROR

THERE IS SOMETHING in the unity of ourselves which, for practical and descriptive purposes, has a sort of masculine feeling about it. Whether you are male or female, you have within yourself the power to envision. This creative faculty is derived directly from the Ancient of Days, of which The Emperor is a representation.

Most of us were raised with the notion that God is a He. I got a large dose of God the Father as a child. I had to go to Catholic mass every morning at 9:30 and to Baptist service at 11 o'clock; also Vespers on Wednesday, plus evening meetings at the Baptist church. Even with all that I always felt something was missing.

The Tarot and the Cabala teach that God is both a He and a She at once, which is also a Hindu idea. The androgynous figure in the final Tarot trump, Key 21, symbolizes this ancient teaching. We make a separation of the powers for analytical purposes only, so that we can see clearly how they work in ourselves. In the Cabalistic view of things, the masculine and feminine elements are in a state of perfect balance. There's no chauvinism on either side. Don't get the idea that because certain things are done first, this means they are more important. Actually, the polarities are eternally conjoined and together they make a totality greater than the parts.

The Emperor is a benevolent figure. The wild Jehovah of the Bible is more like the feminine aspect in the Cabala. The most ferocious part of the Tree of Life is the Fifth Sephirah, which is like a mother bear defending her cubs. In the East they have a fearsome Mother Goddess who embodies this concept.

The Emperor embodies the Logos, the Divine Reason that guides the universe. You might say he keeps an eye on things. Chokmah, Wisdom, is his eye. This single eye is a special feature of the symbolism of Key 4. It's the same all-seeing eye that's on the dollar bill.

Chokmah is the power to look at ourselves, the power of the Self to reflect upon *all* of itself. This is the greatest tool for spiritual advancement that we have. The Cabalists suggest that we try to keep an eye on things all the time, so that we stay awake. We're surrounded by a vast universe we know nothing about, but *poco a poco* (little by little) we wake up to it. Salvation goes on a little at a time.

REASON is the key word in connection with The Emperor. If you wonder about the importance of reason, consider what un-reason is like. Divine Reason passeth all understanding, which means that we can't really understand what God is up to. So the best thing we can do is to apply reason to our own particular universe, the universe of ourselves, in the fond hope that if we get that in order, some special good will come of it. Actually, setting one's house in order is an essential aspect of liberation. In practical terms this means the elimination of things you don't want in your house.

Imagine living in a house with all the doors open, where cats, dogs, mice, goats, sheep, and chickens go marching through while defecating along the way. This is much like what happens to everybody who lives in America and listens to the media. Your life is eternally being invaded by things that don't belong there at all. The first thing you have to do is shut the doors and settle down to making a kind of laboratory out of your life. The Hebrew letter connected with Key 4 is HEH ה, the *window*. You can look out of the window, but you don't necessarily buy all that you see.

The law of life is that you either rule or are ruled. As you know, there *are* people in the world who would like to rule *you*. They want you to be docile and do what they say. If you think it's better that someone else rules your house, that's your privilege, but I don't recommend it.

Key 4 is called the Constituting Intelligence. In practical terms this means that nothing exists without first having been constituted. In the beginning it was constituted by God or the Life Power or whatever you want to call it. Now since we are the sons and daughters of this same power, we have the same ability. Our teachers tell us that when we reach a certain point of maturity, we are supposed to reconstitute ourselves in a very special way, a way that represents our True Self. This requires a conscious act on our part, so in all seriousness we are asked to write a "constitution" for ourselves, on a piece of paper, *in ink*.

The value of this exercise is that it helps clarify what our objectives are and thereby gives some point to our lives. By this act we accept spiritual responsibility for ourselves. This begins a process of accretion that builds from all of nature to express what is in our constitution. Up to a certain point, people live by a dispensation called Mercy. This means that no matter how stupid or childish we are, we're taken care of. When we grow up, spiritually speaking, we no longer have to lean upon the Divine Mercy. We begin to think in terms of what *we* want to do with our life and energies.

You may feel that you don't know enough to constitute yourself, or that you have to make compromises with the world. But you have to start *somewhere*, and our teachers tell us that the best place to start is with a piece of paper and a pen. Just as the fathers of the United States sat down and wrote a constitution—which was ridiculous at the time, because they didn't even have a country—you should sit down and write the story of the marvelous creature you're going to develop into. It might be considered an act of faith by some, but if you're fairly well versed in the philosophy of the Cabala, you can see the reason for this. Instead of being a chip on the stream, you want to anchor yourself in the Self.

Never forget the basic dogma of the Cabala that Reality exists. And that we, as parts of Reality, have nothing in ourselves except powers and faculties that reflect the one basic thing that's going on. There is no difference between you and Life Itself. There is no separation of powers. When you muster all your powers and faculties together—which is what you do when you write your constitution—they become available to you in a practical way so that you can manipulate them in the direction of your heart's desire.

The Cabala believes very deeply in your innermost character and your innermost desires, and it wants to see those desires fulfilled. It is *most* concerned that what you have in yourself be expressed as fully as possible. As you know, the Cabalists have an ennobling view of what we are. Philosophically, there are many reasons for believing in the greatness of Man. People are essentially good, but we get confused by all the outside pressures and our goodness becomes obscured. "Therefore," as it says in the Emerald Tablet, "Let all obscurity flee before you."

▶ **What sort of things should I put in my constitution?**

Concentrate on what you would like to be or what you think you are. Try to express what you want to have happen for yourself. I don't tell anybody how to lead his or her life; that's against the rules. The whole idea is that *you* are the only one who can figure out what you would like to be or what you really are. You say, "Well, I think that I am thus and so." Put that down on a piece of paper. Review it every day. See if it works. Then if you don't like it, amend it as much as you want.

As time goes on, you'll find that by some strange magic, you come to a decision as to what kind of person you really are, what you really want for yourself, and so on. In other words, *you define yourself to yourself*. This is important because the only one you can live with—day in and day out, year in and year out, *forever*—is your True Self. Nothing else will do. My definition of you will not do. Your best friend's definition will not do. The only one to hit the mark is the one you create for yourself. Writing your constitution makes you concentrate on the all-important question, "Who am I?"

▶ **How detailed should it be?**

Details are the amendments. They will change, but I think you'll find that the basic note around which you want to build your life will stay much the same from beginning to end. Finally, you can tell that you have succeeded in this process when you don't want to amend your constitution any more. You are pleased with it. If you can stand your constitution for, say, a year, you're in business. When you get up in the morning you won't have to *read* your constitution because you will have *learned* it. You look at it and you say, "It's okay. I like it! I like me! I can define myself in understandable terms to myself."

▶ **This might turn into a book.**

The process might result in your own private book. However, this is *not* for publication. It can be unwieldy at first, but try to keep it simple.

▶ **What if I can't make up my mind?**

It's quite a job to get your head in order. The psychiatrist Karl Menninger said that everybody is disordered to some extent, what with the stuff we believe about life, relationships, and so forth. Before you have peace in your head, you must do some cleaning up. Be The Emperor of your life. Say, "I live here. I rule this house." Be brave, be strong, and above all be patient. Disorder *will yield* to your efforts, which are coming from a higher level.

Four is the number of order. CHESED, the fourth center on the Tree of Life, is called Mercy. This gives us some idea of what a great blessing order is, according to the Cabalists. They say that it is the love and compassion in Chesed that measures the universe correctly.

► The Emperor looks so stern.

It's unfortunate that the rulership represented by the fourth Key is associated with such a bunch of you-know-what in history. However, you don't need to be at all afraid of this personage. In the Tarot deck, the knights are likely to carry weapons, but the Author of the Universe doesn't need weapons. There isn't anyone outside of himself who could possibly attack him. There's no competition. He's in the same position as The Hermit, who is *alone*.

The Emperor sits in the Mercy Seat, which is also said to be the Seat of Jupiter. His purple outfit is the color of Jupiter, that great benefic of astrology. In the words of Milarepa, Tibet's favorite yogi, "Goodwill and harmlessness his weapons are." In other words, love is disarming. That's the greatest weapon of all, isn't it?

► Why does he wear armor?

His defensive armor signifies that the sacred things in the divine scheme are protected. The old temples always had guards in the outer precincts to protect the Holy of Holies inside. This was the original function of Mars. The armor corresponds to GEBURAH, Severity, the Fifth Center on the Tree of Life, which is the Seat of Mars. It is said to be a ring of fire, a ring of protection.

► What happens if The Emperor is surrounded by tanks and cannons? Does he melt them all with love, or what?

Now wait a minute. We're not talking about Superman here. We're talking about the ultimate abstract masculine principle. It's very remote, a long way from tanks and bombs. Our bombs don't bother him. If you ever saw *Green Pastures*, you'll remember that Gabriel was always for going in and cleaning up the earth, and it was always the patience of God that stopped the archangel from wiping us out.

Our beneficent Divine Father is generous and understanding. What's more, he's in love with The Empress. She represents the good in his life. We mentioned last week that he looks at her in the Tableau. There is a similar arrangement in The Lovers Key. Because she's a wise psychologist, The Empress pays little attention to him, but she knows he's looking at her. He'd *better* show his appreciation if he wants to get any dinner.

The Logos principle can construct a house, complete with the plumbing and lighting. He can build the automobile, and he can go to the moon. He can also go to hell rapidly; he has a lot of talent. However, he can't fill the house with children and he can't cook worth a dime. If all the ultra-Logos type of people had to live together, they wouldn't last long because there would be so little nurturing. So you can see why this person needs to be married to somebody full of love and affection. The Logos principle is way out there, very abstract. The Eros principle of the Divine Mother is right here and now, and breakfast will be on the table when you need it.

Paul Case says that we should study Keys 3 and 4 together. This is more illuminating than looking at them separately because all of us, both men and women, have these opposites in our psyche. If we neglect one or the other, we become unbalanced. If you are an extremely emotional person, perhaps you should cultivate some Logos to shed light on the subject. The Logos light leads to sweet reason. On the other hand, if you are one of Hitler's doctors, then you are way overboard on Logos and you need a dose of raw feeling to bring you out of the trance.

The alchemists used to draw an androgynous person as a sort of diagram showing how the psyche is constructed. Within ourselves we play a game called The Enjoyer and The Enjoyed. The Enjoyer is the Logos, and Eros is what he experiences as pleasurable. Both are conscious. They are combined in a single being. These principles take us back to the Three Supernals at the top of the Tree of Life: One is consciousness. Two is the creative, initiating impulse. Three is the creating, producing aspect.

▶ **Why is it said that the Logos is the Word?**

The Word is a vibration that has all the necessary qualifications for becoming a thing. It is the Creative Word that calls all things into being, but as it says in *The Book of Tokens*, the Word is as truly a *vision* as it is a *voice*.

The power to envision, define, create, to give life, to dream it up, to see what will be—the power to *constitute*—is expressed by the Logos. The scepter that The Emperor holds in his right hand is an ANKH ☥, a symbol of the Life Force. He is the Lord of Life. I won't insult your intelligence by trying to explain to you how powerful Life is.

▶ **I'm an astrologer, so I associate power with Mars.**

That's appropriate because Mars rules Aries and this is the Aries Key. The Mars force is actually derived from the solar force, and back of all the suns in the universe is the abstract Intelligence that envisions the fundamental force and makes it work. The curved horns of Aries the Ram symbolize the whirling force that proceeds from Kether.

It's a little hard for us to grasp the concept of a force that has no physical basis. The nearest thing to it is magnetism and iron filings. You put the filings on a piece of paper and hold the magnet underneath the paper. The filings will align with the magnetic current even though there is no physical connection, as we normally think of it, between the iron and the magnet. An invisible force field makes everything jump around. This gives you some inkling of how everything is energized by the Life Force in a mysterious—you might even say occult—way.

▶ **Our textbook says that the figure of The Emperor resembles a triangle over a cross, and that this is the alchemical symbol of sulfur. What does that mean?**

These Tarot images are complex because the people instructing us in this symbolism are trying to pack in as much information as they can. As we unscramble the symbolism, we discover connections among the Keys and the Tree and ourselves. If you're wondering whether the game is worth it, I'd say yes, because it illuminates ourselves to ourselves.

In this case, The Emperor is drawn so the top of his body forms a triangle, and his legs form an equal-armed cross. A triangle surmounting a cross is the sign of sulfur, one of the three main materials used in alchemy: mercury ☿, sulfur, and salt. These represent *qualities*. They correspond to the three gunas of Hindu philosophy. Sulfur is rajas, the passionate, fiery desire nature. Salt is tamas, the ultimate in rigidity and stability. Mercury is sattva, the harmonizing quality that supplies meaning.

The heraldic colors of alchemy are white, black, and red, in that order. They correspond to mercury, salt, and sulfur. Red comes last because that's life actually *living* itself. Naturally, Key 4 has lots of flaming red. It even says in the Bible that "the Lord thy God is a consuming fire."

The rajastic nature has to *ignite* the tamasic or lethargic side in order for anything to happen. Rajas makes action possible. For instance, if you say to someone, "I bless you," it's different from actually enacting the idea by putting your hand out in blessing. Gestures help to communicate ideas.

The figure in Key 12 is drawn in the shape of a reversed sulfur symbol, with the cross surmounting the triangle. The Hanged Man stands for a certain stage of unfolding consciousness in our spiritual evolution, in which the desire-nature is turned inward. This is not something that The Emperor has to work on; it's humanity's problem to be what is represented by Key 12. The Emperor doesn't have any problems. He's just a papa with all sorts of responsibilities. He's expected to discharge these responsibilities and of course he does. He has all the necessary equipment and that's all there is to it.

In Key 21 the sulfur is right side up again. The World Dancer requires a lot of energy for her expression. Don't take this sign of sulfur in too physical a sense, because it's only a quality; it's not a thing. It's a state, like the difference between hard and soft, or wet and dry. It's artistic. You can say, "I think I'll add a little more yellow and some green to give it a certain quality," but it's not like a brick, not to be approached in a hard way.

I emphasize this because the nature of substance is subtle. *It's* not like a brick, either. It can assume any characteristic, so if you want a certain feeling that comes from a certain quality, you can create it. The gunas—the qualities of mercury, sulfur, and salt—will respond to you. It's important to remember that everything is fluid.

To get the idea of the way The Emperor's vision works, think in terms of the completely *fluidic response of substance* to what he has in mind. This explains what happens when we start to constitute ourselves. Substance, represented by The High Priestess in the Tarot, contains everything in solution. Insofar as we set up a positive pole in ourselves, we begin to pull things out of that great ocean of possibilities. Everything necessary to bring our constitution into expression will come by way of accretion, without any effort on our part. As it says in statement number four in the Pattern on the Trestleboard, "From the exhaustless riches of Limitless Substance, I draw all things needful, both spiritual and material."

This is the true magic of life and mind. If we *use* the philosophy of the Tarot and the Cabala, it will work for us. We mustn't ever, even for one moment, think that we have Reality figured out. By *definition* it's the thing that nobody knows anything about. It's *there* but it defies description. So if we take a pragmatic approach to spiritual matters and stick to what we know is *useful,* we can work with that.

▶ **Are you talking about holding an image in your mind of something you want to materialize?**

Getting something you've imaged isn't so great. What's more advanced in this kind of magic is to realize our own place in the scheme of things, to wake up to our own specific reason for being here in this place at this time.

Even if we don't know how the law works, it works anyway. It is always working, always supporting us. Even if we kick and scream and don't like what we see, still it supports us.

▶ **The average person can't bear to admit that there's anything he can't understand. He just won't take that leap.**

I guess this is the reason that millions of people cling to exoteric religious dogmas, because it's comforting. It's nice to have ten thousand or a million people all telling you the same thing. It's reassuring even if it's baloney. But this has never been the path of the thinker. As Lao Tzu said, if you just use your eyes and ears and what you've been given, by observation you will come to valid conclusions about what's going on. This doesn't mean you'll know all the answers in the universe, but you *can* know what's happening in *your* life.

To explain yourself to yourself is just about the most difficult thing there is, yet that's why we're here. Ninety-nine percent of it is finding out what you *aren't.* One of the strongest steps in discriminating between what you are and what you are not is to try to constitute yourself *consciously* as to what you *are.* This immediately eliminates a lot of what you are *not,* as you can see. Then if it doesn't work out quite right, well, do it again. But at least you get to where you can say, "That's not me. If you want to be that, George, you go right ahead. That's your life. This is my temple, my garden, and this is where I'm the boss."

We're talking about your inner life, what really *matters* as far as your Self is concerned. You are always able to cherish a certain part of yourself that you consider sacred. You keep it strictly private.

▶ Isn't it just as important to work on the outer as it is on the inner?

In order to live in the physical world, you cannot escape the karma of all beings who live on the earth. You participate and you simply say, "So much for *that*."

▶ Does this mean you don't lose any sleep over people starving and being tortured? You just say, well, that's the way it is?

Let me ask you this: What specifically would you personally do about it?

▶ I don't know what to do, but I feel responsible.

What do you think is the greatest thing you can do for the world? What is the greatest contribution you can make to humanity?

▶ According to the Cabala, I should express my uniqueness to the best of my ability.

Do you have any objection to this ideal?

▶ No, not really.

The masters of this particular philosophy say that until an individual has changed, the world will not change. Even though it's a long, drawn-out process, their idea is to change the *person*. Once the person sees the light, he has no further need for police. So isn't the problem to make changes in people rather than in situations? That gets to the root of the matter.

Every one of us has a sphere of influence. We can affect a certain area and that's about as much as we can do. Judge Medina in New York was asked, "Wouldn't you like to do more for humanity?" and he said, "In my court I do all I can to influence my times in good directions. This is the best that I can do." Very often a lot of progress is made through the work of individuals. It doesn't make much difference what the area is. If you get a good idea and stay with it, you can make quite a dent in the whole scheme.

Who knows? You might get fired-up and turn into another Gandhi. It could happen to anybody. Without any question, Gandhi is the greatest man of the twentieth century, perhaps of the millennium. He was a fantastic leader who started out as an ordinary person. By his own account, he was literally afraid of his shadow. Then he went through a startling transformation. You might say he became completely spiritualized and turned into a different being altogether, then properly known as Mahatma Gandhi.

Gandhi's special magic was that the spiritual aspect of himself was the one thing he could manipulate. He certainly wasn't wealthy and he couldn't be bought in any way, shape, or form. His followers were entranced by the simplicity and purity of what he represented. He never deviated from this. His spirit was completely unsullied. The people of India, who are pretty sensitive, soon recognized that they had a jewel in their midst.

Our teachers tell us that the gem in us is very real. The way you identify yourself to yourself is vitally important. If someone asks me, "Who are you?" I might reach into my wallet and read, "I'm Jason Lotterhand, number 526-10-8987." I can give them a thumbprint too. This kind of identification is a convenience for the government. If you don't get beyond this, or even worse, if you identify with what your parents and the local minister think of you, it's hard luck, that's all. It's like breaking your leg, only worse.

The Tarot and the Cabala offer a way out; let's put it that way.

▶ Can you ask The Emperor for a vision of the real you?

Yes, The Emperor within you can see anything. From where he sits, he's got the best view there is. The CUBE OF SPACE, which is to say the whole universe, is his throne. Since there wouldn't be any universe without the feminine principle, The High Priestess is also seated on a cube. Salt crystalizes in cubes. That's why the alchemists say it represents the tamas guna.

The Cube of Space is a convenient arrangement for studying complex relationships. It is constructed from the Hebrew alphabet. Each letter has an astrological connotation, a color, and of course a Tarot Key. The Palace of Holiness, where God dwells, is in the center. The surrounding letters are, you might say, the ornaments of God.

The three mother-letters go out like an explosion from the center. These supply the qualities that characterize the top of the Tree. The line that connects Above to Below corresponds to Aleph and Kether. The north-south coordinate is SHIN and Chokmah, and MEM corresponds to Binah and the east-west coordinate.

One planet is located in the center of the Cube of Space. The six faces are also planets. The twelve edges stand for the tribes of Israel and the zodiacal signs. Based on a conjunction of two faces, each tribe has a certain character that is precisely due to an admixture of related qualities. Secondary attributions come in from the lines that join the edges at the corners, but the main qualities come from the juncture of the faces.

It's as though sodium were one face of the Cube and chlorine were another. These poisonous elements are totally unlike. If you breathe them, you've had it. However, they bond together to form a totally different, third thing: salt, which is essential to the body.

▶ Salt shows up in a lot of places.

It's everywhere. Anything that has to do with structure, resistance, permanence, stability—that's salt. On the Tree of Life it's Binah, the Saturn principle.

▶ Stability seems different from resistance.

Stability is the ability to resist change, isn't it?

▶ To me, it's the ability to hold to the course you know.

When you're sailing a boat, you hang on for dear life because all the forces are trying to knock the tiller out of your hand. If you can't resist those forces, they will actually pull it right out of your hand.

▶ Okay, now I'm getting the point.

There's nothing wrong with resistance. It is the medium of your expression. We are trying to understand the *value* of this principle in terms of accomplishing anything whatsoever. So don't get excited or despondent when you find that there is resistance, because it's an essential part of your creations. Paul Case says to use Saturn rather than having it use you. Don't come at it with the idea that it's an enemy, because nothing is an enemy. It just seems that way sometimes.

▶ Shouldn't we be a little bit paranoid?

The answer to that is no, because you can't sustain the inner harmony in yourself if you have any paranoia in your soul at all. The philosophy that gives rise to this statement is simple: If you are afraid, then you think something outside is inimical and can attack you. If you don't fear anything, you can appreciate that the universe is all one piece, with protection for all of its parts.

▶ **What about the evil in the world?**

Evil is strictly relative (or your relatives, in some cases). What we think is bad is okay with other tribes, and vice-versa. We think they are evil; they think we are evil. It's just a matter of custom.

From the occult point of view, the outer aspect of things is not important. The inner aspect is all-important because energy works directly on the whole affair *from the inside*. A lot of things that we think are permanent, such as the attitudes of people, can be changed in the twinkling of an eye. Depending on how *we* are, so will be the changes outside.

In a world where events are fluid anyway, you may expect that there are plenty of opportunities for change as far as your Self is concerned. If you play the game according to the rules laid down by the wise, you won't need testimonials about it. You'll find out for yourself that it works. And as they say, God or Life works in mysterious ways.

There is an *enormous*, integrating Idea behind everything. The Emperor's head is surrounded by orange, the color of superconsciousness in this symbolism. The orange center on the Tree of Life is the Perfect Intelligence. Although we like to think *our* intelligence is perfect, as a matter of fact it isn't quite. However, Cabalists are very much aware of the colossal brain that God must have, so fabulous that they are awed. They say, "We can see the hind parts of the Lord but we can never see his face." In other words, we can only see what has already been done. This is why The Emperor hasn't shown up in our Tarot travels until now. He is shown in profile because there is an unseen, ineffable side. Paul Case's version of Key 4 is a traditional Cabalistic way of depicting God.

▶ **I know I'm part of this great being, but sometimes I still wonder why He would care about me.**

Perhaps because He put a whole lot of effort into making you.

▶ **How can I relate to this awesome, remote power?**

Like The Magician, you salute it, and you feel it moving in your daily life. The wind of the Tao is always blowing. The Tao corresponds to the Archetypal World. You can always tell which way the wind is blowing by the old sailors' method of wetting your finger and feeling the air.

The Hierophant is there to help you. Key 5 is the connection between the outside and the innermost, in everything. It goes from the bottom all the way to the top. Guidance is a reality for anybody who wants it. We *need* guidance, and consequently we have something that answers the need. The Hierophant is the revealer of the mysteries of life. These mysteries can be revealed to any of us, provided we're willing to accept the idea of revelation. This might be a stumbling block for some, but for myself I accept the idea.

There are times when we might not like what is revealed to us. We have a higher principle in ourselves that conveys the very information we need in the moment, but if we think we know better than it does, then *whisk*, it's gone. That's why it's called "the still, small voice." In order to contact it, we have to shut up. This frees us inside, so we can begin to get important information. As Jacob Boehme said, "If for one moment you can stop all your thinking and willing, then you will be as God was before ever He created the world." That's pretty good.

Nobody is playing games with us along the Path. If it were that kind of a deal, I'd tell you to go home as soon as possible and take an aspirin and forget the whole thing. But it's not a bad deal. Ever since I started in with the Tarot, or even earlier, I never felt I was cheated or led astray in any of these departments we're working with. My work in this field all started when I responded to a magazine ad at the age of twelve. You always attract what you need on the Path.

This week, give some thought to the matter of your intuition. Think of situations in your own life where you had more or less exhausted your reasoning capabilities, and were in a bind, and then all of a sudden a flash from within yourself led to the solution of your immediate problems.

Have a good week, as always. Thank you for making my Thursdays a success.

KEY 5

CHAPTER 5

THE HIEROPHANT

It's always a good idea to be grateful to Life. We can begin by being grateful for our powers and faculties. Chief among our powers, something to be *very* grateful for, is our ability to cultivate our inner life, the invisible world of the spirit. It is possible to experience a source of superior knowledge within ourselves, knowledge that comes from an altogether different sphere than the world outside.

The message of Key 5 is that we have an *inner teacher*. The more we depend upon this inner teacher, the better for us. Without this instruction we would be lost, but fortunately we are not lost. We have lots of instruction. It is coming, of course, from the Inner Self. As we become more familiar with the technique of the Tarot and the Cabala, we find that all the guidance and inspiration and knowledge that's essential to our well-being comes to us from our own INTUITION.

The lotus starts in the mud and thinks, "Oy *gevalt*, what a life!" Then it rises in the water and that's a little better but it's still murky. Finally the plant reaches the surface and opens its flower to the sun. It's the most surprised plant in the world. It looks back and says, "Wow, I remember when I was thinking, 'oy, oy, oy' in the mud." The lotus was *guided* by a power from within.

When I look back at my own life—and I'm no spring chicken—I can't see any *reason* for the improvements. I just grew out of the mud, that's all. I had nothing to do with all the good things that came to me. They just happened . . . while all the stuff I was *working* on was a mess! Up until a certain point things stayed lousy; then they started to get better. I feel that this is what's going to happen to humanity.

Within ourselves we are being *led* to something better. Any improvement in the world situation will come from within some person or group of persons. This is historically true, and it's the way it will happen in the future. Meanwhile, it's true for *us*, *now*. The Hierophant will instruct us in our progress.

Ideally, we would be conscious of the experience of being inspired, which would make it exciting for us. It is said that exaltation is one of the results of success in meditation. Bliss is a major element in the foundation of the universe, according to the wise. So any time we approach Reality, there is an accompanying blissful feeling that makes us feel exalted, and we know we are getting closer to something wonderful.

There is a philosophical basis for this teaching, which is that the universe is a unity with carefully made arrangements for all of its parts. Each one of us, each universal child, has a built-in guidance system that will work if we give it the chance.

This is not to say that we don't learn from outer sources. Many books that we read, especially the higher literature that deals with spiritual matters, confirm what we know inside. If you have an inner experience and then read about the same thing, you find you're not the only one who ever had a certain inspiration. This is good for you. After all, you are experiencing something that is *not unusual*.

Key 5 follows Key 4 because intuition is not called into action until we have exhausted our reason. Reason is supposed to take care of the bread and butter aspects of living. Intuition is necessary when we come up against such large questions as, "Who am I? What am I doing here?" or the troublesome state of mind that says, "Stop it! I want to get off!" The major human perplexities are not concerned with plain old sustenance, especially in a country like modern America. It's generally true that the average person in the United States can get a meal. The problem is getting the Cadillac and sables. If we were to advance from this childish state, we would see the wisdom of not even desiring vast material possessions.

Intuitive guidance leads to wanting all things *needful*, both spiritual and material. You could meditate on "needful" for years with profit. It's a marvelous word that gets to the bottom of real human concerns. What is needful is not necessarily what you might expect. The Tarot and the Cabala are trying to give you *the most possible enjoyment* out of life. You might say, "That's why I want the fancy car, the furs, and the big house. That's the kind of enjoyment I want." Well, unfortunately these things can become impediments. You could get so completely hamstrung with *stuff* that you miss the point of the whole thing, which is your capacity for blissful enjoyment of what life has to offer. The whole emphasis is to get to the point where you don't have to buy constantly in order to get a kick out of life.

Let's say you have discovered that you can enjoy a day at the seashore, in your bare feet. You don't need *stuff* to get a tremendous thrill from what the ocean or the mountains have to offer. Or from what people have to offer, if you approach them simply for the joy of what they represent rather than what somebody thinks about them.

In the confusion of the world, there has to be some guiding light. "The Hierophant" means the one who explains the mysteries to us. The mysteries of life are not related to the educational system, which as you know, is designed to make us useful to society. That's just fine, but the inner teaching is that first and foremost we should be ourselves. This has nothing to do with society at all. If we don't know how to be ourselves or we don't think it's worthwhile to be ourselves, we're in a heck of a fix.

As far as the Cabala is concerned, you haven't any debt to society whatsoever. You come into the world nice and fresh, with a clean slate. Then people start telling you that you now belong to the United States and you can do this for it and that for it. That little spark inside, which is yourself, gets overwhelmed, smothered, ground down . . . *unless* you learn the Secret Doctrine about yourself, in which case you find out that you're not so small after all.

You look into history and wonder, "What was so great about this or that person?" In nine cases out of ten, they discovered somehow that the secret of their lives was not only to *be* themselves, but to *act* like themselves, and not worry about whether anybody liked it. The people who have been the leaders of humanity were not trying to prove anything. They came on the scene, happily did what they had to do, and went out of the scene. That's exactly how it should be with us.

We're not beholden to one another. From an inner point of view, the whole joy of life is in what we can freely bring to one another. If we don't bring ourselves, we're not really bringing anything. *All* that is interesting to human beings is communicating with one another, finding out what each person has to express and to enjoy. If we were all ourselves, I assure you the result would be absolutely, phenomenally beautiful. The Life Power is terrific, and the secret of your life is to express that, to mediate between the inner world and the physical world. When you do, you don't need any credentials. The people who are interested in what you have to offer will be happy to be your friends.

Perhaps your offering will be small. Life doesn't need a tremendous amount from any one individual. If you have a large contribution to make, that's great, and if you have a small contribution that is possibly closer to the widow's mite, that's great too. Don't forget we live in a very large affair. We are universal beings. You are not nineteen million miles away from the heart of the universe. The heart of the universe is inside you! Our Hindu friends tell us that if you get close to the heart of the matter, you will know something (which is what they call knowledge), you will be close to the secret of life, and you will feel absolutely *high*. So if you don't know anything, are barely alive, and feel lousy, these are signs that you could change your track, take another path.

▶ **Do you mean that this particular card shows me the way to be myself in the deepest sense of the word?**

Of course. The biggest mystery that Life presents is ourself. As I said, The Hierophant reveals the mysteries. It's as though we were fish in the sea, trying to understand what water is. Of course we live in air, but we are also in the great space of the universe. We don't know much about it, but it's a sure thing that we're in it! Another sure thing is that whatever the universe is up to, we're part of it. We may disavow this but that doesn't change anything. You can say, "I'm not my mother's son," but it doesn't make any sense to the person who has, shall we say, heard the message about it.

▶ **You mentioned last week that Key 5 is the "still, small voice." That must be what delivers the message.**

Yes; in fact, the sense of hearing is attributed to this Key. In Sanskrit, the word for hearing is also the word for intuition and meditation. The picture of The Hierophant features the listening ear. Listening involves a great stillness of mind, so that we put aside everything that has to do with the world when we listen to the still, small voice. Out of this stillness comes a special message that is precisely for us, wherever we happen to be in the course of our evolution.

The Hebrew letter VAV ו means a *nail*. It's the thing that binds everything together. In this respect it's related to The High Priestess, who is the Uniting Intelligence. You may be sure that all things *are* bound together, that we have a link with everything. Most particularly, we have a link with what's inside us. There is an unfailing *connection* between the Inner Self and the personality, the outer self.

On TV the other night I saw Norman Lear, one of Hollywood's greatest talents, as he received an award. He said the usual, "My collaborators are just as important as myself." Then he went on to say, "I also want to acknowledge another element in myself: the Voice Within." That was unusual for television, to say the least.

You may gauge the importance of Vav by the fact that it is part of the Cabalistic divine name Yod-Heh-Vav-Heh. On the Tree of Life, Yod is placed in Chokmah; the first Heh is in Binah; Vav is in Tiphareth in the center of the Tree, and the final Heh is in Malkuth at the bottom, where we are most of the time. Vav is our passage to the higher realms.

The four levels of The Hierophant's crown and scepter symbolize the fact that he operates in all four Worlds of the Cabala. In other words, the principle of guidance and instruction works on all the planes. It is a thread that goes from the lowest to the highest, and we have to hang on to it all the time. It's not hard to do. If we are willing and desirous, we can hang on to this golden thread and it will take us from Malkuth all the way to the top.

▶ **Among the paths on the Tree, The High Priestess unites Tiphareth with the Crown. Also, both Keys 2 and 5 are in a temple setting. These are more connections between The High Priestess and The Hierophant.**

That's because The Hierophant is the active, teaching element of what The High Priestess represents. She stands for the total wisdom that's inherent in everything. This is promulgated within ourselves through very definite channels. We receive the instruction when these channels are open.

The word "intuition" (in-tuition) literally means inner teaching. The more we depend upon our inner teacher, the better for us. Key 5 is called the Triumphant and Eternal Intelligence. In the Cabala, instruction is more important than we can even *imagine*. The Cabalists say that METATRON, who is the face (appearance) of God, is the angel of instruction. He must consider the education of all human beings. When you think about it, our evolution depends upon instruction. It's easy to be born in ignorance and die in ignorance. Unless we have direction, we're in terrible trouble. We *do* have it, and it will triumph over our ignorance. We may not know where we are going, but Life knows where *it* is going. The Voice of the Tao, as they call it in China, is continually *broadcasting* to all beings in a waveform somewhat like TV signals. In order to hear it we must listen very hard.

▶ **How can I still my mind enough to hear my inner guidance?**

One recommended method is to focus your attention on something, which is called the *seed*. Our teachers say that when you keep your attention on one thing, information about that object will come through your intuition. Eventually, the essence of the object will be made known to you. As Dr. Einstein said, if you're a lover of nature and you settle on some part of nature that you want to understand, in due course you will understand it.

This takes a certain amount of devotion or attention. Meditation won't happen when you've got the old razzmatazz going in your head. However, there's no hocus-pocus about what you have to do. We all meditate to a certain extent; we can extend this practice *greatly*. If you get involved in the practice, you can stay in it most of the time. Insofar as you remain meditative while everything is going on, you see life in a different perspective from the usual, which sort of calms the waters. In this state you have a certain grasp of things that is not ordinary—in fact, it is quite extraordinary. From that perspective, everything changes for the better.

The kneeling figures in Key 5 symbolize the devotion with which we are told to approach our source of instruction. Remember that a good, red-blooded Cabalist is *receptive*. These figures represent aspects of our consciousness that are *learning*. The one on the right is in a position of supplication; he is the intellect asking for the message. The one on the left is the desire-nature; he's reaching for the silver lunar key, called the key to hell because it opens the unconscious. All the wild and destructive powers of Nature are in ourselves. The gold solar key to heaven gives the devotee access to celestial wisdom, which is also within ourselves.

The one reaching out is the Eros principle, which desires an *object*. The Logos or Knower on the other side does not seek an object. We may deduce that the triangle formed by The Hierophant and the two monks is an expression of the Three Supernals at the top of the Tree of Life.

▶ **How about the gesture of The Hierophant himself?**

That is called the gesture of esotericism. He is teaching the mysteries, in contrast to The Devil in Key 15, whose open hand is suggesting that what you see is all there is. According to the doctrine, we live in bondage in a world of images until we receive instruction to lead us out.

One word of caution. We're not supposed to throw ourselves upon the inner teacher and neglect the spiritual precepts we've heard all our lives. Rather, we're supposed to listen and compare, and find out that Jesus, Lao Tzu, Mohammed, Buddha, and so on were talking about things that relate to where we happen to be.

▶ **I'm not sure what you mean when you say we're not to throw ourselves completely upon the inner teacher.**

We could get lost in the personal subconscious and that would be a disaster. So the generous, sweet-hearted guides that I mentioned are not to be ignored, but taken seriously. All the information is free, all the help is free, and the goodwill and blessings of the people who have explored the Path before us are all there, so we don't go it alone.

▶ **So we have outer as well as inner teachers?**

We have all sorts of outer memorials that are extremely important to us. The Cabala is one of these, a great memorial explaining what's going on. We're invited to enjoy the experience of our forebears, who have spent enormous time and energy exploring the very areas we would like to get into. They give their wealth quite freely. That's the point that I was trying to get across.

▶ **Some people get so wrapped up in the inner that they sort of circle back and get into the highly personal. That's dangerous ground because they only hear what they want to hear.**

Yes. Take for instance the person who thinks that because he's had a divine inspiration, he is suddenly God and everybody else is less. That's a *very* dangerous position to be in. The Cabalists make it clear that every person has the divine in himself, and is God in truth. So there's no reason to get excited because you happen to be a god. This is Man's heritage.

It's generally noticeable that most people don't want any responsibility for themselves, so they avoid the issue of their heritage. Irresponsibility is like any other bad habit that people excuse and rationalize.

▶ **That's why people seek a guru.**

Exactly so. And in the Cabala there isn't any guru except your Self, your Innermost Self. This thrusts the responsibility right on you. If you're unwilling to go along with this, the Cabalistic approach is useless.

▶ **What about the imitation of Christ and all that?**

Our late lamented friend Carl Jung pointed out that you are here for a specific purpose. Jesus led his life, Buddha led his life, and so on, but you're here, in the economy of things, precisely to express *yourself*, not some other guy. Your main responsibility in life is to yourself. This sounds like a wildly selfish statement until we understand that the Self of each individual is not something separate. Each is part of the whole. Our elder brothers and sisters on the Path have all recognized this unity.

▶ **In looking for *my* self, I'm looking for *the* Self.**

Sure. And the only harmony we'll ever find is in Self-recognition among one another. In the East, the NAMASTE gesture is a salute to the Self in the other person, which is the same as the Self in your own person, so it's brother-sisterhood right then and there.

▶ **I've heard it said that in order to travel the Path, you need a teacher. What does the Cabala say about that?**

All an outer teacher can do is remind you to teach yourself.

▶ **Don't we need regular teachers, though? People like yourself?**

What's good about the Path, and what's *true* about it, is that nobody travels it alone. As soon as you get interested in this area, you find other people who are also interested.

▶ **Do you agree or disagree that there is a need for an actual one-to-one teacher? Is just having friends on the Path enough?**

The only thing I know about it firsthand is that who or what you need appears. In my experience, there's always somebody around who is a little bit farther along. "Birds of a feather flock together." When I was a youngster, my first teacher just happened to be there when I asked the question. This was in a bookstore in Detroit. I said to the proprietor, "Is there somebody around here who really knows something about this stuff?" and he said, "Yeah, that guy standing right there."

My first teacher wasn't a demigod or anything like that, but he did know what he was talking about. He was a learned man who was helpful to me. He gave me the Curtis Tarot books, saying, "Someday you'll be interested in these." Sure enough, several years later I read them avidly.

I became interested in Theosophy. I went to live in New York City on 72nd Street, and I found out that the United Lodge of Theosophists was *next door*. They were high-level people and I enjoyed that experience greatly. When I had gone as far with that as I could, one of my closest friends literally dragged me to my first Tarot class in Greenwich Village. Then I felt like Columbus discovering land!

▶ **I've never heard you make an analysis of Gurdjieff or Ouspensky or any number of different philosophers and metaphysicians. Why is that?**

There are two things going on as far as the occult is concerned. There is occult science and then there is the Self, which is more than a science. It's a living experience. The occult scientists discuss time and space and this, that, and the other. This is perfectly all right. It doesn't do any harm, but it doesn't get down to the roots. *Living* things are not of the same order as more static things. Here, we're not talking about the laws of science. We are talking about a level that you might say is primary instead of secondary.

For example, let's take the matter of goodwill. Goodwill upsets the whole world, as far as humanity is concerned. Bankers and lawyers never consider it at all; they're only interested in the law. Yet here we consider goodwill a basic feature of our landscape. There's a vast difference. Take love, for instance. Suppose you go to a bank and say, "I want to be loved!" If you have $100,000 security and you want to borrow $10,000, they'll throw their arms around you and treat you like a prince. But as far as real love is concerned, they never heard of it.

▶ **Can you bring love into business?**

Of course you can bring love into business. Look at the Arabian oil situation. The price of oil is destructive to people who are in desperate straits already, as in India. If the people with the oil had any love, they would make some arrangement with India. They'd say, "Oil is essential to some of your industries, and your people are starving. So we'll give you the oil at a price you can afford to pay, and maybe raise it slowly over a period of years." Actually they say, "That's your hard luck. I'm not my brother's keeper. To hell with you."

That isn't exactly our position. As budding Cabalists, we are in an evolutionary trend that is moving *away* from this kind of foolishness. According to the Cabala, love is a very important element. If your heart isn't in the right place, everything gets out of whack. There are all sorts of interesting and clever things that can come from your head, but until you develop a generous heart, you may expect nothing but trouble.

If each individual is only after their own benefit, then it's conflict from the word "go." It's the jungle. And that's where we are—still in the jungle. We shouldn't be too concerned about it because, after all, we're missionaries. We're showing people how to be more hearty and less heady. Being more hearty doesn't mean we're less brainy. I'm not putting down science. It's always fascinated me, but as far as I'm concerned it's a nightmare without the heart.

▶ Is that the difference between a scientist who's just a technician and a real scientist like Einstein, whose heart was in what he did?

Yes, science is a human function and we should think of it in terms of humanity. However, there are other values that are more important than the strictly scientific point of view.

▶ In the meditation on Vav in *The Book of Tokens* it says, "Will is the small point of all beginning, and its coming forth is a search for itself. For that Will is a hunger, and a desire, and a longing." I had the idea that the Higher Self was somebody else, but it's not, and it's not my individual character. It's my connection with that abstract dot, the point that is the beginning of the idea of everything.

Yes, but don't make it too abstract. It's no use thinking of Life as an abstraction because this has no *meaning* for anybody. And neither does the Life Power have any meaning to *itself* except in terms of expression. Your Self is a cosmic phenomenon and consequently it has fantastic qualities. It's hard for us to get it through our heads that the very life we're living is *exactly* the Life Power living its life in us, and at the same time is also our very own selves.

▶ But we must be an expression of that small dot. I mean, an expression must be an expression of *something*.

But the something of which we are an expression is not a small dot at all; it's a very large one. It happens to be the universe. The notion of the dot is simply an integrating thought. You won't understand yourself if you think of yourself in terms of an abstraction. If you think of yourself as a flower in bloom, that would be a fairly accurate representation.

▶ The idea that the Life Power is hungering after itself—that's a mindbender.

Well, isn't it true? Everybody has this sense of, you might say, incapacity, which they want to get over. They know there's something absolutely superior that they want to enjoy and experience. That's the hunger right there. The limitations of ordinary existence are not sufficient while this feeling is in their heart. They are experiencing Severity, the fifth center on the Tree of Life. So they go on and on, expanding their consciousness. Finally they get to the point where they actually begin to taste a much larger life, which has nothing to do with ordinary personal existence.

▶ **It's hard for me to see how we can be our personalities and also the universe.**

You have two sides to your nature, a receptive side and a creative side. We go from one to the other. Insofar as we receive the universe like a communion wafer, we become energized. Then we go into our creative function with that energy. So, you see the show and then you get an idea for another show.

▶ **Where does the original idea come from?**

There is no original idea, no end to it, no "Which came first, the chicken or the egg?" There's all the material and there's all the Life Force, and the show goes on. Then you say, "Oh, we could do it another way," and then *that* show goes on. Thinking in terms of eternity, you would never get bored with so many factors working together.

▶ **Sometimes, when it starts to get cosmic, I get scared. What should I do when I feel frightened?**

Go home to Mother. Mother Nature is an *immediate* support that never changes, despite all the other things that are changing. We hear of some mamas who say, "Get out of my house and never come back," but the Big Mama doesn't do that. If that were to happen, we wouldn't be here at all.

▶ **Is this fright a safety factor?**

At a given point in your evolution, it could be—as the classical story of Arjuna and Krishna shows. Arjuna asked to see the cosmos revealed, but when he saw the way it was, it was too much for him and he begged Krishna to turn it off. This story doesn't infer that you won't be able to look at the cosmos *sometime*. At a certain stage in your development you are quite capable of looking at Reality without coming unstrung, unhorsed, or anything else. Somewhere along the line you're going to see things the way they really are.

With people who are locked up in the ego trip, which is about ninety-nine percent of humanity, you have to understand that this is a sort of chrysalis stage. This is babyhood. It doesn't refer to what's going to happen in the future. But just because most people are wrapped up in a cocoon, you and I don't have to be in that cocoon. We have a choice about getting out. It doesn't mean that we're oblivious or that we don't give a damn. We care very much, but we don't have to be *in it*. If you're in it, then you're just part of it. However, you might be able to do some good from the outside.

▶ **Since I've started studying the Tarot, I've lost some friends because I've begun to think differently.**

To be a companion of the sages, you have to expect to give up lesser companions. Imagine Lao Tzu the librarian, a little guy who shuffles around with all his books. He happens to have the concentration of all the wisdom of China in his head and soul and being. So you're his devotee. You shuffle around after him. All your buddies say, "What are you going around with that dope for?" You say, "Well, he isn't just a librarian; he's a great saint." And they say, "You're a silly jerk!" A parting of the ways is inevitable.

▶ **But what if I want to help these people to comprehend?**

That involves the notion of helping somebody else, and the doctrine says they have all the help they need. It's essential to remember that all the information and all the loving help that anybody could ask for is *available at all times*.

▶ **So just come to them when they want it, when they truly seek it?**

When they are *ready*. The help has been there all along, and when they are ready they will suddenly see it. There's nothing you or I can do about it. In our enthusiasm we might *think* there's something we can do —I've been through all that myself—but it's a waste of time. This doesn't mean that they've fallen by the wayside, or have failed. It just means that they are quietly sleeping. Unless they actually feel a need for something, you have no way of giving them anything. Meanwhile, there are many forces watching and waiting for Joe Doakes to say suddenly, "Maybe life isn't just the way I thought it was; maybe I should get deeper into something." There are a lot of opinions about this. I'm speaking from the Cabalistic tradition, which I think has a lot of sense in it.

▶ **You don't mean that you should keep Tarot a big secret, do you?**

It couldn't be a secret for me because I was on television. People in my business trade saw me and said, "What the hell are you doing in *that?*" But when I was in the textile business and went to sell some goods, I didn't try to give my customer a shot of Tarot or Cabala, because a person can't listen until he asks, and then if he doesn't listen, it's all a waste of time. That's all I'm saying.

▶ **In other words, we can influence people by *example*.**

That's the best way, isn't it? When the world seems to be falling apart but you're not falling apart, people say, "I don't know why when you're around, all my troubles feel less serious."

▶ **Being silent is nice because you have something to say when asked. You haven't already said it all.**

It is noteworthy that the Voice of the Silence is the most eloquent of all. The suprarational is a sort of pressure area above the rational, working down through it all the time. The Inner Voice never overrides reason. That's one of the tests of The Hierophant. It will never tell you something stupid or immoral.

Rationality is based on classification and observation. The Hierophant extends into other areas. The intuitive faculty gathers the loose ends and illuminates the intellectual process, giving it guidance. Intuition opens up the mind. As you cultivate your inner listening, you get used to it and you come alive on that level.

This is the Taurus Key. I'm no astrologer but I do know that my Taurean wife is extremely intuitive. I've watched her steer her ship in and out of all the rocks and bad currents throughout her lengthy career in business. She succeeded year after year and never made a single mistake in her assessment of people. Intellectually, that's impossible.

The Tarot is an inner path, so naturally it emphasizes the existence of intuition. The Tarot and the Cabala tell you a lot of things that people don't usually pay attention to. I intimated earlier that the purpose of life may not be quite what you think it is. Your Inner Teacher is trying to help you get the most out of your life. The difference between enjoying life and not enjoying it is the difference between knowing what life is all about and not knowing what it's about. A person with no appreciation of life has a meager existence. A person who has a great appreciation of life has a rich existence. This is the kind of contrast that's involved. While traveling the Inner Path, your experience broadens into tremendous sensations of what life is all about.

Our Key for next week deals with some aspects of life that touch us deeply. The Lovers Key is a recitation of all our capabilities. On the surface it's Adam and Eve in the Garden of Eden, but really it's a picture of what we are inside. It shows the intellectual aspect of ourselves applying to the intuitive aspect in order to get the message that comes from the Higher Self. This is the major meaning of Key 6. The details are singular and worth looking into, but it emphasizes the doctrinal truth that this particular arrangement of the parts of our psyche brings about a major success in the work. This Key definitely represents *great success*.

As always, you make my Thursdays perfect.

KEY 6

CHAPTER 6

THE LOVERS

The whole meaning of the Cabala is contained in Beauty. Of all the Tarot cards, The Lovers most closely represents Beauty as the central Sephirah on the Tree of Life. When two lovers are apart, nothing happens. Together, they create beauty. A flower and an eye do nothing apart, but put them together and beauty happens.

Beauty is very subtle. That's why this Key is connected with DISCRIMINATION, which refines the senses. We gradually discover that we are missing a lot if we are sensitive only to the gross level.

The angel of superconsciousness is blessing The Lovers, who represent the self-conscious and subconscious within each of us. We are usually identified with one side or the other, emphasizing either reason or feeling. Integration is the blessing. Communication is the beauty. It is said in the Cabala that the whole universe, the whole Tree of Life, is constructed from the tension that exists between the polarities. This tension is *total*, not partial. As in breathing, there's an in-breath and an out-breath. You've got to have both. If you were only to breathe in, you'd die.

Each person is the *entire picture* seen in Key 6. This is a delineation of the different parts of the psyche. The biblical statement, "Male and female created He them," is open to several interpretations, but the one popular with Cabalists is that we are constructed with both feminine and masculine elements in our psyche. The Lovers Key not only displays both aspects clearly but also shows how to establish a fruitful relationship between the various parts of yourself.

You might say that Key 6 is *the* message that The Hierophant has to give, in order for us to arrive at the next stage, the victory in Key 7, The Chariot. We are supposed to pay serious attention to the message coming from the Higher Self through the agency of our subconscious. This is definitely the most salient feature of this Key and it should never be forgotten.

Later on in our discussion, we can talk about what happens when boy loves girl and girl loves boy and all that sort of thing. We're not bashful around here; if you want to talk about how the Cabalist deals with the matter of sex and relationships between the sexes, we certainly have no objection. But without going outside of ourselves to any other person, we have our main source of inspiration and guidance within us. It is this very guidance that will clear up the enormous confusion in the outer world. Without it, we hear one alarm after another. As Matthew Arnold put it, we see "where ignorant armies clash by night," and also by day. In this group effort here, our primary interest is to contact our inner source so that we can successfully deal with the outer.

It is from the subconscious aspect of ourselves, as pictured by the woman in Key 6, that we receive the necessary inspiration to deal with the daily struggle. The struggle, of course, is something we're all familiar with. It's the effort toward liberation from everything that holds us back from our destiny. Our true destiny is to learn to represent the highest aspect of our own selves. The woman who looks to the angel in this Key shows us that the subconscious is in touch with our highest aspect. The connection between womanhood and receptivity is obvious.

It's a matter of common instruction in the books of the wise that you and I as self-conscious beings should direct our attention to our subconscious. Thus, the man looks to the woman in Key 6. He is on the rajasic, passionate side of the arrangement; his other half represents the gratification of his fiery desire. According to the Cabalists, the root of all desires is the hunger to experience the Self. The means of fulfillment is The High Priestess, because all the ladies in the Tarot are aspects of The High Priestess. It is through the agency of our own subconscious that we receive awareness of what we're really about and where our true center is. In the sixth Key this center is indicated by the Archangel Raphael.

There are only three beings in the Tarot: a male, a female, and an angel. The female is always The High Priestess in one form or another. The male is always The Magician. The angel corresponds to our Innermost Self. They wear different masks and costumes throughout the deck, but there are only three in the cast.

Consider the angel as Kether, the male as Chokmah, and the female as Binah. That's the whole story of what's going on in yourself. Kether is the root that divides itself into two branches, the self-imparting Chokmah and the receptive Binah. In other words, the principle of polarity emanates from the principle of unity. The Three Supernals are synthesized in love.

Once it's pointed out, it's easy to see that we have the whole Tree of Life in ourselves. This marvelous inventory is extremely difficult to see on our own, hence the importance of The Hierophant's instruction. To analyze all that you see and hear on the outside and come up with the *truth* is virtually impossible, so inner instruction fills the gap. Key 6 is the Disposing Intelligence, meaning that it places things apart for the purpose of analysis.

In the beginning, the quest for your Self seems like a bottomless pit, but we can make great strides with a little help from our Cabalist friends, who have organized this material over the centuries. This is all very important as far as our individual welfare is concerned. In the last analysis, you and I have to make our own choices. That's what it means to be mature. If we can make *intelligent* choices, with some background—like this—to work from, we're on our way to success.

In occult circles the story is that at one time there were not two sexes; there was just One Being. Then it was considered entertaining to divide us into masculine and feminine. It *is* entertaining, and for writers and movie producers it's been a gold mine. It's hard to write an interesting novel about, let's say, a yeast cell. Life is always trying to entertain itself, and it goes to great extremes in order to do so.

It's the view of many thinkers all over the world that the most ghastly fate of all is boredom. If you imagine God as a great big, happy blob existing all by Itself in the universe, you can see how dull that would be. You can understand why the Divine Being might say, "Hey, let's create merry-go-rounds and loop-the-loops, and let's get the whole thing rolling!" From a dramatic point of view, it makes sense. The polarity you see in The Lovers generates all sorts of fascinating experiences.

▶ **In the biblical Garden of Eden, it wasn't so much fun. They got into trouble.**

We've all been subjected to the story of Adam and Eve. As you might expect from the Cabalists, the real story is exactly the reverse. Adam didn't have a fall. He had an uplifting experience that introduced him into the spiritual world through the agency of his feminine aspect. This is a far cry from the ordinary myth with which we are so familiar. The apples were delicious and enjoyed by all. And, far from being a dreadful creature who was the embodiment of Satan, the serpent represents the power in ourselves that is our very salvation. The angel indicates that the relationship between the sexes is being blessed from on high. Anything else is heretical, as far as this teaching is concerned.

▶ **Does the Cabala believe in original sin?**

The Cabala doesn't believe in sin at all. There is such a thing as "missing the mark," but we always get another chance. The notion of sin is fabricated by the priesthood. It's their way of keeping the sheep in the fold.

This whole philosophy is different from outer religion because it doesn't say, "Don't ever go over there where *she* is. All those feelings and sensations and delights over there are *evil*." That would be considered a stupid attitude. In fact, the Tarot and the Cabala are saying that if you didn't have access to that side, life wouldn't be worth living. You must have both intelligence *and* sensation in your life to make it successful. They are equally important, and you should think of them *both at the same time*. Key 6 is a sacrament in the highest sense of the word because it represents the prolongation of life. Cabalists have great respect for God, for Creation, and for men and women.

Everyone is trying to get back into the area of feeling. At the end of the Tarot, in Key 21, the feminine aspect is uppermost. The World Key is the Tarot equivalent of the Heavenly Androgyne, the unification of the psyche, when there is no longer any difference between the self-conscious and the subconscious. The Lovers Key sets forth this perfected balance between opposing forces. It illustrates an ideal situation. We are fortunate to have this ideal as something to work toward.

Discrimination is our most important tool in this matter. It's connected with the sixth Key through the letter ZAIN ז, which means a *sword*. In the relationship exposed to view here, the Sword of Discrimination is possibly more difficult to apply than in any other area we can think of.

It is positively extraordinary that at puberty we are invited to experience love—dragged in by the ears, as far as I'm concerned. In Key 6 in the Marseilles Tarot, Eros has a bow and arrow with which he inflames people's passions. Love sweeps you right off your feet. This is nothing less than the Life Power itself insisting that we join in the Dance of Life.

In my case, my mother and my wife's mother put their heads together, and who can beat the power of two mothers? My marriage was all settled over a cup of tea.

One thing I have always found delightful about the Cabala is its honesty in dealing with something so basic and so *inevitable*. The Victorians didn't want to look at sex. They wanted to filter out the truth and look at it only from a certain removed slant. Fortunately for us, we live in a happier age. We are welcome to recognize the power and *rule* of Eros. We never get away from this tremendous drive as long as we live.

Through discrimination we begin to see that we cannot upset the natural drives in ourselves. We must recognize the forces for what they are and deal with them as best we can. The real problems arise when we have no guidance in this area. When we are left in the storm of our feelings without discrimination or analysis, we can't tell if they are major hurricanes or just local thunderstorms.

We are all subject to this universal rule, with no exceptions. That includes the Pope, the Dalai Lama, and anyone else you care to name. You can ignore it but you are still subject to the truth about life. It's not just a piece of paper, like a traffic law. This law is written *in us*. We don't have any choice. You can evade your income tax or get away with murder if you have lots of money, but this law cannot be broken. In antiquity the Greeks were so impressed by the power of Eros that they venerated it. What else could you do?

The reason for my long-winded preachment is that without an understanding of this dynamic, you miss the point of the Cabala. This is equally true of any good, solid Eastern philosophy. Life has an intellectual aspect but it is *not* an intellectual affair. It's an affair of *forces* that are big and strong. The sooner we get that in our collective heads, the better for us. It's just plain stupid to think that we can evade, avoid, or deny the way we are made.

▶ So the Cabala says sex is inevitable?

Speaking in theological terms, God has ordained it and God blesses a marriage with children. We have a responsibility for the continuation of the race. I'm sure my great-grandson would agree.

I think it's beautiful that the Cabala has such a friendly, wholesome teaching about the relationship between the sexes. What's more, they say you've *got to put on a coat of skin* in order to fully express yourself. Key 6 rules the sense of smell, biologically connected with sex. A male monarch butterfly can smell his lady-love a mile away.

▶ **How is it that the snake is a good guy in the Cabala?**

The snake is a foreshadowing of spiritual success. In GEMATRIA, which is a kind of Cabalistic numerology, the word for serpent or Tempter has the same numeration as the word for redeemer or MESSIAH. There's only one Life Force.

That's the single most famous piece of Gematria. Every Hebrew letter is also a number. Therefore every Hebrew word adds up to a larger number. NACHASH (serpent) and Messiah both add up to 358, which means they are essentially the same. Hebrew is one of the sacred languages and has a code-like aspect.

It's interesting that Moses placed the symbol of the snake on the cross, or TAV. That's a kind of double whammy, because Tav stands for the Muladhara CHAKRA at the base of the spine, and in the East the Serpent Power is said to rise up the spine to enlighten the chakras. It's amazing that Moses, who never went to college, knew all about such things. Forty years in the desert spent studying the Secret Doctrine can be very rewarding.

When I reflect on more than fifty years in the Tarot, it seems like a very short time indeed. The message that's written in the Keys is timeless. The Tarot is something that was put forth to *help* us; that's its *raison d'être*. And there's no sticky stuff on the back, you know; when you turn the card over there's no bequest form on the other side.

My wife is an Episcopalian and we were quite amused by the mailings she used to receive from a church she belonged to at one time. *Every* communication she ever got from that church had a bequest form printed on the back, saying, "If I die tomorrow, I leave everything I have to the church. Sign here." The Tarot cards don't have this. You'll notice too that the personalities who are responsible for the Tarot are long gone and they didn't sign anything either.

Getting back to the Garden of Eden: Everything you and I call life depends on the polarities. No polarity, no life, no game, no anything. The *idea* of the game is on the Logos side. The game itself is the role of Eros because the game is played in the field of *sensation*. Sensation is a mystery best approached through meditation, which means thinking about one thing for a long time. It's not easy to do, but we can train our intellect to sort of bore a hole into *anything*. We see this happen in science, but we can also apply it to our own psyche. The whole object of the analytical process we go through with the Tarot and the Cabala is to make us more able players in the game of life.

The three figures in this Key represent the three Pillars of the Tree of Life. The masculine side is called the Pillar of Mercy and the feminine side is the Pillar of Severity, named after the Fourth and Fifth Sephiroth respectively. The angel is the Pillar of Mildness in the middle, which balances, integrates, and energizes the polarities. In this connection, Raphael is the angel of healing, which is wholeness.

▶ Do the two trees in Key 6 correspond to the pillars also?

Yes, they do. The Tree of Life behind Adam has twelve flames. These are the twelve different kinds of life expression that have been noted by astrologers for thousands of years. The whole Orchestra of Life is built on the principle that each instrument has something unique to offer. As in a Beethoven symphony, the interplay of all the instruments makes for a tremendous richness of expression that wouldn't exist with just one note. The more different we are in our own special way, the more interesting life becomes. We're not supposed to be the same.

The fruits on the Tree of Knowledge behind Eve symbolize the five senses, which are in the domain of the feminine because they are receptive. Through our senses we can cultivate the remarkable joy of which we are capable. As mentioned in the Bible, *life is a feast* to which we are invited. Enjoyment of the feast takes skill, like everything else, and in the Cabala this skill is considered worth achieving. The enjoyer of the feast is ourselves, our Innermost Self.

Where I live in Marin County it's always cloudy on summer mornings, so I remind myself that the sun is shining brightly up above the clouds. Clouds are made of water; therefore in the Tarot they represent the world of matter, the world of appearance that obscures the True Self. That's what has to be overcome—the total illusion of everything that's going on. When you begin to look at it differently, to see it inwardly instead of outwardly, then you are on your way to getting rid of the cloud of intervening substance that keeps you from seeing the sun.

Nothing stands between us and illumination except this great big hunk of entertainment. There's nothing wrong with the entertainment in itself, but we should not confuse it with Reality.

You and I are trying to poke through the facade and get to what's important. It's not far away, honest! The Real is very close, but people have well-organized ideas about everything, such as: "Some things are holy and some things are the work of the Devil, and that's the way it is!" In the meantime the sun and the moon and the stars are quietly shining ... It's a comfortable feeling to know that *something* is not being elected every four years.

▶ **Mountains are dependable too, and there's a big one in the Key.**

It's dependable, all right. It stands for the Great Work. Due to the fact of evolution, you don't *have* to do anything for yourself and you will still make it to the top of the mountain. That's the doctrine. Still, if you feel like it, you can participate in your own evolution. There's lots of propaganda to keep you in a nonthinking state, telling you that if you've been a good girl or boy you'll get your reward in heaven. Rather than trudge along with this, we must always remember that the work of amelioration and betterment of life in the world can only be accomplished in an atmosphere of love. Changes are brought about not through coercion but through friendly persuasion. That's the way this tremendous mountain of achievement is going to be surmounted.

▶ **Jason, what specifically would you say about personal human relationships?**

In any relationship, both persons have two aspects. *She* has a masculine and a feminine aspect, and *he* has a masculine and a feminine aspect. Ideally, this polarity is opposed in each case. Her masculine is opposed to his feminine, and his masculine is opposed to her feminine, which makes a harmonious four-fold arrangement.

▶ **Does this four-fold thing go on all the time in relationships, even between persons of the same sex?**

All the time, all the time. An example is in communication. We can't communicate without this polarity. If I want to hear you, I have to assume a feminine state of mind, and if you want to hear me you have to do likewise. Key 6 is connected with Gemini, the zodiacal sign of communication. Paradise results from perfect communication, and hell from lack of communication. Key 6 is the opposite of Key 15, The Devil Key. Look at the two Keys together: The discriminating faculty in Key 6 doesn't take anything for granted, in contrast to the typical attitude of the pair in Key 15.

▶ **So, to listen receptively is as important as sending out?**

We need a balanced expression of both. I mentioned last week that the whole idea of life is exchange—each person giving in terms of their own self. Not opinions and prejudices and the stuff you read in the newspapers; that isn't yourself. We're not talking about that. It's the old story —we could make a helluva racket together or we could make beautiful music together. We can create beauty only if the whole area is illuminated and handled intelligently.

▶ **Can a human being be complete without a mate?**

It's important to remember that we each have The Lovers in ourselves, without any outside reference at all. The time comes in our evolution when we no longer have to *have* another person; we don't have to hold on to the feeling that we're just going to *die* if they don't spoonfeed us our granola. You go from that state to the realization that you are yourself and you can give what you please. And the other person is their own self, and can give or take what they please. Then the whole thing becomes an intelligent exchange.

▶ **What is love, according to the Cabala?**

Love is unconditional and self-imparting, like sunlight. We don't have to generate love. It exists as a universal principle. All we have to do is let it flow through us.

▶ **What is bliss?**

When you've made some progress, bliss is what you feel then in comparison to the way you felt before!

When the masculine and the feminine in yourself are in proper relationship, the total effect is called *grace*. There is a descent from your Higher Self that completely engulfs your personality in a blissful feeling. What the Cabalists call grace and what they call love are practically indistinguishable. Remember that this influence reaches from the highest to the lowest expression of life. From the most glorious imaginable aspect to the smallest thing you can imagine, it operates on all levels and remembers all levels. And it inspires all levels. This is MEZLA, the Holy Influence, but thinking of it as love is probably the best way to understand it. Nothing is too small or beneath its notice. You might say that's the nature of the cosmic phenomenon of love. You can tell you're getting close to bliss when little things move your spirit.

▶ Paul Case writes about the sun in this Key as the body of a being.

That's a tradition that's as old as the hills. Whether you have any feelings about it is entirely up to you.

▶ It is said there is a spiritual sun at the Center of Being.

Yes, and the quickest way to get to the center, according to the authorities, is to think of it as a Being and simply throw yourself at that Being. In the East that's called BHAKTI. It covers the shortest distance between where you are (regardless of where you are) and It. This is also the idea of The Hanged Man in the Tarot. You let yourself go and you wind up in the center. There are all sorts of occult sayings about giving up your life to find greater life.

▶ Do you have to define the center?

Well, as I say, you have to think of it as a Being, rather than an abstraction. This is not hard to do. For instance, consider the Cabalistic notion of Father and Mother on a cosmic scale. Since *we* are beings, a being is more meaningful to us. We can't fall in love with an equation, that's for sure. What would you say? "Dear equation, I need a friend?" And even if you don't want to go so far as to say that the cosmos is a being, perhaps there are beings *in* the cosmos who might be helpful to you.

▶ How about the Supreme Being?

This is something that each peson has to define for themself. It's not anything that someone else can lay on you. That's impossible.

▶ Do you believe in the Supreme Being?

Personally, yes I do. But as I say, I wouldn't lay that on anybody because it doesn't *mean* anything, you know. The communication that comes from within yourself, and enlightens you in certain respects—

that's the best you can expect. You don't need anything else. We are capable of the direct perception of Inner Reality, which is what intuition is. When we apply to the inner principle, we get a true intuition for an answer. That's what the man is doing in Key 6 and that's what the Bhakti practitioner does.

▶ **The Bhakti is like the Fool, isn't he?**

Yes, the Fool of God, but understand that the Fool of God is no dummy. Of course, there have been people who made the horrible mistake of telling other people that they were enlightened, and they didn't do too well. Most people don't understand this business at all. It's okay to join the Salvation Army and beat a drum, but it's not a good idea to go around telling people that you just spoke to God because that's not considered sane. In fact, there are lots of people in mental institutions who talk to God all the time. It's a dangerous area to be in.

▶ **When I look inside myself, I'm aware of conflict between the different parts of my psyche.**

This is sometimes called the War in Heaven. The polar opposites can give us a bad time, which is what happens when an individual is not imposing the rule. In general, the parts of the psyche are like the countries of the world; for no good reason, they war and bicker with each other. In Jung's *Psychology and Alchemy* this is illustrated by the picture of a sick king with all the planetary figures fighting around him.

Our emotions are the most challenging part of our composition, which is why you'll find this one of the most exciting fields for investigation in yourself. You need a "steady hand at the wheel" when you get into this kind of journey because the emotions are, by their very nature, "rough waters" and difficult to handle. So the ruler must rule. In the Cabala it's the Higher Self who rules through the Sun Center, Tiphareth on the Tree of Life. The Self holds all other aspects in place. Then each functions perfectly in its own area, and the sick king becomes well.

In practical psychology the passions rule humanity. This is humanity's undoing. Jung prophesied that there would be a holocaust in Europe because of the suppressed passions there. He saw that underneath the surface calm there were extreme, compelling emotions that were going to express themselves in an explosive way. And they did, in World War II.

The Lovers Key beautifully represents the peace that is possible in the psyche. Human beings actually have an *instinct* to work in harmony with the universe—it's built into us. Key 6 helps us to free this natural inclination, showing us that the human psyche is *made* for relationships.

▶ Last week you talked about the dangers of getting lost in the personal subconscious. Discrimination is needed to distinguish the purely personal from the more . . . ?

. . . subtle things. Yes. It's fairly easy to discriminate in this matter, because you *know* what is personal—so all you have to do is be honest with yourself. Easier said than done, I admit, but if you're *honest-minded* and willing to recognize what is personal and what is not, it comes unstuck fairly well. For example, if you have an ax to grind, that's where you are personally involved, which gets into egotism, which is a large area of study. Not always pleasant, but plenty big.

▶ When the Eastern religions speak of "desirelessness," is that the same as beyond Binah?

They are speaking of the Witness consciousness in Chokmah.

▶ You have to go all the way through Binah to get there, in order to satisfy your desire.

Analytically speaking, but not really, because this never stops. It is simply the way the universe operates, so it isn't a matter of going through or beyond something. You'll never dispense with Binah. The goal is to have a good, healthy desire-nature that is also illuminated, so there isn't any doubt in your mind what it is and what its function is.

Imagine that you are a person who loves children. You are married and you think your wife is horrible, but that's the only way you can have children. That would be some situation, wouldn't it? So don't remove the means of getting what you want. No matter how high your objective is, no matter how lofty a constitution you write for yourself, you can't possibly achieve it without involving your desire-nature. Desire actually teaches discrimination. As we advance, we like nicer and nicer things.

▶ Honesty and generosity are nice qualities to put into your constitution.

Honesty is pretty good, but generosity is suspect from an ego point of view.

▶ **If I have an experience and want to share it with someone else, that, to me, would be generosity.**

Not unless that someone else *wanted* to share it with you. It could be laying it on the other guy whether he liked it or not, and that wouldn't be generous. I'm being the Devil's advocate, I admit.

▶ **If you just gave a gentle hint to someone of this lovely thing you have, and they responded at all, it might be safe to go ahead and share it.**

Let's talk about something that takes care of this whole area, which is simple goodwill. The Primal Will-to-Good is the basis of the Cabala. If you affirm the Primal Will-to-Good, that takes care of all difficulties without involving the ego. It brings in superhuman or superconscious aspects that are far above the level of the ego. There's no need for display (which the ego just adores) when you arrive at a higher level. There's just no necessity for it.

Love follows its own gravity, goes where it's supposed to go and does all the things it's supposed to do. This is not a *planned* thing on the ego level. It's much like the way water runs downhill.

I don't want to leave anybody with the notion that generosity is a bad thing, but true generosity is not something you *will*. You might say it's a side effect of love. Truly generous people have no awareness of it at all. It's perfectly natural for them. My mother, for instance, was a truly generous woman. She had no more idea of generosity than she had of quantum physics, but other people were aware of her generosity. It was just natural for her to give of herself, her substance, and everything else. It was lovely. No strain, rather like the quality of mercy in Shakespeare, if you remember.

▶ **It's not strained.**
▶ **And it "droppeth as the gentle rain from heaven."**

Right. And Mercy on the Tree of Life *is* the love center.

▶ **What about Beauty? That's in the center of the Tree and it corresponds to the heart chakra.**

The sixth Sephirah, the Sun Center, rules over the Triad of Personality below it on the Tree. As the Mediating Intelligence, it connects everything above with everthing below. Statement number six in the

Pattern on the Trestleboard says, "In all things great and small, I see the Beauty of the Divine Expression."

In the construction of the Tree of Life, Beauty is the center of YETZIRAH, the World of Formation. This means that the sword of air is placed here. The sword has two uses. First, it delineates and discriminates among the different parts. Then it actually cuts out what you want. Desire is the only necessary control in this. Naturally, we want what we feel is beautiful. Beauty, being central to the whole Cabalistic scheme, represents a goal for all of us. I'm sure we would each have a different definition, but as the bullseye on the target, we can all aim at it.

In the occult doctrine the mainspring of each individual's development comes from that person's Innermost Self. Some of the best information about the Self can be found in the UPANISHADS, which are ancient scriptures from India—highly recommended by yours truly. The Self is always working and eventually will overcome any obstacles. It will continue until it gets its way, which is *your own* way.

As you get closer to your Self, you feel more and more "with it." You don't care any more about a lot of junk that seemed important, because you have something better to take its place. You get simpler inwardly. That's worth money, right there, because to be happy normally takes a lot of money. To be abnormally happy in terms of this doctrine doesn't cost anything at all, so you are moving in the right direction economically.

The total mastery of which we are capable is summed up in Key 7. The Victory Key is a synthesis of all the previous Keys. For example, The Lovers are represented in a state of union by the LINGAM-YONI symbol on the shield. The complexities of the love affair have resolved themselves into a reciprocal working relationship of a permanent quality. The flow is continually going back and forth.

The Charioteer is none other than your Innermost Self, the rider in the chariot of personality. This is the self that you would *prefer above all other selves* if you were capable of making the choice. The whole purpose of self-discovery is to find out what a fine Self you have. Your True Self is *exactly* the way you would like it to be. It might not be easy to find it, but when you do find that Self, you will approve of it very much. You'll love it, and you should, because it's you!

Have a victorious week with Key 7. Thanks, as always, for coming.

KEY 7

CHAPTER 7

THE CHARIOT

JUST AS IN ANY OTHER GAME, we want to move from "Go" to "Home" in the Game of Life. In the *Upanishads* we learn that you can't win the game as long as you *try* to win, because in Reality you have *already won*. Your Inner Self is eternally victorious in the Great Game. Although we extravagantly try to explain the Inner Self at these meetings, we can't possibly describe what it's really like. Despite this difficulty, we shall make our usual noble effort.

The essential feature of Key 7 is that it represents the Middle Way, not the extremes of right or left. The Way of the Self, which is *your* self and *my* self, is in the middle because that's the place of mastery. The Self is the master in you and me.

It's hard for us to understand that the Self is not different from us. For a long, long time it seems as though you are one thing and your essential Self is something else. You feel a kind of dualism inside yourself. It's not actual, but that's how you *feel* about it. There's always the old idea that God is up there and you're down here; God is great and you're nothing. The trouble with this outer doctrine is that it doesn't work for anybody.

We are not God but we *are* the sons and daughters of the Most High, made in the image of God. The Bible says these things, not because of our gorgeous personalities, but because of the remarkable *spirit* that is in us. As they used to say in my old school days, "It's the spirit that quickeneth." We meet here not as bodies, but as spirits. On this level we have a delightful camaraderie. It is the spirit, or Self, in each of us that makes us interesting to each other. That Self is the Charioteer, the triumphant rider in the vehicle of personality. This Tarot image is a *mirror of yourself*.

The Chariot Key is a summary of all the Keys in the first row of the Tableau, which is a sequence of seven meditations dealing with important aspects of our psyche. The Magician is our self-conscious, directive power. The High Priestess represents memory, the all-inclusive aspect of the subconscious. The Empress signifies the power of active imagination seated in the subconscious mind. The Emperor is our ability to constitute our lives in a fashion that is acceptable not only to ourselves, but also to the law of Life Itself. Our intuitive faculty is indicated by The Hierophant. The Lovers Key symbolizes the keen discrimination necessary to unscramble all the different factors that are dynamically interacting in ourselves.

The Chariot is a summing-up. The words RECEPTIVITY-WILL are attributed to this Key, and the notion of receptivity was suggested by The Magician in the first place. You will recall that The Magician's gesture signifies his recognition that all his powers are derived. There's no harm in power as long as we don't get tangled up in our egotism, so we can't acknowledge that our support comes from within. Once we get the message, we can exert the will. Key 7 is the reward for The Magician's mental efforts.

In this Key we see all four Cabalistic Worlds. The stone chariot represents the physical body or outer level. The sphinxes symbolize the senses and the desire-nature on the emotional level. Then we have the invisible reins of the mind on the mental level. Topping it all off is the essential level, where *you are IT*; you are the driver.

I'm not old enough to remember the dinosaurs—but almost! My first car was a Model T Ford. I used to drive it proudly around Central Park when I was eighteen. I'd honk at my mother and embarrass her and her hoity-toity friends. I had a grand time with it.

When you get in your car, you are the driver. Someone in the back seat may also be driving, but the controls are in your hands. You have to pay close attention to everything. When you're driving the chariot that's pictured in the Tarot, you must be just as careful as if you were on the road in a high-powered automobile.

Control of the two dynamic forces represented by the sphinxes is a primary factor in the victory of the Inner Self. The white sphinx is attracted toward something; it's the "I like it" side of the desire-nature. The black sphinx is repelled from something, the "I don't like it" side. These polarized forces use the same energy in opposite directions. Until these creatures are controlled, they will pull us this way and that. You know this if you have lived on earth more than two weeks. How to overcome this basic being-dragged-about by our desires is the problem that's solved in this Key.

The Charioteer's left hand is holding the invisible reins of the mind. The mind is the means of controlling everything in your life, but if you are unconscious, this arrangement isn't going to work for you. When the mind is tuned to the Self, it knows what it wants. Otherwise it just chases whatever comes along. The art of driving your vehicle is like any other art. In the beginning the rewards seem meager, but as time goes on and your understanding improves, your vision, hearing, and other senses also improve. Then you begin to get a different feeling about it.

Again and again and again we think too small, even though we are capable of thinking big. We can't possibly encompass everything in our thoughts, but the bigger we think, the better for us. The Charioteer's body goes down into the cube that represents the physical universe. However, his head is in the upper or inner part, in the cosmos, where it belongs. His canopy of stars indicates the presence of The High Priestess. He is in a state of realization of the faculty of mind.

Suppose you were to think for one moment that your life was caused by your fellow men or women. That would fracture anybody's equanimity right there, but fortunately it doesn't depend on that. All these encumbrances in our heads are simply dreams. They don't mean anything. We are immediately connected with the cosmos, but we don't think about it. We are immediately connected with our total potential, but we don't think about that. We're in the midst of the most exciting experiment about ourselves that we can possibly imagine, but when we start to feel it happening, we want to hide in the hole that we have already dug, just in case, for these occasions. Our mentors keep saying, "Come on out and look at the stars. Keep looking and after awhile you will get the message." That's *your head* in the stars there in Key 7 and it's fantastic if you just let it happen.

Another important part of the symbolism of Key 7 is that the chariot is on the other side of the river from the city. *The other shore* is a metaphor for emancipation. You and I have left the city because it represents the complex conditioning of RACE-THOUGHT, the thing we must analyze and overcome. It's okay to read the newspaper, the news of the city, but we should remember that it doesn't represent Reality. The city is real in the sense that real beings live there, yet to apprehend the One Reality we must remove ourselves from distractions. Concentration is The Magician's chief means of liberation from all the oppressive factors he is born into. He wants to be rid of everything negative. This is achieved through focusing on a positive philosophy, such as the Cabala.

▶ **There's a lot to overcome.**

"We shall overcome." That's our motto.

▶ **How does the chariot get across the river? Is there a bridge?**

In Reality it is always there, as in, "Your limousine awaits, Madame."

▶ **And I come to know this by . . . intention? discrimination? focus?**

It's suggested in the textbook, but also it seems to me that there is a *cosmic* intention. Like the Taoists, the Cabalists think in philosophical terms and they decided a long time ago that there's a certain *impetus* to the Plan of Life. You and I don't have brains enough to go in the right direction, but we have better than brains. We have an inside push that helps us with these special discriminations. We don't know where our evolutionary buttons are, but our Inner Self does know. Once again, we are *led* into these areas that give us more control of our powers and faculties. Hence the importance of receptivity. As it says in statement number seven in the Pattern, "Living from that Will, supported by its unfailing Wisdom and Understanding, mine is the Victorious Life." Seven on the Tree is Netzach, which means victory.

As indicated by the spangled canopy, starlight is raining down upon us all the time. Cosmic rays are constantly zooming through our brains, splitting atoms as they go. We are powerless to do anything about it. We don't know what this bombardment does for us. It may be important in keeping us going. If you want to fantasize about it, you can look on the bright side and say, "This is how we get messages from the cosmos."

▶ **How do the sphinxes, the senses, come into the picture?**

The senses are the connecting link between the Being and the Being's fulfillment. If you wanted to reach across the table and get a cup of coffee and you didn't have any arms, it would be impossible. The senses are like arms, the mechanism by which Life fulfills itself. When the universe takes a snooze, all this sensory mechanism is withdrawn, so the story goes, and the sphinxes take a nap. When the universe wakes up, so do the sphinxes. As long as life is going on, the senses are plugged in. There's no let-up. In the *Sephir Yetzirah*, or *Book of Formation*, all the senses are enumerated because without them there is no life.

▶ **Jason, you said that the chariot is the body. Then you said it's the universe.**

Our vehicle is a portion of the universe, a microcosm. According to the wise, it *represents* the entire universe. This gives us an unlimited horizon.

The one thing that Life is doing at this particular moment is living itself. The Cabalists caution us not to think that Life is one thing and we are another. We are the same as Life; our consciousness is no different from the consciousness of Life Itself. If you think of yourself in these terms it will set up a relationship between the energy aspect of yourself and its medium of its expression, which is your body. Transpose this awareness onto the universe and you can see how it works, eternally.

If I were to greatly identify with the car that I drive, I would think I was part of that car. But I think of it as a vehicle. I'm grateful to have one to get around in, but I know it's not *me*. Awareness is universal rather than particular. We can go out of the personal into the universal, and that's cosmic consciousness. It's as simple as that. When consciousness is not identified any more with a particular vehicle or condition, that's the awareness shown in Key 21, The World.

If you are a human being, it's hard to understand that human life is a vehicle. Nevertheless, it can be done. By the instruction offered in The Hierophant Key, creative will comes into play. You begin to impose this will on the vehicle of your life, as in The Emperor Key. You either impose patterns on your own life or you just take your chances. If you gamble, it's like Reno; you might win and you might not.

▶ **So the Charioteer imposes his will over the pleasure/pain principle as symbolized by the sphinxes?**

Right. That means his mind is liberated from the illusion, so he can drive his vehicle anywhere he wants. It's not driving *him*. He's driving *it*. This is uncommon, because the control is very subtle. Just one persuasive word can move most people in a negative way.

The Hebrew letter here is CHETH ח, which means a *fence* or *wall*. One aspect of this is protection. The Cheth surrounds the sacred inner place that is free from any negative reactions. In classical times they called this the TEMENOS, the holy space.

Liking and disliking are in the category of reacting. The *capacity* for liking and disliking is the important part. When you become aware, you say, "I'm reacting like an automaton, going this way and that. It's *my intrinsic power* that's energizing this. I don't have to go along with this."

▶ **Then you are ruling instead of being ruled.**

You always have the choice.

▶ **What about doing what you like to do?**

Doing is another matter. Liking or disliking something is reacting; that's negative. But if you like to *do* something, that's positive. There's a big difference. If you say, "I like to play the banjo and that's just what I'm gonna do," you are being creative. Doing something for the fun of it is very close to The Way.

▶ **We must discriminate between reaction and motivation.**

Yes. Motivation you've got to have. That's the will in Receptivity-Will.

▶ **I question my motivation sometimes. My ego gets involved.**

Motivation is the toughest part of yourself to analyze. As we've mentioned before, you have to take a hard look at your desire-nature. The Cabala is helpful because it teaches that your desire is part of the cosmos, an essential part of yourself. It's your engine, which is neither good, bad, nor indifferent. It just *is*. The way it works is that it always has an object. This is where you can get fouled up. The desire-nature automatically attaches itself to some object in your subconscious, from your memory bank.

▶ **The Charioteer looks to me as though he has transcended desire.**

The Cabala firmly teaches that you will never get rid of your desire. The Charioteer, the master who is your Self, is able to *look* at desire and see what is going on in this department. When you know what is happening, you are no longer the victim of it. At that point you are free of karma, because karma *is* desire-nature reacting to what's in your memory bank—over and over and over. Since the memory bank is limitless, as long as it works automatically it goes on forever.

According to the Cabala, bless its heart, Wisdom (Chokmah) is our salvation. It is here that Life reflects itself to itself. If we didn't have this superior faculty we'd be in a bad way, but this center in ourselves can look at anything and size up the situation. That's salvation right there—unscrambling all this complicated stuff that's going on. The liberating aspect of ourselves can cut right through it.

The Cabalists are smart; they don't believe in eliminating any part of life, such as desire. They try to find out what it's for, which is a different approach altogether. They understand that in order to enjoy life, you have to comprehend what is really good. As Winston Churchill said, "I have very simple tastes—just the best, that's all." This is the same idea. You do not have time or desire for lesser things when you have something better.

▶ It's hard for me to give up believing in nonattachment.

Part of the illusion is the idea that we can possess anything. We can't. We can *enjoy everything* but we can't possess anything—because it isn't ours in the first place. The Inner Self is always insisting that we learn the true values of life. It's got a bulldog grip on this particular goal and will never give up. Until we know what life is all about and what its true values are, we'll be hounded by our Inner Self.

If you can't get a big bang out of seeing a beautiful mother and child on the street, that's being sick as far as Life is concerned. If all you can think about is the stock market, that's a tragedy, because Life can't get in. You've shut out all the beauty and joy. You're supposed to be open, and when you are, Life begins to permeate you. You can have a heck of a good time for yourself without even doing anything. It's a terrific show, better than Hollywood. No kidding!

It's all in your head, as the Buddhists say, and they're right. That's what Key 7 is all about. We're trying to get our heads straightened out so we can enjoy life in the wonderful way that we are truly capable of. The Chariot Key is the Intelligence of the House of Influence. This refers to a mind, a universe, full of grace and love.

▶ I was brought up to believe that it's wrong to enjoy life too much, so I was shocked last week when you said that sin was an invention of the priesthood.

I'd like to repeat, if you'll bear with me: In the Cabalistic lore there is no excuse for Life except the experience of Life, and there's no reason for it at all unless it has meaning. Under the circumstances, you may be sure that Life is not interested in torturing itself. It's interested in expressing itself and enjoying its own expression. We are the same. According to the teachings, we are a small version of Life Itself.

According to W. W. Westcott, in his book *The Kabalah*, the biblical

Pentateuch (which includes the Garden of Eden story) was compiled and written down in 450 B.C. by Ezra and Nehemiah. They were regular, human men—priests, to be exact. They were promoting a patriarchal religion. Priests and shamans of all religions have a tendency to control their followers through fear.

The purpose of religious teaching is to get all the cows into the barn. The purpose of occult teaching is to get all the cows out into the pasture. The barn is not considered a creative place, and the whole idea of the Cabala is to encourage the creativity, the self-expression, within each individual. It's a different ideal.

Instead of starting out with the premise that we are all sinners—and the only basis for that is a tradition—our premise is that you are glorious, tremendous, and super-duper. You don't know it, so you have to realize the greatness of your Self before you can express it. Gandhi is a good example. When he became aware of himself as Mahatma Gandhi, which was his *real* Self, it began to express itself in literally world-shaking terms.

I'm not saying that every person who realizes himself or herself is going to be a big deal in the world. The point is that a *personal revolution* for each individual is indicated in this process. Great or small is immaterial and irrelevant. The subtle ways of self-expression are just as important as the gross. As long as we move with our own inner impulse, we are traveling in the right direction.

Please do not approach this work with preconceived ideas. You don't *tell* your own nature what it is; you *ask it* what it is. Study everything as though you were from a distant planet. It seems incredible that we are in the world and not of it, but that's the way it is. The essential part of us has nothing to do with the physical plane. The best example I can think of is a magnet underneath a surface that holds some iron filings. We have discussed before how the filings will form into the pattern of the magnet. It is equally true that there is no physical connecting medium between ourselves and the outer world. It is a magnetic connection. We have to be able to operate the body somehow, don't we? The Cabala says that the mind moves the body.

Before anybody actually went to the moon, my daughter sent me a funny card about taking a moon trip. The artist had created an awkward moon vehicle with all kinds of things, pots and pans and everything else, hanging off it. When they made the real lunar module, that's what it turned out to be like. And that's the way we are. We're just as silly-looking as a lunar landing device. The only thing is, we've got a piece of plastic around the whole thing; we've got a skin on the outside. But the driver *in* the module is the important thing, and that's us. The Tarot and the Cabala are telling us, "Win, lose, or draw; you've got to drive this thing. There it is; now run it." If you don't run it consciously, it will run after a fashion because of the input that comes from the outside, but that's not the right way to run it as far as the occult tradition is concerned.

▶ **The Charioteer does it right.**

Absolutely. This is the victorious king in his triumph. His scepter is a combination of the Moon ☽ and a lemniscate ∞. When the subconscious, the means of achieving everything, is teamed with the higher aspect of self-consciousness, direction and discipline are the results. The masculine aspect performs the mental magic; the feminine aspect performs the magic of embodiment.

As a summary of the first row of the Tableau, Key 7 is telling us that in our waking state we are the directors of what is going on. We have to take a stand and not be swayed this way and that. The middle Pillar of the Tree of Life symbolizes the equilibrium that is possible for the Self when it isn't pulled to the right or left but stays where it belongs, in the center.

▶ **What do the moon-shaped epaulets symbolize?**

The comic and tragic moons represent moods. The way to master moods is to create a permanent mood—you might even call it a permanent mode—in your mind. This is like the meditation MANTRAM with which we are familiar from our Hindu friends. If you keep some pleasant thought in your mind all the time, it excludes everything else. This isn't such a bad idea, especially when you consider the problem of conditioning. In contrast to keeping the mantram in your mind, the other possibility is to say, "Oh my God, this is terrible!" This battle-cry can continue in your head from the minute you get up in the morning until you go to bed at night, and you can still be marching to this tune in your dreams. The reactive person is a busy fellow, concerned with his daily Armageddon.

▶ **What is Armageddon?**

It's the big battle at the end of time when God and his angels destroy all evil beings and condemn them to eternal damnation.

▶ **What's your interpretation of that, since you obviously don't take it literally?**

Have you read the *Bhagavad-Gita*? It talks about the same battle. There is only one battle. It is between your Higher Self and the ego with its whole family of illusions. There's no question about the similarity between Key 7 and the image of Krishna, who is the charioteer in the *Gita*. Krishna and Jesus Christ both represent your True Self, the one you must rely on for victory. Because of that Presence, *the battle is already won.*

In this connection, you'll notice that The Devil in Key 15, who symbolizes egotism, has an inverted pentagram on his forehead. The victor of Key 7 wears the pentagram right side up. This reversal indicates the contrasting mental states symbolized by these two Keys, which are polar opposites in astrology (Cancer and Capricorn) as well as in the Tarot Tableau. The Devil is at the peak of wildness and The Chariot is very controlled. The Devil sits on half a cube instead of the whole cube of Key 7. This suggests that the ego has a half-baked notion of what is going on.

▶ **Many people believe that Armageddon will be an actual nuclear war.**

I know. It can get to you. But hopefully, all your adventures in the Tarot and the Cabala will keep your head out of dangerous areas. Such areas, if they are repetitive, can be distressing. My experience has been that the Cabalistic philosophy is totally positive in dealing with race-thought as well as with the everyday bumps and grinds we all get into.

It is important for our health and well-being that we try to figure out, "Am I a social security number, or do I really amount to something? Am I in truth a microcosm, the image of the Most High?" In the practice of these teachings, you have to be hermetically sealed against the foolishness going on in the world. That's the reason for Cheth, the fence, and also the shell of Cancer the Crab. If you are hermetically sealed, you have nothing to worry about. This protects you.

▶ **In Paul Case's *The Tarot* it says that speech is attributed to Cheth, and that the right use of words creates safety.**

We've got to name things and get them into some order before we can think, so classification is the first step in science. If words weren't assigned to things, the mind would be on a primitive level indeed. It's only when things have been named and classified that the mind can process the data. Words become the raw material for imagination. The whole process is an essential part of our inner development.

▶ So words are the way we create the world?

We actually get hold of things by naming them. Apparently this is a stage we have to go through. We learn to more or less *fix* things in our minds by means of words. Then we can manipulate them. They can become either an obstacle or a way to freedom. Speech is our undoing as well as the greatest single advantage we have as humans. In Key 16 (The Tower), speech is overthrown. Notice that one plus six equals seven. The structure of speech that is raised by the ego is a mistake.

The children in The Sun Key have turned their backs to the wall that represents words. This doesn't mean there is anything wrong with the words. Rather, it means that there is something even greater *beyond* words, and of course this something is the creative, perceiving Self.

▶ Then words are like an evolutionary stage that we go through.

That's right. Words are laid on us just as the ego is. God only knows why we have to go through this ego thing, but we do. First we have to acquire an ego, very painstakingly, and then we have to get rid of it. The same goes for words because the nature of the Inner Reality defies description in words.

▶ The city in Key 7 reminds me of The Tower Key.

Yes, they are both complex developments of what you might call the self-conscious element or Logos aspect. Men like to build things—and the higher the pile, the better they like it. "Higher and bigger than anything else!" That's typical happy maleness. They start in with building blocks and keep going.

The river in Key 7 is the stream of consciousness that originates in the robe of The High Priestess. It's the dialogue of the Big Movie that's going on everywhere. Fortunately, we don't have to listen to it unless we want to. If we *had* to listen to it, it would overwhelm us, so by the grace of God we can be selective about it.

▶ What do the symbols on the front of the chariot stand for?

The lingam-yoni is a symbol of sexual union, which in turn corresponds to harmony between the feminine and masculine principles. In this case it is drawn as a stylized flame in a cup, representing the Holy Spirit contained within the Grail. All things are brought forth from this generative conjunction.

The winged solar disk is an indication of the immense progress and continuance of the universe, in spite of everything we do to resist it. In China they call it the Tao. It moves forward all the time, and like Alice in Wonderland, we have to run just to keep up with it.

▶ **The winged sun reminds me of the mystical phrase, "Risen with healing in his wings."**

That means that the Self has a universal healing aspect. To heal the body is to restore the divine harmony that is its natural condition. Disturbing input to the psyche creates turmoil in the soma. Unhappy thoughts are obstacles that can be overcome by stilling the mind. When this is accomplished, the mind will reflect the canopy of stars, that is, the heavenly level of ourselves.

In order to believe that you are made in the image of God, you have to overcome a host of misconceptions that have been planted in your mind by your contemporaries. In addition, your egotism (a perfectly natural phenomenon) has got to go. You can't get a glimpse of truth as long as you're looking through ego-tinted glasses.

The healing power in ourselves can handle a complete range of ailments from a sore toe to a sick psyche. Even that most difficult and sensitive organ, the heart, can be restored to its original state of peace. If you recall that the heart is the concern of The Empress in the Tarot, you will have the clue to the cure.

▶ **I feel hesitant about the emphasis on control in Key 7.**

We're only talking about control of your own team of wild sphinxes. It's an *artistic* kind of discipline. For example, a painter effectively uses control to create an accurate expression of inner vision. Then a viewer of the work can understand the communication. The better the control, the more accurately the message gets across. Paul Case wrote about difficult subjects that are hard to explain, and yet he managed to make a lot of sense. In fact, he was very good at it. This is the kind of control he had.

When we tackle the problem of ourselves, we don't go in for any heavy-handed stuff. No bed of nails, no self-castration. That doesn't prove anything or get you anywhere. We use the mouse approach, which is to just nibble a little at a time. Keep nibbling and eventually you will get it all. It won't be any worse than trimming your fingernails, although you don't have to stop with your nails, if you know what I mean. You start out with what is a fairly poor deal and you wind up replacing everything in yourself that you don't like with something you *do* like. When you get it all exactly the way you want, you feel very good about it.

The Chariot Key is going to travel the Path by going through all of the succeeding Keys and ending up in Key 21. In order for our vehicle to move on, we have to *persist*. Along the way, if there's ever any doubt in your mind about who you are, please refer to this Key and let it straighten you out.

Next week's Key, the Strength card, solves all the world's problems, but nobody pays any attention to it. The solution to our problems is love. The title refers to love as that which overcomes all obstacles. Up to now, force has been the answer to everything in the world. Force, more force, and still more force. The solution to such madness is in this simple Key.

The path of Key 8 on the Tree of Life goes from the Sephirah or Sphere of Love and Mercy to the Sphere of Severity, showing us that lovingkindness can tame the wild beast. The Strength Key is a prophecy of what is to come, because in the future, love will control force. This is *the way* we are going to make life on earth work for the human race.

I'm grateful to you for joining me on Thursday nights. This is the happiest part of the week for me.

KEY 8

CHAPTER 8

STRENGTH

THERE IS NO SUCH THING as a real victory of arms. Whoever wins will later face another knight in the forest and the fighting will start all over again. Tarot Key 8 presents a solution to these mistakes. It foretells a time when we shall overcome the illusion that we can win something by sheer force. Then we may not live happily ever after, but at least we won't destroy each other, which will be a step in the right direction. The symbolism of the Strength Key suggests that force should be mitigated by love. Even though we can't expect the world to be made over in a week, you and I can try mitigation and see what happens. We may be the leaven that will change the world. That's our fond hope.

The Strength card, through its attribution to the letter TETH, is one of the three reciprocal paths that connect the two sides of the Tree of Life. Teth is the central horizontal path. It joins the fourth and fifth Sephiroth, named Chesed and Geburah, or Mercy and Severity. The Mercy Seat is also called Love; this is congruent with the woman in Key 8. The lion typifies the fiery energy in the Seat of Mars on the other side. This Key can be interpreted as the relationship between these two centers on the Tree of Life. Since the smaller number always rules the larger, the message is that the Life Force—a very difficult part of ourselves—is to be controlled in a loving fashion.

There are some philosophical systems that say, "Kill out desire." This is the same as saying, "Cut your own throat." All the instinctive forces within ourselves are part of life. The Cabala suggests that if we handle these matters in a loving way, the lion turns out like Elsa in the movie *Born Free*. That was a true story of a wild lioness who was so trusting of her human friends that she brought her cubs to show to them. An animal that's pushed around will react. The harder you push, the harder it pushes back. And conversely, the more you love, the more it loves in return.

If you take the desire element out of your life, you're left with a hopeless blank, with nothing going on at all. What we call our life is made up of a string of desires. The emphasis on desire in Key 8 is clearly shown by the chain of roses that twines around the two figures. Our textbook tells us this chain is in the form of a figure eight. The sideways eight, or lemniscate, symbolizes the interplay of forces that connect the two sides of the Tree of Life in a harmonious relationship. When your desires are woven into a chain like this, they are not just random desires, but rather form a special, meaningful pattern that has an objective. The desires in this man-made wreath are ordered and directed. Strength results from the control that occurs in the previous Key, The Chariot. We have bridled our desire-nature and are actually learning to ride it.

The Cabala always asks, "What do you *really want?*" When you know what you want, you have decided on the path or pattern you are going to pursue. Then impress this on your subconscious by rhythm and repetition, which are powers of the number eight. Impressing these patterns on the subconscious is called SUGGESTION. Our self-conscious Magician makes suggestions to our subconscious Woman. She in turn controls all the so-called lower kingdoms of nature: animal, vegetable, and mineral. This controlling factor within ourselves is all we need to run our lives. The task of living our own lives is the first duty we owe to ourselves.

We can see *proof of our intent* in our lives. There is inside verification for this. We don't need any judgments, opinions, or advice from outside. From a technical, practical viewpoint it is important to remember that the subconscious is in charge of all natural forces, and that the type of suggestion we give our subconscious determines what is going to happen to us.

Our personal subconscious is also a cosmic function, since all of our powers and faculties are derived from the cosmos. Because the subconscious is so powerful, it's easy to fall into the trap of thinking we are powerful personally. An animal can't suggest itself from one condition into another, but we can. Thus, we are responsible for wisely using the powers within.

The letter Teth ט means a *serpent*, symbolizing that aspect of the Life Force sometimes called KUNDALINI. In this particular approach our emphasis is on handling the serpent fire from the top rather than from the bottom. We are told by our mentors that meditation will draw the Life Force up through the chakras, illuminating those areas.

The more advanced mystics, such as Jacob Boehme, say that when you get to the lowest chakra where the kundalini lives, all you see is a roaring, blazing fire of energy. Now this isn't going to do us any good, any more than the cosmic power in the hydrogen atom is going to do us any good, until we harness it. So our work is to harness powers that are already there and to direct them in ways that are useful to us. The whole technique of the Tarot and the Cabala is to assist you in getting The Force in your hands so that you can use it consciously and intelligently.

The Life Force is an abstraction for us until we transform it into something that has human meaning, something with which we can involve ourselves in an intimate, useful, productive way. We are going to use The Force in the work of our own self-fulfillment. As sons and daughters of the Most High, the flowering of the individual depends on our harnessing this power. When it is used consciously, it brings about the unfoldment that is the goal of individual existence.

▶ **I like to see the Life Force symbolized by an animal because I love animals.**

We are wise, I think, to appreciate the animal that is our vehicle. A lion is generally considered to be a ferocious beast, much to be feared. The fearful beast in ourselves is the animal that we inhabit. Its nature never changes, and like it or not, that's our home in this lifetime. The woman in the Strength Key handles the lion as though it were Elsa, showing us that we should treat ourselves as we would treat a beloved pet.

In the nineteenth century we refused to believe this. The Victorians were absolutely disgusted with the human animal, and pretended they were in some sort of angelic vehicle. However, the fact is that *we must love our animal* body and instincts if we are to succeed. If we don't love ourselves we can never really love anybody else. We have to understand the perfection in ourselves before we can appreciate the perfection that exists in others.

There is no part of ourselves that should not be loved and appreciated. Even today there are many people who look with disgust upon their animal aspect. I can assure you that this is a mistake as far as the Ageless Wisdom is concerned. To a Cabalist it's a ghastly error. We are not supposed to hold such ignorant attitudes about *anything* the Powers That Be have created—least of all ourselves.

▶ **You were talking about the lion as the Life Force and then you started equating it with our physical body.**

We live in a world of energy. Our bodies are made of it. Without our being conscious of it, everything we do depends on the Life Force, which is energizing all the forms in the universe, *including ours*. It's a case of having something from birth, but you just don't think about it if nobody ever brings your attention to it. You began breathing when you were a babe and you've been breathing ever since, so you may think, "Well, what's so great about breathing?" You can also say, "What's so great about energy?"

The engery we use for expressing ourselves in every way is the same energy living in *everything*. This becomes important when we try to orient ourselves in the universe. The Force is one force. This is a healthful and helpful thought in the development of our philosophy. Insofar as we are able to *realize* this force, we can use it more ably as time goes on. Right now we use it but we don't understand it fully—or even remotely. We're working on that. It makes a good bone to chew on in our meditations. The eighth statement in the Pattern on the Trestleboard tells us to "Look forward with confidence to the perfect realization of the Eternal Splendor of the Limitless Light."

The Tarot Magician realizes that everything about himself is a major miracle and that life is a magical process. We inhabit a most mysterious body. The more we understand that we are right in the middle of a mystery, the more we can relate to the whole. Also, the more we can move human nature, which is the hardest kingdom to affect.

▶ **What's the difference between animals and humans?**

If you walked into a doctor's office and asked that question, the answer would be, "Not much." But spiritually speaking, humans have been given a divine array of higher powers. I mentioned the power of suggestion tonight, and the power of speech last week. Human beings have an active imagination and they can make changes. They are creative to the point of being nauseating sometimes. In the ultimate definition, generic Man is the master of the house.

We must discriminate carefully between our animal and our higher element. It's a matter of being *very honest* about what we consist of. Until we understand the animal, which is our pet, our vehicle, and our friend in this lifetime, we can get into all kinds of difficulties. If you've ever had the good fortune of owning a pet, you will understand quite readily that it has certain limitations. For instance, when my little dog gets frightened or excited, he might do something abnormal, such as snap at me. Now if you translate that behavior into the animal in yourself, you can get some idea of what happens in the vehicle.

▶ **How can I learn more about my animal nature?**

The best thing is to study apes because they are practically carbon copies of ourselves, except that they don't have our higher faculties. An extensive study at Yale University concluded that apes have all the same emotions we have. If you understand this, you won't hate yourself when you behave like an ape.

Don't browbeat the animal that is your vehicle. Treat it gently, feed it regularly, let it play outside once in a while, keep it from getting run over, and so forth. If you do this with your pet animal vehicle, it will be happy, and because you're stuck with it, you will be happy too.

▶ **It's probably not a good idea to always diet or otherwise try to fix your body some way or other.**

I have a "pet" theory that the healthiest point of view is a keen appreciaton of what marvels we are. This encourages the body to be at its very best. If you're always poking at it and thinking there's something wrong with it, this irritates and aggravates the body. The ideal situation is to love your body and then just forget about it. Let it take care of itself. It's the work of millions of years of evolution. As a living machine, your body is quite capable of performing all sorts of miracles without any help from your conscious mind. No car can heal a bent fender, but the self-healing capabilities of your body are amazing. Theoretically, with our conscious participation, there's no reason why this self-repair shouldn't go on forever.

▶ **Why do some people have an instinct for self-destruction?**

Practically everybody has a certain amount of suicidal instinct, which is the desire to get out of a difficult situation. It's a provision of nature that there is always a door open in the body by which you may leave. In a state of shock, you may already be half gone. If you're very touchy, you may sort of go into shock over little things, which is a burden on the body. If you think about leaving the body or doing away with it, that's a burden too. When you say, "*Bad* dog!" to your pet, it feels terrible. A lot of people say something like this to the body, putting it down with negative suggestions.

A hypochondriac is an example of someone scaring their body into a frazzled condition. Even when there is nothing basically wrong, they can upset the applecart by continually saying to their body, "Don't tell me you're well or marvelous because *I know* you're *sick*." This is called psychosomatic suggestion.

We all probably know some healthy bedridden people. I recall a woman who spent many years with a box of chocolates and a stack of penny-dreadful novels by her bed. She took care of her natural impulses and ate everything that was set before her, but she wasn't well enough to get out of bed. She lived into her seventies. Her husband was one of the most eminent physicians in New York City. This was his skeleton in the closet—except that it was an elephant!

In another instance, I knew a woman who had been bedridden for at least thirty years. After living in the same house with me for about three years, one day she told me that she'd had an affair with her best friend's husband when she was young. It had preyed on her conscience to the point of affecting her back so that she could barely walk. After she volunteered this information, I said, "Well now that you've got that off your chest, why don't you try walking around a bit?" So she did. She eventually got up enough steam to go to Europe, which was a pretty good change after all those years.

In connection with Key 8, we really can't say enough about the remarkable interaction between mind and body. As always in the Tarot, the woman represents the unconscious aspect of mind. We call it the unconscious or the subconscious, but in terms of *control* it's like a conscious mind. It controls all the miraculous goings-on in the body. The teaching is that *that* mind is just the same as *our* mind. Eventually, when we can stand it, we will be completely connected up. There won't be two minds —the self-conscious and the subconscious—but just one.

There is a reason for our present ignorance about our relationship with the immediate environment that is our body, and with the greater cosmos also. What's going on here is so enormous that it would overwhelm us unless we were more prepared for it. From a conventional point of view, there are dreadful forces at work in the body. Just looking at metabolism might scare a person half to death.

In the average person, the Life Force runs through transformers. It's cut down to size so as not to blow anybody apart. If you unwittingly or stupidly involve yourself in occult exercises before you're ready, you let the cat out of the bag—the cat being the lion, of course. When you fool around with natural forces without the element of control, you're in real trouble. This is the peril of the sorcerer's apprentice.

▶ **What kind of occult exercises are you referring to?**

I'm talking about practices specifically designed to raise the kundalini whether you're ready or not. This can blow the nerve circuits, and has been known to cause incapacity, insanity, and even death. It's just like playing around with the equipment in a high-voltage laboratory—a good way to bow out of the physical plane in a hurry.

▶ **Wow, very fierce!**

The lion is rough, you know, a fearful beast. Fear, or PACHAD, is another of the names of the fifth Sephirah. That fiery desire-nature is a primitive force that's dangerous and difficult to handle. However, "Fear of the Lord is the beginning of wisdom." Consider how fire, when handled correctly, becomes the most useful element we can think of. The Tarot is designed to bring about the gentle, loving cultivation of your inner powers without any rough stuff.

▶ **If we can make the kundalini rise, do we become saints?**

There is no morality involved. The raising of the kundalini is somewhat analagous to puberty. Something natural and remarkable happens to you.

▶ **Does it make you a more loving person?**

No.

▶ **What is it good for?**

It raises your consciousness to a special state. Imagine that you've spent your life between the TV, the subway, and the bar. Then one day someone takes you to the High Sierras. There on a mountain you see the heavens and the earth spread out in a panorama beyond your wildest imaginings. Your consciousness is changed forever by that experience.

▶ **How is it that the Tarot can bring this about?**

Symbols are the language of the psyche, as our dear friend Dr. Jung tells us. The symbolism of the Tarot communicates directly to our subconscious. The lesson of Key 8 is that, given the proper suggestion, your subconscious mind will automatically control the forces within you. Since Key 1 is positioned above Key 8 in the Tableau, this is like superimposing the Magician over the form of the woman. That's indicated by the lemniscate over her head, which is a trademark of the Magician. The Magician points to a garden, the same one growing on her head. This shows that the intellectual powers are at their peak, in full bloom. Eight on the Tree is HOD, Splendor, Seat of the Intellect.

The three levels of the Tableau are said to portray principles, agencies, and results. The agencies in the second row show how you bring the principles into action. For instance, Keys 1, 8, and 15 comprise the first column. To avoid the condition of bondage signified by The Devil, the tricky part is your desire-nature, and the Strength Key shows how to handle that. The desire-nature is the essential feature of karmic bondage. You just have to have some place to put that little old libido. If you throw it away somewhere and go home, it will be sitting there waiting for you when you get back.

▶ **So the Magician makes the suggestions and the woman in Strength responds to them.**

That is precisely the magic of the Tarot. Key 8 is called the Intelligence of the Secret of All Spiritual Activities. The secret is simple. It's the suggestion we give to the subconscious. When the suggestions you make on a self-conscious level reach down to the subconscious level, the entire universal machinery is set in motion. If you *insist* on directing your life and making sensible suggestions for your life, you will experience a mysterious response from your environment. You actually set up a vibration to which your environment responds. Results may not occur within seconds, but they occur eventually. You will be aware of them when they happen.

▶ **Keys 1 and 8 both have a lot of yellow and red. Why is that?**

In this symbolism, yellow has to do with the intellect and red stands for activity. The self-conscious intellect is always creating images and the subconscious is always bringing them into concrete expression. Hopefully, for each of us the images will reflect our True Self to ourselves.

In connection with this work, the Cabala teaches that there are two kinds of people. One kind is called unconscious in a friendly sense, not derogatory at all, just descriptive and clinical. It means that the person is unaware, like a child. The more advanced kind is the person who is *conscious* of what is going on. Both types utilize the same magical mechanism in themselves. They make images and have desires that constitute suggestions, and so on. The unconscious people are not aware of their role in this process. The conscious people are already aware, so they say, "I want the *image of myself* that will be pleasing to me. I don't want any other image." This approach will bear good fruit, because the guidance comes from a deep level.

Key 8 rules the sense of taste. The Cabala can't stress enough the importance of *developing your own taste*. It's amusing that this whole work boils down to *what you like!*

▶ We make suggestions to ourselves all the time.

That is absolutely correct, so we have to be careful. We must remember that negative images held in the mind constitute negative suggestions to our subconscious. We must make an effort—and it *is* an effort—to ensure that we don't slip into negative thinking. We are bombarded on every side with propaganda that attempts to make us fearful about our health, about the future of everything, and so on, *ad nauseum*. It's not easy to keep brushing this stuff aside when it's coming at you day after day. You can't turn on the TV without getting the suggestion that you might have some illness for which you must buy certain remedies. Then the insurance companies come on strong: "Be careful and watch your heart, because if you die when you're not included in our actuarial charts, we're going to lose money."

Even if you throw the television into the trashcan or turn it off to protect yourself, the insidious danger is that you may start working on *yourself* as a result of this progaganda. If this sort of thing goes on in your head, you may get into the psychosomatic realm.

▶ Can you recommend any specific device for mental self-defense, so we don't have to throw the TV away?

You've already written your constitution; you can hold a meeting of the congress regularly, in order to build a positive idea of yourself that you can live with. This is saying, "I'm going to live in my chosen area, and pay less attention to everything else." Then if *you keep busy*, that's your first line of defense. When you are working, you are in effect saying, "Please don't bother me."

You might ask, "What about my duties as a citizen?" Well, you can still vote. What you *really* have to do is find where you're supposed to operate, and then concentrate on that. The main thing is to be busy with what you're supposed to be doing for yourself. This might sound like utter selfishness until you remember Goethe's observation that if each of us kept our house in order, then all the houses in the world would be in order. Our higher teachers ask us to keep our house in order by a constitution. This is a *personal* proposition.

Because we are what we are, we're supposed to create our own morality, which is very different from trying to live up to someone else's. On the level that the Cabala talks about, you simply cannot live by any morality but your own. We must get to the point where each of us is a law unto ourself, meaning that we are not going to kill one another all the time.

As we can see from looking at Key 8, we should be reasonable with ourselves. Repressive measures are not required. According to the teaching, you are going to live a long, *long* time. You have to develop something suitable for an immortal. What can you do forever that won't drive you up the wall? You can keep moving on, growing indefinitely. You've done this all your life, so just continue to change and grow forever.

▶ Does the purple mountain in this Key represent the Great Work as it did in Key 6?

Yes, and here we get more *involved* in our own personal evolution. Even if we're unconscious, the Life Force still supports our evolution. When we get beyond that stage and develop our relationship with the cosmos, we consciously involve ourself with our own subconscious. And the subconscious says, "Oh, is that what you're trying to do? Well, I'll help. Give me some leads and show me that you mean business, and I'll get in the act."

Prior to that time the subconscious had the whole show going anyway, the best way she could. She did her best with what she had to go on, which was race-thought and a lot of foolishness. When The Magician says, "I'm going to make some basic changes. See how my wand is pointing to the Life Power? I'm working for God now," then the subconscious says, "You've told me that a thousand times before. You've got to show me." So then he does something on a regular basis, day by day by day. Now she says, "I don't know what's gotten into you, George, but you certainly have changed." Then it begins to happen. When you're serious about it, then you get a response.

▶ **Why did Paul Case attribute number eight to Strength and not to Justice, as in the traditional French systems?**

Basically, because Leo the Lion follows Cancer in the zodiacal order. Also because of its connection with Teth, the Serpent Fire, and its alignment with The Magician in the Tableau.

Paul Case was acknowledged to be a great Tarot scholar, and God knows, he was. He put the Keys on the Tree of Life the way he thought they should go. Originally, only the Hebrew letters were on the paths among the Sephiroth. Those were ancient attributions.

Once we learn the language of the Tarot and the Cabala, we can communicate easily about the various parts of ourselves that are interesting and useful. The Tarot deals mainly with areas in which we are alike. The mind, especially, is something we share in common. And then each person has a *specialty* that gives you your unique flavor, your taste, your individuality. Leo is a sign of self-expression. When you become clear, with your mind emptied, your specialty has an opportunity to express itself. The inside has a chance to get outside.

There's nothing wrong with the outer world, but it doesn't satisfy us deeply. Just because we can perform the mechanics of life doesn't mean that we are going to feel fulfilled. You can do it all and be miserable because the precious thing can elude you. If you don't get the "nut," you've always got an ache and a feeling that somehow you're missing the boat; and of course, you are.

▶ **What's the "nut"?**

It's the Self. You feel troubled until you reach the area of your Self.

▶ **Why does this elude some people and not others?**

Life is full of distractions. If it's not your destiny to make some effort to overcome that, then you stay "in the soup."

▶ **Why is that?**

I'm not God, so I've never been able to answer the question, "Why do we have to evolve?" The sages tell us that the only way we can reach the ultimate in evolution is through our own conscious efforts.

Surely we are all aware that many people scream a lot over nothing. There are enormous dramas in people's minds about life in general. It's the end of the world, or the beginning of the millennium, or whatever; there's a tremendous racket. But it ain't necessarily so, as the saying goes.

▶ **That's reality for those people. It's not just a drama. It's their life.**

Sure, it's true for them. If you're in a play and you suddenly identify with the role, then the whole situation changes. Once you confuse your identity with the role, it becomes a tragedy for you.

▶ **Isn't this an illustration of people's creative abilities?**

Someone who creates a monster is just as creative as someone who creates beauty. You can't help being creative, whether you do it consciously or unconsciously. Accumulated unconscious creation adds up to race-thought.

▶ **People can turn animals into friends or monsters. You can tell a lot about a person by what his pet is like.**

Yes, and by the way they handle the animal and what they expect from it. The master of the hunting hounds handles his dogs in a very disciplined way. They are never petted, only taught to obey. I know of one case where a master of the hounds told his granddaughter that if she petted a dog, he'd whip it. The animals are fed and taken care of, but there's no affection shown at all. Yet the dogs are highly trained and do exactly what the master says.

▶ **It sounds efficient, but isn't it kind of sterile and rigid?**

It's very rigid, and yet commonplace. You'll find it in business, in the army, and in many professions. In engineering school there is just one exact way to do things, period. In some art schools they say, "Paint this bottle a certain way or you don't graduate." Then you wonder, "Am I in art school or am I in the army?"

There's nothing wrong with discipline. *Self*-discipline is essential to everyone but it's not an end in itself. Discipline isn't just about imposing your will. If you want to engage other people, the correct method is to invite them and give them an option. You say, "Do you wish to do this? If it's a fair bargain, then let's enter into an agreement." You don't corral them and say, "Look, either you do this or I'll beat you up." In that situation there is no recognition of the other person.

The theory of the Tarot and the Cabala is that there is only One Will. This One Will corresponds to the power of consciousness in the universe. Consciousness wills things and makes them happen. That's its nature. As a microcosm, human beings have the same faculty, the ability to will and to create things that correspond to their will. This is why discipline is absolutely necessary for the individual. You and I have to apply the principle of rigor *in our own lives*. This is the woman taming the lion.

▶ **Jason, didn't you say that the woman corresponds to Mercy and the lion corresponds to Severity?**

Yes, but don't forget that they are intertwined.

▶ **Which side is the rigor coming from?**

The rigor is coming from the woman, because she represents the limiting aspect. She is the Saturn power that mitigates and contains the lion's roar. In Hebrew the shortest name of God is EL, which literally means strength. It is composed of two letters: Aleph א, the Life Force, and LAMED ל, the law that directs force to accomplish work.

▶ **How can it be that the feminine acts masculine?**

Every one of the centers on the Tree of Life has a masculine and a feminine aspect. Mercy is the controlling, masculine aspect in relation to Severity. It represents a loving, nonrepressive discipline, but a strong control nevertheless. As you know, love has a peculiar quality that is impossible to describe. The softening effect of love creates a special atmosphere, quite magically. That's part of the message of this Key. As Chaucer says, "Dear Lady, thy sweet spirit hath tamed my raging lion."

Love's sweetness doesn't mean that it's any less rigorous. Love has the power, all right. In dealing with animals, if you control them by love, you control them totally. You can subdue and manipulate them through fear, but the *ultimate* control consists of love, which actually *binds* the pet to the master.

▶ **Does this make the lion feminine?**

Yes, insofar as he is controlled by the subconscious. He is still the masculine element, the fiery Life Force. In alchemy, the lion is often linked pictorially with the sun. He might be shown with sun rays coming out of his head, for instance. Leo, the sign of fixed fire, is ruled by The Sun, Key 19.

All this fire is contained by the subconscious, which explains the Cabalistic riddle, "The fire is in the water." Instead of having an explosion, which is typical of the masculine essence, the force is usefully directed, so that it *energizes a structure.* In this case it's a power structure.

We are witnessing a reflection on the Tree from fiery Chokmah on the right to Geburah on the left, and from watery Binah on the left to Chesed on the right. It's like a mirror reflection in which right becomes left. I once read a story about Gary Cooper. In the movies he was playing a baseball pitcher who was right-handed, and Gary Cooper is left-handed, or maybe it was the other way around. But what they did was, they just turned over the film. Then his right hand was his left hand. Pretty clever. Reminded me of the Tree of Life.

▶ **How do we draw the line between masculine and feminine when everything that's manifested has both?**

The nature of the masculine aspect is self-imparting. The nature of the feminine aspect is receptive. This makes all the difference in the world. The sun shines and the moon reflects. However, *we are not manifested* in our essence. Remember that unity is the source of polarity.

The Strength Key represents a kind of marriage between the feminine and the masculine. The wreath of roses joins them in a complete and happy mixture, a harmonious affair. Each aspect acquires something of the character of the other. This is recognized in the Chinese philosophy of yang and yin, each of which contains the seed of the opposite. There is a tendency for one side to be transformed into the other side, back and forth like a heartbeat. This is a kind of internal attempt to reach the ideal of *unity.* The lemniscate indicates this general tendency toward unity.

Key 9, The Hermit, is an image of the great Unity of All Life. It represents the Inner Self as our spiritual guide on the path of self-conscious effort. This beneficent aspect in our makeup guides us to some understanding of our Inner Self. In the East this understanding is called YOGA. The Hermit is very loving and helpful. We can depend on the comfort and friendly advice that comes from this archetype within ourselves. The closer you get to The Hermit, the better it feels.

Thanks for sharing my favorite night of the week.

KEY 9

CHAPTER 9

THE HERMIT

IF YOU ARE one hundred percent yourself, you have achieved the greatest possible glory in life, according to the Cabala. The Secret Doctrine states that there is One Self in the universe, which is sometimes called God or the I AM. This is the most glorious feature of the universe. All of creation shares in the Self, and through that we share in the Universal Life. The Hermit represents the cosmic Self and also our own true Self *in* ourselves. Our major job is to *identify* with our Inner Self, which in plain terms means to *be* ourselves.

This sounds easy but it's very difficult. In fact it's so difficult that the highest attainment on the Tree of Life is Ipsissimus, he who is most himself and she who is most herself. This Latin word is assigned by the Rosicrucian system of grades to Kether, the Crown. In Hebrew the Self is called Yekhidah, the Indivisible. The Yekhidah is in the deepest reaches of ourselves. Kether is said to be concealed with all concealments, hence the dark background of Key 9.

Our deep, hidden Self is always trying to illuminate us as to the truth. This is the meaning of the lantern symbolism, as expressed in the ancient saying, "I am the Light that lighteth everyone." The only thing I would add to this statement is that the light is *within* every person. First and foremost we have a responsibility to this Inner Light. It's all right to study and listen to teachers, but the real Wayshower is inside ourselves.

We have to get rid of a low opinion of ourselves ... or a mediocre opinion ... or even a fairly good opinion. This may take longer than two weeks. It is hard work to realize the Self within. As we progress towards this goal The Hermit brings us to ever greater Self-expression. When we reach this foundation within ourselves, we shall not go thirsty. The key word here is RESPONSE. Every effort we make to contact the Self is answered. Key 9 is one of the great benefic cards, if not the greatest.

The world and all that we know is in darkness. Everything is created by Binah, the Divine Mother who is the black, yin aspect of the Tree of Life. Even the True Light looks dark to us because it is beyond our intellectual understanding. Just as The Hermit is surrounded by darkness, the Self makes its home in the subconscious. The spark of life is hidden within substance.

The superconscious Self is androgynous. Manifestation is handled by Binah, the Creatrix. Chokmah, our Father Creator, begets the *ideas* of what is to be manifested. You can't see ideas. This inner nature of the Life Power is incomprehensible to us. The Archetypal World is not knowable, which is why the Cabala says that you can see where the Lord has been but not the Lord himself. If you stick to Binah and get to know her, you will find the Father because that principle is within her. If you learn to see into the nature of things, it becomes easier to see the nature of superconsciousness.

The sages tell us that the first level of the Self's expression is the Archetypal World of fire. The letter associated with Key 9 is Yod, which is said to be a flame whose upper point is in Kether. The body of the Yod is in Chokmah, Root of Fire on the Tree. Aleph, the letter of The Fool, is made out of a Yod with two other Yods whirling out from it, one above and one below, corresponding to Chokmah and Binah. This whirling fire exists in the center of each person, empowering their whole life. The entire Hebrew alphabet is born from the Yod, which is why it is known as the Flame Alphabet. And alchemy has been called the Science of Fire.

All this fire symbolism refers to Will. The path of Yod on the Tree of Life is named the Intelligence of Will. That Will is the *only will there is*. The Will is operative throughout the universe twenty-four hours a day—no weekends, no vacations, no strikes—just go, go, go all the time. This is the nature of our Innermost Self. It never sleeps. It never deserts us. We desert *it* from time to time. We are perhaps led away by some of the interesting distractions of human existence, but as far as the Self is concerned, it just stays where it has always been, where it will always be.

The Cabalistic view of Will is like the Chinese philosophy of the Tao. Our own willpower is derived from the One Will. Personal will is like money given to you by someone who actually owns all the money in the world. Part of spiritual discipline is to *remember* that we have been given all we need. The bounty of Life is infinite. The Magician recognizes this fact. He first salutes the Will and then goes about his other business of commanding the elements by thought. We are all magicians, getting our ideas and inspirations from the cosmic level of the vast Self that supports the entire universe. Our lifetime job is to free ourselves from duality and unite with our True Self. If our root is in what is symbolized by Key 9, we are not swayed from moment to moment. We are secure in knowing that our will is part of the One Will.

In his chapter on Key 9, Paul Case points out that the word *will* means primarily *delight* or *pleasure*. This lovely fact ties in with the idea that life is a process of self-fulfillment. It always comes as a pleasant surprise to a penitent that he doesn't have to sleep on a bed of thorns in order to gain salvation or liberation. The emphasis in the Cabala is just the other way around. We're never asked to give up anything except the lesser pleasure for the greater. Insofar as we discover what is truly enjoyable, we naturally move in the direction of knowing our Innermost Self. By following this path it is perfectly possible for us to reach a state of conscious union with That.

When we succeed in knowing who we are, we don't need anybody else to tell us, because *we know*. Then of course when we've reached the top of the mountain, there's only one place to go and that's down the other side. We don't disappear in a greenish vapor or anything of that sort, but rather like Larry in Somerset Maugham's book, *The Razor's Edge*, we ascend and make contact; then we go down the other side and get on with our daily lives. However, we are different now. We have been changed by the experience.

After realizing the Self, you job is to *be* yourself. What you *like* to do is what you're *supposed* to do, so put all your energy into that. There is always an area that's just right for you to work in.

Number nine is the end of the numerical series, so the ninth Key is the culmination of everything that has gone before it in the Tarot. This weighty aspect of the Self is balanced by Key 0, which represents the same thing in another guise. The Fool is the youthful eagerness to appreciate and enjoy life. Life has many different experiences but it never grows old. It starts every new day completely fresh, without any qualms and without turning back. The Hermit, by contrast, is the Ancient of Days, the aspect of consciousness that is very old indeed, and very, very wise. He is the accumulation of all The Fool's experience.

Both of these aspects are working all the time within us. The Cabalists have generously pointed this out so that we don't have to discover it all over again after years of patiently trying to evaluate what is going on in ourselves. We can consider these two major aspects of God simultaneously and strike the balance inside.

▶ That's a lot to think about all at once.

The purpose of life in the Cabala is expansion of consciousness, which is movement toward freedom. This is also typical of Yoga in the East. Many people who claim to know a lot about Yoga have missed its real meaning and gotten lost in the horizontal plane of possibilities. Although human beings are tremendously endowed with endless possibilities, these don't necessarily move in the direction of Yoga. Can anyone here tell me what Yoga means?

▶ Yoga means *union*.

With . . . what? The Teamsters?

▶ "Communion" would be a better word.

With . . . ?

▶ the Higher Self.

What Self is that?

▶ The Only Self.

Spoken like a true Vedantist! Yoga means communion with the Only Self. This is a very special endeavor. All the rides that exist on the horizontal plane are not necessarily connected with the big ride we are continually working toward here. Because The Hermit is clothed in the subconscious aspect of ourselves, he is hidden from the casual glance. We must not expect to find our Innermost Self parading around in Union Square, or in Macy's or the art galleries. Again, this aspect of ourselves is the *most* deeply hidden. As it says in the Bible, "He made darkness his secret place."

▶ In your opening remarks tonight, you emphasized the difficulty of attaining Self-realization. That must be why it's called the Great Work. How may we best proceed to do this work?

The goal is to be yourself. It's hard to be something if you don't know what it is. The work is basically an attempt to explain ourself to ourselves. This means having a detailed knowledge of yourself, not just in principle but in *detail*, with all the ins and outs. It's a long, drawn-out proposition, but anyone in their right mind would be happy to engage in the effort.

In your explorations you might decide that you want to change some things in yourself. Through your constitution, desire, and intention, consciously plant the seed of what you want. Water it and wait patiently. Seek satisfaction in one area, then go on to the next. Dissatisfaction is part of the cycle. We sometimes explore one level of desire for a long time. Eventually we get tired of this and want to penetrate inside. We sense something colossal going on in there. "Seek and you shall find." The only limitation is that which you put on yourself. *You get exactly what you order.*

► **I feel limited, all right.**

Nature doesn't create something for nothing, including us. You are important in the cosmic scheme. You have a unique vibration in the universe. If you tell yourself you don't amount to anything, you will eventually convince your subconscious. If everyone did that, there would be no light in the world. Whether we feel good or bad is entirely dependent on how much light we have in ourselves.

We each have a different route up the mountain because the effort must come from the individual. What's important is that you can become wiser and wiser. When you get to The Hermit—when you find yourself—it's an exciting experience. You actually "see the light."

The Yekhidah guides and urges us in the direction of being totally ourselves. It doesn't want to see us get cheated and it pesters us when we mistake the lesser for the greater. It doesn't want us to buy a piece of junk. It wants us to have the *absolute best*.

Key 9 represents the end of the path of self-conscious effort. Through our own intellectual faculties and powers of awareness, we can observe cosmic principles at work, until finally we see who's holding the principles. We are following the light and then suddenly, "There's somebody there! What do you know?! There's a Being holding the light . . . well, hello!" First we see the light and then we recognize the Being who is The Hermit.

► **It sounds wonderful! I want that experience. My snail's pace up the mountain is frustrating.**

You have to plant the seed of what you want and tend your garden patiently. The power of Yod, or Chokmah, within you is called by our mentors the "Magnet of Jah." Given a proper environment, it continually attracts matter and organizes it according to the archetypal pattern in the seed. Like a magnet, it draws to itself whatever it needs for completion and total fulfillment. All seeds do this.

We are like squeaking baby birds being fed from above. Studies have shown that a mother bird feeds her babies in a certain order, even if one is pushy. Since the universe is very orderly, we will be enlightened when it's time for us to be enlightened. You don't hammer your way into heaven. When the apples are ripe they drop off the tree, and that's God's truth. In the meantime, as the old hymn says, "Lead kindly Light amidst encircling gloom."

▶ **I get the feeling that The Hermit is trying to attract students with his lantern.**

Yes, he holds the light for seekers. We all have Life Itself inside us, trying to teach and guide us. The rays are shining out from a six-pointed star inside the lantern, symbolizing Tiphareth on the Tree of Life. In the construction of the hexagram, the upward-pointing fire triangle corresponds to the Three Supernals and the downward-pointing water triangle represents their reflection in substantiality. This marriage of fire and water creates the Light of Beauty, which is sufficient to guide you through your whole life. Beauty is the very temple of the Cabala. The four Sephiroth that form the central pillar of the Tree of Life spell out the message that the Will to Beauty is the Foundation of the Universe.

▶ **The Hermit's long staff might signify that central pillar.**

The Tree exists in each of the Four Worlds, so The Hermit's wand would certainly stand for the central pillar in the Archetypal World. Will is purpose. The Golden Gate Bridge was considered an impossibility until Joseph Strauss came along and said, "Sure, I can build a bridge here." That original intention carried through the whole cooperative venture to forge a beautiful result.

▶ **The letter Yod appears a lot in the Tarot. In some of the later Keys, the sky is full of them.**

Yod י means the *open hand*, and thus beneficence. It is also a phallic symbol. The nature of will is that it is self-imparting, like the sun shining. This is love on the highest level. It is perfectly content not getting anything. What The Hermit has to give cannot be depleted or diminished. You can depend on it *totally*. It is the Self who says, "Before you call, I will answer." That's a pretty quick response!

Yod is the signature of God. You are a child of God. Note that Yod is the initial letter of YESOD, Foundation, the ninth Sephirah, which is the womb of the Tree of Life and the seat of reproductive power. The Yod is said by Cabalists to be totally encased within the feminine element. There is a definite sexual connotation here, indicative of Key 9's attribution to coition and the sense of touch.

▶ **The Hermit's hat is a blue Yod.**

Since blue is the color of The High Priestess and she represents mind, this means that The Hermit is crowned with the powers of mind. When we identify with The Hermit we get our heads out of the wrong place and into the right place. We come to understand the highest aspect of mind.

▶ **How does The Tower fit in with The High Priestess and The Hermit in the second column of the Tableau?**

The lightning flash in The Tower Key is coming from the Hermit's lantern. In terms of human experience, the inner light is extremely upsetting to the outer world. When you begin to wake up inwardly, it's disturbing outwardly because the principles that operate on the outside are different from those on the inside. This is the basis for "Render unto Caesar what is Caesar's, and unto God what is God's." There's a vast difference between the two areas. The wider life of the Self contradicts the life of the ego. You can't be a cosmic being and an egotist at the same time. You can't be a free bird flying around in the sky if you're in a cage.

We usually think everything is going along well if we are leading conventional lives. Then it often takes a serious crisis to make us look at what is *really* going on. As long as you buy everything in society's brochure, it's dreamy, but if you wake up to the fact that the brochure is a bunch of hokum, suddenly it's wild. If you get rid of the brochure, then what? Where do you go from there? A little training from the Cabala can be helpful in a crisis.

▶ **You've got to handle both the inside and the outside.**

My first Tarot teacher advised being like a rapier, in that you are both flexible and firm. He made a great "point" of this. He meant that there are *times* to be flexible and *other times* to be firm.

▶ **Would The Hermit be an example of this?**

Yes, but unfortunately, most people won't believe there's any good in being like The Hermit. The problem of Self-realization is that people think it's a bum deal. One of the reasons for this is all the propaganda from organized religion. There are people who say you should carry a cross from the cradle to the grave. They think that you've got to go down on your hands and knees, and that it helps to have thumbtacks under them while you're doing this. If you've got a friend there to whip you, that will also contribute to your salvation. Most people don't want to go through all that, so they say, "I'm sorry, God, but I'm just a slob. I'm not even an original sin; I'm just a second-hand copy. I'm nothing but a nothing, Lord, so please just let me alone." This attitude makes it hard to identify with the loving Being that is The Hermit. In the Cabala we're faced with a completely different idea of what life is all about.

▶ **Carl Jung said that people actually have a religious instinct.**

I agree. The root of religion is in The Hermit's light. People who get the most out of their religion are those who have penetrated through the fearful notions to the reality of the inner light. "Churchianity" is difficult, having become crystalized and dogmatic, but the original, essential support on which religion is based is universal. Nothing can take its place.

The things we study here have enormous religious impact, but this is not what we're about in this particular group. We don't deny any of the religious features of this at all. We're just concentrating on trying to realize the Self by these means that are offered to us. This is more of a technical problem than the ordinary business of religion. Still, consciousness of God is basic. If you don't believe in God you are wasting your time in the Cabala. The God that you believe in could be of many different kinds, but you have to believe in some kind of a superior intelligence in the universe. If the word "God" has too many connotations, just think of the underlying Reason For Everything. Your faith is personal to you even though its root is the same everywhere. From the faith of a primitive savage to the faith of the most advanced Knower in the world—it's all the same thing.

It is by the grace of God that we can advance in awareness and consciousness. This is not an advance into something dismal. We are moving into something delightful. The Will is not trying to be a pain in the neck or worse. Quite the contrary. The ever-expanding life is inspired by the God within yourself. This creative aspect is your motivation. The Muses are the *capabilities* of the creative power, but the *creative power itself* is the thing that sets the Muses to musing.

▶ Is there a danger of expanding too much?

No, because life is circular. We don't travel in a linear fashion, but rather in cycles, so we always stay in touch. In a cycle, things change, yet they don't change. This paradox is illustrated by the Zen saying, "First there is a mountain; then there is no mountain; then there is a mountain." As we go around and around, by the power of grace we expand into an open spiral. The closed circle is the crystalized life and the spiral represents liberation. After awhile you get a feeling for the unfolding Self and you develop a certainty about it.

Outer circumstances don't necessarily change in this process. It's the *way you look at things* that makes the difference. The religious mystic Jacob Boehme said, "Heaven is where thou standest." In plain English this means that *it depends on you* whether you're in heaven or in hell. It doesn't depend on anybody else. If you can see, then you're in heaven. If you can't see, then you're in hell.

For instance, we need to get rid of projections and conditioned reflexes in our relationships with other people. We have to reduce ourselves to pure perception of the other person before we can really see or hear them at all. We have to think, "Maybe I've been laying a trip on this person. Maybe I can get myself to where I don't project and I'm not involved in conditioning." It's possible to get into a state of mind where you *intuit* in regard to things, where you're *actually* looking at them. That's *direct perception* of things as they really are, rather than some modified version.

Direct perception deals with the essential character of a thing. It doesn't deal with any learned set of data, or with measurement or classification. Our teachers tell us that there is the possibility of seeing a thing aside from all of these considerations.

▶ Jason, don't you think that a person who is always intuitive would become unbalanced?

Hardly, because intuition does not preclude reason. Being intuitive simply means that you move out of the cellar and go to the top floor where you belong. The intuitive faculty oversees the rational faculty, so it's higher and deeper. This is important, because intuition brings in unity, a spiritual consideration that is not part of rationality. There is nothing in your rational consciousness that would lead you to think of life as a unity.

▶ Are you saying that psychism leads to higher spirituality?

Well, now we're getting into words. Like doctors and lawyers, Cabalists have a special language of their own. In the language we use here, the intuitive faculty is the crown of reason. It doesn't have anything to do with psychism in the ordinary sense. In the special sense that we use the word "intuition," it means the pathway of movement from the Inner Self to the rational faculty. So it has nothing to do with spirit guides and the like. There are lots of beings on your side who would like to help you in every way possible. This is okay, but it's not what we're talking about when we speak of intuition. You can have good teachers and bad teachers, good inner guides and bad inner guides, and so forth. However, your own intuitive faculty, which connects you with your Innermost Self, is fortunately safe from any mistakes.

▶ Is direct perception describable in words?

If you see the essentiality and want to communicate it to someone else, you have to fall back on words. But since words are the tools of differentiation, you will only be able to approximate the original experience. Feelings cannot fully flow into words.

▶ What about communicating intuitively, without words?

On the nonverbal level you can have profound experiences in feeling. There are many stories from the East about people who go to visit a spiritual master. The master doesn't *say anything* or do much, yet people feel different afterward. Something happens to them *inside* that defies description, but it's a reality all the same.

We've all had experiences with other people in which we immediately recognize a harmonious relationship that, as far as our conscious knowledge is concerned, doesn't have any historical background. When we meet someone who feels like an old friend, we don't have to make any explanations about anything. We're already *there* with that person. These become friendships that last all the way down the road.

There's an intuitional basis for the recognition of seemingly old friends, but it's unconscious as far as we're concerned. Likewise, Key 9 represents something ongoing within ourselves that we are generally unconscious of. The teaching states that in deep sleep we're united with this other Self. The Yekhidah, this Innermost Self, is the very *reason* for our being. We have lots of ideas about who we are, why we are, and where we're going, but according to the tradition the real reason *is* the Self. It has certain plans for us that are, strangely enough, our own plans for ourselves. Since we're so complicated and involved with all sorts of things, it isn't always clear to us. No matter how confused we are, we still get back to home base during deep sleep. No matter how goofy our life is, this pulls us back together (relatively speaking, since some people don't get pulled together very well). But if we *are* going to be integrated, we do so around this center.

The Hermit is Virgo, the astrological sign of health and individuation, to use a Jungian term. If the heart is contracted, then the expansive aspect of life can't operate and the person is basically ill. It's quite simple. If you are open to the positive influences in the cosmos, they stream through you and that's all there is to it. It's just like fresh water flowing through you all the time. It feels cleansing and healing.

Sunlight is a good example, but I'm speaking of an inner light, the Lux Occulta, the essence of our innermost principle. If that light is operating in us, it's possible for everything else to work in harmony. Note that you don't have to invoke it or stroke it or thank it. You must be *aware* of it and receptive to it. If you have a small opinion of the Light of the Cosmos, it can't do much for you. If you say categorically, "The Light of the Cosmos is very good for some types of psychic problems, but for most things a drug is better," you limit its power.

We have all heard of instantaneous healings that happen because of the greatness of the power behind the facade. We mustn't think in picayune terms about Life. In Plato's cave, the people only see shadows on the wall. When they come out, they are *amazed* by the light. The Hermit is monumentally tremendous.

▶ How can I be me and also this super Being?

The principle of Being is not only frisky, it's snaky. It's there before everything happens to you and it's there after everything has happened.

I think everyone here would say that they have been aware of a sense of selfhood for a long time. We are aware of this ongoing identity even if we don't explain it to ourselves. The Self persists. It has *continuance*. This is important in realizing the ongoing support we have.

▶ **How can I bridge the gap between my ordinary self and the Great Self?**

There is no gap. If the universe is One, then everything is related. In the Cabala, there are no personal characteristics. Everything that exists is universal.

▶ **If I contemplate the idea of unity, will I eventually "get it"?**

That's one way, yes. If you love, love is in the universe. If you hate, hate is in the universe. Consciousness is in the universe; this is the electric *zap* in ourselves. We are a focus, just as It is a focus. What goes on in that focus is *meaning*.

It always comes down to a matter of instruction, especially that wonderful inner instruction called intuition. We have to be willing to accept instruction and experiment with it to see whether it's true or not. If you are receptive, you can "get it." If you fight it, it can be a lifetime disaster. Trying to get away from yourself creates all sorts of tension inside you.

▶ **Once you accept the Higher Self, you can focus on the path you want and not be diverted by all the potential selves hanging around.**

That's right. Key 9 is success in terms of escaping different roles by getting back to the *source* of the roles. That's why it's the crown of *self-conscious* effort. In order to do this, you must really discriminate between your desires, because they're like wild horses pulling you in sixteen directions at once. You simply have to decide what you're going to do about it. Once you decide, then you become the Charioteer.

The control in The Chariot Key has to do with the mind. According to the doctrine, we live in the mind. Man, manas, mind. It's hard for us to understand that there's another area in ourselves that is *not* mind. It's the *creative* area, represented by The Hermit. All the different roles, all the ten million things—are in the feminine aspect, the mind. You can be very busy with all those things. It's time to do this and it's time to do that and then before you know it, it's time to die!

That's why it's a good idea to dump everything out of your head once in awhile. Don't think about the Tarot or the Cabala or anything you've ever heard of. Then you'll discover, like homing pigeons, which things come back to roost. It's not possible to really empty your mind, but you *can* make room for growth. The Buddhists say that you can get out of the mind and look at it objectively. They call this the mirror-like wisdom. In the Cabala, this principle is Chokmah, Wisdom, on the Tree of Life. The wise old man of Key 9 symbolizes our *ability to look at what is going on* in the mind. Seeing all the choices can be a life saver. If we're locked in, we can't see those possibilities.

▶ So transcendence is seeing where you are in a larger context.

Quite true, and the reason is that you can't leave yourself. We make all these separations here for the purpose of analysis, but in truth there isn't any separation. We're never going to get out of the universe. We shouldn't bother trying. In the Cabala, life consists of being *in* something. Ultimately it consists of being in *ourselves*.

Historically, people who have understood transcendence didn't do anything fancy. No matter how much you understand, you're not necessarily going to become a world leader or some marvel of human expression. But as far as your inner life is concerned, you're transformed. That part is definitely settled, once and forever. You're not the same person that you were before. That's the important thing.

You know, we're inclined to romanticize what will happen when we're triple-ascended masters, like acquiring special powers and so forth. We imagine that when we get to the top of the mountain, we will be able to materialize cash and diamonds. Isn't this sort of a childish dream? What's at the top of the mountain is *the view*.

Milarepa, the great Tibetan saint, foreswore all the occult powers. He saw something else that was much more important. In effect, he said, "Powers, schmowers! Forget it!" I'm not saying you shouldn't acquire these powers. It's okay if that's your destiny. Just be aware that they are not the end or reward of the Path.

There's a delightful story in the *Zohar* about some Cabalists sitting in a discussion group in a simple room, just like ourselves tonight. Some character comes in and says, "Hey, I'm going to show you some magic!" All of a sudden they're sitting in a palace garden with beautiful serving maidens carrying sweetmeats around. "Taste one!" says the magician. But the person leading the discussion says, "Will you take that junk out of here? We don't want any of that stuff."

▶ **Once you get to the top and come down the other side, you come to The Wheel of Fortune. Does that signify perpetual change?**

Yes, change and growth. Once we understand—not completely, but *somewhat*—who we really are, then we're ready to move into a world of continuous change. If you live forever, which *is* what's going to happen to you, you must continually die to the old and be reborn into the new. You have to give up the past altogether. You don't lose it, because you can return to it through the path of memory, but you have to be willing to go from one road to the next. In other words, the thread that connects all your experiences is *you*—going on forever and ever and ever.

The one thing you *can't* do is stop in any one place and say, "Now I've seen the glory of the Lord. Now I have a special throne in the southeast corner of the Bronx." It would be very nice for everyone to come around and say, "How wonderful! Joe made it. Isn't he beautiful?" Then Joe could sit there and gloat over his success. Well, this just isn't possible, because as you grow and change, all your innate capabilities keep expanding, so you get bigger and better as you go along. It's a case of continually busting out of the shell.

▶ **You don't want to get stuck on any one thing, but you've got to have limitations.**

Right. If you live the creative life that's described in the Cabala, that doesn't mean you are going to be a musician today, a bricklayer tomorrow, a baker the next day, and an obstetrician after that. Actually, you might well become more expert in some special field. However, you don't attach yourself to any particular state. You don't want to make *anything* last forever, because you have to be ready to expand, but the liberation presented in the Cabala does not involve giving up skills.

Since The Wheel of Fortune is associated with Jupiter, you should all have a great week. When I first saw this Key in 1933, I thought it was the most baffling of all. My only encouragement was the name associated with Key 10: The Rewarding Intelligence of Those Who Seek. That sounded mighty good to me. *I* found it to be true and I'm sure *you* will be rewarded for your efforts. Thanks for joining me and have an especially fortunate week.

KEY 10

CHAPTER 10

THE WHEEL OF FORTUNE

THE UNIVERSE BEGINS with a whirling that emerges from the Crown of Primal Will, so the sages tell us. Through more and more expansive spiraling, life gradually unwinds into more and more detailed self-expression. All forms of life expression, of which we are a type, are based on spinning. Spinning occurs at the atomic level, the molecular level, and the chemical level. It is found in the biology of the cell and in the celestial movements of solar systems and galaxies. Underneath all these manifestations is the spinning Wheel of Life that supports all the outer forms. Every activity you and I engage in—good, bad, and indifferent—is supported by this inner whirling, this principle of ROTATION.

According to the doctrine, the great Wheel (ROTA) in Key 10 gets tired and stops sometimes, and then starts up again, just like you and me. When it stops, everything withdraws into Original Being, just as we unite with our Higher Self when we are in deep sleep. Key 10 also represents the forces of involution and evolution. Consciousness descends into denser and denser areas of life until it turns around and starts going the other way and ascends into a more rarefied atmosphere.

We are each a microcosm of whirlings. They're like fleas, only worse. They start at your toes and go right up to the top of your head. Five hundred years ago, if I had said, "You are full of whirlings," I would have been thought quite daft. Today, you can open any textbook on chemistry or physics and see it all spelled out. The fact that you arrived here at all is fantastic, once you see what is going on. The subconscious is the ruler of these powerful forces that are spinning around in your body.

The part that *isn't* going around and around all the time is your discriminating consciousness, which is capable of being aware of all these whirlings without losing its balance. This is symbolized by the sphinx in Key 10, and also by the very center of The Wheel of Fortune. Our salvation consists of the fact that *we can look at everything* that is going on without being intrinsically upset by it, no matter how strange it seems. This is the mirror mind of the Buddhists, the attitude that since it's there we might as well look at it. If you do, it gives you a certain point of view about yourself that is very valuable.

You are not the whirlings. You watch the whirlings because you are always going to be living in some sort of a cycle. The Wheel governs all kinds of fortune, including health, wealth, and happiness. Taking the advice of our mentors, it's wise not to go overboard when appearances are good. We should maintain a steady pace because things are not always what they seem. Keep planting the seeds that you want to reap. Do you want to be rich and famous, or do you want to be happy? What do you expect to get out of life? There isn't anything you can conceive of that the Life Power can't produce. The Wheel of Fortune will deliver it to you. *When* it will deliver is a function of the natural development of seeds. In his chapter on Key 10 in our textbook, Paul Case translates the old anagram, *Rota Taro Orat Tora Ator* as "The Wheel of Tarot speaks the Law of Nature." More particularly, this refers to *our own* nature.

After all my years with the Tarot, I still think this Key has a startling appearance. It's a zoo. Of course the lion isn't really a lion; it's the Archetypal World. The eagle is the Creative World. The person is the Formative World. The bull is the World of Result. Literal-minded people may think they need a pet lion (and so forth) for success in this undertaking. But no, all you need is the Tetragrammaton, the four modes of Life Power that are God's expression of Himself or Herself (or Themselves, for all we know).

In the construction of The Wheel we find the same Worlds repeated. The center is the Archetypal World and the three concentric circles are the outer worlds. The result is outermost.

The four sacred animals correspond to the fixed signs of the zodiac, which signify principles that *do not change*. All of the turnings and shenanigans in the universe are taking place within a fixed frame of reference. This is the doctrine; I'm just telling you what I read in the book. You don't have to believe it, but it's worth looking into because a great deal of effort went into the Cabalistic analysis of the way things are done in the cosmos, as symbolized by Key 10.

The four modes of life expression that compose the Wheel of the Law are as different from each other as ice, water, vapor, and energy—which are four distinct states of the same substance. When you engage in any project, you naturally follow the order of the Worlds. First you get an *idea*; you get fired up about doing something. Then you must choose suitable *means*. Next you go through the "blood, sweat, and tears" of the *process*. Finally, there it is—your *result*.

You'll remember that the Cabalistic Worlds are The Magician's tools. The Magician in yourself sows the seeds of what you want. I admit this is a dangerous game, but it's the only game there is. Since you have to play, you might as well play according to the teachings. If you actually do so, you'll find that your efforts will bear the fruit you want.

Key 10 is the Rewarding Intelligence of Those Who Seek. As a rule I don't give testimonials, but in connection with this Key, I will say this: If you do seek, you do get your reward. This has been going on in my life since I first started in with the Tarot. I just wanted to testify to that and I'll stop right there before we all burst into tears.

▶ **Isn't The Wheel of Fortune card a depiction of Ezekiel's vision?**

Yes, the prophet Ezekiel saw the Pattern of Life as wheels within wheels. The four sacred animals of his vision, as described in the Bible, came from astrology, which was part and parcel of the religion of the time. This means that their beliefs were tied to the seasons, *tied to the sun*. The orange color of The Wheel indicates that it is run by solar force. On the Tree of Life, the circle of the zodiac is placed in Chokmah, root of fire. Kether makes it go around.

Key 10 is attributed to Jupiter or Zeus, the Great Sky Father of antiquity, the great benefic in astrology to this day. The clouds in this Key characterize Jupiter Pluvius, the lord of rain, responsible for keeping the earth alive, whose lightning was thought to fertilize the earth. Interestingly enough, it was discovered in the twentieth century that organized matter such as hydrocarbon chains can be brought to life by an electric charge.

Jupiter rules change of form. In the course of the cycles of evolution, energy moves from one form of manifestation to another. This is symbolized in Greek mythology by the way Zeus changes himself into different animals. It also suggests that the spirit of Zeus is present in every form.

▶ **There are people who can do shape-changing too.**

This is the power they would use to do it. This is the power we use to make the greatest change of all, to become the new creature spoken of in the Cabala.

Four alchemical symbols appear in the circle of the Formative World on The Wheel. The top three stand for Mercury, Sulfur, and Salt, which were defined in our discussion of The Emperor. The fourth squiggle at the bottom is the glyph of Aquarius ♒, and also the symbol of alchemical dissolution. This doesn't mean that you should be dissolute. The concept can be explained by what they call the "replacement series" in chemistry. If you put a steel knife in a solution of copper sulfate, the knife becomes plated with copper, while the iron from the knife goes into solution. You end up with a whole new situation caused by replacement. This is precisely what happens when we get ourselves involved in the Path. We don't dissolve and just disappear. Rather, old patterns and thought-forms go away from us as new perceptions and understandings come to us. This is how we become a new creature through the alchemical operation. Becoming *more ourselves*—that's what the new creature is all about.

KAPH כ, the letter attributed to this Key, means the *grasping hand*. It symbolizes the Life Power always in control of what's going on, which is why it's the initial letter of Kether. Kaph also represents our own control and comprehension as derived from the Life Power's ability. The Magician in Tarot grasps the magic wand of this power. In other words, he **takes** responsibility for creating the image of the future, much like putting a seed in the ground.

When you're dealing with a plant, you shouldn't worry and fuss over it every minute: "Are you growing, dear? Oh I hope you're growing." I mean, the cosmos—the sun, moon, stars and everything else—will help the plant grow, just as you and I have grown without somebody being overpoweringly protective. A plant that's smothered with anxiety will just say, "Forget it; this is too much!" So all you have to do is maintain the image in your mind with confident expectancy. Trust that something is going to happen and it *does* happen. You don't have to do anything extraordinary because *life is magical and extraordinary already*. You plant the thing at the top of The Wheel and it goes around and then it just blooms. Very simple.

If you don't form the specific image of what you expect to get, you'll get the average, the same that everybody else gets. You know, whatever food they give you in school or in prison, they just hand it to you and you can take it or leave it. We're on a different track here because we're working to unfold our own Inner Being.

▶ **Which way is The Wheel turning?**

Counterclockwise. Involution is symbolized by the yellow serpent going down on the left. It's as though consciousness jerks a rope at the top, and the energy makes waves in the rope and comes out at the bottom. This is the spirit getting involved in the physical level just for the fun of it, which is the only reason there is. The spirit is like Houdini. It says, "Tie me up, chain me, put me in a box, dump me in the river under the ice, and see whether or not I can get out." That's involution. Getting out of the situation is evolution.

Anubis is the red figure evolving up the right side of The Wheel. He represents humanity having reached three-quarters of the way to heaven. In fact, our ears are sticking up into the heavenly atmosphere. That's about all of ourselves that's up there, but still we're making progress. The ears represent inner hearing; we are headed into the intuitive realm. As we proceed, we understand each other more and more and we find out that humanity is wonderful.

The blue sphinx at the top represents the Self, our Innermost Self, which although outside the Wheel, could be considered equally well at the center. Even though The Wheel turns, our consciousness doesn't move. What's at the center of everything isn't going anywhere. There are some portrayals of this sphinx as a composite being with a lion body, eagle wings, human head, and the horns of a bull.

Identifying with the sphinx can get us off the merry-go-round. We have talked before about the state of awareness of being outside everything that is going on, as a spectator. Although the Self is the master of the game and master of the show, it is above the show. It's the producer. It's got money invested but it's not the show. There's a big difference. We have a tendency to get involved to the point where we forget, and then the show starts to hurt.

▶ **It's hard for me to identify with something that is a hodge-podge of different animal parts.**

Outside the toy store near where I live, they sometimes have a man dressed up as a gorilla, or he might be dressed as a bear. He plays animal roles. The animal roles that the Life Power plays include the human animal, elephants, cats, dogs, and everything else. Each of God's creatures, including ourselves, has special powers and faculties. I used to have a cat that could jump to the top of a fencepost six feet high. He could land right on top, just as though it were nothing. Animals have marvelous abilities that we don't possess. However, we have our own little tricks. If you think of yourself as being *all* the different animals, this creates excitement and drama, which is what a play is all about.

▶ **The sphinx has breasts and she's colored blue. Why is the Self depicted as female?**

Why not? The Self is androgynous. IT can appear in any guise. Here we are looking at what could be called the *super-subconscious*. The control indicated by the grasping hand is usually located in subconsciousness, which takes care of everything all the time. Think about how fortunate we are that this care is going on in our world and in ourselves.

There are only two Major Arcana cards in which a sword is carried, Keys 10 and 11, The Wheel and Justice. In both instances it is the feminine aspect that grips the powers of the Formative World. In fact, the original sword is Binah, the Saturnine power of definition. The sword is a separating influence that works in a two-fold positive way: It cuts out what you want and eliminates what you don't want. The clearer and stronger your desire, the more action you get from the sword.

We have to *embrace* the Saturn principle because the cutting tool is essential to creation. Decide what you want to express and then be quite severe with what disturbs your vision. You can't sculpt a horse, a cow, and a rabbit all at the same time.

▶ **Sometimes the disturbing things are hard to ignore.**

In some old versions of the Tarot, The Wheel has a handle. This is good symbolism because The Wheel represents the law of karma, so the handle shows that *you crank it up yourself*. When you stop turning The Wheel, that's the end of your karma right there. In psychological terms, this means you've stopped energizing old, outworn situations in your memory bank.

▶ **When you stop The Wheel, does this mean you stop living?**

You never stop living. Think of it this way: You can be a superior person but still go to a movie, or dancing, or anything you want. As long as you maintain the separation between yourself and the activity, you won't get lost. You may feel it's a good show or a bad show or whatever, but you have it under control because you are the superior person.

▶ **What if the movie wants to keep on being shown, over and over?**

I'd leave.

▶ **How do you leave? How do you turn it off?**

Just walk out.

▶ **How do you walk out?**

If you are saying that the whole universe bothers you, which is quite possible, as your friend I must tell you that I don't think you *can* walk out of it. You must come to terms with it.

▶ **Can you change the movie, though?**

Well, I should hope so. You've got to be the boss. That's growing up. Certain responsibilities in being the boss aren't exactly funny, but it's better than being "low man on the totem pole." It means you can do anything you want. If you don't like where you are, you can get out. The world is a big place and the universe is even bigger. There are any number of places to go, and that's the truth.

▶ **You might have to compromise.**

The only compromise is to society. The cosmos doesn't run on the basis of compromise. It just runs, period.

▶ **So there is such a thing as being too fixed where you are.**

Being even a little fixed isn't good for a person. You've got to move along. When you are tuned in to the spirit of Jupiter, you become open to possibilities. The cosmos has a tremendous capacity to produce, God knows, *anything*. If you don't have much faith in it, you'll have a rather tightwad notion of what it can do. But if you say, "This is a magical universe, so maybe something wonderful will happen," then you more or less expect that it *will* happen. A discerning person can see that we live in quite a fancy place, with all kinds of remarkable things here. If you have an open mind, you don't come up with negative ideas about what is likely to happen. You've got a fifty-fifty chance *anyway*, so why push it?

▶ **I have learned that karma means you reap what you sow, and DHARMA means the law. What is the difference?**

When our teachers say, "As you sow, so shall you reap," it's like saying, "Don't drive with your eyes closed. *Stay awake*. Watch what you are doing." Dharma is the path of one's duty. It may be your time to be counted among those who "also serve who only stand and wait." The path of duty is a serious question, and to be led in the direction you belong is a matter of *grace*, not a matter of what someone else thinks you should be doing.

Duty or dharma is the law that comes out of Chesed, the Mercy Seat. When you are coming from love, you *create* the law. Then you won't break any laws. You can get up in the morning and live a whole comfortable day without a single shalt or shalt not, *without one*.

When you see the wisdom of the law in yourself, you have nothing to fear from the law. Chesed is the law of love; law *enforcement* is over on the other side of the Tree, in Geburah. This seat of Justice and Severity corresponds to karma and to the mechanical aspect of natural law.

In a sense, Key 10 represents bondage to the laws of nature, until we see that the creative aspect within us can override all else. The main thing to remember about karma is that we may introduce a new element into the cycle at any time and thereby create a different effect. There is something you can do about any situation. Break the cycle. Turn the bull the other way, as it is turned in Key 21, The World. Be creative. Go along *with* natural law; use the mechanics consciously. After all, they're only a veil for the inner light, your Self at the center. This Key's attribution to Jupiter reveals the beneficence behind the *apparent chaos* resulting from the mechanical workings of nature.

Our beloved brother, Paul Foster Case, recommended a pattern for study that has all twenty-two Tarot Major Arcana cards placed around a wheel. In this exercise, Key 0 is placed att the top of the wheel, Keys 1 through 10 descend on the left side, Key 11 is the turning point at the bottom, and Keys 12 through 21 ascend on the right. In this arrangement, Key 10 is opposite Key 21, which is apropos of this discussion. In Key 21 the letter Kaph veils the androgynous dancer's masculine genitals, which are symbolic of creative power.

▶ **In *The Tarot* it says that Key 10 rules Wealth and Poverty. Wealth must be connected with this creative power.**

Sure. Our greatest wealth is knowing that we are complete within ourselves. All of our human problems *without exception* relate to the illusion of not having, or of not being, something that we'd like. These things are all illusory. Lack is a matter of definition. The fact is, we could be happy on the diet of a chimpanzee, but we become deluded and give importance to unnecessary things that may actually be obstacles to our happiness.

▶ **To me, wealth is being able to live here with all the beauties of earth.**

Amen. My feelings exactly. The Cabala agrees also through statement number ten in the Pattern on the Trestleboard: "The Kingdom of Spirit is embodied in my flesh." The word "kingdom" is the translation of Malkuth, the name of the tenth center on the Tree of Life. Malkuth is called the Resplendent Intelligence. It is the completion of any particular round of evolution, the *cumulative effect of power*, or combination of all four elements.

▶ **The Chinese talk about the elements in a somewhat different way from the Cabala.**

There is only One Reality about which both systems are speaking. One of them is talking in Chinese, which I'm no good at, and I'm not much better in Hebrew. Still, the ideas become intelligible after you look at them for awhile. Some of the best minds in the history of the world have spent a lot of time with these ideas.

One view of Malkuth suggests that all the beauties of earth can be thought of as the spectrum of life. When all the colors of the spectrum are arranged in a circle, they form what we call the color wheel—an absolutely *beautiful pattern*, very harmonious and pleasing to the eye.

A mandala of Tarot and astrology fits perfectly on the color wheel. Saturn is black in the center. The three mother letters corresponding to the outer planets and primary colors are arranged around that. The other six planetary Keys and the secondary colors are around that. The twelve zodiacal Keys and tertiary colors are in the outer circle, and that takes care of all of them. This pattern of the spectrum illustrates something that is so true about life: Divisions, as they exist in humanity, are each glorious *complements* to the whole.

▶ **The genetic code is something like the zodiac in its abstract pattern of types.**

As far as this particular approach is concerned, the code would be the *expression* of the idea, the means, but not the idea itself. Anything that we can be aware of from a scientific point of view would be in Binah. Science doesn't reach into Chokmah, into Life Itself. The life areas are the most elusive prey of science. A great many of the things that science deals with sort of trail off; they go over the hill and into nothing. You're watching something and all of a sudden it disappears. That happens in physics quite a bit.

Still, with modern science, we can do a lot of things we couldn't do before. You can make things happen in science as soon as you know the principles. Universal principles are represented by the four corners of Key 10. No principles, no manipulation. Once biologists learned the principles of the cell, they were able to manipulate cells. And when you know all about high-voltage electricity, you can stay in one piece in the powerhouse. What we are studying here is high-voltage too. This is *psychological science*, a real and dynamic thing.

The Tarot and the Cabala deal largely with the well-being of the psyche. Stability in the psyche is the foundation of health. In an unstable condition, life energy constantly tries to keep peace within the psyche. This is not the best use of life energy.

For example, imagine that you belong to a large family with lots of in-laws. You also work at a job all day. When you go home at night, all your in-laws jump on you as soon as you walk in the door. They tell you that you're no good, you're not working half hard enough, you don't make enough money. You're so tired by the time you listen to all this nonsense that you just fall into bed. The next morning you wake up thinking, "I have to go to work, and then when I come home I'll have this horrible situation all over again." Well, this can just suck the energy right out of you.

This is analogous to the state of mind in which something is bugging your psyche all the time. Regardless of what it is, it eats up energy that you could better use in some direction you *like*. Battling with yourself all the time wastes your eneregy and weakens you.

It's important to get our psyche into a balanced condition. This means that we need to know something about it, so that's our primary effort here. Our major goal is to discover as much as we can about ourselves, or the Self. Our second goal, which follows from the first, is to improve the quality of our lives. The more we know about ourselves, the better we can deal with any life situation that comes along, because in terms of the psyche we're all constructed the same way. Insofar as we understand our *own* psyche, we understand the *other person's* psyche too. This psychological science can be very helpful. It gives you a handle on things that you wouldn't have otherwise. As you know, education in this department is singularly lacking in the schools.

▶ **Perhaps it will be taught some day.**

Some day, it will be. But at the present time no guidance is given in school about what is going on in ourselves. If you don't even have an inventory of your powers and faculties—which is the *minimal* requirement—you can't know much about yourself. As God is my witness, I never got such an inventory in school. Like all of us, I got a lot of discipline and I heard a lot of things, but nobody ever delivered the real goods.

▶ **You were talking about inner conflicts when you gave the example of a person whose family is carping at him. Does meditation with the Tarot and the Cabala offer a way of resolving those conflicts?**

If, by meditation, you mean understanding and encompassing what is going on, then I agree with you nine hundred percent. The Tarot and the Cabala present yourself to you in a dynamic way, leaving *nothing out*. For example, anger is right there in the Severity center on the Tree of Life. You have to meet it, greet it, look it over and come to terms with it, because it's part of you. Actually, an extremely valuable part. If you can't get angry about something, you're half dead already. The only way you can make changes in yourself is to be so angry that you can say, "*This has got to stop.*"

There's a funny story from the Middle East about a famous doctor who was an actual historical character. He was the sultan's physician and his royal patient was languishing with some inexplicable illness. One day the doctor said to the king, "I'd like to borrow one of your horses and go for a ride." The king loaned him his favorite Arabian stallion. When the doctor returned, he said, "I rode your horse over a jump and he broke his leg. We had to destroy him." It was a put-up story but the king didn't know that. His royal highness sprang up out of bed, yelling and screaming, ready to kill. At that moment the doctor said, "Hold it. You're cured." That was a positive use of anger.

▶ **What if you're angry all the time?**

Then you have to reach to the other side of the Tree of Life, to the Mercy center that balances Severity. You say, "Hey, wait a minute. What's going on here? I've got all this anger but I don't seem to have much love. I'd better balance myself out." For equilibrium you need both Severity and Mercy, and the heat is just going to keep coming at you until you get it balanced.

▶ **Do you think that the process of meditation continued over a long period of time will eventually resolve most of our conflicts?**

Definitely. *Most* of our conflicts are imaginary. They're not real at all. They have been put upon us, although we're really okay, just as in the saying, "I'm okay; you're okay." But just to *say* that doesn't do the trick. That's like saying "God is love" without coming to terms with anger. You can repeat "God is love" until you're blue in the face, but if you're a mess inside, then God *is* love and you're a mess!

▶ **The Path is not all sweetness and light.**

If you follow the Tree of Life pattern in your meditations, you'll find that the head of the left-hand pillar is not sweetness and light. In fact, it's *black*. Yet it is one of the Three Supernals.

As you get farther away from the top of the Tree, you get into denser and denser situations where the separation becomes more pronounced and the possibilities of misunderstanding become greater. So we aim for the top. If at this moment everyone in the whole world were illuminated in the sense of the top of the Tree of Life, you wouldn't recognize the place. Really, it would be so different you could hardly believe it.

▶ **Does the top of the Tree correspond to the center of The Wheel of Fortune?**

Most certainly it does. If all of us here tonight could see ourselves from that viewpoint, from the level of the Self, if we could literally see ourselves together on the inside, the harmony would be incredible. On the *outside*, we have differences. We're so used to these differences that we take them for granted, but really they're superficial. On the *inside* it's another story. There we're all the same.

▶ **Would you place Eros on the inside and Logos on the outside?**

No, because there's no separation in Reality. There is only One Being who has two aspects. The Innermost Self can turn its face in the way of Eros or it can turn its face in the way of Logos, as the situation demands.

▶ **If you're on the outside and you want to go to the center, do you have to sort of "come unglued" and dissolve back through the various stages?**

Absolutely. To put it another way, heaviness would be a factor keeping you on the outside of The Wheel. One way to proceed to the inside would be to lose a lot of weighty thoughts. Our *psychological impediments* are the things we have to get rid of. As we simplify ourselves, we get lighter and lighter. Eventually we become The Fool; with no impediments, we can be right at the center.

In terms of her psychology, my wife is a very rich person, the kind who says, "If you would like to go *anywhere* in the world *right now*, I'll go! We can pick up whatever we need later, so we don't have to take anything with us at all." This is typical of The Fool, who is qualified to make it wherever he happens to land. That's a simple formula. If we believe that we need a lot of things, then that's exactly what we need. The minute you tell yourself something, that's it for you, so be careful.

In occult circles you may run across the notion that if you can pronounce the Tetragrammaton correctly or if you know the magic word, you will have it all. This mumbo-jumbo completely circumvents the reality of the situation. According to the doctrine, you already *have* everything you want. Your problem is that you think you don't.

The *image* of your Self resides at the center of The Wheel of Fortune. Our mentors say that on the inner planes everybody can see what the image is. For instance, in India the Lord of Wealth is an elephant named Ganesha. You may think that's silly, but it doesn't bother Ganesha because he is what he is. It doesn't matter what your inner image looks like. The main thing is that it is profoundly *true* about yourself and so you are standing on *extremely* firm ground. This is the best there is. The Cabala is eternally trying to explain this to you.

The wise who are responsible for this system of study and education know that when you reach this image in yourself, you have solved all your psychological problems. There's no further attempt to get rid of anything or acquire anything. To quote the Bible, "I have said, Ye are gods, and all of you are children of the most high." As long as you don't believe it, you shut yourself out. It's as if you were a millionaire who said, "I don't want the money." You're overlooking the good you could do with the money. You might use it for some noble purpose. The same is true of yourself, except you can't turn away from it. You're stuck with yourself, but since you're stuck with something wonderful, what's the kick? You can take a negative or a positive attitude about yourself. As far as the wise are concerned, you can take their advice about yourself or ignore it. It makes no difference to them, because they don't want to interfere with your God-given option.

Over the gate at Oxford is the motto, "Let them say what they will say." Some things are true regardless of what people think. I'm just telling you the straight stuff. There's no such thing as a philosopher's stone or any of that occult wizardry, which is unnecessary once you understand the greatness of your Self. Those things are like the hawkers at the sideshow: "Come on in, folks, and see the belly dancers!" Then when you get inside, you're in a psychology lecture, know what I mean?

Don't forget that this Key, which started you off in the first place, will bring you out of all your difficulties. It's "guaranteezata" that Life wants you to flower, in the sense of having complete command of everything that is your birthright. But we're a narky bunch, so it takes awhile, *n'est-ce pas?*

Our Key for next week is in the center of the Tarot Tableau. Justice, Key 11, represents work and action because it balances all the other Keys. Insofar as we work at the doctrine and act upon it, everything comes about. If you involve yourself in an active way, *things will happen.* The sword in Key 11 is the creative weapon that carves out everything. It's the cookie cutter—and we're the cookies. We're the end result of the formative process. Once you start exploring the Sword of Justice, I think you'll find it extremely interesting.

As always, I enjoy your company very much.

KEY 11

CHAPTER 11

JUSTICE

JUSTICE HOLDS THE central position in the basic Tarot Tableau. It is a pivot for all the other Keys in the entire display, an exchange point through which the energies of the Keys are transmitted to one another. It maintains a dynamic balance among them all. The old alchemists used to say, "Equilibrium is the basis of the Great Work." Key 11 deals directly with equilibrium as a matter of central importance.

Manmade justice could be improved; I think we'd all agree on that. Conversely, cosmic Justice is always improving *us*, for which we can be grateful. The Divine Mother in her guise as Justice directs everything that goes on in our bodies, the households where we live. We are controlled and sustained by this supervising agency, which for lack of a better term we call the subconscious (as opposed to the self-conscious principle), although it's not "sub" and it's not "un"; it's alive and well. This is someone you can talk to anytime, even without an appointment.

Our subconscious never lets us down. She's always on the job, day after day and night after night, which is why Key 11 is associated with the Faithful Intelligence. She literally preserves us from all sorts of difficulties, without our bothering about it. In the process of maintaining our metabolism, she performs great feats of magic. She can transform our dinner into poetic inspiration, or even into something as peculiar as goodwill. When we poison ourselves, as we do regularly, it makes extra work for this capable Lady. She has an array of forces at her command by which everything important is sustained and everything unimportant is eliminated. As long as we have this friendly, mighty power on our side, we never need to worry.

It's not surprising that WORK and ACTION are the key words here. This is the Libra Key. Venus rules Libra, so we are seeing The Empress at work. Last week, mention was made of the super-subconscious who sits at the top of The Wheel of Fortune holding a sword, which is one detail among many in Key 10. The sword becomes a major feature of Key 11 because Saturn, the great Sword of Binah, is exalted in Libra.

If I had to point to a handful of prize ideas that I had gotten out of the Cabala, surely one of those would be the teaching that if there is no resistance, there is no art. I'm given to long speeches, so please bear with me while I explain this again, because it is vitally important to understand the positive aspects of the Saturn principle.

An artist must have a resisting medium, whatever the field of expression. Without the resistance, no form could last. The marble was always fighting Michelangelo, yet he knew that its resistance continually increased his skill and power. If we didn't have something to practice on, we'd stay the way we were in the beginning. But we want to advance. Consider the enormous amount of material in the Tarot and the Cabala. The more we practice on this material, the stronger and sharper we get. Thus, we should enjoy the pressure because it means we are advancing all the time.

The Sword of Severity is *the* tool by which you delineate what you want. In the beginning it's difficult, because you want it all. This is understandable but it's impractical. You can't possibly embrace everything. So you narrow it down: "Well, what I really want is A, B, C, D, E, F, and G." Your trial run shows that's still too much, so you take the sword and carve off F and G. After awhile you see that you can live without E. Then D gets burdensome. With a deep sigh you go snicker-snack, and then you are left with just what you need, which is A, B, and C. Everything you could possibly need is in those areas.

This is the *process of elimination* by which you find out what it is you really want. The things you eliminated were actually the obstacles. By this process you learn keen discrimination, the ability to see the difference between what you want and what you don't want in fine terms, not just in gross terms. The whole point is that *your joy and your life depend on no one but yourself*. The choice is yours; no other choice will work. When obstacles are in your way, you are not happy. That's the same as being ill. Around here, we want you to be not only well, but *blissfully* well.

Health is so important that wellness underlies a total experience of the Tarot. You can forget about all the fancy stuff in the last row of the Tableau if you are not well. The Justice Key teaches that the way to cultivate health is by being careful. This means you have to eliminate anything that runs counter to the law of Nature, which is the law of life. If you don't want to eliminate it, that's okay—the law of life will eliminate you!

▶ **What sort of things go against the will of life?**

Overdoing anything, cultivating any aspect of yourself at the expense of other aspects. You can overdo running, eating, having sex, sleeping—all of this is more or less against the rules. However, the Cabala doesn't tell you to abstain from the joy of living. The point is to get the most out of life by approaching it as a gourmet, not as a glutton. The happy medium is taught by Mother Nature in Key 11.

You don't have to think too hard to see that elimination is essential to health. This runs contrary to the common idea of what life is. Many people think that keeping to the status quo is living. According to the Tarot and the Cabala, living consists of being able to *move* through a jillion status quos. Life is never the same from one moment to the next, so we have to move continually in the world of change, or temporarily perish. You should be able to change gracefully and not get bogged down. The Justice Key represents the opposite of being bogged down.

From the time we're conceived right on through the time when we move on to another level altogether, it's a case of getting rid of the old and moving into the new. This sword is the instrument by which you carve off what is useless and outworn *in yourself*. That's easy to say but it isn't easy to do. We all have pet attitudes, so it's agonizing to get rid of something we've petted for years. But we're a brave lot, so we keep on trying. After awhile, if we succeed, we can look back and say, "I'm glad I did it."

▶ **In biblical allegory there is an angel with a great, flaming sword.**

That's Severity, the Mars center on the Tree of Life. Mars guards the Holy of Holies. Geburah contains the four upper Sephiroth. Its flames protect these inner, priceless elements.

▶ **Do we hold the sword ourselves when we're able to apply the discriminating faculty?**

The story goes that in the dispensation of Divine Mercy—when we're metaphorically crawling around in our diapers, which applies to practically everybody—we are taken care of along with the birds and the bees and everything else. When we become more divinely human, all these powers in the Tree are given to us because, as you just pointed out, we're the ones who are supposed to handle the sword. That's part of our job, to discriminate about what we want in our house. The angel with the flaming sword is not there to cut your head off. He simply makes the distinction about who will get through. We don't call out an army to protect the sacred aspects of the Secret Doctrine because in the nature of things there is this automatic, separative element. In mythological terms it's a flaming sword. In biological terms it's the cell wall, which protects the cell.

▶ When you understand what it's all about, you'll simultaneously be past the door.

Oh, sure. Nobody's trying to keep us out of enlightenment, for heaven's sake. Don't forget that the sword is the essential tool of the creator, and *you* are the creator of your experience. In the act of creation, *you* make a division between what is going to be in and what is going to be out. You have to limit your expression but you have *infinite choice* as to what you're going to do. In the Cabala, nobody's telling you *what* you should do. Our mentors just tell us, "If you want to accomplish a particular thing, be willing to eliminate the other things. You can't do everything at once. That's impossible, according to the law."

▶ How much are we actually doing? Sometimes I think that everything was decided when the universe was created.

That's a mechanistic idea of the universe. The Cabala says the universe is an ongoing proposition, that it never does the same thing twice. In other words, it's *creative*.

▶ I've often wondered whether I'm making the decision, or is something else doing it?

Well, of course you're making the decision. Your question is dealing with the matter of how you identify yourself. If you define yourself carefully, you find out that you do have the responsibility of decision. If you define yourself as "just me," then you're forgetting who you *really* are.

▶ I must be identifying with my body.

You are identifying not only with your body but also with your mind and all your faculties. But the Self is not the faculties; this is what I'm trying to get at. Your True Self has nothing to do with your faculties.

▶ **Is it that continually changing thing that flows through the Magician?**

Yes, and that is really *you*; no two ways about it. You may be driving a horse-and-wagon or a high-powered car or an airplane—those are the faculties—but *you* are something else again. As long as you keep centered in that which you really are, and understand that you *have* faculties which you exercise, then it comes out all right. But if you question yourself, "I wonder if I am or if I'm not?" then the whole thing falls apart. You need to grasp what's going on in yourself because it's no fun to fall apart. Self-integration is important to how you *feel*. I'm sure that the reason we're given this vital information about ourselves is because it's so essential to our well-being. Again, it's a matter of *health*.

Who you really are hasn't *anything* to do with what someone else thinks. Nothing! You know yourself. You know who you are and that's all that matters. The garbage that's thrown at you every day can be eliminated by the Lady of Justice. She takes it outside right away, before it smells up the house. There's an outer conspiracy against the individual because the individual is just too hard to handle. The system wants sheep; lions are not encouraged. In the Cabala it's the other way around.

▶ **Every day I think of things I want to do, what's right for me or not, and every day it all keeps changing.**

That's good. As I say, it's a process of elimination. It takes great patience and a good sense of humor.

▶ **Does it last indefinitely?**

Of course it's indefinite. It's like Zen archery. You're not going to hit the mark the first time or the second time or even the thousandth time, but eventually you're going to hit the mark *every* time. In other words, it becomes automatic. That's the supreme skill. It's not a matter of *willing* yourself to hit the mark.

It's the same with your Self. If you keep trying, eventually you will be yourself, which is the supreme goal of occultists all over the world.

It's easy to say you can be yourself (I just said it!), but it's much more than you dream of. As I've told you a thousand times here over the years, it's very hard to realize how great each one of us is. We haven't yet reached the colossal potential of ourselves, but if we do, it's an *irreversible* condition. We'll no longer fall back to what we were. This is encouraging. The reason we don't fall back is that we *like* being ourselves. Before, we didn't like ourselves. That's the inner impetus to keep working toward liberation.

▶ **Should we follow our own personal standards even though they seem completely "off the wall"?**

Yes, because the masters say that in our essential being we are good, not bad. Our personal satisfaction is not different from what's good for society.

Lamed ל, the letter connected with Key 11, represents inner discipline and self-regulation. As a verb it means *to teach*. As a noun it means *ox-goad*. This is what keeps life on the road of meaning. If we stray from that road, Lamed brings us back. Our individual lives *must have meaning*, otherwise we're really *gesunken*—we're sunk. The scales also symbolize this principle. If we go too far to one side or the other, inner instruction puts us on the Path again. This is the Saturnine face of the Divine Mother, in her constricting and restricting aspect.

Aleph-Lamed spells El, the name of the Lord, which is the shortest way to sum up everything that's going on. Aleph represents the expansive aspect of the Life Power, the free-wheeling spirit. Lamed is the contrasting aspect, wanting to express itself in countless different forms. It's like a marriage. You can guess who is full of grandiose ideas and who wants to maintain a home and feed the children.

Some undiscriminating people consider Saturn an enemy but really it's a *friend*, especially when we understand how it works. Within ourselves the spiritual Aleph aspect creates a kind of evolutionary pressure. Over a period of time the response of the restricting Lamed aspect within ourselves brings about a complete change. The process is so magical that it's hard to believe, but it does happen.

Justice is said to be crowned with the cap of maintenance. On this crown there is a red circle in a white square. The circle corresponds to Aleph and the square to Lamed. Saturn is symbolized by the indigo T or

Tav which Justice wears on her breast, and by the T-shaped handle on her sword.

▶ **I am one of those people who thinks of restriction as something to rail against.**

One of my daughters used to work for a newspaper where they piled on so much work that she was in despair. At that time she thought she couldn't get another job. I advised her to quit, and she said, "Nobody else would hire me." Finally, she went through the trauma of quitting. Then she went down the block and got a good job at another paper. After a few days she said to me, "You know, Daddy, this job is so great that I feel as if I died and went to heaven." The point of this story is, the resistance was *in her own mind.*

▶ **Isn't there a connection between work and karma?**

Karma is the Sanskrit word for work and action, and this Key has a lot to tell us on the subject. Going back and forth on the scales of Justice is the same as going around and around The Wheel in Key 10. This is the action and reaction so typical of karma. Key 12 (The Hanged Man) is stability, the pendulum come to rest. Here, Key 11 shows us how to get from the state of karma to the state of rest.

The mechanisms of nature, as symbolized by The Wheel of Fortune, veil the truth from the uninitiated. Violet is the heraldic color of Jupiter and of Key 10. Here in Key 11 the violet curtains are drawn aside so we can see the light. This is where we get into the creative intelligence that takes us out of the repetitive situation altogether, into the complete reversal of The Hanged Man, who is *free of karma.* Karma takes place in the world of cause and effect. If we are participating in the One Will, we are operating on a higher level than that of karma. It is quite possible to lead a normal life without any karma because you function on a whole different level.

▶ **In your daughter's work situation, quitting was the creative act that broke the pattern.**

Exactly. Karma is not merciless or vengeful. The Life Power will stretch it out for us so we can live and learn.

One of the goals of the Tarot, especially in this Key, is to teach us *how* to work. The proper way to work was set forth a long time ago in the *Bhagavad-Gita*, which says that we should work without being concerned about the results. Wisdom tells us that although work is a necessity, we should not be workaholics or work ourselves to death; yet there is no harm in achievement or skill. This is not the same as ambition, which is just egotism. Whenever the ego is involved, the scale is unbalanced; then a reaction must follow. The *spirit* in which you perform work is the secret of success in the Cabala.

Lamed the ox-goad is that which incites us to action. In order to realize our goals in a concrete way, we must work and act. In the central column of the Tableau, the archetypal masculine energy of The Emperor directs the feminine power of Key 11 in unfolding the evolution of the organism depicted in Key 18 (The Moon). The Empress works out The Emperor's ideas on the substantial level. As always, this is happening *in ourselves*.

The teamwork of Mars and Venus is seen in the colors of the garments that Justice wears. Red, as you know, symbolizes action, and in our system green is the heraldic color of Venus. Venus is the particular goddess of everything of a vegetative nature. By stretching your imagination you could say that we are walking vegetables, but really Venus rules all things organic, what we call living creatures.

The Justice Key illustrates the *economy* of nature. This is the law of parsimony, the notion that there shall be no lack or excess—just enough, or as we say in the Pattern on the Trestleboard, all things *needful*. Some lusty characters must get it through their heads that what is needful is not as much as they want. There is also the other type, with a niggardly idea of what is needful. We try to strike the proper balance.

Economy operates in the mind as well as in the body. At one stage in our career we think that if we could just stuff our heads full of all the knowledge in the world, that would solve all our problems, but this is not so. All we need to know is where to get the right information when we want it. Like The Fool, we want to travel light, taking with us only what is useful. Our teachers keep telling us that we don't need a great deal in order to succeed. What we need are the *really powerful tools*. In the magic of the Self, just a few principles accomplish everything. That's why there are only four implements on the Magician's table. That's not a lot but it's enough.

There is really only one instrument required to bring about all transformations—the magic wand of the will. The question is, "What do you *want?*" If you can find out what you want, you can get it. Experiment until you find something that really suits you, that you are happy with year in and year out. That's the proof right there. *You* are the proof. You've gotten to the point where you can live with yourself. There has to be something delicious and delightful in yourself, which you can relish eternally. Of course that's the Self, your Innermost Self, which is absolutely gorgeous.

▶ **The thing that suits us is like a calling; it's what we're supposed to be doing with our lives. Isn't that a decision that has been made about us?**

Yes, it's a decision that you made yourself. According to the wise, decisions are not made on the level of personality. All decisions are made by the Inner Self. Apparently, the only reason it lets us get into all sorts of tangles is so that when we finally settle down to being ourselves, we're perfectly content to stay there.

▶ **No greener grass.**

That's it. It comes as a surprise, because we tend to think of God or the Self as being "over there" while we're out in limbo someplace. Actually, the whole thing is One and it's all inside us. When we become acquainted with what's inside ourselves, we have no desire to go anywhere else. I'm talking about where you want to be, where your heart is. That's always tied up with your desire-nature. The will is just another way of talking about your desire-nature. We've mentioned before that what you will is what you delight in.

▶ **Aren't there two kinds of desire, though, one from the personality and one from the Self?**

No, they're just different levels of expression. There is only one kind of energy. It may express itself in various ways that are good, bad, or indifferent, but the power is the same. The Cabala excludes nothing from examination. Everything is to be looked at, neither in a friendly nor an unfriendly way, just looked at clinically for what it is. When you look at your desire-nature in this way, it becomes understandable. Then you realize this is going on with *everybody,* and that makes you feel you have a lot of companions.

Little by little you come to see how energy works and how it can be useful to you. Instead of having it work you, you work it. The way you do that is by *directing* your desire with this Saturn power we're studying tonight. The Magician consciously directs his desire into a certain channel. It doesn't make any difference *what* you do with your desire because sooner or later you will decide what you *ultimately* want to do with it. In the meantime you learn how it works by practicing the conscious use of it. Later, you narrow down the field and say, "I don't think I want to get involved in this or that use of my desire-nature." Key 11 comes in handy again and again. The main thing is to see how desire is the *drive*, the *power to act*. Take the desire-nature away and everything stops right then and there.

Our desire leads us along what is often called the Path. When you start out on the Path, you don't know what the heck it is, anyway. Your Inner Self knows the answer but the personality doesn't. The personality just knows *something* is going on. So it's blindman's bluff. You feel around . . . read a couple of books, hoping to find something meaningful . . . maybe you meet someone who can tell you a few things . . . and eventually a polarity builds up inside yourself. By withdrawing your attention from the outer world, the positive force inside yourself starts to build up strength.

As long as you're in the jet set you can't be a mystic because you haven't got the time. If you're not putting your energy inside, you're not getting any result. Once you start attending to the inner, it can speak to you because you are receptive. That's basic, as you know. The Cabala has to do with receptivity all the way through.

If the world is so important that we can't pay attention to inner things, then we are creatures of the world and that's the end of it. That doesn't mean we're going to hell. It just means it's the world that makes us tick. Our life consists of reactions to what he said, what she said, what he did to me, what she did to me, over and over. Nothing is ever settled. There's no peace, no rest. Finally they put you in a nice padded coffin and you have a long sleep and maybe start all over again someplace else. Nothing is going on as far as your Inner Self is concerned. You're just banging around like a billiard ball. Here, we're making a noble effort to reverse the whole affair. Next week's Key means just that: reversal.

▶ **What is justice, really?**

Justice is the way things work.

▶ Since things work in a just fashion, according to a just law, does that mean I don't have to worry about how things will work out?

That's what the Cabala teaches and that's why this Key is called the Faithful Intelligence. One of the most difficult things for us to understand is that the universe runs itself. It just does. Most people think that we run it. Instead of involving ourselves in the creative act—which is what the universe *is*, morning, noon, and night—in our own small way we try to run it. If you ask someone point-blank, "Do you make the sun shine?" he would say, "Of course not." Yet he acts as though he were God. He isn't, in this sense. We are the Life Power in a certain special way and as individuals we need to know precisely *how* we are *That*, but we must never think that we are the Lord of the Universe, because there is a slight difference.

Father Divine said that he was God and a lot of people believed him. They gave him everything they owned and worshipped him. Other self-appointed people have said the same thing. They didn't say that they were channels or expressions of the Life Power. They stated in plain terms that they were God. Well, this is dangerous because, "You is and you ain't."

You see, in the realm of the imagination, in the mind, we have tremendous power, but if we think that we are *the* power in the mind, that's a mistake. As Jung pointed out, a mind that doesn't recognize anything superior to itself is an unregenerate mind. That's his definition of the Devil. When we identify with the mind, we're on an ego trip. We must recognize that the mind is only a faculty, which doesn't take away any of its power. The *essential* part of Man is Being. Man is a being in Being.

The eleventh Tarot Key represents the Path of Duty—Karma Yoga—very difficult. We all have within us the knowledge of just what to do. The hardest thing to do is the *little thing*, because it goes contrary to what the world says. The world says the little thing is not important. You should go out and beat the drum, be the mayor, be a Big Man. Some people end up thinking they should be God. But to do the little thing because it's the right thing—that's not easy.

▶ Especially when nobody knows you've done it, even if you've succeeded.

That's what I *mean* by a little thing. That's what I'm talking about.

▶ So how do you do Karma Yoga?

In the *Bhagavad-Gita,* you just throw up your hands and holler, "Krishna! For Krishna's sake, what's going on here?" Krishna represents your Innermost Self, so if you channel your energies in that direction, it will carry you over your difficulties.

To direct all your energies into Krishna is technically correct but not easy to do. Another method, promulgated by our particular teaching, is to mind your own business and stick to what you're supposed to be doing. You don't generate any harmful karma by doing what God designed for you in the first place. In order to succeed by this method, you must learn to live creatively. This means that your viewpoint is totally apart from what most people think is important in the world. You have your root elsewhere. When your guide is your Innermost Self, you act from that basis and you haven't *anything to do* with what's normally called karma at all. You just *do* it and then it's done; you're no longer involved in it. It's possible to go on like this forever, and as I say, we're trying to learn how to do that.

▶ So we are not supposed to be attached to the fruits of action?

Once you're concerned with the outcome, you're hooked. That's the karmic tie, right there.

▶ What's the connection between your constitution and your karma?

Writing your constitution is a creative act. It represents the way you want to lead your life. The creative act is the same thing as Life Itself, and Life Itself doesn't have any karma, for the simple reason that there isn't anything else. If there's only One Life, there's nothing else to react. Now, Life has polarity, and apparently it likes drama, so it writes all kinds of plays, but it Itself is not involved in karma.

▶ If I experience something in my life that seems unjust, what should I do?

Your question boils down to, How are you going to respond to observable phenomena? What's your *attitude* going to be? There are attitudes like that of my dear departed mother, who was annoyed at God because the fish eat each other in the ocean. She had a continual complaint with God about these creatures eating each other. If that's the way the world was run, well, she didn't like it—even though she ate *her* roast beef and chicken regularly.

On the other hand, the attitude of a trained Cabalist would be, "Who am I to say whether anything is good or bad?" From a Cabalistic point of view, to judge life when you don't know all the answers is just a joke.

▶ **So the problem lies in my *reaction* to the thing that I'm not happy with.**

That's right. You write your story. You control what's in your own life. That's all you have to do. Never mind what's in someone else's life. If everyone would just do what's right for them, then as Alice would say, the whole world would go along a lot faster. The sages agree that if each individual does his share about himself, then we've got it made. We would all communicate on a beautiful level, rather than the level of "Do it my way! You're wrong and I'm right! It is written, blah, blah, blah." We don't need that. Direct your energy toward bringing yourself the greatest possible rewards. If you want *nothing but the best,* then you're on the right track. Don't take shoddy merchandise or shoddy thinking. Just don't accept it. Insist on the best.

When you try to find out the best that is known about yourself, you'll be amazed. For thousands of years the wise have been saying that what's inside you is tremendous and marvelous. Politicians don't tell you that; educators, TV, and newspapers don't tell you that; but the *wise* have been saying it for a long time. What's the difference between Joe Doakes and a sage? A sage is a Joe Doakes who's *become* wise. The sages were just like anybody else. Each of us can move in an inner direction, but it takes instruction. Fortunately, instruction is available, especially Self-instruction. Begin to see things for yourself. This makes you strong.

The Pillar of Establishment, the left-hand side of the Tree of Life, shows that what starts out in a floaty-floaty way does become quite firm. But I must honestly tell you that in the beginning it's a will-o'-the-wisp. Now you see it, now you don't. The experience of the Self comes and goes. There may be periods of a day, a week, a month, or even a year, when it gets weak. Then it comes back again. It's an accumulation over the years, or some people get a large dose of it all at once. The important part is that eventually it becomes your foundation. Then it's there for keeps.

Mind you, all of this is done while you're leading your regular life. The inner experience goes on in parallel fashion to whatever else you are doing. You know, you have to keep moving, especially in the West. If you go into deep meditation and stay there, somebody's going to pick you up and carry you away to the nearest mental institution. However, you can train yourself to more or less meditate all the time, while doing the laundry and everything else.

▶ **Martial arts are a kind of moving meditation.**

There's a Zen story about an eager young man who goes to a sword master for instruction and says, "I want to be a great swordsman." The master says, "Very well," and he takes a large wooden staff and whacks the student with it. Then he says, "Come back tomorrow." The next day he hits the student as hard as he can, over and over. Naturally, the student starts to duck and dodge. The master continues to swing at him, and eventually the student gets very good at dodging. Finally, when he *can't be hit*, he is ready to become the best swordsman in Japan. *Then* he gets his sword.

We'll explore the fascinating Hanged Man next week. Key 12 represents a complete reversal of attitude in terms of how you look at the world. You no longer accept its surface appearance. It's not a rejection of the world, but a recognition that there is an inside and an outside to things, and that you have to look at both of them. Our Tarot education has brought us to this point, so now we have something with which to form sensible judgments. We can distinguish between what is of this world and what is not—what is transitory and what is everlasting—what is illusory and what is real.

As always, you make me happy on Thursdays. Have a good week.

KEY 12

CHAPTER 12

THE HANGED MAN

THE HANGED MAN represents the *power of stillness*. Pressure from the outside always demands that you should be moving in the world. Doing absolutely nothing is unreasonable, immoral, and bad for your circulation. There are thousands of outer reasons why we should not be still, and yet, it's imperative for us to find the stillness within ourselves ... stillness that is not related to words or things ... just *quiet*.

The way you can tell when you have reached the stillness is that you are not concerned about anything. This technical achievement does not mean you have withdrawn from life. Being not-concerned means having very deep faith. You can be still because you are depending on Life Itself. That's exactly the symbolism and the whole idea of Key 12.

Perhaps more than *any* other Key, The Hanged Man emphasizes the Inner. All twelve branches have been lopped off the zodiacal tree from which he hangs. This means that the grab bag of ordinary experiences inherent in the zodiac is put aside in this particular state, so that a different consciousness altogether can be brought forth in the individual. In Hindu philosophy this superconscious state is called SAMADHI, which is success in Yoga. Yoga, or union, means "losing your shirt" in the vernacular. In order for union to come about, we have to give up all our powers and faculties and concentrate on just one. That's what the figure in this Key has succeeded in doing.

The Hanged Man typifies a cocoon-like phase of spiritual evolution. In a cocoon, the caterpillar disappears into a lump of protoplasm. Later, it will emerge as a glorious butterfly. In other words, we start out one way and end up very different. The cocoon phase is quiet but not solitary, for Life Itself does the transforming. Believe it or not, you will be transformed into a superior creature. Despite your doubts, you will eventually unfold and succeed in this work. That's the nature of things.

The main Cabalist principle represented by this symbolism is REVERSAL. Basically, the reversal is one of attitude. It's a turning-away from the world, not in the sense of rejection, but rather to interpret it in inner terms that are opposite from the usual outer way. The outer way assumed that you know all the answers, while the inner way depends *entirely* upon the Life Power. Everlasting principles underly all the outer phenomenal aspects of life. If we make a noble effort to acquaint ourselves with the eternal verities, our interpretation of life becomes transformed.

Key 12 carries Key 11 to its logical conclusion. We discover that everything hangs from the center. Our balance depends upon none other than Life Itself, to which we are intimately connected, like a baby in the womb. It's easy to imagine that The Hanged Man is in the womb, or in the birth canal.

In this connection, note that the letter MEM מ, attributed to the twelfth Key, means *water* or *seas*. We are born from our personal mother's womb into the Womb of Nature, moving from one fluid environment to another. All life originally came from the sea, and water remains essential to biological life. Atomic structure is fluid. Our environment is fluid because it is always changing. It nourishes us because it is a manifestation of the Divine Mother. If we do not see how we are dependent upon Nature, then we are in need of a reversal of thinking.

You can *practice* the reversal of thoughts. It is a purposeful exercise in values that helps you appreciate the subconscious. The Hindus undertake such practices for their own edification. They call it TAPAS, or spiritual discipline. The main idea of the reversal exercise is to break the habit of believing that certain things are so and other things are not so. *Everything is so,* as far as the Cabala is concerned. In this way we learn to accept what's going on in the proper spirit. For example, I try hard to put myself in my son-in-law's position. He's a rock-solid Republican. When we work to understand each other's point of view, we get insight into each other.

Jacob Boehme, a mystic who lived in medieval Germany, said, "Walk in all ways contrary to the world." Be suspicious of externals. Don't take them at face value. Reversal is the most useful tool for overcoming our main obstacle to perfect freedom—our own attitudes. Only we ourselves can free ourselves. It is not the responsibility of God nor of any religion. We are equipped with a full panoply of powers that range from the mundane to the divine.

The average person operates in a small space, simply refusing to believe how great he is. He needs to reverse his attitude toward *himself.* At the point of Key 12, you accept the fact that you are going to do something with your Inner Self. You are willing to put aside the world for awhile and experiment with inner experience. You learn to *empty your mind*, putting all its contents elsewhere. It's like leaving all your concerns in the house, and going down by the river, out in the open under the trees and sky. When you are in that composed state you are exactly where you *belong*. Once we become centered in ourselves, we can hear, feel, or in some way *sense* the message, and the rhythm and beauty of the universe around us.

▶ **Does reversal really have nothing to do with outer changes?**

It's a foregone conclusion that when you begin to heed your own inner instincts and intuitions, your outer life will vastly change. An example that comes to mind is Bridgeport, Connecticut, near where I used to live. At one time Bridgeport was the corset captial of the world because of the whaling industry there. The whalebone was an important part of keeping a woman together in the old days, as you know. The fact that she could hardly breathe was neither here nor there. With the coming of the freedom that women have today, and the fashion changes that went with it, Bridgeport became a dead city, block after block of empty factories. This is the sort of thing that happens when there is a major change of any kind. Similarly, when your values change, which they are *certain* to do if you become involved in inner matters, then your outer life is going to go through the same sort of process as Bridgeport. You can expect a *lot* of your habitual life patterns to be a dead city for awhile.

Transformation is typical of the Tarot. By the grace of God it's coming up next week with Key 13, Death. Our teachers tell us to always move toward the *new form*, to always have somewhere to go and something to take the place of what you had before. People who follow this path discover that there's always something to replace what they're leaving behind. You're not just left there with your foot in your mouth. Sometimes in psychoanalysis, people get analyzed out of their own minds and then left without knowing what to do with themselves. Ours is a gentler method than that.

▶ **There are times, though, when you have to step into the dark.**

Sure, you need that excitement. Life without suspense would be extremely dull.

▶ **What happens when you give up your addictions?**

You get new ones. You have to have addictions because they represent your desire-nature. You can't give up your vital mechanisms, so you simply switch from one thing to another. What actually happens is, you become more refined as far as your Self is concerned. You begin to lead a more subtle existence. You don't need a jolt in order to feel stimulated; you don't have to be hit with a baseball bat to get excited. You've still got to have those kicks—that's basic—but now you begin to pick up on *subtler vibrations* that give you just as big a bang.

We're not on any schedule here, so if you haven't suddenly taken up violin playing or smelling flowers constantly, this doesn't mean you are a spiritual failure. It's not a case of la-de-da refinement. It's always a gutsy situation when you strongly desire something better. As you mature spiritually, you find something that represents your *ultimate* heart's desire. When you find that, you will *know* it. This is always the case. In the process you move naturally from gross enjoyments to subtle enjoyments, but the *principle of enjoyment* underlies everything. The Cabala states that the reason for existence is delight, not misery.

▶ **Do you go from "forever seeking" to "sometimes finding?"**

Yes, and then to finding more, and then still more. The treasure isn't something that you get once and for all. There are no final rewards because if you're going to live forever, your life is dynamic in a way that you can't exhaust. The only thing that's even remotely inexhaustible is a change of tastes and scenes that gets progressively better. That's what's in store for you as you become refined and your horizons expand. In astrological language, Key 12 is Neptune, the watery planet of inner awareness and hidden, subtle changes.

▶ **They say that Neptune rules illusions, too. Sometimes I can't tell the difference between fantasy and reality.**

It's like answering the question, "Are you ignorant?" We can *all* wholeheartedly say "yes" because, even though we know some things, basically we are enormously ignorant. On the other hand we do have analytical powers, and by using them we can overcome some of our ignorance about what is fantasy and what is reality.

▶ **What is the difference between fantasy and reality?**

There's a fine line between fantasy and what's called reality. At a powerful theatrical performance, a good audience just lets the theater run over it like a truck. When you let the performance penetrate you fully, it's close to the experience of reality. When you identify with the characters on the stage, they can move you mightily. After it's all over, it doesn't hurt any more and it's made a tremendous impression on you. The Greeks were aware of this; they used the theater in a remarkable way.

The theater is a creation. In other words, it's a fantasy. It's not reality and yet it's so close to reality that the experience can shake you. Consider your own myth. Your own fantasy is actually where you live all the time. We're perfectly content to live in a world of our own making. The occult teaching states that, as you become more advanced, you get better at making your own world. You improve your fantasy. Instead of living in a hovel, you live in a palace, psychologically speaking. As we always say, it's better to be a king than a slave, and the choice is yours.

▶ **It's hard to see what anything is, other than what you think it is.**

I agree. This is why you have to play the game of reversal. The starting point in the game is to say, "Everything I think is wrong," and then you say, "Well, what else could I think?" Eventually you can find something new that was not in your head in the first place. The problem is your conditioning, which is a mixed-up view of what's going on. Your mind is confused because it contains reality and illusion, and you don't know which is which. The only way to overcome this is through meditation. Meditation will take you out of yourself, and then you can see yourself. To meditate, you must be very still.

▶ **The Hanged Man has ceased to go along with what the tribe calls reality.**

That's correct. And that means he has exercised all the powers in the first row of the Tableau. This is where *it happens* in you. You have unfolded to the point where you are no longer what you were. In fact, you are the *opposite* of what you used to be.

▶ **The human race seems to like its illusions.**

We believe we haven't got anything else. We want our security blanket, even though it may look like a piece of Swiss cheese when it's held up to the light. It may be full of holes, but we're hanging on to it.

Fortunately for him, The Hanged Man has been able to get back to the Truth. That's precisely what illumination consists of.

▶ How would you define illusion?

In our society it's a manmade creation, like the notion that you're nobody unless you own the latest turbo-charged Mercedes that goes two hundred miles an hour, when the speed limit is fifty-five. This kind of hypocrisy is typical of humankind. It hasn't anything at all to do with Reality.

▶ Is there a Reality?

Of course!

▶ How would you define it?

Well, as Einstein said, "Something is *moving*." If you can get out of your personal problems long enough to look at the universe, you may not *understand* it, but one thing you'll be sure of, it's *there*. *It is real.* If you are a patient observer of what goes on, you'll see that Reality is not the possessions or the wealth or any such things, but That which supports these things. And apparently, whoever is running the show has a great sense of theater, as though IT were the audience having a really great time—and it has an extremely generous viewpoint—because we *are* asinine. Just as George Bernard Shaw said, this is the madhouse of the universe.

The Bible tells us that we are as gods. But when we do not accept our place in the scheme of things, we become stupid. As gods, if we want to act like Nero, that's our privilege. Our tremendous potential is still there. The Cabala goes even further and says that our relationship with Reality is an intimate one, because we derive our marvelous powers and faculties directly from the universe itself. We don't have to be dignified if we don't want to, but if we assume our dignity as humans, we can reach very high indeed. The Hanged Man has become truly human in the best sense of the word, being the image of God on this level we inhabit.

Key 12 is a major statement in the Tarot. Mem is one of the three MOTHER LETTERS of the Hebrew alphabet. Aleph, Mem, and Shin stand for *air*, *water*, and *fire*. *Earth* results from their combination. The Hanged Man is looking down into the earth and *seeing* that it is composed of the mother letters. His illumination results from his dependent attitude.

All energy in the body is unified. By directing your attention to inner things you *energize* this area in yourself. Any student will see this in time. If you direct your energies inward, you are going to succeed in the same sense that is meant when you speak of raising the kundalini. Historically, illuminated people in the West have succeeded in raising the kundalini energy to the head through meditation.

Just to raise the kundalini by force, which can be done, is no cure-all for personal problems or anything of that sort. It's much like an orgasm. You can have nine million orgasms if you're lucky, but this isn't going to illuminate you. There is a parallel, however. If you persist in meditation, what you are doing is taking the basic energy that's flowing through your body and bringing it up to your head. Then it becomes possible to see many things otherwise unnoticed. Seership depends almost entirely on this process. Your understanding of life depends on this process.

The arms and head of The Hanged Man form a downward-pointing equilateral triangle. This is known as the water triangle, which is appropriate because the whole Key symbolizes water through its connection to Mem. This triangle is surmounted by a cross, formed by his legs. In Keys 4 (The Emperor) and 10 (The Wheel) we looked at the alchemical symbol for sulfur, in which an upward-pointing fire triangle surmounts a cross. Sulfur represents passion, or rajas guna. In Key 12 sulfur is *reversed* and *still*. In the usual situation, the passions seek outer objects. In this disciplined situation, fire energizes the forces that bring about the splendor, the illumination.

All the fiery power of the Mars force is involved in this successful attempt to achieve perfect union. It is concentrated in one point, the head. The same thing is represented another way in Key 0 by the red feather coming out of the top of The Fool's head. The Hanged Man is concentrating on the point of communication between the personality and the Self. The Cabala calls this Kether, the Crown, and Yekhidah, the Innermost Self. Illumination occurs when the consciousness seated in the personality and its root in Yekhidah become One.

The watercourse allows The Hanged Man's head to extend below the level of the earth and actually penetrate, so to speak, into the mineral kingdom. Thus the mineral kingdom also becomes illuminated by the process taking place here.

If you've read the textbook, you know that the gallows from which the figure hangs forms the letter Tav ת. Tav signifies the Palace of Holiness in the center of everything. Thus, the being is suspended within a sacred space, and the twisted white rope clearly represents the whirling force that descends from Kether. The Life Force comes down the rope, through the body, and out the head. It is said that a Yogi in samadhi seems almost dead except for a hot area on the top of the head.

▶ **Does he hang himself up there? It looks scary.**

Life Itself does everything; when it comes time for you to hang up in a cocoon, it's Life that's calling the shots. If we cooperate with it, it will cooperate with us. We are always building a clearer and clearer *feeling* about this support, which is magical and mysterious. Whoever is in charge here has created a remarkable thing, which is *us*. We can appreciate this and depend on the intelligence involved. Thinking that it's scary can actually serve to remind you of how close you are to the sustaining factor in life. You have a one hundred percent *definite connection* and you're supposed to use it, not in any vainglorious way, but modestly.

Regardless of how you define God—whether it's a primitive representation or a sophisticated one—it's essential for everyone to rely on a superior power. You really can't trust your own capabilities if you don't understand where they come from. Knowing the nature of your support system makes you more sure of yourself.

▶ **Does The Hanged Man hold his hands behind his back out of modesty?**

Having negated the ego, The Hanged Man is well acquainted with modesty. He is thinking, "Of my little self, I do nothing." The Path really isn't a manual thing, because it's an inner reality. Hands govern the outside, in no uncertain terms. That's why his hands are literally "out of the picture." When you're on the inside you don't need them. You are working with your inner faculties.

Key 21 is the opposite of this Key because The World pertains to outer expression, including dancing as the ultimate in physical activity. In the Cube of Space, both Tav and final Mem are attributed to the center of the Cube. There is a direct connection between Keys 12 and 21. Note how the numbers and postures mirror each other, just as reflections are reversed in water. Twelve says, "Be still and know that I am God." Twenty-one says, "Keep moving and know that I am God, yet maintain that inner stillness." Thus we see the importance of Key 12 as the foundation of the success in Key 21. When studying these two Keys together, place the Being above and the mirror image below. Then you have the true picture.

▶ What happens if I negate my ego?

You affirm some other rule of life than that of the ego. The soul that is freed of ego delusion doesn't go into a world of emptiness. On the contrary, it goes into a world of fullness that reveals the ego as the empty world. The ego seems all-important when you're in it, but it's a tiny dot with respect to the universe. The ego is separation, whereas real Life is not in separation. When you get out of the ego viewpoint, you go into the realm of infinite relationships. The experts tell us that in the inner world, the spiritual sun is always shining and you are always aware of it. On the ego trip, you can and do get into desperate straits because you can't see the light. The Hanged Man can see the light that never goes away. He has reached an inner stability that is not going to change.

The Twelfth Key depicts the Stable Intelligence, which refers primarily to a completely quiet mind. Stillness isn't easy, but it has a big lesson for us. Most people have problems with their mind going around and around, following association trains within the subconscious. Many psychiatrists make a living from this widely recognized feature of the mind. They call it free association. You go into the psychiatrist's office, and sit or lie down. The psychiatrist says, "Apple." You say, "Adam and Eve ... big snake ... big trouble," and so on. At the end of forty-five minutes, he is seventy-five dollars richer and you are no closer to illumination than you were when you walked in.

▶ Jason, what technique would you suggest to begin quieting the mind?

If you're going to use the Tarot, just do what it says in our textbook. Look at a Key for five minutes, devoting your entire attention to it. Then put down in your Golden Book of Ideas any reactions you have. Practice with all the alertness and awareness of a cat watching a mousehole. This is an essential feature of the discipline, not only in the West but also in the East. After awhile you get used to focusing your mind on one thing and leaving it there for some time. Then you take the Key away and your mind is in just the right position to become illuminated ... but this might take a week or two.

Intrinsically, we all have the same capability as anybody who ever lived to become a great soul or a master of life. The only thing that keeps us from fulfillment is the filter we put in front of our perceptions. We can get rid of this filter through practice, just by emptying the mind and then *looking*. Most of the time we're viewing judgmentally. We classify and compare everything. However, when you use your intuition you are able to perceive *directly* what is going on.

▶ **Is that a kind of acceptance?**

Yes, but acceptance is an *intelligent view of things*. It's not the resignation of the whipped dog, "Here I am, God; do anything you want with me." No way! We don't have to be overassertive or anything, just recognize that we all have a remarkable powerpack inside. The idea is to *liberate* that power, to get it going. At the same time, we mustn't forget that the universe *gave* us everything we have. We don't sit down and invent new powers and faculties. We're not that smart, but we have a big powerpack *anyway*. In the scheme of things there comes a time—Key 12 is the time—when we wake up to the fact that there's a vast difference between the way we're living at any given moment and the way we *might* live. There's a big spread there, real "gulf-itis" as far as our potential is concerned.

▶ **The Hanged Man is in that sublime situation where he doesn't have to worry.**

As Lao Tzu pointed out, we don't have to wind up the universe every morning. That's fortunate. You can do what you have to do and then stop right there. Nobody's asking you to do the whole thing. You must take a wise measure of how much energy you're going to put into the universal pot. You know, a good executive gets more and more into a position where she or he does less and less. The last Key in the Tarot is the Administrative Intelligence, meaning that you do practically nothing. How can you possibly be the joyful dancer of Key 21 if you have the burden of responsibility on your back?

In some versions of Key 12, the person is being shaken upside down. Life gets you by the feet and all your change jingles out of your pockets and your lunch and your pens fall out. Your worries fall out then, too. That's a big part of emptying your mind.

▶ **This reminds me of the Yoga posture called the headstand.**

I discovered that you can take this pose very easily in water. As long as you can hold your breath, you can be in this position. It's kind of amusing that it's so easy to stand on your head *in the water*.

On the other hand, please remember that the Tarot images are spiritual and psychological symbolism. The ramifications of the Tarot certainly do proceed into the outer, but the emphasis is definitely on the inner. So in case there is someone very literal-minded who might make a mistaken interpretation, don't hang yourself upside down physically.

▶ **I know by now not to interpret Key 12 as nonattachment; still, it looks that way to me.**

You *can't* become nonattached. You may think so but you're just kidding yourself. The only hope that the wise hold out to you is that you can become attached to something greater, rather than to the lesser. But you can't extricate yourself from what is.

▶ **I don't want to do that. It just seems more relaxed to give up caring too much.**

That's intelligent, because once you understand that the whole tremendous universe is working for you, you don't get so excited about everything. If you think that nothing is working for you, then you can get panicky.

▶ **When you know what's going on, you love people and things but you don't cling to them. You don't get jealous.**

Jealousy represents a big hole in yourself. You feel incomplete without the desired object, but you are *by definition* complete. Although it's hard to convince yourself of this, it's true. *You don't need anything at all* to complete yourself.

If someone comes up to you and says, "You're glorious; you're magnificent," you're trained to suspect, and think, "What does this guy want? Is he looking for money? Does he want me to sign my life away?" Yet if I were to say that you are less than magnificent, I would be a liar.

Historical data about the remarkable men and women who have lived down through the ages is there for your encouragement. This does not supplant your own experience of yourself, of course. One of the very hardest things to do is to define yourself accurately, without falling into egotism. Then it's well to remember that we all share this (fortunate or unfortunate) life condition of being tremendous. Knowing we're all cut from the same cookie cutter makes it easy to avoid ego inflation, and gives us profound respect for one another.

▶ **You've said that creative expression can keep a person out of the ego trap.**

When you're creative, you're not concerned about *anything* except the creation. It's your pleasure to create. The act is sufficient. This can occur on any level whatsoever, including the social level.

I'm sure that the Most High God has no guilt feelings about creation, and we're not supposed to either. The creative act is balanced in itself. What happens in the world is something else again. The world may adore your creation or hate it or whatever, but don't get involved in what other people think. Make your masterpiece or your floperoo or whatever; just spew it out and that's that. See the event in the entire matrix of what's going on.

▶ **Does this Key symbolize the phrase, "in the world but not of it"?**

Yes, it certainly does illustrate that.

▶ **Key 12 is like being in a traffic jam and not minding it.**

Right. You can sit back and listen to music on the radio or whatever you want to do, but the one thing you *don't* want to do is involve yourself in the mess. The minute you do, that outer situation fastens upon you like a tick.

▶ **A lot of people take drugs to escape from tick-like situations.**

Drugs are not a real escape. Once you're on the flypaper, you're stuck. You can take drugs or booze, but you're still on the flypaper. It's a problem that has to be tackled in another way. That's all there is to it.

You are responsible for your own life. Humanity is said to be placed higher than the angels because we have the power to create our own circumstances. Insofar as we can discriminate between circumstances of our own making and those being laid on us, then we're getting smart. I'm talking about people, not God, because God is merciful with us no matter how screwy we are. Still, the character of our own existence is strictly up to us. We create heaven or hell on our own.

You can make anything of yourself that you want to. It's like you're a sculptor doing a monumental project called Making Yourself Over—and maybe you're a hundred feet high—so you have to get up there and carve it all out. The scaffolding in Key 12 supports you while you are busy hammering.

The Tree of Life is God's design for Man. The Tarot and the Cabala come in handy for putting yourself in good working order. You got a kit when you were born, and this is the "How To Do It Yourself" instruction book. If you didn't do it yourself, you wouldn't be able to *command* it, and you're suppsed to be in command. Sounds quaint to say that the Cabala was sent down from heaven for the redemption of Man, yet it certainly is a very good system for getting out of the mire. There are other paths, of course, but I think this is a good one.

▶ **I'm getting the idea that meditation is essential.**

It's basic to all the great teachings. In meditation, you look at everything you are, and as they say in alchemy, you dissolve it. In Latin SOLVE. Then COAGULE, and away you go. But only if you *want* to. Nobody's going to make you do it. You can coagulate into anything or any form you want. You name it and that's what you can be. Writing your constitution means that you really want to get someplace ... or that you don't. You could say, "I'm gonna be the biggest bum on the block." That's okay, because you are *doing it consciously*. This is what you want to do *yourself*—good, bad, or indifferent. You may make a blooper but at least you know you're not being driven to doing it Bill's way or Mary's way.

▶ **So you give up all the ways ...**

... except your own ...

▶ **... and suspend all action.**

That's a good idea until you make up your mind what *you* want to do. If you don't know, the best advice is to do nothing.

Through meditation you will discover what to do. In the basic Tableau, Key 12 is directly under The Hierophant, the Inner Teacher in ourselves who supplies all superconscious information. Continuing down the same (fifth) column in the Tableau, The Hanged Man's head is in The Sun Key, where his mind is regenerated through illumination.

▶ **He reminds me of the Christ, who is associated with the Sun center on the Tree of Life.**

Yes, this represents the Crucified One. In mystical terms it is the purified Ego, which is One for all humanity. The Compassionate Buddha is a real, honest-to-God being, and by the same token the Christ, the total Ego of humanity, is a real being also. In the inner teaching of the West, the cosmic Christ represents, you might say, the king of humanity as a unit. His rulership is over the individuality of the human race. The function of the Buddha is a bit different, because his compassion is directed not just to humans but to all beings in the universe.

There's nothing wrong with imitating Jesus, but we're still stuck with the problem of ourselves. The imitation of Christ is easy compared to knowing your Self. Reducing yourself to original protoplasm and achieving absolute stillness are difficult tasks. Fortunately, we have Life on our side when we try.

In Tarot, the Death Key is actually the release from the cocoon, and the emergence of a completely new being. You have been through the amorphous condition in which the things you thought were important turned to slosh inside yourself. Then a new structure began to build around your constitution. This geometrical arrangement inside yourself became the skeleton for your new life as a transformed being.

Key 13, Death, is specifically a picture of sunrise, not sunset. It symbolizes the concept that life depends upon transformation, moment by moment. You are constantly being transformed, otherwise you *would* be dead. Death of the old is necessary for new growth to come about. We create the new by exercising our creative imagination. We imagine ourselves into a better life situation. If we stay with it like a good artist stays with a composition, then it comes to pass.

Thanks, everybody, for coming. Thursday nights mean more to me than I can say.

KEY 13

CHAPTER 13

DEATH

THEY SAY DEATH is the last enemy to be overcome. Why wait? Let's overcome it right now. Let's not make the mistake of looking at it in the conventional way. The Big Whatsis has determined that life is *change*. In the Tarot, Death signifies change. As the Key of Sunrise, it symbolizes rebirth. We don't weep when the leaves fall off the trees in autumn, because we know they will reappear in the spring.

The skeleton in Key 13 is a symbolic representation of your Self, the essential part of yourself that is beyond your attributes and vehicles such as personality and body. The faces are our old friends, the self-conscious and the subconscious, representing the two roles you can play. One is King Logos and the other is Queen Eros. The Innermost Self is beyond role-playing. As master of the whole game of the phenomenal universe, the Self lives far beyond any phenomena. That's where *you* live. That's where you *always have* lived. You forget this when you get caught up in the illusion of the world. That goes for practically everybody, so cheer up; you have lots of company. We're all in the same boat.

Being poetic, it could be said that everything in the body hangs upon the skeleton. This rather Halloweenish character is the fundamental support for everything that goes on in your personal vehicle. Remember this when you think about *who you really are*. Despite the fact that we command remarkable—I am serious—*remarkable* powers and faculties, these are just *vehicles* of expression.

Even though it might stretch your imagination to think of yourself inhabiting some other vehicle, sure enough it's going to happen that you *will* be in another vehicle. You're in a vehicle now that is well suited to your total understanding of everything that's going on, which is true for all of us. Farther along, you'll be in another chariot that will express a still greater grasp of everything that's going on. It won't look anything like your present one, but it will be home for you and you'll like it just as much. It will still be hung upon the essence of your Self. Once you thoroughly understand that you never were the vehicle in the first place, it becomes easier to understand *how* you might have a life that isn't attached to any particular form. This is important if you are going to overcome the last great enemy.

The body that you inhabit on the physical plane exists by a burning process we call metabolism. We know that our cells are always dying by the jillions, and that new cells are being born all the time. These facts don't seem to bother us a bit. We are constantly falling apart and at the same time also building up. In other words, there are two sides to the life process in the vehicle. One is constructive and the other is destructive. If it weren't for this fluctuating pattern of life, we wouldn't be able to change, and then we would have a serious problem.

Movement, change, and TRANSFORMATION are the meanings of Key 13. We actually *thrive* on change. The better things that we all devoutly wish for *depend* upon transformation, which makes the Death Key important to us. If we didn't have this pattern of being able to change, we'd be stuck. There's nothing worse than feeling enmeshed, with no way out. The thirteenth Key is crucial to our emancipation. It teaches us that perpetual change is at the root of everything. As the old dies, the new appears. Take science, for instance. Max Planck, the founder of quantum theory, said that science progresses not by convincing the adherents of outworn theories that they are wrong, but by allowing time to pass until a new generation can arise, unencumbered by the old errors.

The consciousness attributed to Death is the Imaginative Intelligence. If you have an unhappy situation that you want to change for the better, the way you do it is through your imagination. It's essential that you imagine yourself as you would like to be if you expect the Powers That Be to support you.

We are told by our masterful mentors that Life Itself exercises its imagination all the time. That's why it is creative, never repeating itself. Since we are a microcosm, we have to act the same way. I might add that for our own sakes we had *better* be imaginative, since we are going to live forever. As we go along, we have to imagine what we want to be next, otherwise not much happens and we get bored absolutely stiff. Using what our friend Carl Jung called *active imagination*, we can deliberately picture the future in terms that would be suitable for us. As always, devotees of this philosophy know that nobody is telling you *what* you should be. *You* have to take that responsibility. It has to come out of your own insides. As we continually think about this, the situation evolves. We move comfortably from the worm into the butterfly, then into the bird that ate the butterfly, and so on and so forth . . . no problems at all.

Always there is dissolution of the old form as the new is created. The whole ongoing process is represented in occultism by the Ouroboros, the serpent swallowing its own tail. We see this symbol around The Magician's waist in Key 1. This transformative process makes it possible to liberate ourselves from our misperceptions, so Death is called the Key of Deliverance.

I recommend that you keep a diary or that you write your autobiography, for your own personal use. These records are illuminating because you can see the state of your mind five or ten or twenty years ago. You can observe your transitions. As we move from one level of our life expression to another, it becomes clear that all the *preceding* ones were fundamentally *important* in producing the level that we happen to be working on now. We continually transform ourselves through the agency of the death principle.

▶ **I see there is a big forward movement toward change, but there seems to be a strong pull *away* from change, too.**

The people who *like* change are disturbing to those who don't like it, so there you have a lot of drama. Negative attitudes are built in by society, which always says, "If you want to be a good girl and 'belong,' then don't be an innovator; that's not good." You have to ignore this, and everything else of a negative nature. This is like ignoring a broken leg and a fractured skull; it's not easy.

▶ **When I'm approaching something new and expanded, a part of *myself* resists the growth.**

That's the part that comes out of the Stable Pillar on the Tree of Life. It is on the side of the Divine Mother, who will eliminate anything that tends to destroy the structure of her creations. A physical example of this principle at work would be when the body rejects blood of the wrong type.

In the Hindu pantheon, God has three aspects: the creative, the sustaining, and the destructive. VISHNU is the preserver in the middle. The universe would be absolute bedlam without a preserver. In the Cabala, the preserver is Mama.

▶ Isn't the Mother also the destroyer, the Black Kali?

Yes, the Mother is in charge of the whole universe, and more particularly, in charge of her babies. They have to have enough to eat, and after they've eaten they can raise a ruckus. But if the kids raise too much hell she puts them back in line. *Both* construction and destruction are in the nature of the manifested.

I mentioned metabolism, a basically destructive process that liberates energy. We destroy food, we destroy our bodies, simply to be able to express ourselves. Then we have to rebuild our bodies. As is pointed out in the teaching, destruction is the foundation of being able to move and create. Every time you move, you destroy cells. To live is to live on top of a heap of destruction. This is literally true, and we have all kinds of mechanisms in the body to eliminate the dead matter that we accumulate in the course of a day. Again, Key 13 shows that our *power to destroy* is a *liberating influence* if we want to use it that way.

▶ Still, death is scary. I'm afraid to die.

I'm trying to tell you that you aren't going to die. You are going to *change*. You'll just have to get used to being immortal.

▶ How am I going to live forever? I can't even stand it today!

By moving into a less reactive, more creative way of living, it becomes okay. After all, we only have to live one day at a time, so the problem is, how do you live one day in Eternal Life? You really don't have to worry about forever and ever. The secret is in doing it *one day*. Then it's easy.

Exoteric religion puts a strange emphasis on eternal life. It tells you that if you're burned to a crisp and ground into a powder here, then you can be reformed in heaven when you die. All the goodies are in the hereafter. On the other hand, the occult teaching is that you're going to have to make it *wherever* you are. Don't assume that there's no existence except earthly existence. We could live very well in other dimensions besides this one. I suggest to you that these other dimensions are contained in your mind. You can have experiences in your mind that have little to do with your body, as we know from meditation, dreams, hypnotism, and the like. The more you know about the inner world, the less you will be upset by thoughts of death.

As far as fear is concerned, death is the *big* one, the biggest phoney-baloney of them all. The Cabala tells us to deal with it. We're not supposed to be ignorant about this most fearful experience; we're not supposed to have *any* fear in us. Anything we react to in a fearful way is an obstacle, but it can eventually lead us to an *awakening*. If something doesn't bother you, you pay no attention to it. Since death bothers practically everybody, we work on it. If we weren't *ambitious to know*, we could get locked into this fear, but by trying to find out what is really going on, then little by little we can unlock the mystery of death.

If you are blessed with an inquiring mind, then all obstacles lead toward knowledge and ultimate liberation. When you're not afraid of death, you don't waste energy on fear. If you *are* afraid of it, then you're always fighting it subconsciously in the psyche.

Our teachers, who are well-versed adepts, tell us that if we persist in our study and practice, sooner or later we will actually *experience* our Self apart from the vehicle, and stop worrying about physical death. The Judgement Key, located under Death in the Tableau, symbolizes this type of experience and describes the precise nature of our spirit. This is a promissory note given by the Tarot.

▶ **You have said that fear belongs in the Tree of Life.**

Yes, Fear is one of the names of the fifth center. The reason for it is that it's *protective*. For example, fear makes us defensive drivers, to keep from getting clobbered on the road. We know it's a healthy fear and it's done in full consciousness. The danger is from *un*conscious fears. As occultists, we don't want to energize anything that doesn't move forward the work on ourselves and The Work in general. We want to direct our energy *consciously* as much as possible.

The way to overcome unconscious drains on our energy is by looking at them. The Buddhists study death. They sit by a corpse or a skeleton and after awhile they become quite clear as to what's going on. They say, "I used to think death was horrendous, but now I see it going on all the time in myself. I'm not so afraid any more." Then inside, that energy is *freed* and can be directed in any desired way.

The only request that our elder brothers and sisters make is that we direct our energy toward being our True Selves. You can't complain about that. It's *your* Self. It's what *you* want. That's purification; that's the white rose.

The white rose appears twice in the Tarot, once in The Fool's left hand and once in the Death card. Keys 0 and 13 have this similarity: A joker can upset the game and take all the cards; Death comes unexpectedly and does the same thing.

In both Keys the white rose refers to the purification of the desire-nature. This has nothing to do with Victorian attitudes but refers to a not-this, not-that process of getting what you really want. It means eliminating the secondary and getting down to the primary. Purification is freedom from admixture. We learn to *focus* our desire-nature on some aspect of life that is near and dear to us above all others. The Magician is number one, and concentration is his operating technique. Our will becomes like a laser beam, a coherent light that can cut through metal.

Trial and error are coming up next week with Key 14. You try everything and eventually you become discriminating about your desire-nature. You say, "Hey, wait a minute. I did that before. Now it doesn't seem so important. Now maybe I'll *concentrate* more on this." Finally, when you get to the area that you really want, you're aware that this *is* what you want. The single white rose is associated with illumination because, "If therefore thine eye be single, thy whole body shall be full of light."

▶ **What is the symbolism of the white rose growing out of the black earth?**

It means that the spiritual light is rooted in the subconscious. *Everything* emerges from the Divine Mother, the magical ground that contains all the secrets of life and reproduction. The entire Tarot is an exploration of the subconscious. In Key 0 the rose is plucked, but in Key 13 it is growing on the bush, thus ensuring its reproduction. This is similar in meaning to the letter NUN ׃, which is associated with Death. As a verb, Nun refers to *sprouting*, to life springing up—in *you*. This is the regenerative force symbolized by the zodiacal sign of Scorpio, the astrological attribution to Nun.

The symbol in the upper left-hand corner depicts a seed, the promise of the new thing that is to come. All seeds have their source in Chokmah, the supernal fire. If you meditate on what a seed is, what it contains, what it does and how it does it, and so on, you will understand the spirit of this Key. As the saying goes, the seed dies in order to become the plant. Something has to die *in us* as we progress on the Path. After awhile we get used to letting it go. Without this death trick, this opportunity to grow, we might hang on grimly to things we don't need. That would be another obstacle, which is the last thing you and I want, right?

In my estimation, there's no greater magic than what goes on in embryology. The intricacies of the physiology are staggering. If you think deeply about conception and embryology, you will comprehend the *power* of Life. Never forget that, in the tradition, *you are* Life Itself, so you don't have much to worry about. My personal recommendation is not to consider death as a problem, because it's obvious that we already have passed through stage after stage in our evolution.

It's remarkable that when we're born, someone takes care of us. As babies, we are totally dependent on our mothers. Whoever or whatever organized life in the first place (certainly not ourselves) made some arrangements about how we would be cared for, having been born so helpless. My feeling has always been, well, if it's able to do that, why shouldn't it be able to look after us when we drop this vehicle and go somewhere else? Why should we think life is any less powerful in terms of this transition than it was when we came here in the first place? According to Cabalistic tradition, what happens after you leave the physical vehicle is *better* than what happens here.

Some things about this Key are so *happy*, rather than the other way around. The River of Life is flowing toward the sun, returning to the source. The sun is in the east, always rising, symbolizing us looking forward to the new. This is truly an optimistic Key.

Please don't forget that the major character in Key 13 is yourself. Your skeleton is the basis of your ability to move about, which sure beats being a spineless jellyfish. The skeleton features the spine, the passageway for raising the kundalini energy. *Bare bones* can be associated with meaning. They're what's left after all else is gone. Bones also come first, since bone cells are the first to develop in the fetus.

▶ Do you think immaculate conception is possible?

Nature is One Being that produces males and females and everything else at will. Exceptions to the rules are part of the whole paraphernalia of reproduction. Never in my wildest dreams would I say that anything is impossible. Even though science doesn't like the idea of immaculate conception, I wouldn't kick it out because I take a broad view of Nature's capabilities. Parthenogenesis (virgin birth) happens with insects all the time and it's been observed lately in lizards of the Southwest.

▶ **Speaking of the magic of nature, Paul Case says in his chapter on Key 13 that subconscious response to new patterns of thought will transform cellular consciousness in the body.**

That's the power of suggestion that's taught in the Strength Key. Thought has an immediate effect upon all the cells in the body. Today we are aware of the physical world in a way that was completely unknown to medieval people in general. We don't *suppose*; we *know* that the body is a manifestation of radiant energy. This is not "just metaphysics." This is the truth, the way it is. Cells are composed of atoms, and the structure of the cell is similar to that of the atom. The cell has a nucleus and a periphery, and we know it is electrical in nature. The thought that is characteristic of the cell determines what the cell is going to be like.

▶ **What do you mean, "the thought that is characteristic of the cell"?**

From an occult point of view, mind is constructive; it winds up in a physical phenomenon. In its own nature, mind is quite different, not at all physical. You might say it's a vibraton, but it's not even a vibration, really. It's a *nothing* as far as science is concerned. For lack of a better word, it's usually described as an *idea*. An idea doesn't have any material basis at all, yet we *seem* to think in physical terms. The mind has a formative power that is unlike anything we deal with in physics or chemistry. Atoms could be considered thoughts. The nature of mind underlies cellular structure. If the structure is a human body, the thought that's energizing that structure has an immediate effect upon it.

▶ **Jason, is there such a thing as a "bad seed"? I'm asking because I work with disturbed children.**

You are talking about something that is strictly a social problem. From a larger point of view, these children are just different, not really disturbed at all. They *do* disturb *us* but they are not disturbed by themselves. Now, whether we like it or not, in the grand scheme of nature the seed that's malformed rarely does well. If idiots and imbeciles were left free to run around without society to look after them, they would die. So the problem is in how society thinks, not in nature itself.

▶ Our society tries to ignore death.

We are abysmally ignorant about the subject of death. Yet the more we think about it, the easier it becomes to handle the whole situation. The Cabalist teachings always equate birth and death. This is the key to the puzzle. You've died nineteen thousand times already but never thought about it. You've been half dead all your life during sleep, yet somehow you've revived, regularly.

Death is like going to sleep. When you go to bed at night, you never know whether you're going to wake up in the morning or not. That little prayer, "If I should die before I wake, I pray the Lord my soul to take," makes sense. You get used to the idea of becoming *totally unconscious* during sleep. If you didn't have some degree of faith that you were going to wake up in the morning, you'd be in a condition of terror when you went to bed. The dramatist would say, "Do anything! Pound on me! Stick pins in me! But don't let me go to sleep—I gotta live! I gotta live!" But we say, "Oh, forget it," which is wisdom.

You see, underneath the superficial information that we live by, there's an instinctive knowledge of what's really going on. When we go to bed at night, we know inwardly that it isn't a matter of supreme importance whether we wake up in the morning or not. We know that it's all okay somewhere inside of ourselves. This truth about our Self is something we're trying to contact, trying to know in a conscious way.

Poets like to write, "When I go into that great deep, that's it. I'm finished, done for." This simply means that they have not made a profound study of the matter. It's sensational to talk about the awesomeness of death, but this won't do for the occultist. A person who won't *investigate* what is going on is not capable of understanding it. Fortunately, we are investigators.

Whereas the West is not particularly psychologically oriented (although we're getting interested in it now), the East is another story entirely. The renowned "wisdom of the East" is the wisdom of the psyche. People everywhere in the East believe in reincarnation. They've spent *ages* studying and investigating it and have been meticulous about it. It's not a romantic proposition. In India the government will actually spend money to verify whether, for instance, a child remembers a lifetime in another locality. They have amassed tremendous amounts of evidence that we are free to look at. We don't have to accept their conclusions, but we should at least consider them.

As a youngster I studied hypnotism, in which there seemed to be a dissociation between the soul and the body. Surgical operations may be performed painlessly under hypnosis, but it's not used much because the process is too slow; it's easier to give you a jab with a needle. I asked myself, "Is there such a thing as a soul?" I looked into psychic phenomena, life after death, and so forth. I didn't have wild psychic experiences myself, but I decided that those who did were not lying. I learned that we can function in the mind apart from the body. After much exploration I felt it would be ridiculous to conclude that there was no astral body.

Then I got interested in the Tarot and the Cabala specifically. It became clear to me that there's a lot more going on than we have any idea of. When I asked, "What kind of a place am I living in, anyway?" the answer was, *a very magical place*. Now that I'm facing possible transition any moment, I have a great deal of respect for the incomprehensible Power that creates and sustains the universe.

Please *dig* into this. The truth makes your faith strong. The Cabala does not ask you to just repeat some beliefs. It wants you to see for yourself. With the help of God you take over at a certain stage and pursue your own awareness. As the dean of the philosophy department at Columbia University used to say, *"Look* until you *see."*

The subject of death offers a lot to look into. You might say that your lives are like the grass that the skeleton reaps. The fruit of all your lives is an integral part of your Self and remains in your Self. This makes it possible to evolve, so that you never go back, you never regress. Since the universe is infinitely large, you may expect a limitless supply of experiences.

▶ There are people who believe that reincarnation is something to avoid.

That idea is not in the spirit of the Cabala, which states that this level is the ultimate expression of all your powers and faculties. There's nothing wrong with the physical life, but it's completely misunderstood by the average person. This state has *more possibilities* than any other level. In Cabalistic philosophy, the physical world is the climax of all the efforts of the inner world. As total manifestation, it's the glory of God. The earth plane is the gift of God and that makes it holy. Don't forget that the body is basically made out of *light*. Light, as you know, is both a particle and a wave—a paradox. It's fascinating to think of your incarnation in these terms.

▶ **Do you think someone could be contacted in the spirit world even after they've reincarnated?**

I don't know whether this is a contradiction in terms or not. The teaching is that we never leave the spirit world. We just *think* we do. Tonight we've been looking at the fact that the mind, the consciousness, can be dissociated from the body. *Consciousness is not the body*. It is The Knower *in* the body. Once the mind becomes involved in everything that's going on in the world, it loses sight of its own Selfhood. The mind becomes attached at birth to the qualities of the vehicle. Then it *assumes* it *is* the vehicle, which is like believing you are the automobile that you happen to be driving.

According to the occult teaching, the Self has three aspects. It has the aspect of unity as well as a discriminating aspect and a mental aspect. In the Hindu philosophy these are called ATMA, BUDDHI, and MANAS. This eternal triad is represented on the Tree of Life by Kether, Chokmah, and Binah. It is said there is a gulf between these three and all the rest. This gulf is the abyss in Key 0. It symbolizes the fact that the True Self in ourselves is always Itself. It can come down here and be a human being; it can be anything, anywhere, but the Being *inside*—that never changes.

We have inner experiences all the time but nobody calls them that. For instance, think of the exaltation you experience when you hear a favorite piece of music. Thanks to evolution, now there's a whole generation of people who are interested in the inner life. They will persist like a dog with a bone until they get the answer. They are suspicious of leadership and of outworn, useless ideas. That's the end of the Piscean Age right there, the end of the status quo. It's not the end of *life*. Actually it's the *beginning* of something halfway decent. Because Pisces rules the feet, the foot in this picture symbolizes this time of entrance into a new age. As it says in the song, "This is the dawning of the Age of Aquarius."

The scythe in Key 13 is our tool for getting rid of old illusions. The T-shape of its handle suggests the Saturn principle of elimination. Everybody here has some pet notion that they don't want to give up, so we really need this scythe. Sometimes it's the idea of *living* this lifetime that people hang on to.

▶ **What's the difference between elimination by the sword in Key 11 (Justice) and the scythe in Key 13?**

Key 11 is technical and measuring. There the Divine Mother maintains a balance in the body through the process of metabolism. In Key 13 the fertile imagination is inspired by the Self to make sweeping changes. If you are to be renewed, the old stuff just has to go. The changes are wonderful and exciting because transformation lifts us up; it does not bring us down.

Look at the field of ecology. When I was in college, no one had ever heard of it. The point of view at that time was ruinous for the world, and didn't care at all about the next generation. It was strictly for itself. Our generation says that this is untenable and we're not going to put up with it anymore. Big Business doesn't like it, but the ideas of youth are entering into many different areas and won't be stopped.

When you want to make changes, you have to be knowledgeable in your specialty. Our main specialty here is finding out what a human being really is. In other words, we are trying to identify ourselves. This particular philosophy emphasizes that the human being is a divine creation hardly understood. Now, you can take a diamond and throw it into a fireplace and turn it into carbon dioxide very quickly. By the same token, you can take a perfectly glorious human being and under certain situations you can make a mess out of him too. We want a deep understanding of what a person really is, so that we can be helpful in the process of humanity's awakening to itself.

▶ **We need to be able to see the God in people.**

Quite true, and while we are identifying ourselves, we need a better identification of God, as well. Based upon history, we have a limited, outworn concept of God. We have to come up with a more satisfactory God-idea all over the world, a rock-bottom concept that we can all agree upon. This will be a most interesting process for humanity.

▶ What part will the Imaginative Intelligence play in this process?

The imagination of Life Itself dreams up things like bodies and powers and faculties and so forth. We are familiar with these because they are all enumerated in the Tarot. Our *own* imagination is something that we can exercise independently. We can use it to make refinements in our basic equipment. Nature does things automatically, but if Man interferes, then things can be changed. The world of imagination solidifies around us all the time. When we are in harmony with what Life wants to do, then the forms around us are satisfactory—including our concept of God.

▶ What's the difference between imagination and intuition?

Imagination is manipulation of existing data. Active imagination is an act of will. Intuition can't be willed. You can dwell on a problem for a long time, but only if you are lucky will you get an intuition, an inspiration.

▶ Why is the number thirteen associated with bad luck?

Since thirteen is the number of Death, it looks bad from the outer point of view. In the Cabala, which presents the inner viewpoint, thirteen is the number of love and unity. The Hebrew words AHEBA (love) and ACHAD (unity) each total thirteen when you add the values of their letters. Thirteen follows twelve, the number given to the Key of Reversal, and its meaning reverses from the outer to the inner. If we look at Death in the conventional sense, we miss the inner meaning.

▶ I'd like to hear about our "dearly beloved, late lamented brother," Paul Case.

Paul retired from this plane in 1954. He was a charming, warm, and modest man. As far as the tradition is concerned, he was Arthur Edward Waite's successor. Crucial information is always preserved. The function of those who have the knowledge is to pass it on. It used to be conveyed from mouth to ear but now it can be told in print.

Paul started out as an orchestra conductor. That's how he made his living. Then he got the word that he should spend some time on the Tarot and the Cabala—the rest of his life. So he did. And he became a world-recognized authority on the subject. He edited the highly respected *Azoth* magazine. He was the first Prolocutor General of the Order of the Golden Dawn in America. Then he founded the School of Ageless Wisdom in Boston. Finally he established the Builders of the Adytum (B.O.T.A.), an educational institution in Los Angeles.

Until recently, not many people were interested in either the Tarot or the Cabala. When I met Paul in 1937 he had already been in it for over thirty years. To the outer view Tarot was a kind of side show back in those days, so Paul Case was a pioneer in America in this field. His powerful writings are a legacy for us. His researches connecting Tarot with Cabala demonstrated convincingly the role of the cards in preserving the Ancient Wisdom of the West.

▶ How does Death relate to the next Key, Temperance?

Death is the overture to the Path. Key 14 is the first Major Arcanum to actually show us the Path. Temperance says symbolically that there is a *guide* in these important inner matters. You can't succeed on the Path without help. That's the teaching. It's a puzzling affair, but you won't get far off the track if you stick with this angelic being, representative of your own Higher Self. You will never be lonely if you understand the symbolism of Key 14 and avail yourself of the services of your Guide.

I hope that all of us pilgrims on the Path will have a good week. Thanks for coming tonight.

KEY 14

CHAPTER 14

TEMPERANCE

THE PATH OF LIBERATION is a matter of choice and a matter of taste. Nobody's going to drag you onto the Path. Fortunately, if you are *inclined* to travel the ancient Way of Return, the good Lord provides an inner guide to whom you may apply for assistance. Key 14 symbolizes the principle of guidance. It states that, as you traverse the Path, you will have the company of your Inner Self. It faileth never. It's comforting to know this, because you *surely need a guide* on the Path.

Angels are not new to us in the Tarot. In Key 6 (The Lovers) we met Raphael. Tonight we will get to know the Archangel Michael, who represents your Innermost Self. It's impossible to lose your Innermost Self. Just remember that you have it, so you can turn to it any time you wish. You can commune with the Inner Self whenever you feel lonely. It's there all the time, twenty-four hours a day, unceasingly, in the middle of the night, in the middle of the day, in all your affairs, good, bad, and indifferent—*it's there*. It's a *reality*. That's the main message of the fourteenth Key.

On the Tree of Life, the path of Temperance goes right up the middle pillar and resolves itself into The High Priestess, which joins Kether, the Yekhidah or One Self at the top. The High Priestess represents the basic characteristic of mind, which is memory. We are told over and over again in this work that success depends upon remembering your Self. The effort here is to remember who you are *truly*, which goes beyond the ordinary into the extraordinary. To remember yourself in Cabalistic terms is to relate yourself to Life Itself. That's a large order. That function is presided over by memory, which leads to your perception of yourself in the unity of Life. The Tree shows that Temperance is very much a part of this procedure.

They say in the East that the Path is without moving. If you think of the Path as being in your mind, it makes this statement understandable. The problem on the bottom level of mind is all the race-thought, conditioning, and automatic phenomena that occur regularly every day—a murky proposition. On that level the mind is not critical. It just reacts in the old stimulus/response routine. There's no deliberation, no thought. When you react immediately without considering what's going on, you're unconscious.

Present company is always excepted, of course. We're talking in broad terms about the general public. Most people have an immediate, *voluble* response to anything that appears on the scene. You may have seen the Steinberg cartoons in which he draws people's ridiculous pronouncements in a monumental, architectural fashion. Enormous, meaningless things issue from the mouths of his characters. He's pointing out the funny side of unthinking response.

As we become more analytical and discriminating, we don't react in the same way. Eventually we get to the point at which we look at the phenomenal world as a philosopher would. This doesn't mean that we withdraw ourselves from the world. You can be in it as much as you please, in a *conscious* way. Because you have been educated, you act in a more skillful fashion, and this improves the condition of your life.

As we proceed inward, the mind becomes brighter and brighter. The two mountain peaks in this Key stand for Wisdom and Understanding, Chokmah and Binah on the Tree of Life. As you know, wisdom and understanding are *mental achievements*. The shining crown in the picture illustrates Kether, the light at the end of the tunnel. We become more human—more alive, sentient, responsible—as we advance up the Path. When we become completely human, we are glorious indeed. You won't hear this generally, but one of the things you'll get here if you're persistent enough, is an idea of your own *glory*. That's not a compliment. It simply states what is held to be true about all of us in the philosophy of the Cabala.

We have to try everything to see what is true, so Temperance is a Key of experimentation and VERIFICATION. This is the Intelligence of Probation or Trial, which invites us to participate in the great experiment of ourselves. Trial and error is not a dull trip. That's for sure.

The gorgeous Rainbow of Promise is placed in this Key for our eternal encouragement. As you'll remember from the story of Noah and the ark, it's the sign of the covenant between God and Man. In spite of Noah's problems with his personality (drunkenness), the Lord made a pact with him. As a symbol of this pact the rainbow represents a promise, a guarantee, from the Inner Self that you *will succeed* with the work that you have to do on yourself.

Of course, you won't succeed by your ordinary human efforts, but you will succeed with the help of the angel. You will traverse the Path, including whatever difficulties seem to be in the way as you go along. You can see in the Tableau that there are all sorts of interesting adventures ahead. The Devil and The Tower are coming right up in the next two Keys. So—welcome to the Path!

▶ **Do we get medals as we advance through the difficulties?**

Most people on the Path to God go through a phase where they think, "I'm gonna be a hero, a saint." Well, that's not the way it works. The way is so simple that it's difficult. I feel that to be yourself is the *most* difficult thing you can accomplish in this life. If you really believe in wisdom, you have to *live* wisdom. This has nothing to do with competition or comparison with other beings, nothing to do with egotism. You do not have to fight your way to God.

▶ **Isn't Michael the warrior angel?**

Yes, and the fight is against *ignorance*. Since we are ignorant about the Path, we can't proceed without a guide. The ego is not a guide. When the time comes for you to find out who you are, a Voice inside yourself will tell you who you are.

▶ **I don't mind the idea of a guide, but the idea of angels is hard for me to swallow.**

Just think of them as beings like yourself who exist on higher vibratory levels. It's interesting that all over the world, in occultism as well as in religion, there is always some talk about either angelic beings or gods. They usually operate in the unconscious; we don't normally see them fluttering around. Yet even though they are beyond the range of our outer senses, they are real in terms of the areas they administer. Occult doctrine says that the universe is efficiently run by Intelligences. We are generally not aware of this, so we think that we are the only ones who have any intelligence at all, which is a serious mistake. The angels you see in the Tarot are real beings who are busy as all get-out.

Michael is your mountaineering friend. He is a *part of yourself* who can teach you to fly, to leave the everyday and soar into higher realms.

This Key illustrates what the Cabala rather prettily calls "Conversation with the Holy Guardian Angel." This is just talking to ourselves, which everybody does all the time anyway. The Tarot is telling us that we can improve the quality of the communication.

▶ **Once I had a kind of vision of this angel. He was standing there holding out his hand, and I knew that I could go with him if I would give up my conditioning, but I wasn't ready to give it up.**

Well, we have to go one step at a time. We don't just jump over all the squares. That's what the Tarot is all about. It shows that this is a *procedure*, a *process*. That's why "the Path" is a good name for it. No path is straight, because everything is cyclic. As you progress, you have lots of adventures, and out of these experiences you get the material, the data, to make decisions. Ultimately, you *must* determine the course of your own life. There are plenty of people who will tell you how to live your life, but that's not living *your* life, is it? That's living the other guy's life, and we're not buying that here. We want to see each person lead the proper life for that person.

▶ **I guess you're ready to give up your own soap opera when you stop enjoying it.**

You never give up anything as long as you're happy with it. Until you're ready to try something else, until you feel dissatisfied, you'll stay put. The ubiquitous clam is happy being a clam and so it stays that way. Just know that when you *want* to change, you will have all the help you need.

In Key 14, your holy companion is wearing all the regalia of power. The Tetragrammaton is on his robe, the star of mastery is on his breast, and the solar emblem is on his brow. The name "Michael" means "Strength of God." He is the Angel of the Sun and he governs the direction south, where the sun reaches its zenith. His authority is summed up in the Yod-Heh-Vav-Heh that's embroidered on his robe. It's like a Jewish delicatessen that puts up the sign, "Kosher," so you know what it is. In this case the Name of God lets you know that this Being is definitely someone from on high. If you're religiously inclined, that should wake you up a little bit. If you're not religiously inclined, you can still grasp the idea of the overpowering strength of the solar aspect.

If you're historically inclined you probably know the enormous role of the sun in religion. In the old days, the priests and priestesses were the receptacles of knowledge and enlightenment, and of all the arts and sciences. It came to them through illumination, as a sacred trust. Their illumination, they believed, came to them from the sun itself. This is a powerful idea.

▶ Does the gold background in Key 14 stand for illumination?

Gold is the metal of the sun. Symbolically, gold represents the most valuable thing, the thing of great price. Its actual worth is not the point. The thing of great price is the sun, which corresponds to *light*, as you pointed out.

There's an old saying, "The Path that leadeth on is lighted by one fire, the light of daring burning in the heart." The zodiacal sign associated with Key 14 is Sagittarius the Archer, an idealistic, adventurous sign that rules religion, philosophy, and higher learning. The path of the arrow takes us from this room where we are now, right up to TIPHARETH at the center of the Tree of Life. The life of the separate ego is spent underneath Tiphareth. When we arrive at the center, the Sphere of the Sun, then our consciousness becomes identical with everyone else's and we are in a state of unity with all our fellow men and women. For Christians, this is the Christ, the central Ego of all humanity.

When we get to this stage of unfoldment, we have advanced beyond being fascinated by what's going on in ourselves and our own immediate environment. The Temperance card treats specifically of getting to this state of consciousness. The angel is going to assist us in a kind of *rebirth* that will take us once and for all out of the realm of the separate ego. This is a special kind of operation that's going to take place in ourselves, and we need all the help we can get. Since the help is already *inside*, we don't need to look outside for it. This is a great boon.

We can get a lot of instruction from books—I have a pile of them and you probably have a pile of them—but when it comes down to the subtleties of the Self, and to all that goes on in the life of the individual, there isn't any book that can sort this out for you. You have to turn consciously toward your highest aspect in order to get the correct answer. If you're not involved in the inner life, it would never occur to you to do this, but when you *do* turn within, you discover that you've got something in there that works like the Temperance angel. It will lead you all the way home.

▶ **What do you think about other types of inner guides?**

There are many kindly beings on the inner planes who are happy to help us, a tremendous layering of beings of all descriptions, just as in the outer world. They are real enough but they are of a more subtle substance. We must perceive them with our inner senses. We have a lot of learning to do on inner levels. If an inner guide presents itself, the traditional challenge is, "If you be of God, then stay." Apply your own best standards. Get another guide if it doesn't work. In the spirit of trial and error, why not verify this inner guide idea by trying it out?

▶ **Would you say that the angel guide has no sex or both sexes?**

It's described as an androgyne. It has both sexes because it represents unity. The Creative Whatever is not bound one way or the other, but expresses itself either way. You see this in nature.

The wise, including our noble master, Paul Case, explain that *each of us* has a masculine *and* a feminine aspect in the psyche. This might be a shock in the beginning but it makes sense when you think about it. Human beings have a feeling side that is Eros, and a reasoning side that is Logos. These two are supposed to be more or less balanced. There's nothing wrong with that!

▶ **I thought angels were not supposed to be of any sex.**

In the Cabala, *everything* has sex. It's loaded with it. To unscramble the philosophy of the Cabala, to understand the *dynamics* of what it's talking about, you have to see that polarities are at the root of everything. For example, when the elements in chemistry are joined, they actually *embrace* each other. It's like a sexual union. The Cabalists say that this is the correct way to look at it. Plus and minus are combining everywhere. They maintain a dynamic union throughout the universe. This can be explosive in chemistry and it can also be explosive with people. The point is that *forces* are involved, and they *act*. We're not playing with tinker-toys here. We're talking about the Real Thing.

The fire and water being manipulated in Key 14 symbolize the polarities as they are summed up in the Tree of Life. The torch would be Chokmah and the vase would be Binah. Our mentors say that the relationship between these two aspects is just about all you need to know. In Key 10 (The Wheel of Fortune) we saw that the lion represents the Archetypal World and the eagle symbolizes the Creative World. So this alchemical funny business going on here represents a modifying of the archetypal and an enlivening of the creative.

▶ Please translate that into practical terms.

You may have heard the business phrase, "pouring cold water on a deal." Someone gets enthusiastic about a deal, and then the controller comes along and points out very neatly that the whole thing is going to fall flat on its face in the first three months. That's the cold water treatment. On the other hand, there are people who are full of what you might call "negatrons," who can't get started because their imaginations dwell on negative possibilities. These people need to be fired up.

When you look at yourself at any given moment, you can always see these simple energy relationships at work. They never cease. When you get up in the morning, you can examine yourself: if you don't feel full of energy, you're sick and you can do something about it. Just as in static electricity a single charge can change the polarity of the whole, so in the morning you can charge yourself positively and say, "Now I'm ready to go." It's just like a bank account. If you've got one cent in the bank, you're okay. If you're one cent short then it's not okay. Your inner equilibrium works the same way. It's a delicate thing. That's why the Tarot gives plenty of instruction on how to charge yourself up, how to plug into the system and get your juices flowing so you can go on about your business. If you are depressed, you need fire, and if you are manic, you need water.

▶ Fire and water symbolism can also be seen in the red and blue of the angel's wings.

That's right. This picture tells us that the Higher Self has both aspects. Blue and red are the colors of Chesed and Geburah, so these qualities are what give the angel his flying power.

The balance between the polarities *in ourselves* is critical insofar as our health and well-being are concerned. Once someone explains it to you, it's not difficult to see that: "Now I'm being *this* way, and now I'm being *that* way." Anyone can do this who *wants* to do it. It's important because if you see what's going on in yourself, you can make the necessary correction. If your boat is shipping water, you can turn on the pump.

For inner equilibrium, we always turn to the other side of the equation on the Tree of Life if we're getting out of balance. For example, if we're stuck in trying to work everything out in a logical way, which would be the right side of the Tree, then we have to introduce the feeling elements that come from the left side. This is a completely different approach from anything that is taught in the schools or in exoteric religion. The Cabala says that there's another side to life besides just straight reason, and we'd better listen to it. Then of course if you've been living totally on the Eros side, a little reason wouldn't hurt, either.

When you're just in the soup, that's not intelligent, and if the Cabala preaches nothing else, it certainly tries to impress upon us that we should be intelligent about what's going on. It doesn't expect you to master the faculty of intelligence in a week or a month or a lifetime, but it says, "For goodness sake, *try* to be intelligent, because whatever success you have in this area will be a *boon* to you. It makes your whole life a lot easier."

It's interesting to note that all the fundamental ideas in the United States came from a small group of men who put their heads together. They were not sheep. Whether you like their ideas or not, they gave a wonderful demonstration of what a few individuals can accomplish with an awareness of history, and by *knowing* what they want. All that's being asked of us is to be intelligent about our wants, so we don't let some character soft-soap us into accepting something less than our true desire.

There are plenty of leaders who will get up and say, "This is the way to go! The Lord decrees, 'This way, this way!'" Then everybody says, "Yeah, yeah, let's go. Where do you want us to go?" This can lead you straight to Jonestown. That's being a sheep, and you're not supposed to be a sheep. What *you really want* always comes from your Innermost Self.

The willingness to go all-out makes you become what you want. Gandhi is a perfect example of a dedicated person who became his own ideal. Like him, we want to become involved in outer expression of the inner idea.

▶ **I'm interested in the concept of synergy, the third thing that is created when two things work together. What would be the Cabalistic equivalent with Chokmah and Binah?**

The cosmic Father and Mother create a baby we call the Universe. Or in terms of personal relations, the creation would be love. Love is not possible for either side by itself. The third thing is the *unifying* element.

There is really just One Thing going on all the time, but we look at it analytically to clarify certain areas. Actually, the creative impulse is inside Chokmah, which is inside Binah, so it is *One Being* we're talking about. The separation is an artificial one. It's like dissecting an animal body. You can take out all the parts to see what's in there, but it's not a living body.

The reason we go through all this analysis is so that we can peg what happens inside ourselves. If we have the tools for self-diagnosis, we won't need to go to an analyst. "What happened? Why do I feel so bad?" are questions a therapist *may* be able to answer, and maybe not.

▶ **It's a good thing we have inner help!**

The Path is no easy journey, as we all know. It's a tricky affair. It's hard to control our faculties and get everything working properly in a harmonious relationship. All the major world teachings agree that we can't succeed in this task without relying on our Inner Self. We are most fortunate to have this ever-dependable, constant companion. Although we are learned and powerful and so on, compared to the Universal Intelligence we don't amount to much. So we needn't be ashamed to ask for help. The more we depend on this guide, the better it works. Some very famous people have admitted that they had inner guides. Socrates is one example; Carl Jung is another.

Once you think about it, it's obvious that all our powers and faculties, our creativity and intelligence, and so on, are continually supported. It's not a conscious effort on our part. We don't get up in the morning and purposely energize all our faculties one by one. It's not like starting a car. Our faculties are already there and already turned on. This total, never-failing support of the Life Power is symbolized by SAMECH ס, the letter attributed to Key 14. Samech is a *tent peg*; in other words, a prop or foundation. This reminds us that we are never alone. We will never be without support.

It's not always easy to remember this, and the Tarot can help us. When we look at the cards they remind us of the principles of Ageless Wisdom. The sages' message for us is easily reviewed by means of the Keys. The Tarot is a device to help us understand and remember the deeper wisdom of the Cabala.

▶ **I don't understand the title, "Intelligence of Probation."**

In general, you can think of it as the Intelligence of Trial and Error. That's an honest and helpful statement on the part of the Tarot. Sure as shootin', if I'm a witness, the Path is trial and error. In a sense, my trials became easier as I went along. There are always trials, but with training you can make it. You sort of need training to deal with this whole business.

The word "probation" applies to a special initiatory Intelligence that guides aspirants who are emerging from the experiences of Keys 12 and 13. After death comes transfiguration. Only if we reach a certain point in our evolution are we going to be involved with this sort of subtle operation.

▶ The word "temperance" reminds me of the Women's Christian Temperance Union.

To temper simply means to regulate, to mix properly. We have discussed how the Inner Self regulates the cosmic forces within ourselves. In the WCTU, temperance is confused with abstinence. That's dangerous! Asceticism is unacceptable in the philosophy of the Cabala. From time to time we ask the question here, "If you were God, would you make yourself miserable?" Misery, frustration, and denial are not what life is all about.

The idea that we are made in the image of God is basic in the Cabala. It's all very well to accept this highfalutin' expression, but how do you apply it in everyday living? What are your rights in the universe? How can you operate? What is the law of the universe insofar as it's given to us to understand? If we don't know anything about our own psychology, we can be victims. The object of the game is not to be a victim or a loser, but to be successful and victorious.

▶ Do you abstain from abstinence?

Whether you should abstain or not abstain is entirely up to each individual. In this philosophy you are supposed to live your life according to your own lights, which are ample. Once you know that you have sufficient light within yourself, you'll do just fine. The Cabala suggests that we appreciate whatever is available to us for our own enlightenment, enjoyment, and fulfillment. It's there to *use*, not abuse.

You have to be patient about all this. You can't just sit down and say to someone, "Hey, Jack, I've got to catch a plane in half an hour, but I'd really like to hear about the Cabala. I want to know what it is and I want to be able to utilize it. So you've got thirty minutes—sock it to me." It isn't that kind of thing at all, because it has to do with *experience*.

You have to *live* it. In order to have any kind of *feeling* for it, you must literally put yourself into each and every one of the areas pictured in the Tarot; immerse yourself in them and see what happens.

This attitude is part of the practice of meditation. As the Hindu yogi Patanjali said, whatever you put your mind on, the nature of that thing is conveyed to you. So when you put your mind on these teachings, after awhile they begin to speak to you in terms of experience.

▶ So experimentation is in order.

Experimentation and verification are very much in order. *What* the experiment is going to be is something that will be divulged to you as you go along. There will be different experiments and each one will tell you something new. You have to go along with them. If you resist them, then that stops your progress. In other words, you have to be *willing to be led*, not by an outside force, but by your Self. When the time comes, your guardian angel will tell you *exactly* what to do. Fourteen reduces to five, the number of The Hierophant, who symbolizes intuition. Key 14 is a function of that faculty.

There's a tribe of Native Americans in the northeast who get a picture in their minds of where the fish are biting. That's where they go and that's where they find fish. They don't read the morning news and they don't get a Coast Guard report. They literally get it from inside themselves. The Knower in you knows everything. Even though *you* don't know it, *It* knows it. Sounds absurd, but that's exactly the way it is.

Paul Case had an expression that he used quite a bit as a kind of joke, but at the same time it was true: "Don't get too worked up about learning the Tarot and the Cabala. Don't worry, because you already know all about it!" That's hard for most people to grasp—that they have this kind of knowledge inside themselves.

In China it's called knowing the Tao. You can tell from within yourself which way the wind is blowing in your life, and whether you should or shouldn't do something. The more you make the superconscious factor work for you, the more interesting your life becomes. Not necessarily dramatic, but interesting. There may not be much for others to see outwardly, but it can be exciting *for you*.

▶ How do we know if we fail the test of the guardian angel?

There's no failure in the Cabala. There's only what is called "missing the mark." It's like the marksmanship of the Zen archers. They don't punish you if you happen to miss. They just put you back to work until you *don't* miss.

▶ **How do you know if you *pass* the test?**

When you wake up every morning and feel that *your life has meaning*, that's success. Ideally, your life should be like eight-track stereo, where many things are happening at once. In the art of living, you don't want to let the nice, juicy states of consciousness get away from you; you want to keep them all the time. Rather than sliding in and out, you want to keep them going all at once. This is why The Magician is sometimes pictured as a juggler. Inside, in your head and heart, you have to stay *awake* consciously all the time.

▶ **I hear about something called "going through the grades." What's that?**

The idea of stages or grades was popular in occult societies in the last century, and for a long time before that. There was a heavy emphasis on one-upmanship. Instead of saying, "You're doing a wonderful job, George, and you're just going to unfold like a flower," they would say, "It's uphill all the way, so don't expect anything but that." This is not true and yet it was promulgated for a long time. This approach was useful to the people who dished out this baloney because it gave them a handle on the other fellow. You can't control people if you tell them, "Look, you're a perfected being already." But if you've got someone going through the grades, whether it's the Army or the Masons or anything else, you've *got* the person, don't you see? You can say, "If you want to advance, you'd better do this and that, otherwise you're not going to make it."

▶ **Why does the angel have one foot in water and one on land?**

The pool stands for Yesod, the Sphere of the Moon on the Tree of Life. We know that in occult science, water symbolizes mind, the foundation of all. This pool sums up the whole marvelous procedure of life renewing and reproducing itself. Michael's right foot is in this life-sustaining aspect, and his left foot is on the stabilizing aspect. The earth plane is the outer world in which you can reap experience. For a well-rounded existence, you might say we should have one foot in heaven and the other on earth. We are told not to neglect either side of the mind/matter equation.

The concepts of mind and matter cover everything we know. Then, in the Cabala there is *something else*, which we *don't* know anything about, and yet we deal with it anyway. That's the creative aspect, the "Mysterious Mo" that's hidden in the equation. As far as mind and matter go, we can deal with that. We can see mind in ourselves, and of course we're familiar with the material aspect.

The physical world actually glorifies God. I preach this regularly. Cabalists see *into* the physical life. Ensouled by the spirit, it's very beautiful. Uneducated, uninitiated people only see the outer aspect. They are taken in by the facade and don't look behind it. They don't see the beauty and the magnificence of the structure. Actually it's fantastic. It's a wonder. Anything is a wonder if you have the eyes to see it.

► The "Mysterious Mo" is Chokmah, right?

That's correct. You might think that wisdom is just knowing everything in the book, but really it's a *living* thing that's hard to describe. As Lao Tzu said, if you *can* describe it in words, then that's not it. Wisdom is the first emanation from the Crown at the top of the Tree, and when you're talking about the Creative, about the Tao or God's Will, you're not talking about logical things *at all*. Kether comes out of the Ain Suph Aur, which is like saying it comes out of nothing.

On Binah's side of the Tree, everything is neat and tidy. She's the Queen of the Universe in no uncertain terms. Once the Creative reaches the conceptual level in Binah, it's locked in and proceeds just like clockwork. From there you can see divine order all the way down the Tree.

We are just like Binah. In ourselves we depend upon inspiration and intuition. The thing that brings the conception about is something we don't control. As far as the initial blast of energy is concerned, we can't unscramble that one. That comes from the Infinite. In terms of what we think of as order, it would be chaos by comparison, because of the infinite ways of which it is capable. For all practical purposes it is indefinable. It comes out of a black hole and energizes the whole Tree of Life by causing conception in Binah. Then hers is the face of God that's turned to us, the face we can see and understand.

► Jason, would you explain the connection between the three Keys in the last column of the Tableau?

In Key 7 (The Chariot) there is an analysis of the desire-nature, which is a black-and-white, yes-or-no proposition. In Key 14 there is a *mixing* of the polarities. Finally, in Key 21 (The World), they are *blended*. They become One in the World Dancer. So there's quite a story going on in the last column.

Next week we will begin on the bottom row of cards in the Tableau. These last seven Keys represent a summation of life experience. The Path is not some kind of wizardry or something apart from life. The Path is Life Itself. Its culmination in Key 21 results in a complete change of consciousness and character.

Key 15 (The Devil) begins the process that will lead us to that total success. The Temperance angel appears in his guise as The Devil. You've heard of Lucifer the Light-Bringer. He's like the doctor who says, "You're drinking too much, you weigh too much, you've got to stop smoking, etc." He's a light-bringer all right, but he's not very popular. You might want to say, "I think I'll go to another doctor, one who will tell me to drink more and eat more." In problem situations, the Cabala says you are dealing with the Adversary.

In this friendly Key, the people involved are not unhappy. They're in Las Vegas or Reno, and they're not complaining. The only trouble is, you can't keep up this sort of thing. The Devil always had a pitchfork in the old days, and in the cartoons it was applied where it would do the most good. In the Tarot, the pitchfork is actually the ox-goad of Lamed, from Key 11 (Justice). This is the *prod*. You know the old tune, "Ya gotta get up, ya gotta get up, ya gotta get up in the morrrning!" That's what The Devil is all about.

A sense of humor is essential to an understanding of Key 15. Mirth is the function of consciousness attributed to The Devil in the Tarot. In his remarks on this Key, Paul Case says that the priests in ancient Egypt used to get up in the morning and "wash their hearts with laughter."

Thanks very much for coming. I hope you will have sun and laughter with your morning meditations this week.

KEY 15

CHAPTER 15

THE DEVIL

The Devil is humanity's favorite excuse for all the evils in the world. According to Cabalistic doctrine there is no such thing as a Devil. Yet somebody *says* there is a Devil. Now why would anyone say something as nasty as that? There are demons in all religions. Devil-talk is a popular pastime in shamanism and the priestcraft. This fabrication of words works very well to control an unruly tribe through fear.

Our job is to overcome this utterance, to liberate ourselves from this ghastly spell of words. Discrimination in speech is one very real aspect of liberation. We should not accept speech as having any validity whatsoever until it has been examined.

You might say, "Don't tell me there's no evil in the world. Look at him and them and them!" To be sure, they oppose you because you don't happen to be on their side. You came here as a perfectly crystal-clear-minded babe, and right away all the old influences began to act on you. Soon you acquired a whole headful of dualistic judgments about "right and wrong" in the world and in yourself. This is not an easy situation to overcome, but you can do it if you understand that men and women created this myth, and that you're the victim of it.

Anything that opposes our personal will is a Devil to us, no matter what form it takes. Key 15 pictures our Innermost Self in its guise as the Adversary. It will chafe us every time we try to do something incorrect. This is galling to us because we think we know all the answers. Anything that challenges our intelligence is anathema, so we hate and detest this dark angel.

The main Cabalistic teaching in connection with The Devil Key is that nothing in the universe is inimical to Man. I use the term "Man" generically, meaning all of us. The Adversary is our *best friend*, since it helps us to evolve. Our Inner Self keeps bothering us because it is determined to free us of illusion and delusion.

The Adversary is much more than conscience. Conscience is a learned thing, but this is an inner, evolutionary urge going on in all of us. It simply will not give up until we become illuminated. Tradition states that the last row of Keys in the Tarot Tableau pictures the seven stages of spiritual unfoldment. Key 15 is the first stage. The Path is full of difficulties at the beginning. We must recognize that we are in BONDAGE and that we need liberation. According to the occult teaching, the average person is living in a state of almost total unconsciousness. Unless they are instructed, people base their entire lives on what they see outside themselves, with no inner life to speak of.

Buddhism, the third largest religion in the world today, is preaching forty-eight hours a day that the main problem is world illusion. As a practicing occultist I have a profound respect for the Buddhist psychology, which I think is second to none. However, the Cabalists feel that it's not just a matter of getting out of the world illusion. It's also a matter of discovering *what it's all about*. The goal of the Cabalists is to find out as much as possible about Reality, which of course includes stripping down the illusions to get to the *facts* of the matter. Appearances are deceptive and misleading. For the sake of our individual spiritual evolution, we simply *must* progress beyond accepting everything we see.

The Devil's open hand, on which is imprinted the glyph of Saturn, is saying symbolically, "What you see is all there is." This is in contrast to the gesture of esotericism made by The Hierophant. Key 15 is telling us that if we insist on believing in *appearances only*, we're going to be in serious trouble. We'll have to be hit over the head with a baseball bat, which occurs in the following Key, The Tower. The "bat" happens to be the principles of the Cabala, which come as a great surprise to anyone who is locked into the general view of the world.

Astrologically, the fifteenth Key represents Capricorn, the sign ruled by Saturn. Saturn itself is Key 21 (The World), the seventh and final stage of emancipation. The Tarot is saying that the entire Path of Return, from bondage to freedom, begins and ends with Saturn. The power that seems to limit us is the same power that liberates us. The Devil's pitchfork is not shown in the picture, but we know he's got one, since we feel it. Saturn is that good old goad that keeps us on the right track. It is the very loving, wise power of our Innermost Self working to keep us from making ourselves ridiculous. This is a difficult and trying task, somewhat like teaching a goldfish to sing. It takes years and years of patient training and communication to make us see the light—which obviously isn't in this Key but is coming next week.

Not being God, I can't answer the question, "Why aren't we born knowing that we're made true and perfect in the first place?" Our teachers say it all begins with the ego. We save some money and buy a few things; we get bigger and fatter and stronger, and eventually we say, "What a big boy am I!" Then Life says, "Wait a minute. How big are you? Are you a hundred miles high? Do you own the world? Suppose you didn't draw your next breath; where would you be then?" You never think about your life-support system when you're a Big Fella. The unthinking person is very vulnerable. When he comes to Key 16—*crash!*

Life supports *all* of us, regardless of what we're up to. If it didn't, of course that would be the end of us. This means that it is really God who is causing all the trouble in the world. As it says in *Isaiah* 45:7, "I make peace, and create evil: I the Lord do all these things." The author of the piece is God, and The Devil is a *blind* for God. The giveaway in Tarot symbolism is The Devil's white beard and pentagram. White is always a reference to the One Self on the Tree of Life. The pentagram is reversed, meaning that the Devil is God looked at in an inverted way, *but still God.*

A lot of people are afraid of God. There is a fearsome aspect of the All-Power that has been promulgated for a long time, but we don't *have* to think of God as a sort of great big thing out there just waiting to clobber us. In line with the Cabalistic view, we may rather think of God as our Father and Mother, the Source of ourselves and everything that's going on.

▶ **It's hard not to believe in the Devil when everyone around me does.**

Explain to your good friends (those who want an explanation, otherwise it's a waste of time) that they are under the spell of words. It's an hypnotic state, and we are the sleeping princesses in a fairy tale. Until we go through a convulsive sort of inner revolution, we are in the grip of an idea.

Ignorance exists, and inertia, and an unwillingness to proceed. But in this philosophy The Devil only exists as a *disguise* of your Innermost

Self. It's reminiscent of those devilish Japanese theatrical images that are made *for fun*—which brings us to the fact that the function of consciousness attributed to this Key is mirth. According to the Cabala, The Devil is a joke.

We tend to think of limitation as adversity, but our actual needs are one thing and our fancied needs are something else. We can get caught up in this very easily, especially with Madison Avenue working overtime. As Americans, our karma is that we are materialists.

The letter AYIN ע is the *eye*. It asks you to look more deeply. Don't judge by appearances. If you see into things, you will find, to your amusement, that many things you thought were a certain way, turn out to be quite different. This is true for everybody.

One time, back in New York, a study group presented the Tarot to a child, and recorded his reaction to each one of the Keys. When they got to Key 15 the child said, "Oh, that's a funny-bunny." He recognized right away that this was a put-on, an oddity.

▶ I don't see anything funny in this picture.

The funny part of the picture is that some people think this is true. If you *think* that there is a Devil at your heels, there *is* a Devil at your heels, but you have created it yourself.

If there were no Devil, Billy Graham wouldn't have anything to talk about. He makes a great profit by telling everybody about it, how he has seen it in the kitchen and so forth. And you'd better look out, because the Devil is after you! He's going to use every possible means to make you sin. Then he's going to grab you and take you down to hell and keep you there forever and ever, and burn you and freeze you and stick you with forks. The only way you can get rid of him is to go up there and have Billy give you the old hocus-pocus, right?

Key 15 is a caricature of Key 6, The Lovers. Fifteen reduces to six. These Keys are opposite sides of the same thing. The Lovers Key is associated with discrimination, and the Bondage Key shows what happens when we don't discriminate. The Devil card is a *cartoon* of life, rather than life itself.

I'm told that I'm a triple or quadruple Capricorn, or something like that, so this is my home ground, my ballpark. The mirthful side of this Key has always appealed to me. When you study the Cabala or Zen or whatever you're into, the incongruities of the outer levels of appearance become apparent, and you can laugh. Most of what you consider terrible obstacles in yourself are illusions. Once you get to a certain point with yourself, the illusions become funny.

Mirth brings a sense of proportion into things. Will Rogers was a popular comedian who proved that you can always laugh at politics. He got all his material from the daily newspaper. He was a very witty, brave man.

If you read widely and experience life fully, you will come to the conclusion that God has a sense of humor. In order to succeed in any of the inner disciplines it's essential that *you* have a sense of humor, especially about yourself. When you take your personality too seriously—the Great Me—then your goose is cooked. If you grasp the fact that you share human frailty, you're not likely to become too involved in the ego trip.

▶ **The ego is the real Devil.**

From an occult point of view, your observation is entirely correct. In *Psychology and Alchemy*, Carl Jung describes the Devil as the unregenerate intellect, which is another way of saying the same thing. Key 15 is the Renewing Intelligence. People need renewing when they can look at the universe and say, "Gee, look at them stars up there . . . real pretty . . . uh . . . I think I'll have another beer." The *idea* of the universe doesn't appeal to them, the fact that it has some history, that it's an *order*. "Yeah, well, it hasn't fallen down yet. I guess it'll be there in the morning." This is the real Archie Bunker approach. Don't laugh; there's plenty of it.

▶ **What's the difference between egotism and loving yourself?**

Self-love is the simple appreciation of yourself as a work of the art of God. Apprehend with wonder your dog, your cat, yourself, and all other people. Egotism has no philosophy and doesn't consider the miraculous qualities inherent in all Life.

It was St. Paul who said, "Be ye transformed by the renewing of your mind." The glyph of Mercury on The Devil's navel indicates that he-she-it is an intellectual concept born in the mind. Through the power of imagination, our own intellect produces this phenomenally funny character. Bondage is an unnecessary and nonsensical part of our mental programming. It is sometimes called race-thought. The Adversary inspires us to go inside and sift out truth from illusion. In the process, our minds become enlightened.

▶ **In reading a layout of the cards, Key 15 sometimes represents a state of frustration and dissatisfaction, when you don't know what you want out of life.**

That's hell, isn't it? There's only one Reality. It's the way we look at it that makes a heaven or a hell. Our *attitude* determines what we see. In psychology this is called projection. From within yourself, you project onto the scene of life a certain emotional content—plus or minus, good or bad, whatever. Beauty is in the eye of the beholder and so is evil. If you tell yourself The Devil is in charge, you have projected that on the "movie screen" of life. You could take a more reasonable view. You could say that Reality is, was, and will be—and the best thing that you can do is to try to find out something about it.

Look at the path of Ayin, the eye, connecting Beauty and Splendor on the Tree of Life. We know that there is something mysterious and wonderful here because this is the twenty-sixth path, and twenty-six is the number of Yod-Heh-Vav-Heh, the Name of God. This eye is like yang, the masculine principle in Chinese philosophy. It's The Emperor's power to *envision*. When vision is used negatively, it's a snare and a delusion. When used creatively, the eye is the very means of producing the splendor that is rooted in the vision of beauty.

We don't know enough to make judgments about life but we have all the equipment we need to make an analysis, to learn, to understand, and to become wise. Then the phantasms that exist in our heads will disappear and the clarity of our creative essence will shine through. That's what the Tarot promises, anyway. The Tarot can be used as an extremely critical instrument. To think deeply about what is going on is a great advantage.

We're in a dangerous situation when we don't think, because we have this capability and we're supposed to exercise it *mightily*. We *need* to exercise it! Never mind the fancy occultism. Just ask, "How come? What's really going on? What's it all about?"

The Devil was superimposed on Pan, the goat-footed nature god. Pan means "The All." Nature is The All. Nature is exactly what it is, and you may be assured that it doesn't give a hoot what you or I think about it. *It just is.* We have to be willing to look at what is, and not come along with some fanciful notion about God and Satan. When you can say, "This is the way things are whether I like it or not," then it will explain itself to you. As a *student* of nature you can see things firsthand.

"Nature in the raw is seldom mild." That was a slogan on cigarettes in the old days. We're very much part of nature. If you think you are one thing and this ugly brute of a nature is something else, then it's easy for it to surprise you and grab you, because in your mind you are separate from the Reality you are actually part of. We all have natural propensities, do we not? They are supposed to be alive and well in us. They can also get out of hand. If we want to *think* of them as evil, we can *call* them evil. In fact, we can say they are the work of the Devil. We can say anything we please.

During the nineteenth century no one accepted the fact that we are living in an animal, and this led to long novels full of people who were anguished about having instincts. The Tarot says that we have a menagerie in our makeup. The sacred animals in Keys 10 (The Wheel) and 21 (The World) are an indication of this. You've got a lion, an eagle, and a bull inside, and somewhere in there is a human. It's like panning for gold. If you're patient and careful, you'll find the honest-to-God human being inside. Keep shaking the pan and eventually a fine line of gold will appear on the rim. That's your truth.

The Devil's half-cube represents a partly understood reality. It's a half-baked notion of what's going on. The whole cube in Keys 2, 4, and 7 (High Priestess, Emperor, and Chariot) represents what is *really* going on. The people in Key 15 are chained to a miscalculation; they are the slaves of illusion. But you will notice—and this is one of the fun things—their chains could be lifted off easily if they *cared* to free themselves. Their bondage is voluntary. They actually like this situation. They're getting by, so why should they do anything that involves effort? That's why the following Key (The Tower) is necessary.

▶ **What is illusion?**

Technically, in this system, illusion means thinking "this" is "that." It's being completely mistaken. If you think this is that, you're making one heck of a big mistake. It's like saying square is round. The people in Key 15 don't think. They just go along with the lie that everything is okay. Everything is *not* okay in Key 15.

To get the chains off, you have to *want* to get them off. Freedom can only be attained by *self*-liberation. Once the chains are off, the option is yours. It's okay to *act* attached, providing you know what you're doing.

▶ **What did you mean earlier when you said that nature can grab you?**

Let me give you a couple of examples. I was once thrown bodily out of the Connecticut DMV office by two highway patrolmen, landing on my face in the gravel. I was so angry at that moment that I wanted to kill. It was lucky I didn't have a gun because I would have shot somebody. That incident showed me that there's a murderer inside me.

Jung predicted the Second World War. He could see that society was whitewashing itself and repressing its dark side. So then the instinctual nature came roaring out and swept everybody away. In that instance there were guns aplenty, which resulted in a horrendous bloodbath.

Nature is a mighty proposition. The only thing to do with a mighty proposition is to come to terms with it, to understand it. That means effort. You have to *study* nature, especially your *own* nature, to find any peace in yourself at all. You can't just forget about it, because sometime you're going to find yourself face to face with nature, and if you're unprepared it's like having no insurance. When you're suddenly faced with yourself, that's what is called meeting "the Dweller on the Threshold." It's seeing yourself as you really are, for the first time.

▶ **The Self unexpected is the Dweller on the Threshold?**

Exactly. This happens more consciously when you are on the Path. When you make certain inquiries about yourself, what you see first of all is darkness, the unknown. When you're trying to find answers and you look into darkness, it does anything but lift your spirits. Then the next thing you discover when you look into yourself is all the accusations the world has made against you in the course of your lifetime. That doesn't improve the situation, either. What you are seeing is The Devil as the personification of guilt.

You are not born with guilt feelings, but they get laid on, just like somebody building a wall, layer after layer of bricks, until you're all walled in. So here you are, going into a dismal area of yourself that is *absolutely unknown* to you. You are the *total explorer* going into a black cave. Jung describes the fear that everybody experiences when they come up against the unknown. To most people, the mind is an especially terrifying mystery.

▶ **Jung said that your Shadow consists of the things you don't like about yourself.**

And why don't you like certain things about yourself?

▶ **Because they are bad or wrong.**

Why do you think that?

▶ **Hmm. Because somebody said so.**

Yes. People *told* you you had done something wrong, so you assumed you *had* done something wrong—which is perfectly natural.

▶ **Do you ever have the secret fear that these accusations just might be true?**

The act of thinking you have done something wrong has already created a Devil. It is possible to emancipate yourself from this type of monkey business. If you proceed, the time will come when you realize that guilt is a common experience of the human race. These things you see inside are universal, not just specific to yourself. You are no better or worse than anybody else, so there's nothing to get excited about.

You may have heard the Hindu parable about the blind men describing an elephant. One feels the tail and says it's like a rope. Another feels a leg and says it's like a tree. The trunk feels like a snake, and so on. Well, all the pictures in the Tarot are different parts of the same elephant, the One Thing or Life Itself—Key 15 included. As you advance on your inner path, you learn to reconcile all the things you discover within yourself. You begin to understand that, like Reality, *you are what you are*. When you find all that you truly are, you're quite happy with yourself.

The Dweller on the Threshold is said by occultists to be the Guardian of the Gate of the Sacred Mysteries. All the Nature Mysteries are involved with Key 15. This was the horned god of the old religion before Christianity got hold of him.

In mythology, Pan is the god of sound. In the ancient philosophy, sound is the basis for everything that happens in the universe; it's all *done* by sound. Consequently, Pan is a high god in the hierarchy. Pan can cause pandemonium and strike fear into the hearts of anyone. This ties in with the biblical Jehovah, Yod-Heh-Vav-Heh, who could scare anybody anytime, with no problems at all. This is that same idea of *power* that can grab you and shake you very hard and scare you half to death.

Fear on the Tree of Life is Pachad, located with Geburah in the fifth center. Fifteen is three times five, so fear raised to the third power is bound to make your hair stand on end. We've heard that the fear of the Lord is the beginning of wisdom, but that's only the beginning. It's on the other side, in love, that you actually *find* wisdom. Chesed reflects Chokmah, the Wisdom center on the Tree. What this boils down to is that the fearful Jehovah is in fact your benevolent Innermost Self.

▶ It felt kind of weird and bizarre when I first got interested in the Tarot. Was that the Dweller on the Threshold?

Sure, that's an aspect of it. It can be spooky.

▶ Why is there this element in the occult that seems to scare people?

Race-thought, or cultural indoctrination, is just as alive as you or I. When you emerge from the womb, this race-thought grabs you right away. You get it with your mother's milk, you get it in school, you get it in church, you get it from the President of the United States. You get it all over the place. And if you're born in Timbuktu you get another version of the same thing. It's been accumulating for thousands of years, so it puts a lot of pressure on you.

You were told that there were spooks and goblins that come out of the *dark*. They are associated with things like the Tarot, and astrology, and witches, which are said to be slimy and creepy. On the other side it's Lord Jesus and all the saints and prophets. They are all shining brightly and they have on white suits and sing like crazy.

▶ So you're explaining it just in terms of superstition.

Yes, but that's a force, you know. When you talk about God Almighty, you're talking about a super-dooper power that's got the universe in His grip, and He's very much interested in what you're doing, and you'd damn well better do the right thing or He's gonna come right down and blast you.

That's why the Secret Doctrine is secret. Not too long ago it was a quick way to the eternal. If you said anything about the Secret Doctrine, you'd get your head knocked off. You'd be stoned, burned, or something else painful. We're not the gentlest people, you know . . . humankind.

▶ Do you believe there was a time when the populace as a whole was more enlightened than now?

No, I don't think so. There were times like the Golden Age of Greece when they produced their miracles of art just as we produce our miracles of science. But the spiritual aspect is still ahead of us. As the Hindus say, this is the Kali Yuga, the Dark Age. If you have two eyes in your head you can't miss that one.

▶ I have a question about the process of materializing an object of your imagination as a living person.

Yes. A projection.

▶ A woman in Tibet decided to materialize a mental construction. It was an amiable little monk, a companion. She said at first no one could see it but herself. As it got stronger, other people could see the figure. Then it started to take on its own lifelike qualities.

That's what the Cabala calls the GOLEM. In Tibet it's called a *tulpa.*

▶ As its behavior became more complex, it took on a negative autonomy. It started becoming insolent and even threatening. I don't understand that.

She was energizing the whole thing. It was her Shadow self drawing something out of her that she probably didn't want to recognize in herself, and presenting it to her.

▶ You mean the spirit was actually hers even though she didn't know it?

Yes, *yes.* In psychology, if we saw a demon or something like that, our first thought would be that it is an outside thing, but it isn't. We are looking at our own Shadow. This is exactly what The Devil represents in the Tarot—along with a lot of other things.

▶ Isn't it that reluctance to admit to the dark side of humanity that makes witch hunts so popular?

Of course. It's much more convenient to hang it on the other fellow than on yourself. In the Tarot, the main key to unlocking the mystery of The Devil is not to have a scapegoat. Face up to what you consist of. When we can see, we are saved.

▶ **Do the people in Key 15 have horns and hooves because of our animal nature?**

These symbols show that our animal propensities are emphasized at the beginning of our spiritual evolution. As a race, we're just emerging from the jungle. It says in Paul Case's book that these people are bestialized—a somewhat old-fashioned word. The thing to remember is that this is a passing stage. As we proceed, the hooves turn into toenails, and so on.

When we're unconscious, the only thing going on is our animal nature. There's nothing wrong with being an animal if that's *only* what you are, but there's something very wrong with humans who don't recognize their *humanity*. Animals have certain instinctive rhythms. People have their minds. They can do anything they please with their minds, including inventing ways of being more animal than the animals.

The spiraling horns on The Devil signify divine grace. This piece of symbolism is like the white rope that upholds The Hanged Man. The Cabala says that all force works in a spiral that comes from Kether and sustains the universe. If you think of the One Self as unwinding and expanding, then you have the shape of a horn, the cornucopia. From the Horn of Plenty come all the experiences and awakenings on the Path of Life. It is a kind of continuous feast.

▶ **Isn't The Devil inciting the man to lust?**

He's certainly firing up the man's tail, but let's face it, lust plays a very important role in life whether we like it or not. Who designed lust in the first place? Remember that there is only One Life energizing everything.

The woman's tail is ornamented by the grape—wine, women, and song—a real party doll. This picture represents our happy adolescence before we move on to something more serious. It depicts fun on an adolescent level. At least I had a pretty good time. The Devil's red eyes remind me of my overindulgence in bourbon during my college days.

The torch in Key 15 symbolizes the Life Force. It is said to be burning wastefully. We are quite capable of using this force unwisely, which is what these characters are doing. Overindulgence results in exhaustion and boredom. We must find a balance, because we *must* live, and not deny ourselves life experiences. In order to swim, you've got to get in the water and get wet.

▶ The posture of The Magician is similar to that of The Devil, but The Devil glares outward while The Magician looks down modestly.

The Magician is a white magician. He is modest and disavows his egotism. His gesture shows that he understands he's simply an agent of the higher intelligence. The invocation of grace is part of his magic. His heart is in the right place so he can't get into any serious trouble.

The Devil is a black magician, and anything but modest. He thinks that the power comes from himself. In a *profound* way it does come from his Inner Self, but he thinks of it in terms of ego and personal achievement. He says, "I can do this," and he *can* do it, so the more he does it the more he's convinced that it's his own power.

We have a perfect example in Hitler. The more he exercised his power, the more power he had. You never heard him say publicly, "All my powers are derived from God."

▶ Hitler practiced occultism.

So did his opponents. One occultist that I know of was Louis de Wohl, a crackerjack Hungarian astrologer who worked for the Allies.

Ego inflation is a real danger in occultism. Misused power is not only destructive to others, it's *self*-destructive and self-devouring. It can turn you into a monster of egotism. Of course, power itself is perfectly harmless. It's great!—fantastic!—wonderful!—if you use it constructively in the right channels.

▶ How would you define black magic?

Black magic consists of using all the occult powers for personal ends. White magic uses the same powers for the good of humanity. An example on the ordinary, everyday level is the telepathic transmission of curses instead of blessings.

▶ Are you saying that to think negative thoughts about someone is to do black magic?

That's correct. Now, if you are on the receiving end and negativity is being directed at you, remember that goodwill and harmlessness are the *weapons* of the sage. This was the teaching of Milarepa in Tibet, who started out as a black magician and ended up a great saint.

▶ Is there a Cabalistic definition of evil?

Missing the mark. Generally, evil is the result of an unenglightened approach to life. This is a touchy subject, but evil is relative. For instance, if I were to kill you and eat you, that would be considered horrendous in this society, but in another society that would be acceptable. You would taste delicious! Aside from social evils which are defined by the tribe, there are crimes against *life*. One can be socially correct and still commit a crime against life out of ignorance.

The Hindu philosophers use the concept of tamas, which is darkness, ignorance, and inertia—everything that would hold us back from the clear vision of life. Black is the color of tamas. It surrounds everything in Key 15. The people are immersed in darkness.

▶ **I like black. Why does it have to be the color of ignorance?**

I like black, too. On the Tree of Life black is the color of Binah, the mind. It is our minds that need illumination. The illumination comes from *within* the mind, so in the Cabala there is always light in the darkness. Buddha's final words were, "Be a lamp unto yourselves." There is no other light.

The mind is very tricky. There are all sorts of levels of enlightenment in the mind. There are also levels of ignorance. You can be a little ignorant, you can be *very* ignorant, or everything in between.

Mind is substance and substance represents darkness, in the basic sense of being the opposite of light. But the material aspect has no meaning whatsoever in itself. It's *real* enough and it's *necessary*, but meaning has to be *given* to it. Imagine that you have a stage, you have actors, lights and everything else all there, ready to do it . . . but there's nothing to be done. That might be all right for a two-second skit, but it's certainly not a play. Until some meaning is introduced into the situation, there's nothing going on. Still, it's all ready and waiting. This is the nature of mind.

▶ **Then Binah is equivalent to the Prima Materia in its chaotic state. How does that connect with ignorance?**

They are the same thing, if you want to look at it that way, because ignorance is an absence of meaning and enlightenment. An ignorant person doesn't know anything. The Materia you're speaking of doesn't know anything, either, but please understand that we're only talking analytically. As far as Reality is concerned, there is *no time* when the Materia is actually in this condition, because the Life Power is working on it all the time. Complete darkness is *symbolic*. It doesn't really exist, but the symbol gives you a feeling for the nonsensical nature of substance by itself.

The tangible aspect alone is just a joke, really. It's the Coney Island fun house. Somewhere along the line, there has to be an illumination that makes it understandable and gives it meaning. On the Tree of Life this light comes from Chokmah, the Illuminating Intelligence. This is the highest level of the solar aspect. The highest level of the lunar aspect is Binah, which is the Sanctifying Intelligence and the *temple* of the sun.

▶ **People also have their own darkness, the dross that they create within themselves.**

As Emerson said, we all have the defects of our qualities. When you start to think about yourself, "Yuck, ick, bleh," just remember that the special way you're constructed emphasizes some things and de-emphasizes others. Don't worry about this. It doesn't matter whether you're an elephant or a crocodile or a canary. Whatever you are, there is a deep reason for the powers and the faculties and the vehicle you have. Without specialization you wouldn't be you, and you have to give up some things in order to specialize. Don't get alarmed and think that certain things "should" be there. *There's no immorality* about insufficiency in certain areas. All you need is a heart of gold and tremendous efficiency in your own area, and you've got it made. Don't try to be all things to all people.

▶ **What should you do if you keep running into obstacles on the Path?**

That's not pleasant, but there isn't any particular approach. You just put up with it. In time you begin to see the wisdom of the Adversary. Key 14, Temperance, taught you about trial and error, and that is *mostly error*. The more errors you make, the faster you learn. This whole philosophy is one of learning. Never is it a philosophy of withdrawal from life, or anything like that. Life is something that *proceeds*, and we proceed right along with it.

The pressures brought by the Adversary are great. They have a tendency to split everything wide open. Key 15 represents the static aspect of the personality before it begins to emerge into the area of understanding. In Key 16 the status quo is relieved very rapidly. You can't stay in hell forever, and The Tower Key shows the way out.

Key 16 is the birth passage from a hopeless situation into a glorious future, right next door in Key 17, The Star. Any birth is traumatic, but it's over in a comparatively short time. The baby will be born healthy and live happily ever after, which is what the rest of the Tarot is telling us.

Thanks for joining me as we share the treasures of the Tarot and the Cabala. Have an exciting week!

KEY 16

CHAPTER 16

THE TOWER

In the words of Hermes Trismegistus, "The soul cannot long endure its nymphal prison." It's interesting to note that the dragonfly *backs out* of its old, dead, nymphal form. Just like the people in The Tower Key, he doesn't see where he is going. Life calls and he goes.

In order to rid ourselves of something old or undesirable, we *literally* have to get rid of it so that something *much better* can come along. Life won't stand for the half-baked understandings of Key 15. The Tower represents rationalizations, excuses, and intellectualizations. Its bricks correspond to words. Like the Tower of Babel, it gets nowhere, so Life takes responsibility and helps us out of this gross mistake.

If the Powers That Be wanted to eliminate us, it would be easy. Apparently they have something else in mind, like our unfoldment, as pictured in the remaining Tarot Keys. If Key 16 were the end, it would be sad indeed, but really there is a marvelous sequel. This is comforting and encouraging to anyone on the Path of the Tarot.

As I mentioned last week, Key 16 is the birth passage from The Devil Key into The Star Key. Actually, it is *rebirth*. Spiritual rebirth is emergence from what could be called ordinary, everyday consciousness, into a more positive atmosphere—a type of consciousness that is completely different from environmental conditioning and the race mind. We have to pass from a state of almost total ignorance into knowledge of what we truly are. Emancipation of the spirit is a dramatic change in our evolutionary progress. The key word for this card is AWAKENING.

A lot that goes on with the birth of a baby is not appropriate for dinnertime conversation. Still, it's an essential process. The Tower process is also essential. Spiritual rebirth engenders at least as much trauma as a regular human birth. Let's face it, this is the most traumatic Key in the whole series. It pictures the wild and woolly passage from unconscious egotism into a state in which you become related to life. At least you make a beginning in this direction, and then you proceed into the glories of cosmic consciousness that are to come to us in just a few weeks. After all, here we are and here's the cosmos, so why not communicate with it?

If for any reason you have stumbled upon the Path of the Tarot (which, of course, represents *the* Path), you must go through this transformation, this revolution within yourself. You're going to leave behind something near and dear to you. It's a two-letter word: "m-e." You're going to leave behind this fascinating "me" and move into something even better. This is hard to believe, but truly there *is* something better than "me." That's the main message of the sixteenth Key.

You erect The Tower in your head when you think of yourself as isolated from everybody and everything that's going on. You have a tendency to pile up a sort of structure of words that makes you feel important and *builds up your ego*, as the saying goes. Then after you get your tower built, you sit in there and read everything you're supposed to read, wear everything you're supposed to wear, and drink everything you're supposed to drink. You're real sharp, real keen, you're right in style ... okay, that's Key 15, The Devil.

It's not our fault that we are egotistical. Society prods us in this direction. There's nothing *wrong* with this, as far as the inner teaching is concerned, except that it's *limiting*. The intention of the Tarot and the Cabala is to get us *out* of anything that's limiting or obstructing to us. If we are living the sheltered life of the ego, it's a bit small, know what I mean? So our Innermost Self says, "You can't stay in here forever. You've got to *expand*. You've got to get rid of those old clichés and move into something more exciting, more aware, more related to life." Then, like the hermit crab, when your house begins to cramp your style, you get the hell out.

A bolt of lightning once hit a drainpipe in the wall behind me. The next thing I knew, I was all the way across the room with no recollection of how I got there. It's always a thrilling experience to have a near miss with lightning.

This is a different kind of lightning. It traces the descent of the Life Power through the Tree of Life. This symbolism shows that the Hidden Wisdom of the Cabala is destructive to your pet notions about the world, your relationships, and everything else. Wisdom has never been popular, but somehow it has survived through the millennia. Wisdom is always interested in the total picture. It's a heavy blow to your intellectual pride to find out that there's someone or something that knows much more than you do—and that you're going to have to make a choice, either to accept or reject the truth. If you've gone this far in the Tarot, you don't really have much choice. There's nothing to do but accept the fact that there's something smarter than you are. It's a terrible come-down, but that's the way it is.

The thunderbolt is the weapon of Jupiter. In the old scheme of things, Jupiter was God, so you might say that this is a message from God that goes *Bang!* It's banging on your head, which is where The Tower is, in order to get rid of obstacles to your advancement. The ego trip is a useless edifice of rationalizations. The ego finds a reason for everything. The only problem is, it's the wrong reason. So at a certain stage in your career the Light comes *from within*—an uncomfortable awakening. But these three dark windows, the three kinds of consciousness in yourself, are about to become *illuminated*.

The spiritual weapon that destroys egotism is the Cabala itself. The impact of the divine idea, the reality that is in this scheme, is more than sufficient to get rid of the problem. That's why this is called the Exciting Intelligence and the Key of Awakening. It says, "Wake up! Become aware of *inner* things." It doesn't involve physical destruction at all. It only destroys illusion, and God knows there's enough of *that* around.

The divine light is the same radiance that shines from The Hermit's lantern in Key 9, located directly above The Tower in the Tableau. It seems destructive because it's so upsetting. If you have been living on the outer, ego level, and you suddenly become aware that there's something going on in the universe besides what you *thought* was going on, this is disturbing to you. But without this new way of looking at things, you're only kidding yourself.

Instead of despairing about this transition, we should *welcome* it. We are being born *out* of the everyday world with all of its problems, *into* the inner world with all of its joys. In the inner world, principles remain, much as the stars remain in the heavens. Things go along swimmingly there. The Tower is not an experience to be dreaded, but rather something to be *happy* about. You can get through this difficult period and come out on the other side into something wonderful.

▶ I feel queasy when I see how "upset" the people are in the picture.

These topsy-turvy figures represent inferior aspects of yourself that are going to be redeemed. The self-conscious and the subconscious are having a nightmare. Fear is written all over these characters. Key 16 is Mars. The seat of Mars on the Tree of Life is in Severity, otherwise known as Fear. They are afraid that this is the end, that they will hit bottom and never get up. Of course they *do* get up—and start dancing around—but in the meantime this pile of nonsense has got to go. Luckily, Zeus steps in and saves them the expense of having the thing carted away.

Again, the notions that have to go are in your head. It's there that the Battle of Armageddon is going to take place—a knock-down, drag-out fight between the ego and the spiritual forces of the Innermost Self. As far as I know, the Inner Self always wins. It will be like the debate between Krishna and Arjuna in the *Bhagavad-Gita*, except in our everyday terms.

▶ **Is this a conscious battle?**

Oh, yes. You're very conscious of it because you identify with the ego. In this battle, you're constantly losing everything on the level of the ego. In the *Bhagavad-Gita* this corresponds to killing your relatives. Arjuna has to kill his precious "relatives," all his prides and joys. The ego can be very subtle. "I'm going to save a little, just in case." The answer is, "No, nothing. That's finished. You can't take any illusions with you."

▶ **I'm wondering about the role of desire in all this. We are instructed to fulfill our desires, but sometimes the ego is screaming, "I want, I want!"**

That's when the desire-nature is out of hand. Now, there's one important thing I want to emphasize. When you go through this Tower experience, you don't lose your desire-nature. *You don't lose your ego.* It just becomes subordinate.

As we've said many times in these meetings, you're here in order to lead a creative life, but you can't unless you *want* to. If your desire-nature is not involved, then it's impossible, because you don't have any steam. "Maybe I will and maybe I won't..." shows a lack of *drive*. You *need* that drive. The same thing is true with the ego, because the ego controls everything in the physical world. Its job is to be the controller, but only on commands from above. It's like an executive taking orders from the boss, or a prime minister carrying out directives from the king. The ego and the desire-nature are not supposed to *originate* any orders.

► So we just remember who's boss.

Yes, that's the secret of harmony. We remember that the Creative in ourselves is the boss. We touch it in Chokmah. We're over in Binah, the Holy Grail. The Lord fills the cup; it can't be filled any other way. The Lord inspires us or we're not inspired at all.

► What is the ego?

The ego is a reflection of the Self in the mind. It's what we call our self-conscious, waking self, which is a reflection of our Higher Self right in the middle of our mind. It tends to think of itself as a separate entity. There are plenty of reasons why this seems logical. The only problem is, eventually it becomes a trap. It's a completely unworkable proposition to be dragging around a great big fat ego. One never dispenses with this reflection of the Self. What has to go is ego*tism*, which is a pernicious form of ignorance.

Don't ask me why we have to go through this stage. I haven't the remotest idea. But everybody goes through it, and the sooner we do, the better we feel. At first everything tends to make us as egotistical as possible. Then the next step is, we have to get rid of egotism. This is a painful process. It can be devastating. If there weren't something beyond this battle that was worthwhile, it would be a terrible situation. But there is something better than the life of the ego.

► Enlightenment?

Well, it's even better than that, in the sense that when you get to a certain point, you're living for a creative purpose, not for any specific result. In terms of your Innermost Self, whatever you want to do is an ongoing thing. It doesn't depend on any immediate gain. It's like true artistry. True artists enjoy creating; that's what makes them happy. This does not necessarily have to do with any particular art; it might be just living life. The person who's following his or her own creative purpose completely discharges all the inner energy that's available, in a satisfying way. On the egotism level it's a win-or-lose proposition. You win sometimes and you lose sometimes. In the creative situation, you *always* win, because you're not trying to play any games.

Now, mind you, I'm not telling you what to think; I'm just reporting what the Cabala states quite clearly: There "ain't no such animal" as my personal will or even my personal little finger. To involve yourself in the illusion of ownership is a waste of time. We have all things to *use*. They are not ours to *claim* as our own. The universe is very generous. It gives us all kinds of interesting things to amuse us and keep us more or less occupied. We're not supposed to make the asinine mistake of saying, "It's mine." The air isn't ours, the sunshine isn't ours, the energy we expend isn't ours. All these things are gifts. They are part of the general fun.

You can't define yourself properly as long as you grab things. You are something that *inherently* owns, operates, controls, and so on—but only in terms of being *part of the universe*. In the final definition of yourself, please remember that you are a cosmic person, in every sense of the word. If we love God and are God's children, then we are divine and the rest is easy. Jesus is the leading authority on this in the West; he said, "Behold, the kingdom of God is within you."

▶ **I don't understand how The Tower is a structure of human speech.**

Paul Case introduced the idea of having twenty-two levels of masonry in The Tower. These correspond to the twenty-two letters of the Hebrew alphabet, representing the foundation of speech. The letter specifically connected with Key 16 is PEH פ, which means the *mouth* and the power of utterance. All the definitions and decisions in human life come from the mouth. Starting with twenty-two letters, you can prove *anything*. Words are tricky. If you're a clever lawyer, you can literally get away with murder. It's done every day of the week. In Key 16 the words prove, "What a big boy am I," like Little Jack Horner. His comeuppance is represented by the crown toppling off.

In our discussion about The Devil, we spoke of the dangerous power of words. In hypnosis, if the operator *says* you are a dog, you behave as if it were true. Mass hypnosis is even more effective. Millions can be put into a trance.

On the positive side, speech is *creative*. When we learn how to use speech creatively, we don't waste it on foolishness or the kind of oppressive statements that characterize the media.

▶ **The media sow erroneous seeds that come from false premises, which grow into monstrous plants that look like The Devil.**

That's exactly what race-thought is. One generation after another perpetuates nonsense, but with a very serious face, backed up by force: guns!

▶ We also give erroneous suggestions to ourselves.

Yes, we talk to ourselves all the time, and we should be careful about what kind of suggestions are contained in this inner dialogue. It would be better to give ourselves *no* suggestions rather than to supply a lot of erroneous ones, for our tendency is to perpetuate foolishness in our own psychology. We just keep repeating our prejudices and passions over and over again. So we've got to be discriminating in this matter of autosuggestion. It's much better to be a *student* of life than to be continually fiddling with yourself. *Life will communicate itself* to anybody who is interested. IT will make the right suggestions.

Language can be inspiring. The wizards of the Cabala have attached the Hebrew letters to inner principles. The letters have had eons of meaning poured into them, so they are powerful agents of communication. They are charged with a message that is backed up by powerful minds trying to get the message through to us. This information is important to us as individuals. The letters are gateways into what our spiritual forebears are trying to tell us—very handy tools.

We mustn't get the idea that we can only receive inspiration through Hebrew. There is nothing wrong with the English language. Our letters are just as good as anybody else's, but they do not represent images as they do in Hebrew, where the imagery is symbolic and important from an inner point of view.

For instance, the male figure in Key 16 is said to be in the general shape of the letter Ayin ע, which precedes Peh in the alphabet. As the letter of Key 15, The Devil, it represents the eye looking outward to the world of superficial appearance. Self-consciousness assesses the outer world and, using the power of human speech, dictates what's what to the human subconscious.

The quality of your conversation with your subconscious depends on how much you know. If you only look at outer appearances, your conversation will be strictly from television and the daily news. In other words, you are making a trashcan out of your subconscious. If you have more of an *approach* to life, then you're going to introduce something different.

The reason we have to be watchful about what we tell ourselves is that our subconscious not only *believes* us, it also *acts accordingly*. Let's say we join the John Birch Society or some fool thing, and we dump this into our subconscious. It says, "Hey! this is the greatest thing since TV! We've got to get with it and really pour it on." It goes ahead and makes you so birchy that after awhile you have white bark that splits. Or if you're a hypochondriac, you can talk yourself into being sick. This is nothing new; it's just the way it works.

As one of the double letters, Peh is associated with a pair of opposites. In this case it's Grace and Sin. Grace is consciousness and Sin is ignorance. That's old-fashioned language. Actually, ignorance is more like a disease that leaves you handicapped.

▶ **The twenty-two Yods around The Tower must symbolize the alphabet.**

That's right. They stand for the letters as seed images. Like seeds, these archetypal ideas have sufficient energy within themselves to bring their expression all the way down or all the way out to completion on the ultimate level—our world. An excellent example of this is Wernher von Braun and his rockets. In the beginning the rocket was just an idea. Herr von Braun hung on to it and mustered continual support for it until at last it found total expression in physical terms.

These Yods are tongues of flame that represent *the word* of what is going to be. A theologian might call it divine fiat. The Yods are organized to show the Logos at work. Ten on one side form the pattern of the Tree of Life and twelve on the other side signify the zodiac. Each archetype has an energy unique to itself. When our awareness connects with the archetype, we receive its special energy.

It's quite obvious that there is a great deal of intelligence being displayed in the universe, even though a) we don't understand it, and b) we may not like it. It's very important for us to see that the intelligence is there. We should be careful not to put it down and call it stupid or wrong. We can reserve our judgment until we know more. In the meantime, we're stuck with a universe that is obviously a fantastically powerful affair. It says in the Bible that Joshua made the sun stand still. That's fine, but personally, I don't find this reassuring.

When something happens to us, sometimes we're able to overcome it and sometimes not. I just lost a friend a couple of days ago. He had a sudden heart attack. Maybe his Inner Guide or Friend said, "You ought to be doing something else." Who knows? The point is, he couldn't do anything about it, and I couldn't do anything about it, and his dear wife couldn't do anything about it. We live in a shaky, quaky universe.

You might think that this viewpoint would be oppressive, but not so, because the more you see the universe as a powerhouse, the more you realize that something is looking out for *you*. The scarier it gets, the more you see there must be something taking care of you. You're not that big in the scheme of things, yet *you are important* or you wouldn't even be here.

There are tremendous cosmic powers flying around in the breeze, just like the Yods in Key 16. This is no joke. It's all pure science. You can look right at the power of the sun, this "thing" that's bubbling and boiling and energizing the whole solar system. For all we know, it could blow up tomorrow and that would be it . . . and this is our Daddy!

▶ **How would you define power?**

In the ancient teachings, there is simply one power, which is *The Power*. In the movie *Star Wars* it's called The Force. It doesn't belong to anybody. It belongs to everybody. It energizes everybody. It's behind every energy phenomenon in the universe. That's the only power there is. All you have to do is *look* and you can see it.

We talk about a power shortage here, but the universe is *loaded* with power. Even though we may be in a bind at the moment, there's ample power. We just don't know how to use it right now. We'd undoubtedly blow ourselves right off the map if we got the power all in one jump. But it's coming. It's coming fast.

The universe is like a coiled spring that's ready to release at any moment. The tensions involved are tremendous. *Man didn't make the power.* He didn't make the universe. He didn't make the atoms or their nuclei. These things are just *there*, and he's fooling around with them. He's either too dumb to know better, or has brains enough to discover how to work all this stuff. Through our cooperative efforts we went to the moon, and we'll be going somewhere else too. If we don't blow ourselves up, we'll turn the whole place inside out before we're through.

Then there's the power of the biological realm. A couple of crop failures and we've had it. The whole life-supporting mechanism of nature is out of our hands (at the moment), yet its power supports us all the time. Some people think the Native Americans are silly, but they were very close to truth with their corn god. They knew perfectly well that if the spirit of the corn gave up, they'd be dead. So why not worship the corn god? We don't have to take all of these sustaining energies for granted. We can think about them, relate to them.

As far as the Cabala is concerned, The Power is a collection of all sorts of conscious energies expressing themselves in the universe. Every expression of power has to be limited, otherwise it runs all over the place. The limitation is where the intelligence lies. That's what keeps everything defined.

▶ What about people who always want to use power for war? After all, Mars is the god of war.

There's a negative aspect to *everything*. Originally, Mars was the protector of the tribe and the flocks. On the Tree of Life it's the protective Ring of Fire. As for war, the school I went to as a youngster preached that nobody wins a war; it's an unintelligent exercise. In fact, the only constructive comment I ever heard then about war was that it improved the techniques of surgery.

In spite of the fact that a few centuries ago they spoke of the Age of Reason, we haven't even come close to the *hem* of reason. We live in a very unreasonable world, but individually and collectively we can do our best to make it a more reasonable place. If you and I were to make war on a personal level the way we do on a national level, life would really be a disaster. We're trying to get some measure of how we treat each other individually to happen on a world level.

Unfortunately, the leadership is not always heroic. In general, the leadership is purchased. It's a front for those basic things that involve everybody in the pocketbook. As long as our criterion for what makes a happy world is a buck or a kopeck or a yen or whatever, there's bound to be trouble, because on that level economics is a function of the ego.

▶ Jason, what if nuclear weapons get out of control?

The universe is a big place; if we fail here, we are not finished as spiritual beings. In the movie *Oh, God* George Burns (as God) says, in effect, "I gave you everything you need. If you don't have sense enough to put it together right, then—goodbye!" If your vehicle is obliterated by those who are mucking about with cosmic energy, you will just wake up as a being somewhere else.

There are three kinds of people: good, bad, and indifferent. The tamasic kind don't give a damn. The rajasic types are the wild, ambitious ones like Napoleon and Hitler. The sattvic people are those who care. If each individual straightens him or herself out, this is a small beginning, but it's the only way. If enough minds get themselves together, they will simply cast off the bunk and that will be that. Having armies is a *habit*, as though we couldn't live from day to day without having a mortal enemy. In this mad world there's a way out and we're supposed to find it.

The crowned woman in Key 16 illustrates a psyche that is ruled by subconscious programming, current conditioning, and the instinctual nature. This is acceptable to society. In fact there are people who take advantage of this unconsciousness, as you well know. They hoodwink people in this particular state. Having no awareness of Self, they ignore Ageless Wisdom and do as they bloody well please. You can go through college and law school and become the President of the United States and *still* be unconscious. You may laugh, but it's happened.

▶ We've all been brainwashed.

We've all been brainwashed, but happily there's a cure for it. The cure is simply to look at the data and to *discriminate* among all the things we were ever taught or told. This is not to say that everything we were taught is no good—that's not the case—but we do have to decide *for ourselves* what is pure balderdash and what has some genuine value.

All the faculties that made it possible for you to become educated were there at birth. Given the material, you educated yourself. No one else can instill knowledge in you; if that were possible, morons could become geniuses. You have perceptive faculties that are functioning beautifully, so you can begin to *observe*, which is completely different from being told. Then you actually move into a different world. When you start asking God questions, which is a perfectly normal pastime, then your intuition will come to the rescue.

Under the present system, you have the vote, which is very important. You can write. You can speak. Your capabilities are great enough. People have everything within themselves that is necessary to make a wholesome life. They have justice in themselves. They have mercy and love in themselves, everything that is beautiful and wise. These wonderful qualities are not something acquired by reading a book. They are *intrinsic*. Aside from the judgments that are made all the time, we are in ourselves okay. Thus, when we truly become ourselves, we manifest these qualities: we are just, we are loving, we are intelligent. We are like the ones about whom it is generally said, "Oh well, those are special people." To that the Cabala says, "Baloney!" Once *any* person attains the

Inner Self, a transformation takes place, and he or she goes beyond the usual life situation.

▶ **Just wanting to be good doesn't make it, somehow.**

You've been taught that being good is desirable. You can be good by obeying all the rules, regardless of whose rules they are, but that doesn't mean that you are *yourself* as we mean it here. That kind of person is not creative, and creativity is the *essence* of what this system is about. Just being good in the sense that you don't break the rules is not good *enough* in the Cabala. One way to obey the rules is to get up in the morning and eat your breakfast and then go lie down in the corner. Then eat your lunch and go lie down in the corner again. Then eat your dinner and go back to bed. You don't cause any trouble, and you're a really *good* person. You never do anything wrong and you never will.

What's more difficult than being good is to do something creative without causing trouble. We have some people who are creating a whole lot of trouble for everyone else. I won't mention any names, but you know who they are. They're in the news all the time. They think they're doing a great job but they're *not*, because they're leading people by the nose. All you're supposed to do for the other guy is tell him how great he is and try to help him find himself. Because, as Lao Tzu said a long time ago, people are okay. The Cabala says the same thing.

▶ **It looks as though humanity is going through a Tower phase on its way to the New Age. Could you say something about that?**

No, because there are over four billion people in the world now, and it would be the greatest conceit on my part to say that I knew what was going to happen to this tremendous range of different kinds of people. But one hopeful thing I *can* tell you is that communication today is highly developed, which means that the *mechanics of enlightenment* can take place a lot quicker now than formerly. So that's certainly good.

Another thing that I think is going to help a great deal is the energy revolution, which is definitely in the offing. Cheaper energy will lift the economic level of practically everybody. When you have advanced communication together with abundant energy, you have a whole new ballgame in the world.

People being creatures of habit, it may be a long time before we see the end of separatist religions and the beginning of what might be called the Religion of Man. Religious institutions are deeply entrenched. I don't think they are going to go away in a couple of weeks (in case you were hoping for that), even though the inner groups in the major religions already want to join together, because they're talking about the *same thing*.

▶ **The end result—enlightenment, or whatever you want to call it—is the same, but the way each person gets there is different.**

It's not as different as you might think. Religions have it all covered up with this, that, and the other, but it always boils down to KNOW THYSELF, which is true all over the world. Fundamentally, this means that you have to know yourself psychologically. There's nothing standing between you and me and Reality except a lot of absurd ideas. You have to just brush aside the antiquated, institutionalized religious notions.

As far as your *salvation* is concerned—which should be of the utmost importance because it's your own hide—it's imperative that you become discriminating and selective as fast as you possibly can. This is something you have to do yourself. Here in this room tonight we're exploring and perhaps buying the idea of salvation through discrimination. I think that's wise. The ordinary human condition is insufferable. It's unconscious in the technical sense, and ridiculous because it's mechanical. There's no need for people to be mechanical. This breeds all kinds of problems in yourself that are very difficult to handle.

If you so choose, you can become a philosopher. Using the Wisdom Philosophy, you can defuse The Tower situation within yourself. Instead of waiting for this tremendous explosion to knock you down, you can de-energize it by doing something about it. Philosophy anticipates the problem, so that when it arrives it's no problem at all because you're ready for it.

Let me congratulate you on getting through the perils of passage connected with the early stages of unfoldment. When The Tower falls, it releases energy that can be used in meditation. In other words, now we're ready to move into the world of Key 17. What a magnificent change of pace!

The Star card represents the activity of meditation. If you succeed in meditation, you will feel better and have *more light*. The Tarot is saying that when you meditate, certain things are revealed to you that could not be communicated in any other way. By this time, you've hopefully acquired enough faith so that you are willing to give the process a try. That's all that's necessary. If you try meditation, you'll find that it pays off.

Everybody can enjoy this faculty of revelation. Although you won't learn all about the universe in ten, twenty, thirty, or forty years of meditation, you will find out what *you need*. You all need something *right now* to get you through the experience of life that is currently engrossing you. Meditaton gives you precisely enough steam to get you on to the next square. Occasionally, you get some special piece of information that makes you feel very good.

We shall try to get the technique of this across to you next week, because it has a great deal to do with your health and well-being. I hope that you will find this Key inspirational, as I have over the years. You should have an absolutely delightful week under the auspices of Isis. Thanks for coming.

KEY 17

CHAPTER 17

THE STAR

When we graduated from The Tower and renounced egotism forever, we thereby gained the key to heaven and all the inner kingdoms. We found that we must go into the darkness in order to see the stars, that is, the cosmos in all its glory. Now meditation will reveal the structure and beauty of the physical world: Isis Unveiled.

In The Star card, the Divine Mother is pictured as supplying us with that distinct function of consciousness called meditation. Meditation is an elaboration of the lightning flash in Key 16. This special awareness is a possibility that lies open to all of us. The godlike ability to meditate is an extraordinary power built into us as a *gift* from the Great Goddess. The Cabala teaches that the Life Power Itself is meditative, and we are invited to participate in the eternal meditation of Life Itself. That's a large statement, I will allow, and I wouldn't dare take the responsibility for it. I'm just repeating what's in the book.

The worship of Isis can be traced back to ancient times. Those of you who like to poke around in history will find that for thousands of years Lady Isis was a mighty goddess indeed. She is Mother Nature, who gives birth to the earth, the stars, and the whole universe. The Virgin Mary isn't nature. From the church's point of view, there's something "iffy" about nature. It's a bit dirty, especially in certain spots. We can be more reasonable and *respect* Isis because she is the power within which we live and move and have our being. We can bow in her direction and say, "Pretty *good*, what's going on."

In Hindu lore, the mother principle is named the Savioress, the Illuminatrix, and She Who Carries the Divine Revelation. Here in the Tarot, REVELATION is expressed in pictorial symbolism as a beautiful, naked woman. There is nothing better to meditate upon than Isis, because nature reveals itself to us any time we pay attention to it. To look at Isis is to observe what's going on in the universe. The universe is not only a highly edifying affair, it's also very enjoyable.

Usually people are busily trying to twist out some bit of information from nature that will bring them a couple of extra bucks. Our purpose is different from those who exploit nature in order to acquire something. We look to *interior* nature with the goal of knowing ourselves. We want to be able to *define* ourselves.

We are progressing through the seven stages of spiritual unfoldment as pictured in the last row of the Tableau. Key 15 (The Devil) was bondage and Key 16 (The Tower) was the passage from bondage to enlightenment. With the power of Key 17, we may now proceed through the remaining Keys and all attain cosmic consciousness a few weeks from now. This is the gate to our success. There's no doubt about that. Only by meditation will we get to Key 21. We won't find "the lost word" and the secret mysteries lying around in the workplace or the amusement park. This is an inner journey.

When you start meditating you stir up a part of yourself that has hitherto been untapped. Until you get into meditation you're one kind of person, and the minute you get into it, you experience a reversal of a special kind. You become polarized *inwardly* instead of outwardly, and you maintain your new polarity through the act of meditation. This is an *exercise*. If you don't exercise this faculty, then you stay polarized in the outer world with its continuous reactions. We're not supposed to be pushed around by the world. We're supposed to be in control, but that doesn't happen until we learn to meditate. When you take on this new function, a drastic change occurs. You become a different being and your experience of the Path is revolutionized.

One of the things that happens is, you become able to accept revelations. These revelations are not necessarily going to change the world overnight, or anything of that sort. What you get through the channel of meditation is what you *need*. It's like money. You don't need all the money in the world, and by the same token, your spiritual needs are not limitless. You need *certain* things very much, and if you follow the path of meditation—which is close to contemplation, which is close to thinking—you become open to a lot of helpful information that is a revelation *to you*. Usually your revelations are not meant for others. You can try to ram them down someone's throat; some people do this all the time. What's important, however, is that the information you need for yourself can come to you gracefully, without any strain at all.

Those of you who have faithfully journeyed thus far through the Tarot know perfectly well by this time where the revelation comes from.

It comes from your Innermost Self. If this deep aspect of yourself isn't approached tenderly and lovingly, it won't work at all. We're trying to become acquainted with this fountain of help that we have within ourselves, and to make use of it.

▶ **I have trouble accepting the idea of revelation.**

If you do not believe revelation is possible, please study it for awhile and see if you can learn to accept it, because everything that has happened of a positive nature in the evolution of humankind has come through the gate of revelation and no other way.

For example, suppose the Wright brothers had said, "We're bicycle makers. We couldn't possibly build an airplane. What a silly idea!" A negative statement like that would have stopped aviation dead in its tracks. *All* inspiration for *all* human progress has come from within men and women able to accept revelation.

We have reasonable guarantees on an historical basis that we can do just about anything. Before something is discovered, it exists in the subconscious. Isis is the source of a *limitless* supply of inspiration and raw material. She is Binah on the Tree of Life; she delivers the goods. We're allowed to manipulate this substance-aspect of life to quite an extent. Man is a creative being who is given charge of bringing in the new, but he often forgets to honor his Source.

Great mysteries underlie the matter-of-fact appearance of nature. The only way to understand them is to become a devotee of Isis. We have this on no less authority than Albert Einstein, who said that you have to *love* nature in order to get the message. It is possible to become spiritualized just by looking at nature. When you have learned to appreciate her and to approach her through the avenue of meditation, then you may see Isis Unveiled.

In this connection, notice the bird sitting on a tree in the background of Key 17. The branches and trunk of this tree are said to symbolize the brain and spinal column. The ibis is the bird of Hermes, representing the intellect, which has its seat in the brain. Its red color shows self-conscious activity. From the bird's perspective, he can see *some* of Isis, especially the vibratory movement of her hair. We see *all* of Isis because we approach her through love. If you are strictly an intellectual, sitting by yourself in the dark corner of intellectuality, you'll see something, but you won't see all of her.

Key 17 is the birthday-suit rendering of The Empress, who heads the third column of the Tarot Tableau. The Empress represents Nature as the Mother of All. She is veiled by the next Key down in that column, The Wheel of Fortune, which presents the mechanical facade of what appears to be happening in the universe. Then comes the Key of Meditation, by which the veil is drawn aside. It is said that no person can lift the veil, but that Isis herself will reveal her beauty to her lover.

▶ **The facade never really goes away. Are you saying that we learn to see through it?**

Yes. Understanding *penetrates* the veil. Einstein was looking at the veil in a very special way. Because he loved it, some of what was going on became apparent to him. He was particularly interested in what makes The Wheel go around. One of his prize statements was, "Something is moving." He came to the conclusion that what was moving The Wheel was far beyond his reach. It's obvious that *something* was making it go around, and he stopped right there, which is a good idea from the Cabalistic point of view. You don't have to beat your brains out when you know before you start that the answer is beyond you.

The great central star in Key 17 is symbolic of the Life Power, which is the energizing principle of the entire universe. Life Itself is a large proposition, and it's generally understood among Cabalists to be an enigma. This enigma is represented by The Wheel of Fortune in Key 10, which has eight spokes, just as The Star has eight points.

The smaller stars stand for the seven chakras, which are congruent with the seven original planets of astrology and the seven alchemical metals. All seven are energized by the main star, which is the Ain Suph Aur expressing itself through Kether on the Tree of Life. Key 17 illustrates the universal order that we see in the heavens, and in the higher levels of being, as well as the reflection of that order in ourselves. The doctrine of the Cabala states that there is no intrinsic difference between the greater and the lesser. It's simply a matter of scope. The universe is the macrocosm and we are the microcosm that mirrors all the powers of the universe. The seven levels of the Tree of Life also correspond to the chakras. These psychic centers operate all the time within us and sustain us every moment.

▶ **If the chakras are so important, why don't we ever hear about them outside of esoteric circles?**

In our materialistic civilization, it's hard for us to believe in the spiritual or inner side of things. We have difficulty realizing that the invisible spirit is just as *real* as the ignition in a car, for instance. The electrical system in a car is much more advanced than the mechanical system, and of a completely different order. This is analogous to the Life Power that animates our bodies. Most people take life for granted, but we can be more appreciative, knowing that the Intelligence that created us put some remarkable mechanisms inside us.

▶ Our textbook discusses the "nerve force" in the chakras. Is this the same thing as kundalini?

Yes, kundalini is a Sanskrit term for the Life Force within our nerves. Each chakra corresponds to a major nerve center. In the kundalini's upward passage, you become aware of these various centers within yourself. You could think of The Star goddess as Mother Kunalini herself. She ascends to embrace the Supreme in the sixth chakra. Their relationship, their unity, is the seventh or Crown chakra.

The best possible way to become aware of your chakras is through meditation. Tarot students are asked to meditate on the Keys that correspond to the chakras, rather than to say, "Now I'm going to concentrate on the base of my spine, and I hope it doesn't come apart or blow me into the next room." If you're familiar with the literature on kundalini, you know that it can burn you to a crisp unless the wiring is good.

▶ I feel leery of kundalini and I'm not about to raise it by myself.

You don't do *anything* by yourself in this particular school of thought, so there's nothing to worry about. No one is saying that you should concentrate on raising kundalini because, as a matter of fact, it's going to raise *itself* as you progress on the Path. It's just like a flower growing out of the ground.

Does anyone have any specific questions about meditation? It's so vital to our success that I'd like to explore it with you futher.

▶ What is meditation, anyway?

Even though it is a most remarkable ability, meditation is an ordinary human faculty. Basically, it's training your mind to stay on one particular subject for a long time. It's lengthening your attention span a great deal, so that you can sink your awareness into something over an extended period. When your mind is able to sustain its concentration, it can penetrate to the real nature of whatever it is placed upon and come up with some *meaning* that is helpful to you.

The letter T<small>ZADDI</small> צ is a fishhook. In his remarks about The Star Key, Paul Case explains that we can actually fish around in our inner world by a conscious effort. First of all, we have to be still. We can't be thinking about this, that, and the other thing, and succeed in the practice of meditation. It is possible to *acquire* stillness through training. The Hanged Man is our example of a well-trained, emptied mind. When we are in Key 12 condition, it is possible to get information from the superconscious area within ourselves—an area that we need to get used to and practice with. Then we can be balanced and guided in our earthly existence, which is otherwise a completely complexing riddle. Without our Inner Light the outside is overwhelming.

When you're fishing on the inside, in ninety-nine cases out of a hundred you'll catch a fish, because that's the nature of the game. There are plenty of fish in the sea, so you're not likely to be disappointed. Key 17 presents an unlimited horizon for finding answers within yourself. Your spiritual welfare and unfoldment are matters of serious concern to your True Self. It has things *arranged* so that you will *succeed* if you make certain efforts. You're not supposed to do anything else. The rule of thumb for recognizing success in meditation is the same as that for intuition: If you think it's good and it feels good, then it's good. You are the governor of your practice. Successful meditation leaves you feeling better than it found you. Ultimately, meditation is how one knows oneself, and there isn't *anything* better than *that*.

▶ What can I read about meditation?

A book that goes into the matter of meditation quite thoroughly is Patanjali's *Yoga Aphorisms*. It's a classic on the subject.

▶ The yogis speak of meditation with and without a "seed."

What our friends in the East have to say is to the point, because after all, the truth of things—the Reality that we're exploring together—is One and not two. In this case, the seed is an object of concentration used to train the mind. The mind becomes habituated to the meditative state when it is consistently focused on some particular area. It attains a technical stillness that is not typical of the ordinary waking state. As meditation practice proceeds, the mind takes on a different character. It becomes very receptive. Then when you take the seed away, it *continues* to be receptive. By then the mind is *able* to turn deeply inward and contact superconsciousness, which is a term for all there is to know. The Supreme Intelligence communicates with us, otherwise we'd never be able to advance at all.

▶ What seed should you use?

It could be anything. I would encourage you to observe *closely* what is going on in your immediate neighborhood, with a view to gaining insights that you wouldn't have otherwise. Of course, the Tarot offers the Keys for meditation. Alchemy suggests that you pay attention to your body. In general, all the major questions that have perplexed people from the beginning are suitable matters for meditation. Any specific questions that you have about yourself are also suitable.

▶ Could the worship of Isis be considered meditation with a seed?

Absolutely. Isis worship is concentrating on your source of support. Mother is the immediate source of meals, instruction, and a certain amount of discipline. In Key 17, the right angle formed by the leg symbolizes truth. Pragmatically, truth is what *works*.

▶ What can I do when I get sleepy during meditation?

You can call upon the Will in yourself to keep your mind focused. Simply keep returning to your object of meditation. No matter what your meditation seed is, the important thing is to keep your self-consciousness in a watchful, wakeful condition. Sometimes meditation is described as the cat waiting for the mouse—very alert, not moving, just staying completely concentrated. If you can make this state of mind *permanent*, that would be excellent. We're not supposed to get *into* and *out of* meditation. We're supposed to *stay* in it. This keeps you always with one foot on the water and one foot on the land, so that you are continually in contact with the deeper aspect of yourself.

▶ Even when your plans fall through and your car breaks down and your wife leaves you?

That's right. The facade is always out there, but it's on the edge of consciousness. Ordinary events of the world, such as things breaking down, are peripheral to the really important things that are going on inside. This state occurs when you have learned that the outside is a vehicle. Then your meditation is constant and you're not distracted inwardly by *whatever* happens to the vehicle outwardly.

▶ **When you meditate on what's going on around you, do you try to be open to everything?**

You try not to *react* to it. You let it speak to you in its own terms. It's a frame of mind in which you're not making judgments or categorizing. You're simply looking and perceiving. If you get personally involved, you disturb the perception and can't see straight. We're trying to get rid of all conditioning and preconceptions about *anything*.

▶ **Is this really possible?**

Yes, it's possible. For instance, consider the animals. It is likely that some appeal to you more than others. Some seem funny, others ugly, and so on. But as far as the animals themselves are concerned, they *all* think they're beautiful. We're trying to realize that these beings are doing the best they can. We want to accept them just as they are. This is seeing nature as she is, instead of trying to fit the world into some smart scheme of ours.

Don't forget that our consciousness is imprisoned, and we're trying to get it out. Life is an organic affair, a creative, living thing. It can't be put in a box. We certainly should question our beliefs about it.

Einstein's theory of relativity shows us that we don't really know what's going on. For instance, time is based on relationships. It can be stretched out or compressed. If you're having fun, time flies. If you're going to hang, it drags. Many people have experienced their whole life in a few seconds. Time is a useful concept but that's all it is. You know this world is like a play, and time is whatever the author says it is.

From the point of view of wisdom, space is a concept too. In dreams you can see tremendous vistas. In meditation you can look out at the whole universe. How big are these visions? We say that the earth is eight thousand miles in diameter, but what is a mile? We're trying to get to where we can say we don't know how big the earth is. We *don't* know. We don't know where we are; we only *think* we know. What *appears* to be so is *not* so.

Work in this area corresponds exactly to work in the physical plane.

By practicing Hatha Yoga, a person can become physically capable of doing things that seemed *incredible* in the beginning. By practicing control of the psyche, what starts out as a seeming impossibility becomes a mental capability. For example, in the beginning, the emotions are uncontrollable. They are something that just *happens*. Eventually you get a handle on your emotions and you are able to say, "Enough is enough." Emotions are entertaining, but you want to keep them within certain limits. Otherwise, they are perfectly capable of tearing you in half.

Practice is essential. In order to achieve the desired results, you must meditate daily. The instruction in the Tarot and the Cabala is like a map or a blueprint, but that isn't IT, is it? IT is when you *live* it. Musical notation is not the music, and a cookbook is not the food. Until we involve ourselves in it personally, with our own enthusiasm, there's nothing happening. You can talk about meditation until you're blue in the face, but if you don't *try* it, it's completely without any meaning, just a waste of time.

If you experience ups and downs in your practice, think nothing of it, because that's typical of doing anything new, regardless of what it is. Don't be surprised if the practice works for awhile and then doesn't work, and so on. If you persist, after a time you will find yourself stabilized in this frame of mind. The stabilized consciousness is described as samadhi, but if you don't want to get that fancy, you can say that it's beneficial. Meditation is wonderful for you.

▶ **Even if you don't do it every day, is some practice better than none?**

Yes. Since most people are practicing nothing, any effort in this direction will lead you away from total materialism. Still, it's the steady effort that gives the greatest rewards. If you do it every morning and night, it becomes like tuning a fine instrument, which must also be done daily.

You have to save time for your spiritual desires—not sell them down the river. There's no limit to the possibilities for your inner growth. Remember Who designed the idea that we can improve our situation. In *The Book of Tokens* it says that the divine understanding that comes to a person who succeeds in contemplation is like a lake of fire into which the Devil is cast. All your ignorance is burned up, along with all your guilt and suffering.

In the consistently meditative state, you have a grasp of things that is quite extraordinary. According to our teachers, there is no other way for us to unlock the universe. It has to be revealed to us, and it *is* revealed to us when we believe that can happen. Our faith can be bolstered by the experience of countless generations. And through practice we eventually prove it for ourselves beyond any doubt. When you succeed in meditation, it's like being in love; it's always there. A glow persists that changes everything and makes it more beautiful.

▶ **The Devil Key is one of our twenty-two facets. What happens when he's thrown into the fire of wisdom?**

Then you realize that The Devil is always a possibility, but that's all it has to be.

▶ **Can meditation reveal "the lost word"?**

That's the magic word that makes everything happen. In *Morals and Dogma*, Albert Pike says the lost word is "Man"—the human race, the manipulator of mind. We've lost the deeper meaning of that word, but through meditation we can learn the correct definition.

▶ **Why does the Temperance angel in Key 14 have his foot *in* the water while Isis has her foot *on* the water?**

The foot in the water shows that the polarities are more *involved* in Key 14. They are being mixed. The Temperance angel is amphibious.

In Key 17 Isis is resting her weight on the physical earth and she's using the water, the inner life, for *balance*. This symbolism suggests that the inner *explains* the outer. We need to meditate in order to find out what is going on. If you are continually taken up with your own problems and outer interferences, this isn't possible.

▶ **Why is the water in the vases being poured in two different ways?**

We have learned that the Cabala uses water to symbolize mind. Everything we know has to do with mind. In the Tarot, the blue robe of The High Priestess flows down as the stream of mind that runs through everything and unites everything. Mind informs everything, *including itself*, because it has the peculiar characteristic of being able to look at itself.

The way Isis pours the water in Key 17 shows that mind flows in two directions. We can direct it to the inner or the outer, toward heaven or toward the world. These two functions are sometimes referred to as higher mind and lower mind. In Cabalistic deliberations about Moses it is pointed out that he was adept at turning his mind inward, and consequently this gave him a position of leadership. Most of the people with whom he was associated at that time had their minds glued to the earth.

In this Key the pool is a bay in the ocean of Universal Mind. The teaching states that our mind is directly connected to the Universal Mind. In fact, it's altogether the same sort of thing. In the act of meditation we explore the Great Sea of Binah and communicate with it. The water coming from the vase in the Lady's right hand (her primary strength) symbolizes what happens when we meditate. We actually connect, consciously, with the Universal Mind. We elicit a *response* from this source of inspiration within ourselves.

The self-conscious area of ourselves is only a small part of what we're capable of perceiving. The subconscious is far and away the greater part, as is the ocean to a bay. When we *attend* to the inner area in ourselves, when we are receptive, it will speak to us in terms that are intelligible. It might speak through dreams, hunches, visions, or voices. It might come through the avenue of prayer. Every kind of information is available in various forms. Most of the time the messages might be drab, but if we don't pay attention we're going to miss the big answers. You may have been catching minnows on your fishing expeditions, but suddenly you could hook a big tuna.

As for the water coming from the Lady's left side and flowing out into the world, this symbolism presents an important Cabalistic doctrine. It is said that the mind is capable of moving outward through the senses in order to enjoy the earth plane. The five streams represent the five senses. In the nonmeditative state there is a continual flood of sensation coming in *to* you. When you reach the level of meditation, you generate a reverse flow and begin to see *from within,* outwardly. You bring your higher consciousness into the interpretation of what you see on the outside. This changes the picture. You actually transform the data that you're sensing.

▶ **So there is a correspondence between the way our senses work and the actual reality of our existence?**

According to the reports of the wise, this is not theory; this is the way it is. We live through the agency of the senses and no other way. Your consciousness doesn't mean anything unless it has channels to work through. In order to be conscious, you have to have something going on all the time. The senses are the support system for consciousness. Each one has a special quality. Like the organs in our body—the heart, spleen, liver, pancreas—they function differently, yet they function together.

Looking out through the senses means looking through the intuitive faculties. If water flows strongly out through a pipe, nothing can come in. Nothing will come in to disturb you. When we no longer have outside stimuli hammering away at us, the senses become channels of *direct perception*, the means by which we contact Reality. This is what I meant when I said that Key 17 can change your life drastically.

▶ **You actually see, hear, taste, touch, and smell differently from other people?**

That's exactly correct. So don't be surprised if, in the course of your meditations, you look around and see the world in a new light. That's typical of work with Key 17. At the end of this expansive movement of our consciousness through the senses, we will have technically achieved, at least somewhat, the state of cosmic consciousness.

The function of the Divine Mother is to dispense grace. That's what Isis is doing in this card. When the senses work appropriately, her grace enriches the earth and makes it blossom. That is *love*. And on the inside, she brings grace to the mind. Love in the mind creates peace, joy, and illumination.

▶ **Then you are at the top of the purple mountain.**

Yes, on the mountain of mastery or inner attainment that is also pictured in Keys 6 and 8 (The Lovers and Strength). This is something that we're all climbing *together*. This is the Aquarius card—Aquarius is the sign of humanity. The route we travel is the Path of Liberation. When we get to the top, we join forces with our True Self.

▶ **What do you think about this Key in connection with the Aquarian Age?**

Everybody has something to contribute to the New Age. Everybody's important. Everything God created is important.

We live in hope. Astrologers say that Aquarius governs hope, and this is sometimes called the Key of Hope. Eventually we'll have to realize that we're trying to run a planet in space. Aquarius is an air sign and this Key rules the atmosphere. Starting with our breathing, our life experience is based on the atmosphere. Aquarius is ruled by Uranus, the planet of inspiration—a word that literally means "breath." And remember that the atmosphere delivers the water. No water, no nuttin'.

Isis has an occult connection with the star Sirius, which is said to have an overseeing, helping function for Earth. Sirius is like the main star in Key 17. It is much bigger and brighter than our sun. It's the only star that we can see in the daytime (when conditions are right, of course).

The seventeenth Key represents the Natural Intelligence. We're all naturally intelligent. It's inborn in us. We're trying to get this particular element in ourselves quite *clear* and free of as much nonsense as possible. The New Age will be an intelligent epoch when it gets under way. *Intelligence will rule*, and that will make the world very different from what it is now. We have a marvelous future to look forward to, when humanity wakes up.

Since the Mother creates us, her intelligence is the encompassing intelligence that understands everything about the way we are made. God works in mysterious ways Her wonders to perform. Your body is made up of *zillions* of atoms, all of which are organized. And you're the boss of all this!

The act of meditation has definite physical effects. The Moon card rules the function of sleep, and we are told that mental changes due to our waking efforts will be built into the body during sleep. On the Path in Key 18, going *up* means going *in*. There have to be physical changes in order to make this kind of experience possible, and these changes are instigated by—you guessed it—none other than meditation.

By the time you get to this point in the Tarot, you certainly have ample material to meditate upon. There's a terrific power drive coming through all of the previous Keys, so you have a great deal of support backing you up. The authors of the Tarot promise that, if we practice faithfully in the daytime, at night our inner nature will transform the vehicle. The refined body makes it possible to advance into newer and better states of consciousness. The inner *potential* becomes *actualized* as the body responds to our spiritual progress. The psyche and the soma are so closely tied together that we may *expect* considerable physical improvements if we involve ourselves with the discipline of the Path.

Thanks for your company. Have fun with body-building this week.

KEY 18

CHAPTER 18

THE MOON

WE ARE "fearfully and wonderfully made." I don't think there is anyone here who would disagree with this inspired biblical statement. The more we consider how fearfully and wonderfully we are made, the better it is for us. The structures and processes of the body are far and away the most important observable phenomena in the whole universe. Alchemy considers the body to be the key to understanding. In terms of science, everything imaginable happens in the body—physics, chemistry, *everything*. Key 17 taught us that we should meditate upon nature. Now Key 18 suggests that the most fruitful place to examine nature is your own dear bod.

The body is made of atoms. This fact in itself is the basis of a powerful meditation. An atom is a little solar system. Electrons are whirling around like planets, but at an alarming rate. Nobody knows where the perpetual motion in the atoms is coming from. The matrix for these little marvels is space—what Cabalists call the magical Ain Suph Aur.

The next step takes us to the mysterious molecule. On that level we are mostly water. Then to the cell, which is an enormously complicated array of molecules. Cells have the ability to divide themselves in half. The daughter cell has all the elements of the original cell *plus* the ability to specialize. The whole fabulous, star-like aggregation interacts to produce the ongoing result we call the body. It's really a *universe*. The kingdom of heaven is literally embodied in your flesh. A masterful power of ORGANIZATION holds it all together. How does It do it? God only knows.

For many years I have recommended the study of embryology. You could just look it up in an encyclopedia and be impressed. You've heard of boy meets girl. Well, in embryology, sperm meets ovum and the most extraordinary things start to happen. The egg splits and multiplies and a baby is on the way to being born. All of a sudden, by some inexplicable means the creation of a new creature has begun. I think the only way to understand this phenomenon is from the spiritual perspective.

Under the auspices of The Moon, the Path takes you up through an evolutionary process to the Peak of Understanding. In this philosophy, spiritual evolution and physical evolution go hand in hand, because psyche and soma are intertwined. The sages promise that insofar as we make any effort in the direction of spiritual unfoldment, we are going to get a physiological result. If we use all the instruction we've received from the Tarot thus far, our bodies are going to become more subtle and more finely organized. This is guaranteed by those who have had the experience. They come right out and tell you that you can change your body through meditation. This may sound weird at first, until you remember psychosomatics.

Outer physical evolution is proceeding steadily but slowly. By applying the suggestions offered to us, we can speed up the process inwardly. We advance our consciousness beyond the average, creating a higher vibratory rate, which is reflected in the body through the workings of the subconscious.

New attitudes are actually built into the body during sleep. Then, as our physical capabilities improve, these in turn make it possible to advance our spiritual growth, and so on. Our evolution increases in this happy, cycling fashion, until we get so much farther beyond what we thought was possible for ourselves that even *we* can see the improvement!

The usual view of evolution looks at what has happened long ago in the past. The Ageless Wisdom is very different, in that it emphasizes the evolution of *ourselves, now*. Every human being is at a certain stage in his or her spiritual progress. Whoever and wherever we are, the Tarot and the Cabala can be extremely useful in forwarding our personal evolution. Like God, occult science is no respecter of persons, so nobody is looking down any noses at our level of development. Occult unfoldment is strictly a matter between the individual and the Innermost Self.

The work of Self-unfoldment is *always* an ongoing process. There are a lot of things to consider—we surely know that by now—but there is always one integrating aspect. The whole matter concerns the blossoming of the Self in ourselves. As we move along, certain qualities that were just potentials become actualized, and we discover that we are basically magnificent beings. This is one reason why the wisdom teachings place so much emphasis on being yourself. The masters of the Cabala know that the True Self of Man is a very worthwhile affair. Therefore they are anxious to get it going and off the ground. We have their support in this development. We have every possible opportunity to participate in the experiment of Self-evolution.

▶ Do you ever feel urgency about evolution?

Evolution is going to happen anyway, so there's nothing to worry about. We're not God, you know. The latest scientific evidence substantiates the *forward* movement of the universe. We can't stop it. Evolution is something we can *count on.*

Without the support of evolution, Gandhi would never have made it. He had something pushing him, a tremendous impetus that was bigger than Gandhi. His demonstration will never be forgotten. It was a big load on one man, but he carried it.

▶ Can I trust that forces greater than my intellect are guiding my evolution?

In this philosophy, that's a wise point of view. Of course, as I said, we can *participate* consciously and speed up the process. The Moon is the Key of Evolution. It represents the power with which we cooperate. The face of The Moon shows the *brooding* of the feminine power over evolution. This is an aspect of the cosmic meditation.

As you know, in the Cabala all the departments of life have their executive Intelligences, just as in a big corporation. When you realize the amount of intelligence that goes into the construction of your body, you begin to grasp the importance of the eighteenth Key. When I first started with the Tarot, it came as a shock to me that there was such a thing as a Corporeal Intelligence, an intelligence of the body. (I hadn't heard a lot of things at age twenty-two.) After many years of observation, I decided that this power really and truly exists, and that I'd better give some *credit* to the Corporeal Intelligence, not just take it for granted.

There is an abundance of bodies on this planet. All sorts of constructions are flying, swimming, walking, gnawing, dancing, and prancing around. All we have to do is mentally dissect these magical creatures in order to see an amazing intelligence at work. It may be foreign to *our* intelligence, but nevertheless it displays an enormous know-how of structure, organization, design, instinct, and so on.

In all the books I've read about this subject, mind has never been mentioned at all. Science doesn't recognize that the occult principle of mind underlies all physical forms. There is a separation between the scientist and the phenomenal aspect he is looking at. To him, it's "over there," so his ability to see it is more or less accurate. On the other hand, we can make a big excursion into this area. We should look into these matters because they teach us respect for the kind of mind that creates these goodies. We find that these powers vested in the Great Unconscious are both real and remarkable. We discover that *we* are magical constructions of the unconscious.

The moon is an extremely ancient symbol of the Divine Mother, the feminine aspect of the Life Power. It's not surprising that among her vast talents, *she* is the lord of bodies. The entire physical domain is ruled by Binah, the third emanation on the Tree of Life. Number three controls the concrete, as opposed to the ephemeral.

▶ I don't quite get the meaning of the key word: "organization."

The primitve person thinks of his body as something solid. He doesn't think of it as being made of radiant energy. If you said to him, "Did you know that your body is made of light?" he might punch you in the nose and say, "How's your light feeling right now?" This materialistic approach does not negate the fact that the body is made of living, intelligent *Light*. The only reason it reacts to punches and so on is that it's *organized* to respond. As Shakespeare said, "We are such stuff as dreams are made on." Take away the space, and you can put the body's material elements on the head of a pin. There's really nothing there. It's all organization.

When "a body meets a body coming through the rye," then you have one organization of radiant energy meeting another organization of radiant energy, which is already *geared up* to react. This bunch of nothing is systematized to react to another bunch of nothing. Strange it may seem, but it's true just the same. This was highly classified information in the ancient mystery schools.

Another remarkable thing is that the organization produces *qualities*. Resistance, color, motility, and so forth, are all based on an inner structure that is a collection of whirlings. After all, the atom is just a whirling dervish. When many dervishes dance together, they form a framework that is a girl or a boy or an elephant or a giraffe. They form a *plan* that is *alive*. As atoms become arranged, they become beings. Because of the extremely clever organization of these atoms, they can smile and sing and do almost anything.

This is all the expression of the Life Force in motion. This energy coursing through us all the time is the basic whirling coming out of Kether at the top of the Tree of Life. Subconscious organization is a fantastic mechanism *enlivened* by Life Itself.

▶ **The eighteen Yods in this picture symbolize a lot of Life Force.**

Right you are. Eighteen is the number of CHAI, the Hebrew word for Life. As symbols of the Archetypal World, the Yods in Key 18 represent the *ideas* that are actually the guiding principles of evolution. The Moon is the agency that *develops* ideas, while the ideas themselves provide the spark that makes the whole thing happen.

This archetypal root of power is in Chokmah, the Divine Father, second center on the Tree of Life. Because of the placement of the Tetragrammaton on the Tree, Yod is the signature of this particular Sephirah. Chokmah inspires everything that's going on. Just for your own comfort, so you won't make the mistake of thinking that God is one thing and you are another, this is *your own* Yod, which is *your own Self*, which inspires everything to do with *you*.

The power is raining down in a rather enlarged fashion here because it's not just one idea. *Many* ideas are sustaining your corporeal existence. There are numerous organs and functions in your body. All sorts of weird and wonderful things are coming to you from the Archetypal World, fueling the vehicle that you are driving in this incarnation. In other words, these Yods illustrate the descent of *grace*.

▶ **This picture looks spooky to me. The animals could be the forces of ignorance, bugaboos of the darkness.**

You are touching upon the current psychological view of the *personal* subconscious, which is a mish-mash of feelings, beliefs, influences, and experiences—everything that's going on in a person's life. Underlying that level is *the* Unconscious, which really isn't unconscious at all in the sense that we ordinarily use the term.

Consider healing, for instance. When you cut yourself, there is no way you can do anything about it with your conscious mind, but your *un*conscious mind can go right ahead and heal that cut. This happens in a regular, systematic way, just as though there were a doctor inside.

When we get to the Collective Unconscious, we're on the level of what religion might call the Divine. This what-seems-to-us limbo is actually sustaining us. We're playing around on the surface of things. *Behind* the surface is a tremendous organization that is very much alive and "with it." We don't pay much conscious attention to it, but in certain dreams and meditations, we're allowed to participate in this underlying intelligence. Then it could be said that we are divinely inspired, but it's not necessary to get theological about this. In a simple, direct way, such experiences can be very helpful to us.

The road that's pictured in The Moon Key leads us into these deeper realms. There are two mountain peaks, one on either side of the wolf's head. These are the peaks of Wisdom and Understanding, Chokmah and Binah on the Tree of Life. Our way leads to the left, which is Mother, mind, substance, and Saturn. The Path of Understanding is a Saturnine path. In the Cabala, the mystic path is actually a technical discipline. When you know your own mind, the light of Wisdom will be revealed from within. Your mind is a moon, reflecting the inner sun that shines at midnight.

▶ **Key 18 gives me a mystical feeling.**

In the zodiac, Key 18 stands for Pisces, sign of the mystic, to whom everything is God. At this point in time, the Path of Understanding is not trodden by many. Most people aren't interested. It just doesn't appeal to them. Go into the hotel around the corner and ask anyone, "Excuse me, are you on the Path?" They're likely to say, "I'm going to bed. Is that what you mean?" They just don't know what you're talking about.

▶ **Those who do know about the Path may be very attracted to it. Like the yellow brick road in *The Wizard of Oz*, it's an adventurous journey through dangerous territory into a land of glory.**

Ah, yes, for devotees of this philosophy, nothing compares with the thrill of traveling the Path. The yellow color corresponds to the intellectual, conscious principle. As beings evolve, they become more conscious. If you *like* being conscious, then this is for you. Yellow is the color of the middle way that goes between fire and water in Key 14 (Temperance), and between art and nature in Key 18.

Because it's an example of human adaptation, the dog represents art. The wolf typifies a feral, natural condition. The consciousness that goes in between *manipulates* the situation when you become an active agent in your own evolution. You can turn yourself into just about anything you please, somewhat like Alice in Wonderland. Nibble on one side of the cookie and you become tall; nibble on the other side and you become short. Eventually you find what is just right for you in this plastic situation.

Whatever a person is going to become is that person's own responsibility. In the art of living, the major material is *yourself*. An artist must *concentrate*, which means that you must *decide* what it is you want to be. The Tarot is the artist's manual, a set of instructions outlined by our more advanced fellows. The main key to the art is meditation, which helps you discover what is and what is not true about yourself. It puts you in touch with your Innermost Self, which is your *guide* in all this business.

► What does it mean that the wolf is wild and the dog is tame?

Your feral aspect and your domesticated aspect are like poles. You sort of wobble between them. You like to go wild sometimes, and then the pendulum swings back to domesticity again. Key 18 tells you not to go too far either way. When you're running a household, you want it to be reasonably clean, but you don't want it to be sterile. Once you begin wiping the doorknobs with disinfectant when anybody enters the room, then you're definitely on the wrong track.

► I'm skeptical about evolution. I don't see people getting any better as they get older. They don't get any smarter. They certainly don't get any prettier.
► CLASS: Boo, hiss!
► I guess I'm talking about myself.

A person who is wise in the occult sense doesn't accept much of what the world labels as beautiful. If you can't make a *game* out of society's antics, then you're caught on the flypaper right now. You simply must not get your head into all the foolishness that's going on. You have to concentrate on your own psychology. Try to get the most accurate definition of yourself that you possibly can.

Our truly wise teachers have made a statement that runs counter to the world. We have to look *deeply* into things, especially into ourselves. We can look at ourselves as a person from another planet would view us.

The Cabala is an extremely useful instrument for introspection without going overboard. The Tree of Life explains yourself to yourself without driving you crazy. It's a valuable anchor. Insofar as you understand yourself, you understand other people.

▶ Jason, are you saying that worldly things don't get any better?

The conditions of life are always there. In the Chinese alchemical text, *The Secret of the Golden Flower,* there is a picture of a sage who is peacefully seated in the midst of the conditions. You're not supposed to get excited about conditions; you're supposed to get excited about yourself. It's not easy to realize that you don't have to *have* something or *accomplish* something. The doctrine states that the way we are intrinsically is perfect. There's nothing wrong with us. We're just fine.

In the highest teaching, there is no difference between yourself and the Great Self, except in degree. If you believe this, you have to practice humility. You also have to *laugh,* because the difference between your naturally limited self and your True Self is just ridiculous. However, you are still *like a god* compared with people who are the unnecessary victims of ignorance. When you see the whole Tree of Life working in the smallest event of your life, then you've got it made. Once you become yourself, you are not upset by conditions. A master in Cabalistic terms doesn't feel that he or she *has* to do *anything.*

▶ As the Path undulates we naturally experience highs and lows.

It's a rising path, but as you say, it has its ups and downs. Looking back over the experience of years, we find that our present lows are above our past highs. Once you gain some understanding—once you grasp the *meaning*—it never leaves you. It becomes the ground for your next advance.

▶ Sometimes we forget to practice what we know. We fall back.

Our problem is to become integrated, so that we *remember* ourselves *completely.* As we get stronger inside, we become able to sustain a certain state of consciousness throughout the day. This takes real concentration, because there *are* just one or two distractions around! Nevertheless, the goal is to have our special music going all the time, underlying our outer activities, so that we don't take the world too seriously. We brush our teeth and all the rest of it, while enjoying the inner accompaniment of another sort of song.

The Path symbolizes the ascent of the Tree of Life. It is the scientific approach for getting from the outer to the inner. The Cabala does not de-emphasize the outer at any time. The universe is not so bad or nasty that we can hardly wait to get away from it, but there is a *challenge* to understand it better. Our teachers tell us that the *only* way we can understand it is by including the inner—the psychological and spiritual side of life.

If we keep working at it we will inevitably acquire wisdom and understanding. Then we will get the prize, the crown that's shown in the Temperance Key, representing Kether at the top of the Tree. In other words, the prize is that you become yourself.

You might ask, "Am I not always myself?" The Cabala explains that you are only *partially* yourself until you have traversed the Path. In order to be complete, you must learn wisdom and understanding. Then, for the first time in your whole life, you know precisely what to do with yourself and you proceed to do it.

When we start out on the Path, we are like the crayfish pictured at the bottom of Key 18. Its hard shell represents egotism. When our orientation changes, this shell cracks open and a new being emerges.

▶ **Purple is an unusual color for a crayfish.**

In the Tarot, purple (or violet) is a symbolic reference to Yesod, the Foundation on the Tree of Life. The pools in Keys 14, 17 and 18 (Temperance, The Star, and The Moon) all correspond to Yesod. The Foundation has to do with the propagation and evolution of all forms. When the Tree of Life is diagrammed as a person, Yesod is assigned to the sexual organs. It is through sex that reproduction occurs, so that various forms of life are carried forward from one generation to the next.

Yesod is also the seat of automatic consciousness. From our point of view the pool of unconsciousness is extremely mysterious. Our textbook calls it "the great deep of cosmic mind-stuff." Lots of things are somewhat impalpable, such as electricity, magnetism, and light. And lots of other things are *altogether* impalpable. Our mind is okay, but it's small and has limited scope. The Great Mind is the miracle worker that creates the universe. In its *most* magical aspect, it is the machinery of reproduction. The magic of the unconscious is not goofy in any way. It works scientifically. People who investigate this kind of thing gradually come to some understanding of it. But they didn't invent it. It has always been there. If you want to see it, *look!*

The teaching about The Moon Key states that evolution proceeds through the five kingdoms evidenced in nature: mineral, animal, vegetable, human, and superhuman. The last category includes our elder brothers and sisters who are advanced on the Path. They are sometimes referred to as Those Who Have Gone Before. They reach out to all those who come after.

▶ **Why are there no people visible in the picture?**

You are the one who is walking the Path. Although you have a body, you are not a body. A spiritual being doesn't leave any footprints.

The gates are wide open to the Beyond, but first we must pass between the towers, which are *battlements*. They instruct us in the warlike nature of the ego. The people in there have a tendency to get overprotective and spend all their money on the military budget. So we shall pass through them quickly. In fact, we should cast fear aside and *run* through, escaping the arrows and the hot lead. Then we can proceed up the Path into superconscious areas that are beyond ordinary human experience.

▶ **Why is the bodily intelligence so intimately connected with the Path?**

The change from egotism to liberation will be brought about by our conscious efforts, yours and mine. We will envision a better future for ourselves, and because of that vision, it will happen. The Emperor, Justice, and The Moon form the central column in the Tableau. (The Fool is outside—in between the Keys—like space.) When you imagine yourself in a certain life situation, the Universal Subconscious immediately sets to work to bring it about. Sustained by your own desire and will, your mind—like water—takes the shape of whatever vessel you put it into. This is where you *become involved* in your own evolution. Key 18 is the outcome of your constitution. If you are brave enough to hang on to your dream for yourself, it will manifest.

▶ **Why is this a matter of fear and bravery?**

We have an instinctual fear of the unknown. In this connection, the letter of The Moon Key is QOPH ק. It means the *back of the head*, a reference to the medulla oblongata. Qoph is the *old brain* that contains all of the body's instinctual energies and controls. It is the seat of the animal that we inhabit. One of the problems we humans have is understanding that we live in an animal body. We must make due allowance for this truth. But a human being is not an animal; this we must remember also. The animal is our means of experiencing this level of life.

Without any exception, bodies operate on an instinctual basis. They are designed to react to their environment according to survival programming. This has little to do with the higher and finer things of life. "I'm for me, and that's what counts. I've got to survive on my own." In the animal world, this makes a lot of sense. If something is going to *eat* you, you hightail it out of there. You don't get a lawyer and go through appeals.

Fear is one of our natural, animal tendencies that we must learn to use properly. On the instinctive level, we're always trying to defend ourselves *whether or not* there is anything to be afraid of. We are on the defensive until our faith or experience is strong enough to change our level of perception. Instincive fear is an obstacle we must definitely overcome. We can elaborate, rationalize, and embroider it with our emotions as much as we please, but there it is, until we know better.

The Tarot and the Cabala offer excellent instruction in this task of taming the animal nature and getting it to work for your evolution. Any individual who is thoroughly saturated with this particular discipline is going to advance, in a relatively short time, to a level that will be widespread for the masses in the future. This is sometimes called the Short Path. Instead of taking thousands of years to evolve, it's possible to advance a long way in one lifetime, so that you will be Self-governed from inside. All the *controls* of yourself are inside. Self-guidance is latent in most people, but through effort you can bring it into expression.

▶ **The Cabala says the body is a temple, a place of worship. What does this mean?**

A temple is a place where the Presence is to be found. If you go to a good, honest church, you will undoubtedly feel the Presence there. The indication is that our bodies and our personalities are temples for the Presence of the Most High. The most high thing that we know about is our own Inner Self. It's really a *Super Self* compared to the personality or little self.

▶ **Is the little self the temple custodian?**

It's the high priest. Bit by bit the personality learns to represent the God Within. If we pursue the Path when we're awake, then the body reaches toward the newer state when we're asleep. Our subconscious makes the necessary physical changes when our waking mind is out of the way. Whatever your inner, secret goal is, if you hold to it and give it some attention every day, that's when the body responds. The rhythmic effect of doing something every day is very important. Whatever your goal is, you have to keep at it in order to build it into your body.

▶ **But we shouldn't feel guilty if we miss a day?**

Nobody just trudges from the bottom to the top without getting sidetracked. After awhile your practice gets to be second nature, but even then you have your ups and downs. The undulating Path is characteristic of cyclicity. Your whole life is cyclic and the sooner you recognize it, the better it is for you. Then you won't get all upset when it doesn't go in a straight line. You may say, "I hate to go to sleep at night because there are so many other things I'd like to do," but you *must* sleep. There are things we just have to accept.

It is said that when we are in *deep* sleep, we are connected with our Higher Self. This intimate connection with our divine aspect is what makes it possible for us to get up in the morning. Hopefully, the more advanced we are, the more happily we will rise with the dawn and get on about our business.

▶ **Can revelations come in the dream state?**

Revelations can come in any state, sleep or otherwise. The Tibetans say that when you can't tell the difference between waking and sleeping, you are making progress. When you and I are walking around, we're in a dream just as much as when we're asleep at night. It's a little different, but still, we're *always* in a dream. What we're trying to do is make our dream coincide with Reality a little more, because it's exciting to do that. As they say, Reality is stranger than fiction; what's more important, it's more *fun* than fiction.

If you keep a journal in which you record both your waking and dream experiences, you're likely to find there's not much difference between the two after some time has elapsed. It's a good idea to try to remember your dreams. As time goes on, you will be able to remember them better and better. Taking a hint from our friend Carl Jung, I've been paying attention to my dreams for some years. One thing I've discovered that might be of interest: If you make a sort of shorthand, a little sketch of a dream, in your journal, then years later when you concentrate on it a bit, the whole experience returns in detail.

▶ What do you think about prophetic dreams?

As far as I'm concerned, the value of prophetic dreams is that they loosen up our hard-and-fast views about what's possible and what isn't possible. Some dreams are revolutionary. A dream can be like the road to Damascus for us. One minute you are one kind of person; then you have a dream or a vision and suddenly you're a different kind of person. It makes a profound impression and can completely change your feelings.

The Moon Key is followed by The Sun Key in the Tarot series. Alchemy is often called the work of the Sun and Moon. If the Sun has nothing to shine upon, then the Sun doesn't know itself. The substantial mirror we call physicality is *evidence of the Sun.*

The main theme in Key 19 is joy. Many people look askance at joy. They believe that being joyful leads to anguish when you have to stop being joyful, so why go through with it? Why not just be sad all the time? Tarot and Cabala have a strange answer to this problem: We're supposed to be joyful all the time! As Lao Tzu said many years ago, if we were to stop torturing each other, we'd feel pretty good. In fact, we'd be on a real high.

The sun plays an enormous role in keeping us joyful. Our entire earthly existence is completely supported by solar energy. The Tarot indicates that we should have *due regard* for the source of our life and consciousness. Just to make it exciting and unbelievable, Taroists and the Cabalists say that the sun is a living creature. That idea is so incredible that you ought to have a perfectly marvelous week thinking it over. Thank you for joining me tonight.

KEY 19

CHAPTER 19

THE SUN

THINGS ARE GETTING better all the time. The lovely Sun Key reminds us that we are involved in a *joyful process*, a flowering of the Self. This is not one of those grief-stricken practices where you sweat it out here and get your reward in the hereafter. The Cabalistic method of attainment, as pictured in the Tarot, aims to bring us to the point where we can enjoy the simple and beautiful things in life right now.

Spiritually inclined people have a tendency to get excited about the inner light—the more abstract it is, the better they like it—and they take the outer light for granted. From the viewpoint of the Cabala there is no difference between our inner and outer light.

I'd like to ask you a question. Has anyone here ever had friendly feelings toward the sun? Yes, several of us indicate friendly feelings toward the sun. Have you ever felt a response from the sun? Yes, we have experienced communication with the sun. Have you felt better afterward? Yes, yes. That's because it's *family*.

In the Middle Ages you could lose your head if you didn't subscribe to the idea that the earth was the center of the universe. Our civilization had forgotten that we belong to the sun's family. The sun is our parent. You could go so far as to say that it's the very God of the Earth. In ancient Egypt this was the viewpoint of Akhenaten, who was a very intelligent and far-sighted pharaoh. In one of his hymns to the sun he wrote, "You fill every land with your perfection."

I'm not talking about the physical ball of fire. I mean that the *being* whose body is the sun is an advanced spiritual being. And I'm not suggesting that you fall on your face and make blubbering noises at certain times of the day. All that's necessary is some recognition and appreciation. That something so benevolent could be completely ignored by religion is very shortsighted.

The earth responds to the sun in countless marvelous ways. Just look around and you can see the whole miraculous interaction. In fact, like the children in Key 19, we can just look at each other and see the whole thing.

This picture of a girl and boy dancing in front of a wall follows the old Tarot Sun Key tradition. The wall represents accumulated wisdom. These kids are having a wonderful time because they have advanced beyond the accumulation. I'd be the last person in the world to disparage Ageless Wisdom, as you probably could imagine, but there is something *beyond* wisdom: there is the Now. What happens in the Now is special, and the children are living in that.

Key 19 takes us a giant step closer to home base and the climax of the whole Tarot series. In moving from the fearful to the creative, from the known to the Now, we enter a wondrous new world of experience. This movement brings about a REGENERATION of the spirit. Any way you slice it, regeneration is good for you. It makes you feel young and strong and glad. It makes you want to sing all day. First you get old and gray and decrepit studying the ancient teachings. You're practically doddering by the time you get done with it all. Then suddenly you get a new lease on life. You feel rejuvenated by something inside yourself.

After you are spiritually regenerated, what do you do with yourself? That decision comes in Key 20, Judgement. Then in Key 21, The World, you go ahead and do it. You *must* be creative. you can't live with your present furniture forever; it's going to wear out and fall apart. Conditions are not going to last, but *you* are going to last and you don't want to face immortality with nothing to do. Perhaps you want to cook, or play the piano, or run up the mountain. Whatever you decide, that's your Self speaking. That is what restores joy to your life. Outer things—the price of eggs or the outcome of the election—they make no difference. Our Innermost Self wants us and expects us to see that our own particular approach is the right one. Nothing else will work.

You may say, "This is all very well, but if I do what is pictured here, if I just go out in the park and dance around, pretty soon I'm going to starve to death. If I leave the church and stop being a Republican and don't believe my books any more, what's left?" Well, what's left is the companionship of your intuition and the illumination that is your birthright. The Sun Key presents the happy balance between your self-conscious and your subconscious aspects, which are seen to be enjoying each other to the utmost.

By this time all of us are depending on our intuitive faculty, whereas in the beginning perhaps we didn't even know we had such a thing. I don't want to get too fancy here, but I'm talking about how Life supports us, otherwise known as the Presence of God. We don't have to get down on our knees and pound our chests. Our inner attunement simply means that, in an intelligent and conscious way, we understand that we are directly sustained by the cosmos itself. Therefore we depend upon it. We just have to *remember* it. This is the awareness of the children in Key 19.

Our intimacy with the sun is one feature of our cosmic support we can readily grasp. In Key 14, your guardian angel is identified with the solar Intelligence. The more you meditate on that, the more you become aware that it's a *real* power.

The sun is the source of the regeneration of your spirit. That's the crucial part of the matter. If your spirit is sick, then you are sick. If your spirit is well, then you can put up with a lot of nonsense and still manage to be quite well. If your spirit is in the best of health, you don't need to worry about your body. The body is a marvel anyway and it's under the direct control of your spirit, so you might say that this is a poor man's way to health. If we are careful about the state of our spirit, never letting any distraction interfere with our concentration on this vital element of our lives, evolution will bring about the regeneration that's spoken of in this Key.

All you have to do is meditate on the sun, which is a fun thing to do. Don't look at it with your physical eyes. Just *consider* solar energy. Once you realize the constant support that's coming to us *all the time* from the sun, then you have a good idea of what this Key means. For instance, the thoughts we are thinking right now are supported *completely* by solar energy.

As you experience more and more inner development, you will eventually come to the Great Sun Initiation. You will find, to your utter joy, that all the peanuts and cornflakes you've been eating, which contain marvelous amounts of solar energy, *also* contain the element of your own personal illumination. The Initiation of the Sun is as simple as that. All we have to do is to sort out the Intelligence that lives within energy. Meditation is a technique that gives us an opportunity to taste the illumination that comes to us from the sun. The sun is not the ultimate source, but it is the *direct and immediate* source of our enlightenment.

Aside from the fact that it energizes *all* of our activities, it specifically energizes our occult initiations.

▶ **Let me get this straight. You're saying that what science thinks of as a bunch of hot gas is the actual source of our spiritual awakening.**

You've got it. In the Cabala, sun energy is different from the scientific definition. It's a dogma of occultism that the chain of sun energy, which comes into our bodies all the time, actually contains the inner light. Illumination is everyone's birthright. The main thing is for us to get to it as soon as possible. This is an unfamiliar area for the modern scientist.

▶ **If the sun is the immediate source of illumination, what is the ultimate source?**

The ultimate source of *everything* is the Ain Suph Aur, or Life Itself. This is symbolized in Key 19 by the zero figure where the children dance, which is said to be a magical fairy ring. In the Cabala a circle always stands for the great No-Thing, the underlying Reality from which life continually draws in order to move forward. The regenerative aspect of life doesn't come from what's already there. It comes out of the Big Zero. From our conventional point of view, this is negative existence. From a philosophical point of view it is the ultimate positive, the matrix of everything. It is the source of all the apparent representations in the universe. This is very much like the concept of the Tao in that a) it's mysterious, b) it's indescribable, and c) it does everything.

This harks back to Key 0, The Fool. Like the children in The Sun Key, The Fool of God knows that if you have the Ain Suph Aur you don't need anything else. The zero epitomizes freedom. This ellipse is the children's infinite *playground*.

▶ **There is a sun in The Fool Key, too.**

That sun is the *first symbol* in the Tarot. It's the white sun of the Limitless Light, the mystical, spiritual source of which our solar friend is a direct expression. Our sun is a *palpable* agency that's operating (fortunately for us, in our present condition) twenty-four hours a day, three hundred and sixty-five days a year, and has been for millions and millions of years. The most uneducated person anywhere on earth can relate to the sun: there it is. It's our day-star, the cosmic instrument for maintaining life in the three-dimensional world, which it does faithfully and well. And as I explained, it does much more than supply energy like a mechanical robot. It supports the intelligence of beings from its own Intelligence.

▶ Some day the sun will burn out.

Your mother and father will die someday, but still they had a profound effect on your existence. Even if the sun burns out, its energy will not be lost. It will exist in another form. Take yourself, for example. Once you were a little baby. As a matter of fact, once upon a time you were a tiny cell. The *particular form* that you were in at that stage is *gone*, but all the *energy* involved in that form is *here this evening*—and thank you for coming. So the sun may go out but then something will take its place. Another form will be extended from it.

The sun as we know it today will exist forever. Everything goes through changes, but remember that, as the Cabalists say, whatever is, *will be*, and whatever is, *was*. The whole continuum is a permanent proposition. In the East they call this the AKASHIC RECORD. There's plenty of room. We are limited, but the universe is not.

▶ Does this mean you could rephrase the first statement in the Pattern on the Trestleboard, "All the *things* that ever were or will be are here now?"

Yes, exactly. There's no question about whether a thing is going to live or die. If it's here, it will exist forever, just the way it is now. Then there will be *another* expression, which will be an *extension* of it, which will be different, and that will exist forever too.

We mentioned that the children are living in the Now. Believe it or not, that's where *we* are living all the time. This is why we have unlimited capacity for transformation. We can last as long as we wish, providing that we are willing to emerge from our present state into something different.

▶ Where is the beginning—the creation—in Cabalistic cosmology?

The sages tell us that "beginning" is a time-oriented concept, a projection from any given point in the scheme of things. In actuality the creation is constant. God is *always* moving a hand over the waters, and if He didn't, or She didn't, that would be the end of it. The creative energy within anything has to *continue* in order to uphold the creation. It never stops for a moment. We are *participating* in this constant support that comes from He-She or She-He. It is the basis of any creativity we have. There is no separation between ourselves and That.

▶ What do the sages say about the concept of "future"?

The future already exists. All works of imagination look into the future. If it weren't there, it couldn't be seen, and we wouldn't have any works of imagination. A creative person doesn't sit down and say, "I'm real smart; I'm gonna dream up the future." Oh, no. He *envisions* it. That means it's handed to him on a plate. And it's precise. It works out in a fantastic way.

▶ Imagination is the way to get out of a locked-in condition.

So true. A very important point. The other side of the wall is the locked-in condition. The children are in a *new* area. You get there through the creative use of fantasy, or what Carl Jung called the active imagination. In his work as a psychiatrist, Dr. Jung found that imagination can take you out of a neurosis or a psychosis. In the new area you may have your ups and downs, your good days and bad days, but they don't compare with the agony of being on the other side of the wall. Once you get into a closer relationship with Reality, you can't stand the old condition. It's absolutely *horrible* to feel stuck . . . no way out . . . same old stuff day in and day out . . . nothing new coming in . . . (shudder).

The new elements come through creative fantasy. You take the old elements and look them over; you sort through the junk pile and say, "Maybe I could make something worthwhile out of this, but that has got to go." You must have a vital imagination in order to stay healthy and move on to new arrangements for yourself.

▶ I am afraid of becoming so unattached that I will miss out.

You might let the sun be your teacher. It shines without attachments or expectations. Unconditional love is not looking for anything. It just *is*. Love in the Cabala happens when you reach the level of Chesed, the Exempt Adept, and that means you are exempt from all attachments. You have learned to let it all float through you.

Being afraid you will miss out is a kind of attachment. If you try to clutch life and hang on to it, it's like dream money. The more you grasp it, the more it disappears. On the other hand, if you can consider life a spectacle for your enjoyment, then you get the most pleasure out of every minute. You see, you don't lose anything. As a matter of fact, you have *more*. If the thought, "I'm going to lose it," is preying on your mind, this spoils the fun. If you simply say, "I'm going to *eat* it," that's much better.

You have to depend on the Power of Life to bring you *the works* because this power goes beyond your wildest dreams. If you get in the way and say to life, "I'm afraid of not getting enough," you ruin the deal, you really do. If you take it easy and think, "The whole thing is going to be spread on the floor in front of me, like Christmas when I was five years old," *it will be*. That's the way it works.

You know, with our raving mad intellects, which know practically nothing about anything (my own included), we lay all sorts of nonsense on life. It's like telling an elephant that it weighs too much, or a redwood tree that it's too tall. As one friend of mine said, "I don't like the beach. It's too sandy."

▶ **In order to let the life energy go through you . . . ?**

. . . You've got to get out of the way. The ego has to *allow* it to happen. This sounds great, but it's not so easy.

▶ **What about the parts of life that you don't like?**

It's the ego that says, "I don't want everything to go through. I'll take the diamonds and some ripe bananas and leave the rest." The idea that it's *all* going through is abhorrent to the ego, because it wants to be king. In our discussion of Key 15, Jung was quoted as saying that the Devil represents the *un*regenerate intellect. The *re*generated intellect doesn't see life in terms of itself. In the Now, you are an invisible line that goes across the stream of life—the stream pictured in the Tarot. It's rushing through you like crazy. As Lao Tzu said, all you have to do is sit there and enjoy it.

▶ **Can you ever get to like all of it?**

You don't have any choice. The problem with Reality is that we have to accept it. But we only try to do that by degrees, otherwise the shock would be too much. We have mentioned how Arjuna made the nearly fatal mistake of saying to Krishna, "C'mon, Lord, let me see it all." The experience almost blew him away. So for us it's here a peek, there a peek, and as we get stronger we can see more of the Big Show.

▶ **I don't understand why the wall represents wisdom, or why we want to get beyond wisdom.**

The wall symbolizes words and speech, or wisdom built up in the form of language. There's nothing wrong with this. It's extremely important up to a point, but it's a *boundary*. Beyond accumulated knowledge is direct experience of Life Itself. The children are advanced to a point where the Self is sufficient.

The things that are known already don't offer any hope. That's obvious if you look at the daily newspaper or if you read history. Knowledge becomes antiquated. Some of us are proud of our learning, but that doesn't make us happy. You can be extremely learned, able to quote chapter and verse, yet be absolutely miserable in your heart.

So you've gone through all the books and accumulated all the wisdom of the ages. You're as smart as Mohammed, Jesus, and Milarepa put together. You've achieved samadhi, McNadhi, spaghetti, whatever. That's the end of that movie. What do you do next? That's the point of Key 19. You start on an altogether different basis, which has nothing to do with knowledge or techniques. When we reach the point of regeneration we are having an experience that is beyond words.

Again, it's sort of like love. Love is *eternally youthful*. This particular aspect in ourselves doesn't age. Life just doesn't get old, period. Inspiration doesn't get old, either. All of us have this marvelous ability to see something *fresh* about what's going on. And so, as they say, let's do it!

▶ **Do you think that sunspots are freckles on the sun's face?**

But of course. The letter RESH ר means *face* or *countenance*, so freckles are in order. The sun with a face is a favorite subject of children's art all over the world. The ancient Egyptians used to draw hands coming out of the sun. The Yods in Key 19 are essentially the same symbolism, since Yod means the hand opened in blessing.

▶ **Thinking back to the meaning of the number thirteen, these thirteen Yods must be a reference to love and unity.**

Yes indeed. The six Yods on either side stand for the entire spectrum of the zodiac, and the single Yod in the center represents the loving relationship which this delightful couple has developed. In general, Yods symbolize the archetypal world. They are cosmic impulses that come to us from on high, from the sun. They are attractive ideas that lead to *action*. For instance, if the idea of regeneration appeals to you, then you do something about it. This Key says that you have the inner capacity to renew yourself along the lines that you most desire. The promise is: Whatever you want to be is within your reach.

▶ **In astrology, the sun's placement in the zodiac determines a person's sign, or basic personality type.**

The zodiac is terrific in expressing the *variety* of what we can do, which makes life so exciting. Everyone has special talents, and in the right spirit this is a fantastically interesting situation. We entertain each other, which is the biggest entertainment there is.

▶ **Why are the children pictured at the beginning of puberty?**

The children are still in bud, like the young flower in the background that's said to be growing into the fifth kingdom. The sunflowers represent the same five natural kingdoms that were mentioned in The Moon Key. Four of these realms are in full flower. The fifth or superhuman kingdom is still in bud, in a state of evolution. There is a correspondence to Key 10, because the section of The Wheel of Fortune that starts at the ears of the jackal and proceeds upward in the final arc represents the future perfection toward which humanity aspires.

The bud turns to the sun. This is the heliotropic action of people like ourselves, who are actually paying some attention to the Sun of Life. Insofar as we don't take everything for granted and look into what is going on, we are part of an exalted group. We are trying to get *everybody* into this level—all of humanity. *That's our job*, yours and mine. The Sun Key is the Collecting or Collective Intelligence. It gathers us all in one warm embrace, shining equally on everyone.

As far as you are concerned, the Collective Intelligence within you is a *focus* for all the powers that exist. Cosmic forces are brought together and expressed in a joyous dance. This is a lofty summit in any individual's career because it signifies emergence from a whole set of obstacles. One of our major problems was fear. Now love takes the place of fear.

▶ **The Moon and Sun Keys form a pair much like the girl and boy.**

Yes. The Moon depicts the Path of evolution and The Sun shows the result, the evolved human being. The Path starts off in Key 18 with a crayfish and ends up with something that resembles ourselves.

The Moon governs the *mind* aspect of things. The Sun is the *heart* that is literally pumping life into us all the time. We must always remember that these two are not separated. The mind evolves bodies, but the only thing that makes this possible is the indwelling spirit. This Moon/Sun team has done a remarkable job of evolving nine zillion, four billion, five million, seven hundred twenty-two thousand, three hundred and eighty-six *species*, let alone bodies!

Fertility and Sterility are the pair of opposites assigned to the letter Resh. Sterility happens when spirit lacks substance. The sun without the moon is a big waste of time. Occultists all over the world understand that it's the fire *and* the water that bring about the life process. Add water to the sterility of the desert, and you've got the incredibly fruitful Imperial Valley in California—a really going concern. You and I should own it.

▶ **The boy and girl seem to be in love.**

Yes, this is the alchemical betrothal. The vow is coming in Key 20, and the marriage of fire and water is accomplished in Key 21. This might not mean much to someone who isn't "in the business," but it means a great deal to an occultist. It's the result of tremendous effort. In practical terms, two difficult aspects of oneself are finally understood and controlled. As the perpetrator of egotism, our self-conscious has got to be tamed. And our subconscious memory bank is a dangerous element that can be a real thorn in the side.

Mind is so tricky and so creative that the first thing you know, you're in a jungle of your own making. It happens unconsciously. Energy that you have locked up in your memory bank can come out in strange ways at odd times and make you miserable. Until you put new material into your memory bank, you are stuck with yourself.

It's touchy all the time because your *feelings* are involved, and your conscious reaction to your feelings sets up a tension that goes back and forth. It fills your days and nights with a continual clatter in the psyche. When you get all this calmed down, you have a completely different atmosphere to live in. When the self-conscious and the subconscious harmonize as set forth in this Key, you have *free energy* to work with.

When you get into self-analysis with the intention to grow beyond your little self, you have to look at *everything*. And when you look at everything, you need a sense of humor. One way to keep smiling is to realize that we're all tarred with the same brush, and that's the truth. If we're all lepers, why worry? We're not going to catch anything—we've already got it!

▶ **The children look like they're laughing.**

Their worries are over. They've buried the hatchet forever. There can be laughter and playfulness because there is no longer any conflict. We've seen the masculine and the feminine elements all through the Tarot. In classical terms they represent the Logos and Eros aspects of ourselves. To get the complete picture, we have to think of ourselves in a dual capacity. The two functions are not only complementary, but are also *essential* to each other. In the nineteenth Key there is conscious recognition of the reason for separation of function.

▶ **Both straight and wavy rays are coming from the sun.**

They illustrate the dual capacity that is *in light*. It radiates in straight lines and also moves in waves. It has an energy aspect and a substance aspect. Light is both a thing and a non-thing.

▶ **Why are there sixteen rays?**

In the Cabala, when you want to understand a number, you work with associations. For instance, you think of everything that's concerned with sixteen—it's The Tower Key, it's four times four, it's the number of invisible paths on the Tree, etc. Then you consider how six operates through the agency of one. Then you add six and one, and think of all the meanings of seven. And so on and so forth until you're out of breath. This is an intellectual exercise. The general idea is to bring your intellect to its knees, which will happen eventually.

▶ **I've been stretching my intellect with the Pythagorean solids, and I've found that the tetrahedron is associated with gold and the sun.**

The tetrahedron is the simplest three-dimensional form. One point is a focus, two points make a line, three points establish a plane, and four points form what we call space. Fill in the points with four equilateral triangles and you have a solid. The connection with the sun indicates, once again, that substance is made of light.

In chemistry, gold crystalizes in tetrahedral form. Salt crystalizes in cubes. In alchemy, gold is the metal of the sun and salt is connected with the watery moon.

Your gold is the solar energy that is poured into you, in order for you to express yourself in life. You get up in the morning and eat your breakfast, and for the rest of the day you spend that energy in the best way you know how. That's your *wealth*, the gold you have to spend.

▶ **Why is the sun symbolically associated with the Christ?**

Symbolism tries to explain how things operate in connection with ourselves. It's educational. The Rosicrucians have an expression, "*Jesus mihi omnia,*" which means, "Jesus is all things to me." To the Christian mystics, Jesus symbolizes their Inner Self. This is the all-encompassing *truth*; they don't need anything else.

In occultism, the Christ corresponds to the Hermes principle that saves us from world illusion. The higher mind is the instrument of salvation.

▶ **Jesus said that we must be like little children to enter the kingdom of heaven. However, we forget the innocence that we're born with because so much happens to us as we're growing up.**

A child is like a bulb that is planted deeply in the ground. Its job is to get through the soil and up into the light. Children have to push hard because most of their learning is negative—you don't do this, you don't do that, etc. In spite of everything their parents say, they grow anyway. Eventually they can look at their parents' negative suggestions and ask, "Where did they get *that* information? Who told *them*?" There's no law against getting to the age where you can *think* and *look* and form intelligent opinions about life.

My father died when I was four. Cheer up, I'm not going to tell you the story of my life. This is just by way of example. I didn't have a chance to get well acquainted with my father, and all I heard about him was no good. He happened to be a brilliant man, but from my mother's point of view, he was a large, heavy-set louse. While I was growing up, I began to suspect that there had been some negativity between my mother and father. The older I got, the more suspicious I became. Now, in my seventies, I've decided that they just didn't get along well.

For some reason, there's a general conspiracy on the part of parents to make themselves like gods. They have these happy little sayings like, "Honor thy father and thy mother." However, they could be a couple of drunks, or whatever. You come home and have to push them out of the way to open the door, but "In your heart, you must honor them." Sooner or later you're going to wake up and say, "Well, I *understand* them. I know they've got problems, but so it goes." You can be happy and secure because you know you are a *child of the sun*.

You have made the effort to understand *yourself*, especially in the all-important matter of self-definition. When we arrive at the correct idea of what we are, regeneration takes place. We become *new creatures*, as the mystics say. We open our minds to the idea that there is intelligence everywhere, and we realize that the entire universal energy display is for the enjoyment of the Self.

Liberation is an ongoing proposition. The Judgement Key shows that there is an ever-present power that can lift our minds out of the three-dimensional situation, represented by the coffins. The angel teaches us to fly. We experience immortality, in the sense that we see the physical vehicle for what it is. We have advanced to the point where we begin to sense another dimension in our lives. Some people see it; some people hear it; some people feel it. If you begin to sense this other dimension, don't tell your psychiatrist, because he might misunderstand. However, to a person who is advancing on the Path of Liberation, the angel in Key 20 is a real presence.

Judgement is the Key of fire and of Pluto, the risen Mars-force. Fire is the ongoing pressure from Life that frees us from any situation that would confine us. We are moving up into a wider dimension. This is the prelude to cosmic consciousness, and I know you can hardly wait for that! So have a good week. Thanks for bringing me joy on Thursdays.

KEY 20

CHAPTER 20

JUDGEMENT

AFTER SPENDING MUCH TIME and effort on the Path, we have finally arrived at the point where we are no longer bound by the conventional universe. Key 20 represents our emergence from three-dimensional consciousness and all the stuff and nonsense we were locked into on that level. The spell is broken and we are now awake in the fourth dimension. We're flying. It's beautiful.

The Judgement Key symbolizes our living and experiencing on a completely different level from the ordinary. This does not mean that we are no longer participating in the third dimension; we have not passed away or anything of that sort. It's just that our consciousness has expanded to include an inner awareness of the truth about ourselves. It is this REALIZATION of the True Self that liberates us from all restriction. No longer separate from the One Life, our connection with That is like the tie between lovers asserting itself across physical distance. We find this relationship more real than the passing vibrations we once called reality.

Three-dimensional existence is represented by the coffins in this Key. We get boxed in by the illusions that arise from the interplay of all the things in three-dimensional experience. Once we are born into the human condition, we get more and more intricately involved with it. However, there's a way out: the way is *up* into a higher level. Remember, there was a time when you *weren't* born into this condition. Your Higher Self is so superior that you need not be caught in the illusion of outer things. Sure, we have to put our shoes on or take them off, depending on what's happening in the outer world, but the inner or fourth dimension is where we really live. That's *home*. It's always open to us, always beckoning.

There are a lot of forces at work in the outer world. It will take us a while to straighten them out, so we do the best we can. Since we are the *boss* in our inner world, we are at liberty to *do* something about *that*. When we get a sense of our own Inner Reality, we see what possibilities it can hold for us. It's nice to know there's a place inside of us where we can be joyful and free no matter what's going on in the world. This is why the people rising from their coffins look so happy. They are at *right angles* to their three-dimensional boxes. That's the fun of infinity.

As always in the Tarot, the mother and father represent the subconscious and the self-conscious aspects of ourselves. The baby symbolizes the regenerated personality that we spoke of in Key 19, The Sun. You are the parent of your own new self. Since this is a psychic performance all the way through, it doesn't make any difference whether you are in the body of a man or a woman. The psyche is going to bear a child of your own making. You literally recreate yourself by imagining yourself as different from whatever you happen to be in the scheme of things when you begin the process of transformation. This is *quite possible* for us to do, using the mechanics of our creative imagination and the discipline of the Tarot. Key 20 shows the actual transformation. This is the gorgeous butterfly emerging from the chrysalis.

In the Tableau, Judgement is the last Key in the sixth column, underneath Death and The Lovers. The mountain in the Lovers card represents pregnancy. In the Death Key the male and female are pictured with their heads growing out of the ground, and a rising sun takes the place of the mountain. Death is the Imaginative Intelligence, the agency of creation. The Tarot and the Cabala offer a basis for using your creative imagination *on yourself*. Through the interaction of your psychic components—the alchemical marriage of your animus and anima—the child of your regenerated self is produced. The Lovers Key reminds us that this is a work done in love. The process is impossible unless we love and appreciate ourselves.

Astrologically, Key 20 is Pluto, the planet that rules Scorpio, the Death Key. When you discover that you'll never really die and that death is only change, then you have overcome the last great illusion. You are a Being, not a body. You are free to live forever in the boundless universe. That's why Judgement is called the Perpetual Intelligence. It's the guarantee of immortality.

Transformation has a gruesome side. Your old self has to die and putrify. The part of yourself that is an obstacle must be entirely eliminated, and you may be sure that it feels like the most precious part. If you succeed in burying it in the coffins, then on Judgment Day you emerge as a new being altogether.

▶ **The Last Judgment is supposed to be a time when some people get to go to heaven, and the rest are eternally damned.**

According to the Tarot and the Cabala, there's no such animal as *that* kind of last judgment. The whole notion is surround by a tribal taboo. The tribe called it a sacred teaching, so people let it alone and didn't criticize it. That's one of the problems with orthodoxy.

In the occult sense the Last Judgment is actually a *final decision*. Without any help from anybody else, you make an inner decision that is completely revolutionary as far as your spiritual progress is concerned. When you have the experience that's represented by this Key, then everything is different. *You* make the judgment, *you* make the decision, based on your experience. That's the bottom line. From that time forth there is no going back.

This is a final initiation. Your Higher Self drags you through about a dozen rebirths and metamorphoses until at last you are *done*. You're a baked cookie. In terms of life supply, you have everything you need in the new state, just as you had everything you needed in the old state. What's more, the Cabala says that this kind of judgment *always* lands you in heaven. You go into another dimension, from bondage into freedom. The people in the picture are not cringing, weeping, or gnashing their teeth. The Resurrection according to Key 20 is *delightful*.

▶ **The Tarot is heretical.**

Well, I should hope so. But you know, as they say about chicken soup, it wouldn't hurt you.

▶ **In the Tarot deck by Arthur Edward Waite, there are three more figures in the background of Key 20.**

Apparently Dr. Waite wanted to get everybody into the act. Paul Case felt, in view of the fact that the main emphasis in Tarot is on the *individual*, that it would be clearer this way. With nothing extra to confuse the issue it becomes obvious that the new being in the center must be the result of a relationship between the self-conscious and the subconscious.

Some people would say that this is confusing, using three figures to represent one person. Why have three if there's really only one? Well, the types of consciousness that make up the personality are still separate in Key 20. And there is still a separation between the person and the cosmos. The One is coming up next week. The World Key shows the figure that has it all together in total union. That's successful synthesis. The Judgement Key depicts successful *analysis*—being able to see what's going on in oneself. Analysis breaks things down and synthesis puts them back together again. You've heard about *Solve et Coagule* from me before.

▶ **What happens when you've reduced it all to rubble and you don't know how to put it together again?**

The wise people who invented this system don't take you apart any faster than they build you up. The new being is built *right from the start*, because you are presented with the responsibility to *remake yourself*. So you make a simple beginning in whatever way you can. It's a lot like embryology. The original fertilized ovum is a primitive affair compared to what's going to happen later on, yet it has the peculiar power of drawing from its environment everything it needs for full growth and development.

Sometimes we feel so small and helpless. It seems incredible that the Will in ourselves could attract all the necessary materials for our growth, but it does. When you've been in this work for some time, you'll notice that the things you need come to you in a magical way. You "just happen" to meet the people and read the books that will help to fill out your new life. So let it come! Be optimistic about the seed you plant in yourself. Given half a chance, it will grow in quite a miraculous way.

▶ **I'm getting used to the idea that growth is change.**

When you look at the matter philosophically, you see that there is no way out. You are stuck with the law of change. Bit by bit you must learn to adapt to change, because *this is life*. If you want to live, then you must be willing to change. Like everything else, the more relaxed you can be about change, the easier it is. Be as relaxed as possible. There is absolutely no reason to fear, because of the nature of the power that is bringing about the changes.

We need to learn how intimately we are supported by Life Itself.

Life is not trying to play tricks on us or anything like that. It's trying to lead us in the correct direction. We can't get out of Life even if we want to because it doesn't have an "in" and an "out." The more you meditate on the nature of yourself, the more you realize the chances are that you're going to live forever. This would be a ghastly situation if you couldn't change, but if you *can* change, then it's *easy*. You can lean on Life because it's all-powerful and all-knowing.

▶ Can we lean on the fourth dimension?

Yes, because the fourth dimension (sometimes called the astral plane) is nothing less than your mind, which is an aspect of your being that doesn't *have* any dimensions. Dimensionality belongs to constructions, which have height, width, and depth. And what is the *mother* of all constructions? Sure enough, it's your mind. Mind is a great sea of pure nothingness, which can construct anything you like. This sea is shown in Key 20 as the ocean on which the coffins float. It is the end of the stream of consciousness that began in the robe of The High Priestess. Next week Key 21 will bring us to the fifth dimension, which is a point.

▶ How can I learn to relax and enjoy living in this vastness?

During my recent visit to the Monterey Aquarium, the fish looked quite happy. We are like fish that swim in the sea of mind. As we develop an appreciation for the constant support we receive, we become *mindful*. We move up from the cramped view in the coffins. With the mind's eye, we can see much more than with our physical eyes. When we're liberated, we're able to move freely in limitless space. This is comfortable and very pleasurable.

This process could be thought of as an upward progression through the four worlds of Cabala. In Key 20, the four states of water are a good analogy. The icebergs represent the *earth* in the water. The liquid state is obviously *water*. Clouds or water vapor symbolize the *air* in water. The electrical, inner aspect is the *fire* in water. This fire in the water is the essence of mind—your fundamental Self.

In one of Key 20's most important attributions, it is called the Key of Fire. Its letter, SHIN ש, is among the three mother letters in the Hebrew alphabet, the one given to the fire element. Aleph א and The Fool Key are given to air; Mem מ and The Hanged Man are attributed to water. You've heard until your ears buzz that the two basic tools in alchemical work are fire and water—conscious energy and conscious substance. Air is the consciousness of their interrelation. Earth is the container and expression of the other three elements.

For technically inclined students, I'd like to mention something about the Cube of Space symbolism that the Cabalists have used for a long time. Mem and Shin are the two horizontal coordinates. They are in opposition on every plane of the Cube. They move up and down the Aleph coordinate, the string of consciousness that connects Above and Below.

Occult fire is the Fire of Being. Our life depends on burning. The eternal burning of the One Life sustains the universe. When something burns it releases energy. Fire is expansive: Its first impulse is to *break out* in radiation, to demolish all bonds and be free. In Key 20, the life in us breaks free of the coffins. The problems and obstacles of mind are overcome through the liberating agency of fire.

In the Pattern on the Trestleboard, the third affirmation refers to the Path of Liberation. That path ends right here in the twentieth Key. The angel is your own Self, the Being who rescues you from drowning. The outer self is saved by the Inner Self. Once you get pulled out of the water which is the mind, you become aware of what happened to you and how dangerous it was for your well-being. Then you'll always wear water wings. You won't take any rash chances with the watery medium any more.

Tradition says that this is the Archangel Gabriel. If it's a bit confusing that he is called the Angel of Water, just remember that water contains consciousness. Think of the Tree of Life arranged onion-style, with each of the Sephiroth as one of the layers of the onion. Approaching the central rings you come to Binah, Root of Water. Inside her is Chokmah, Root of Fire. Kether, the Self, is innermost. Polarity exists between each of these levels; that's what makes them distinct.

Gabriel stands for the mind's ability to *look at itself*. This talk of getting out of water, out of mind, is *symbolic*. You always live in mind—there is nowhere else to go—but you need not *identify* with what goes on there. Through Self-realization you stop confusing yourself with your experience. You become identified with the Experiencer. This doesn't mean that you are forever barred from fantasyland. But if you spend your entire time in a fascinated state, that precludes your advance to wisdom and understanding. Once you make the proper Self-identification, you are free to choose how you will involve yourself in three-dimensional experience. There's a vast difference between making a conscious choice and being bound *un*consciously.

▶ **Once I make the choice, should I pour myself into experience or stay detached?**

It's up to you. The idea is to get out of the illusion and be yourself. Like everyone else, you go out and "break the stone" in the workaday world, but out of that situation you must pluck the flower of your creativity. Nobody else is going to cultivate it for you. Your Self is your first duty, as exemplified by Ipsissimus at the top of the Tree of Life.

You are supposed to be the master of life, not the slave. What if your car said to you, "You want to go to the market? Well too bad, I'm going to San Francisco." You would say, "I'm trading this car in today!" Don't let the world get the better of you. Rule or be ruled.

▶ **The rectangular coffins on the left and right remind me of The Devil's half cube.**

They must be the same thing. That's a good observation, because we tend to take all the productions of the mind at face value and consider them real. The objects we desire seem to be the most important things in life. Sometimes it's an attractive bunch of junk, to be sure, but you can get attached to it by the chains in The Devil Key. Really it doesn't *mean* anything. That American dream, the gold-plated Cadillac, *doesn't mean anything.*

According to the inner teaching, what's important is not that you possess things, but that you are *well* in yourself. As a matter of fact, the more junk you have, the more of a burden it is. So at last you can cast off your burdens. You're happy! (It can make other people unhappy to see you happy, so keep this a secret.) There's a saying in the Bible: "Seek ye first the Kingdom of God, and all these things shall be added unto you." The reason for this is, if you don't get your insides untangled, nothing outside can make you well.

As a vision of the Higher Self, Gabriel represents Kether. He's surrounded by a cloud that's composed of water, of mind. The onion analogy illustrates how Kether is hidden in the mind. Without instruction we would never find the Self.

▶ It looks as though the sound of the trumpet is rousing these people from their 3-D attachments.

Yes, that's exactly right. Gabriel's golden horn gives forth a *blast* in order to awaken us from the sleep of unconsciousness. His horn blows continuously with the power of the Life Breath. When we are ready, we hear his message distinctly. It's like the sound of an alarm clock in the morning. The only way to stop the darn thing is to *get up*. Wings symbolize your power to *rise*.

An important area is the inner sound of our *thoughts*. We choose our own thoughts, which can then be heard in populated inner spaces. This is where we are the judge and the jury, where we make our ultimate decisions.

The Cabala emphasizes the occult significance of sound. The seven tones, drawn as lines coming out of the trumpet, correspond to the seven chakras in the body. *The Tarot* by Paul Case gives some technical exercises, such as intoning with a pitch pipe, using sound to activate and harmonize the chakras. These procedures are not a hit-or-miss proposition. If you are interested in practicing, they *do* work. The book hasn't lied to me yet.

▶ Does the trumpet blast represent a life situation that is difficult and shocking, that wakes you up and shakes you up?

That idea is attached to Key 16. The Tower is definitely a shake-up. The lightning flash is temporary enlightenment. Then we revert to Key 15, The Devil. But if we proceed, we will get through the intermittent stage and into the permanent presence of the Light.

▶ How do you experience Key 20 when it appears in your life?

You get a sustained message, loud and clear. It corresponds to the Buddhist idea of total liberation from the Great Illusion.

Here's a story, by way of illustration. This is a take-off on something that actually happened in the South Seas during World War II. Let's think of ourselves as bushpeople, all out there digging up roots together. Along comes a gang of Americans with a portable theater. They say, "Come on in and see a movie." So we see a movie of ourselves digging roots. All of a sudden, the movie starts to show an attack by an unfriendly tribe. Since we've never seen this before, we get up and start fighting the enemy, throwing spears at the screen and so forth.

Now let's suppose that in our group we have a wise old medicine man, because there's *always* a medicine person. He approaches the Americans and says, "This is incredible. This is big magic. You've got to show me how it's done or I'll never rest easy." So the Americans take him in the projection room and show him the *mechanism of projection*. Once he sees where the movie is coming from, he is illuminated about it being a trick. Once he knows it isn't for real, he doesn't have the same *feeling* about what's happening on the screen that he had before.

▶ **The picture is still real.**

There's a certain measure of reality to everything in the three-dimensional world, but when you get behind the picture and start looking at the principles, it becomes a different matter. For one thing, you can see the power of nature in operation. Normally we play that down as much as possible, because nature is rather uncivilized.

▶ **What's the symbolism of the flag attached to the trumpet?**

The same equal-armed cross that's on the breast of The High Priestess now appears on the Banner of Salvation. If you're like me, you've been exposed to long harangues about salvation. Maybe they threw in a little hellfire too, to make it more exciting. "Come and be saved—*or else!!!*" As you know, occultists do not get saved by marching up to someone, or taking a dive in a tank, or anything of that sort. They undertake a *prodigious labor* to save *themselves*. The Tarot and the Cabala offer us this same opportunity.

The banner indicates the way to go. It raises stimulating questions which, if you think about them, will lead you in the direction of your Self. Why should anybody want to be saved? What are we being saved from? How do we go about it? This flag suggests where we can find the answers.

Even if we don't take advantage of our opportunities in this particular round, *we will be saved* sometime in the course of human evolution. This is a declaration of the Ageless Wisdom.

▶ **The man looks passive about salvation and the woman looks active.**

The male is active in a new way; he is *actively receptive*. He has set aside the typical, reactive ego trip common to self-consciousness. Now he's accepting the One Reality instead of his own mistaken interpretation. His folded arms are reminiscent of The Hanged Man. As is always true of the woman in us, the female reaches toward the inner. The subconscious has been in communication with spirit all along. She's the *channel*.

By their gestures the three figures are spelling out a Latin word, "*lux*," which means "light." This is a reference to the Inner Light that illuminates *oneself*. This illumination is a *complete statement* of what started in Key 16 (The Tower) as a lightning flash. In other words, the Divine Idea conveyed by the Tree of Life brings about a permanent resurrection of consciousness.

The gestures are a salute to the Light. When you know the Light is there and you accept it, you are naturally in harmony with it. Recognition is all that's necessary. We have to undo a lot, but we don't have to *do* much in practicing the tricks of the trade, so to speak.

▶ **You can recognize something and still not be in harmony with it.**

This particular kind of recognition brings understanding. According to the Cabalists, understanding gives you power and control. In this case, if you understand the way Light works in yourself, it gives you power over yourself. This is very important, because power over yourself is the highest freedom there is.

It's interesting that at this point in the evolution of humanity, light is becoming more useful to us. We can now bore a hole with it or use it in surgery.

▶ **What do you think of using sound in affirmations?**

Affirmations are an excellent use of sound as a means of lifting your consciousness from one level to another. Sound vibrations profoundly affect the vehicle we happen to be dwelling in at the moment. Believe it or not, when you make a physical sound, it is communicated to every cell in your body. In an affirmation you must have *feeling*. Therefore, whenever possible, make *your own* affirmations—do not go down to your local metaphysical center and buy some already made.

Mantras are another effective use of sound. There's a marvelous Tibetan story about a peasant and his mantram. The peasant's spiritual life was guided by a lama who coached him in how to keep his balance, how to feel the presence of the Powers of Life, and all sorts of things that kept him happily on his path of being a peasant. Then it happened that his lama had to go away for awhile. During this period, our hero was working in the fields while chanting his mantram. One day a different lama stopped him and asked, "What are you saying?" The man replied, "Oh mommy had my pum." The lama got all upset. "What? That's a sacrilege! You should say, 'Om mane padme hum.'"

"Thank you very much for correcting me," replied the peasant, and he started repeating it the so-called correct way. Well, everything went wrong. He broke out in boils and felt terrible. His yaks got sick and his crops died. Finally his own lama came back and found out what had happened. "My son," said he, "just say your prayers the way that's *right for you*, and all will be well." And it was.

▶ **What does the Bible mean when it refers to The Word?**

The Word that God speaks is a sound, a message encoded in a vibration. It has formative power. Your words are creative in the same way. Generic Man is an expression of universal formative power, therefore Jesus—an archetypal man—is called The Word.

▶ **We've learned that sounds are also colors. I've noticed that in Key 20, the colors come in sets of three. One set is black, white, and gray. The other set is red, yellow and blue—the primary colors.**

That must be because of the letter Shin ש, which means a *tooth* or *fang*. It looks like three flames, suggesting the devouring nature of fire. The Being that is yourself *eats up* experience. Shin carries three flames, (also a reference to the Three Supernals) in a sort of boat-shaped base, as if it were a ship of spirit. This divine vessel is the ship of *your* spirit. It provides your support, guidance, and everything you need for your life's voyage. And it gives you the appetite to go ahead and enjoy the journey.

▶ **So it's good to be hungry for experience?**

Sure. I know I'm repetitive, but it must be said: Without that hunger there would be nothing happening. Since it's such a powerful force in ourselves, we have to learn how to use it correctly. The Cabala is a discipline that prepares us for a delicious appreciation of what life is all about. Our Inner Self is dead set against any obstacle that stands in the way of our enjoying life to the *fullest*.

▶ **Isn't that hedonism?**

No, because hedonism gets out of balance, which the Adversary will oppose right away. If we get out of alignment by involving ourselves in some pleasurable activity at the expense of everything else in life, we have a battle on our hands. As the wise say, equilibration is the basis of the Great Work.

▶ Sometimes it's fun to go overboard.

You'd be surprised at how much fun you can have when you're in balance. When you are strengthened by Cabalistic practice, you can stand a tremendously greater amount of experience, which in a balanced way is more exciting than having your head stuck in the rum barrel, or whatever. It is possible to ascend in consciousness so as to be *very pleased* with your life experience. The way to do that is to *appreciate* life fully. If you pursue a deeper appreciation of what is going on, you'll find the rewards are extremely great.

For one thing, as you might expect, your powers of sensation *increase* if they're cultivated in a sensible way. Not only that, but the occultists say that your *inner* sensorium is going to improve also. When you're well-balanced, you become more sensitive and your experience of life becomes heightened. You can literally *thrill* to things that would not have made the slightest impression on you before.

There's always more to appreciate in life. We'll never have it all or know it all; it's too big for that. So it is possible to go through the process that's pictured in the Tableau many, many times. Each time you come to Key 20, you break through to greater awareness. Like the water that has frozen into ice, the mind becomes frozen and *still.* Then you can see that special Something Else going on beyond the activities of the mind—the inspirational, immortal part of yourself, beyond all forms, beyond death.

When preconceptions are put aside and perception is clear, obscurity is removed. Then God looks out through your senses. You realize who you really are. You make correct judgments based upon true discrimination.

▶ Do you go from hedonism to sainthood?

As Cabalists, we do not take sides in the play between the polarities. We stick to the Middle Way. We should not try to become saints. We should just try to become *sane*. On the level of the true individual, we are brothers and sisters and we love each other. We want to do everything we can to help each other. *By our very nature* this is the way we are in Reality.

▶ **I've often felt that way, but then it seems like a dream.**

Everybody can make something out of nothing, and the main thing you make out of nothing is your Self-discovery. When you start off, you're nothing. God's out there and you're here all by yourself. Then when you get through, you're something. You dream up a fitting definition of yourself. This is a dream that *works*. If you get this dream about yourself correct, well then, you are a completely reconstructed person. To *establish* yourself as a Being in the universe, and to know *absolutely for sure* the connection between the universe and yourself, that's the number one proposition. That's the cosmic consciousness of The World Key.

▶ **Is there a difference between superconsciousness and cosmic consciousness?**

Superconsciousness can read what's in the Ain Suph Aur. It's a helpful term used to indicate the awareness held by the True Self. Cosmic consciousness describes a state that may be experienced by people like ourselves. It's a little piece of the big superconscious awareness.

There are two stages in the work of the Self. The first stage *ends* when you are liberated. The second begins thereafter; it concerns your expression. Key 20 reveals your *creative purpose*. Key 21 represents the act of *carrying out* your purpose in the world. The World card illustrates complete integration of the Self, the ultimate in Self-knowledge. We have great difficulty in identifying with this joyful figure. It's a tremendous effort to see ourselves the way we really are. We have to keep working at it. At any rate, that's what we're up to here.

We have a little ritual that we perform every time we get to the end of a twenty-two-week cycle. I hope you'll join in next week when I ask how many of you have attained cosmic consciousness. I'd like you *all* to raise your hands, so that no one's feelings are hurt. Thanks very much for coming tonight. I hope this week will be your *best yet!*

KEY 21

CHAPTER 21

THE WORLD

WHEN WE REACH THIS climactic Key in our career on the Path, it is our custom to take a vote as to how many of us have achieved COSMIC CONSCIOUSNESS during the past week. We ask that *everyone* raise his or her hand, so as not to embarrass any souls who have not quite made it, and to whom we wish every success. All right—everybody who had cosmic consciousness this week, raise your hand. Unanimous! Great! See what twenty-two weeks of applied Tarot will do for you? It's amazing!

▶ **Class: YEA!!** (cheers, applause)

We have advanced mightily in the seven stages of spiritual unfoldment. Key 21 is the crown of our efforts. Here we have a picture of our True Self in the most delightful presentation imaginable. This is the new Being whose development we have followed all through the Tarot. This is *you* when you are feeling good. Of course it's a symbolic picture, because not many of us look like this. This is how you *feel* when you are free to enjoy yourself and improvise in the Dance of Life. In plain terms, cosmic consciousness means that your ego trip is over and you are living in the wide, wonderful universe.

The total experience of being one's Self is expressed as a dance of joy in The World Key. It's the joy of freedom, of liberation from bondage as shown in The Devil Key. This is not a dance where the choreography is all set out for you. It's not a ballet or a fox trot. Your dance of life and my dance of life are something that we have to design for ourselves, in some particular area of expression that appeals to use as individuals in the deepest sense of the word.

Our astrologer friends tell us that we are all different. Each one of us is a unique piece of Life, so some like to cavort wildly while others choose a more stately step. The idea is that we shall move to our own inner music. When we do, we are absurdly happy because this is the way we are supposed to be. You have to make your own way in this business but you have a lot going for you, helping you—the cosmos, to be exact.

You can't have a conversation with the cosmos over dinner, yet it's *right there*. It is pressing on you 14.7 pounds per square inch *right now*. There is no separation anywhere in life. There is no separation between us and the authorship of Life. We can surely *join* ourselves to this authorship in our thoughts, and appreciate it and feel support coming from it.

When we are born, the illusion is that we have left a nice, cozy place for a very uncomfortable one. We squawk about it, but actually we have just moved from one womb to another. We never left Mother Nature. We *can't* leave the universe. We go through many different changes in our experience, but according to the occult teaching, we cannot fall out of Reality. If we are here, we have been here and we will be here. Whatever is, is. What is not, is not.

The ellipse around the dancer is nothing more nor less than Life Itself in the form of a victory wreath. There are twenty-two bundles of leaves in the wreath. We can surmise that this is symbolic shorthand for the Tarot Keys, the Hebrew letters, and the paths on the Tree of Life. Each of the twenty-two is a specialized energy called an Intelligence, which has power over a distinct area of life. Each of these powers has a triple aspect: constructive, preservative, and destructive, just as in the Hindu TRIMURTI. This marvelous complexity of life surrounds us like a wreath. It is our womb, our environment. We should never neglect thinking about our profound relationship with That.

The dancer, your Innermost Self, is the master of all thirty-two Intelligences, associated with the paths of the Tree of Life. You might say, "Are you trying to tell me that little old me is a master?" Well, I'm afraid it's true. It's very hard for you and me to believe that we are the master of all the forces of the cosmos. We have to keep pondering that startling biblical statement, "Ye are gods." The more godlike we are, the more we can appreciate life and the more exciting and meaningful it becomes. If we involve ourselves only in superficial views of what is going on, all this escapes us and our True Self escapes us also.

The doctrine of the Cabala states that we are a microcosm. There is a one-to-one relationship between all the powers that are inherent in the cosmos, and our own powers and faculties. Self-realization in terms of power means bringing these cosmic forces into expression in our personal lives. This is a *stupendous* theory of the Self, but a very helpful one, I think. After all, there is nothing to get ego-uppity about. If we all have it, we can enjoy it together, with all of us microcosms getting together for a big fish fry.

Everyone has the capability of moving into a different kind of existence. In the ordinary way of living you have to have an object, a goal. You have to want something. In the other existence you are completely satisfied and living very happily without wanting anything, because your consciousness has assumed a different character. It is capable of penetrating all of life. Then *all of life satisfies it*. The whole thing is the object, rather than any specific immediate object. That's cosmic consciousness.

It doesn't hurt us to think in a big way. Progress in our profound studies may be slow, but it's *not* painful. We gradually outgrow egotism, which *was* painful. When you are dealing with this kind of evolutionary process in the development of yourself, you discover that the Powers That Be are not inimical. They are there to *assist* you in whatever you want to accomplish. That's the message of this Key. You have to be willing to dance with these forces and be confident in this process. By now you should have had some experiences leading you to believe that Life Itself is bringing you closer and closer to your heart's desire, which is the name of the game.

Meditation on the twenty-first Key can unlock your inner awareness of mastery. The Tarot Keys have a penetrating psychological effect *if you use them*. The way to use them, of course, is to look at them. You will find that they do stimulate certain feelings and states of mind that are desirable. If you look at this Key with understanding, it produces a joyful feeling of total freedom.

Also recommended in Tarot practice is the exercise in which you put yourself in the position of the figure and identify with it as much as possible. In this case, try to feel that *you are the dancer*. If you balk at the idea that you are going to dance your way through life, then you can *sit* your way through life. You have a choice.

▶ **It's fun to identify with Key 21 when I'm actually dancing.**

Sure, why not? Dancing is splendid exercise. It's exhilarating, and great for the circulation. Dancing is an integral part of worship in many religions all over the world. It is even one way of inducing trance. If we overlook this widespread pleasure, we might miss something wonderful for ourselves.

Dancing itself is a *creative act*. The World Dancer is free to perform in any direction without falling down. This Key symbolizes the center of gravity from which balance is maintained and all sorts of turns, leaps, and gyrations can be controlled. Key 21 is associated with the letter Tav and the planet Saturn. These are placed in the center of the Cube of Space. This central point is called the Palace of Holiness. It is also the fifth dimension or the Now. We are trying to learn to live in the Now— not the then, not the was or will be, but the *right now*.

Some people talk as though your future were assured, and other people talk about your past as though it were something you could not escape, but the Cabalists will tell you that the *important* part of your life is the Now. This is the precious part, the only part you are ever going to live in anyway. What you *do* in the Now is enjoy being yourself as much as possible.

In practicing to be yourself, you develop the creativity that comes from *your center*. Life says, "Here is your creative ability. Enjoy it. Express yourself. Trust in the Power that gave it to you and don't worry about what anybody else says because what other people think about your creations is *not relevant*." Total independence of your spirit is very much part of this Key.

▶ Is the fifth dimension a kind of consciousness?

Yes, it's superconsciousness. Cabalistic philosophers think of the fifth dimension as a point wherein the unity principle is concentrated. Everything is encoded in that point and all creation issues from it.

Everything is connected in an *immediate* way, held in one totally united universe. You can understand that there is communication within this unity, much like communication within one's own body. If something is wrong, or especially good in any spot, your whole body knows about it. When you have succeeded in meditation, your whole body is aware of a beneficial effect.

In general, the human race is headed in the direction of basic unity, which is becoming less and less theoretical as time goes on. We are in the midst of an accelerating, monumental change in the world. Values are changing, and when that happens, everything changes.

▶ My company sent me to an "Achieving Your Potentials" workshop recently. Some Cabalistic teachings were being presented as newly discovered techniques. There was even a diagram with three circles corresponding to the Three Supernals.

That reminds me of the time a fellow came to Los Angeles and announced that he was going to read some newly discovered, ancient scroll over the course of a week. He hired a large hall and filled it with the patient suckers who came to be enlightened. He had the scroll right there and he read it off, putting on a good show and collecting a handsome sum. There was only one hitch: The contents of the scroll, word for word, were Paul Foster Case's *The Book of Tokens*! People said to Paul, "Aren't you going to go after this guy and sue him?" To which Paul replied, "It's okay. It's a great way to get people to read the book." That's a true story.

▶ Speaking of Cabalistic ideas in new format, the research on DNA and RNA describes manifestation very much like the dancer's two spiral wands.

It was Dr. Case who added the spiral detail to the wand symbolism in The World Key. He explains in our textbook that these spirals are spinning in different directions, representing involution and evolution. The dancer maintains a dynamic balance between the constructive and the destructive processes that go on in the body, making it possible for us to do what we call "living."

These same two wands are seen in Key 1. It's as though The Magician has picked up the wand on the table, which represents the feminine polarity in his pair of wands. You have to be in the condition of Key 21 before you can wield that wand and control its powers.

The dancer may be placed in the center of the Tree of Life, in the Sphere of Beauty. (Why not? The dancer *is* beauty, *n'est-ce pas?*) In that case, her two wands are the two sides of the Tree. Integration comes from the Pillar of Mercy and disintegration from the Pillar of Severity. Fortunately these two forces are found in all life expression. There is always an energizing force putting things together, and also a de-energizing force pulling things apart. It may take anything from one day to millions of years.

This is the operation of the principle of change. The advantage of it is that everything is recycled. This keeps the world from filling up with what happened yesterday. The world is a shifting place, and we're shifting right along with it. We have to get used to this fact. However, it's a beautiful feature of the landscape that our True Self does *not* change. Ideally, we never lose our sense of Self when we reach the point of equilibrium indicated in the final Tarot trump. This valuable stability is the center of gravity for our psyche.

▶ **It's quite a feat to dance in midair, as our Self is doing here.**

It may seem to us that we are bound by gravity and so on, but don't forget that the whole planet is suspended in midair. You are supported by what seems to be nothing, yet it is sufficient to maintain you at the center of things. The wreath that surrounds the dancer is shaped like a zero, indicating the Ain Suph Aur, the No-Thing. This is a symbolic statement that all the power that ever was or will be is *here, now*.

The blue background is important in this connection because that is what actually touches the figure on every side. As you know, blue is the heraldic color of The High Priestess. She is responsible for everything that happens in the universe, including the flowering of ourselves represented by The World Key.

There is an occult cross-reference between Keys 2 and 21 through the final Hebrew letter, TAV ת, which means an "x" or a *mark*. The original form of the Tav was an equal-armed cross, like the one on the breast of The High Priestess. It symbolizes the balance and interchange of opposing forces in the universe. As a mark or signature, the Tav amounts to a *promise* from the Powers That Be that all the imagery in this Key is true and will serve you well if you study and explore it at length.

Jacob Boehme wrote a book called *The Signature of All Things*, in which he sees the Creator's signature of unity within all diversity. Like him, we want to see *through* an object to the Creator of the object. You don't see that on the outside. You have to penetrate to the inside to *see* it.

I have a picture of a snowflake on my desk. I copied it from a photograph. It continually amazes me that there are interlaced triangles forming a six-pointed star in its center. The frontispiece in our textbook is the zero contained within a hexagram. Paul Case calls this diagram the Key to the Cosmos. To have this fall out of the sky . . . isn't it as though God put his signature in a snowflake?

▶ **When the baby of Key 20 "learns to read" God's signature, it grows to maturity in Key 21.**

That's right. Maturity includes the Cabalistic concept that when we are on the level of our True Self, we understand our human limitations. Limitations are perfectly natural. We will not chafe at them if we understand the nature of the vehicle we inhabit on this level of expression. For example, I have an automobile. It's not a flying machine. It belongs on the road and I try to keep it there. When it comes to my body and personality, I recognize that they too have certain limitations. It would be ridiculous for me to attempt to do things that are not in the cards and not in the law.

Maturity also requires the development of self-regulation. The creative dance of Key 21 isn't just a flailing around. Like any art, it involves tremendous discipline. This dance exemplifies *perfect control*. Our efforts in this direction are supported by the fixed modes of the Life Power you see in the corners of Key 21. As in Key 10 (The Wheel of Fortune), the sacred creatures symbolize the four Worlds of the Cabala. These in turn suggest the process we use to get the results we want.

▶ **Why are they *fixed* modes?**

They are like the elements of grammar. If you're going to have a language, it must have a *structure*. You need some rules. The fixed quality represents basic principles, undeviating laws. Structure is Saturnian, as the gallows in Key 21 (The Hanged Man) and the skeleton in Key 13 (Death) remind us.

The universe is a remarkably orderly place, considering its size and complexity. According to our mentors, the four Worlds represent *the order in the universe*. As you've heard many times here, the Archetypal World is *muy misterioso*. It's straight from the Godhead, not a concrete matter at all. It's not even part of anyone's awareness until it strikes the Creative World in us, which is our mind. The Archetypal World is the *impressor* and the mind is the *impressee*. The idea impinges on our mind and we say, "Hey, that's a great idea! Let's go over to Tarot class tonight!" The machinery of getting here is the Formative World, and our being here together is the World of Result.

▶ **The bull that turns outward shows a new result.**

That's exactly right. The bull turns outward when the mechanistic cycles of nature are broken. Automatic cycles can go on for literally millions of years. If there is nothing to stop them, they just continue forever, like clams in the ocean or stars in the heavens. By a creative act we interrupt the cycling of *ourselves* in Key 21. The Self is not in any cycle. Like the queen in chess, it is free to move in any direction. This total freedom to act is an essential ingredient in our success.

Mechanistic cycles are summed up by The Wheel of Fortune Key, which represents the great merry-go-round that's going on all the time. The veil around our dancer is shaped like a Kaph, the letter associated with Key 10. This is the veil of appearance that hides the true identity of Life Itself.

▶ **So you see something besides your illusions when you get to Key 21?**

You see that illusions exist, but that they are not Reality. This is where Saturn masters The Devil.

▶ **Sometimes I think that no matter how hard I look, I'm never going to see anything but illusion. Can I figure it out from that?**

As long as you are thinking in relative terms, you can't possibly grasp the Real. The World of illusion is so enormous that it can keep you busy forever. Illusion is the realm of *effects*. It's not the world of *causes*. If you go from one effect to another trying to find the answer, it's endless and hopeless. You just go around and around.

▶ **In some way, I am the cause of these effects.**

Absolutely. That's the point.

▶ **You often talk about a kind of seeing that's not involved with illusion.**

That's the view from the top. The reacting mechanisms which are reflected in Key 10 (The Wheel of Fortune) are a far cry from the creative life of Key 21, where you may be sure the Life Power *knows what it's doing*.

▶ **The letter Kaph in Key 21 veils an exciting part of the anatomy.**

Yes, that's the *living* aspect. In Cabalistic tradition, this is an androgyne who represents the union of the feminine and masculine elements in ourselves. The two are balanced, but the uppermost, leading element is feminine. This symbolism indicates that in our ultimate condition, the *feeling* or *inner* aspect of ourselves will be emphasized more than the outer. Like the woman in Key 8 (Strength), love masters force. The rational principle is always important but it becomes subordinate. Intuition is the superior function in Cabala. The intellect has limits to what it can grasp. Intuition has no limits.

We've discussed many times how people have both a masculine and a feminine aspect. Modern analytical psychology can see both aspects in all of us. In the final Tarot Key the relationship between these opposites is one of *total harmony*. This is the place in the Tarot where it becomes clear that the feminine and the masculine never really function by themselves. They function *together* as a *unit*.

▶ **Why is there such a split between men and women in society?**

Humanity is only about one-fourth of the way to its goal. We are abysmally ignorant about ourselves and our relationships. We have barely scratched the surface of our own psychology, so we have a *long* way to go. Abuse of womanhood has occurred throughout the ages but it's changing now. If our society were working beautifully, the sensitive aspect would be uppermost, and that would result in more intelligent assessments of what's going on in the cosmos. Eventually, out of desperation, we shall become sensitive and reasonable.

▶ **Is that the victory the wreath is celebrating?**

That's a big part of it. The wreath's red bindings are figure eights, the same symbols that you see over the heads of The Magician and the Lady of Strength. A lemniscate stands for the rhythmic interplay of opposing forces. In this case it binds the two sides of the wreath into a whole. One on top and one on the bottom tells you "As above, so below," which is something you think about if you are an accomplished occultist. In exploring the realm of the psyche, you get hints from the realm of the soma, and vice-versa.

The principle of correspondence is beautifully illustrated by The Hanged Man reflecting The World card. Key 12 is the beginning and the root of our transformation.

▶ **What happens to the desire-nature in that state of surrender?**

It's operative in the same way that the intellect is operative, but both are subject to the intuitive aspect. It's not the main thing any longer. Limited by a certain focus, it becomes a tool to express intuition.

▶ **This view of Saturn is radically different from what is often considered a malefic in mundane astrology.**

In the Cabala, Saturn is not a malefic. It is a *necessity*. Saturn is the *ruler* of Capricorn, The Devil. In Key 15 we see the difficult aspects of the principle of limitation, but the whole problem is *ignorance*. You must *master* all the wonderful principles that are presented in the Tarot in order to be able to use them. If you don't understand them, they are useless. They become oppressive when they are part of the landscape that you don't understand.

Understanding means knowing how to *use it*, how to *do it*. On the Tree of Life, the seat of Understanding is also the sphere of Saturn. Throughout these twenty-two weeks we have stated frequently that Saturn is the resistance that is necessary to any life expression. If you were an artist and you had no medium, you'd be in a terrible fix. The Divine Mother provides you with the paint, clay, or stone that you need to express yourself. In a very real sense, we are all artists. We can acknowledge that there will always be resistance to whatever we are trying to do. What's more, we can recognize it as indispensable, not as something that is trying to hold us back.

▶ **Sometimes you meet so much resistance that it gets complicated.**

If you're fishing with a drop line and it gets all snarled up, the only thing to do is throw it away. The solution is in *simplicity*. The major lessons of the Cabala are simple but profound. It's a challenge for us to understand that when we *limit* ourselves, we actually have *more scope*. When we are distracted, we lose energy. When we involve ourselves in a particular area as part of the Judgement Key decision-making process, we find our chosen area has an unlimited horizon.

Saturn makes progress possible. Once you make an advance on your spiritual path, it is a *permanent* change. Using this principle, in time you can overcome all the difficulties in yourself. Now there's really something to be said for inertia!

▶ **Jason, what is your view of the myth about the god Saturn devouring his own children?**

I think it refers to a superior aspect in ourselves that can consume inferior things. In your own experience you are likely to find that there's something inside you that sort of eats up the obstacles in yourself. The obstacles are your own creations. I don't know why we have this large progeny of obstacles, but we *do*. Fortunately, the mind has an ability to consume and digest them and to pass them out of the system altogether. In successful psychoanalysis, for example, you take the sting out of your inner problems by *airing* them and recognizing them for what they are. We understand that the old self is a block in our path, so we assimilate it into a new being.

▶ **Sometimes the planet Saturn is attributed to Malkuth on the Tree of Life, is it not?**

Yes. When the Three Supernals are taken as one thing, the other seven centers correspond to the ancient planets, the alchemical metals, and the chakras. Malkuth, the tenth center at the bottom of the Tree, is the Daughter of the Cabalistic family. She represents the earth plane. Naturally she has the same vibration as her Mother, Binah, the seat of Saturn. (The Father is Chokmah and the Son is Tiphareth.)

Through this relationship between the Mother and the Daughter, we are reminded that the substantial basis of the earth is *mind*. Therefore the earth is the earth literally by *definition*. By saying, "Some things are going to be round and some are going to be square," the mind makes it so.

This is Saturn at work, the great cookie cutter delineating what is to be. This is *you* when you limit your creations to *what you want* and kick everything else out. What is beyond the cookie cutter is not any part of the cookie. This is precisely the *positive* aspect of the Saturn principle. To make full use of this power you must have a clear image of what you want, so you can eliminate anything that doesn't conform to your picture.

▶ **Is the earth plane real or just an illusion? It seems to be both.**

Think of it as a *limit*. It is extremely transparent. The minute you move *into* it and penetrate the outer appearance, you're going on the Path of Return back to where it started. In other words, you're going in the direction of mind. The mind holds it all together, and any changes in the earth plane are mind changes. We get ideas, and with these we mold the earth. We're always redefining things.

▶ In one sense, the words "earth" and "world" are synonymous. Do I see a connection between this fact and the title of Key 21?

You've hit the bull's-eye! In the Cabalistic point of view, this plane that we are on is the most exquisite of all. This dirty old materialistic plane is the most sacred, most terrific level in the whole universe. It's the *perfect medium* for life expression. Its capabilities are beyond our comprehension. According to the doctrine, it is in a body that we can reach the ultimate in terms of sensing the beauty of the universe. That's the *reason* for the earth element. It's the end of the line, the final expression of life. Tarot calls it The World.

▶ "Heaven is where thou standest."

That's right. Wherever you stand, you are in an earthly vehicle. The Tarot has been telling us all along that the body is a marvelous instrument. Not only is it a vehicle for the senses, but it also has the ability to dance. The dance in Key 21 is a shorthand way of expressing all of the body's incredible possibilities that come to us as a free gift.

Somebody went to a lot of trouble to figure out how to make a body. Even though I happen to be the father of two children, I can't take any credit for knowing how to make it work. It's still a miracle to me. Once we understand that we are a miracle and decide to look for the miracle in ourselves, then we really get to enjoy what is going on in the universe.

The letter Tav is the Administrative Intelligence. It governs the pair of opposites, Dominion and Slavery. You won't be surprised to hear that this refers to *Self*-administration and management, which is the opposite of bondage to your own ignorance. The technique for getting control of yourself is meditation, because meditation is how you know yourself. Patanjali called it an unbroken flow of ideas on a subject. In plain English, this means that you can keep your mind where you want it. You don't get knocked off balance or wander away from the center of yourself.

▶ What else besides meditation can help me realize what I really am?

Education about the Self is of immense importance. There is a great deal of material available on this very important subject, but if you don't avail yourself of it, you can't learn anything. For thousands and thousands of years some of the best minds of the human race have wrestled with this problem, and they have come up with some answers. I won't say their conclusions were all equally good, but for sure they were all people like ourselves who sweated the problem out.

When it comes to the question, "What is a human being?" the scientific viewpoint has much to offer, let alone the occult or mystical approach. If you discover all there is to know about a human being from a study of the nature of the beast, then you will be very close to the answer of what you are.

Approach the problem and do the best you can with what you have, and by the process of elimination you will learn, among other things, what you are *not*. What's left after that is your Self.

The whole purpose of the technique of the Tarot and the Cabala is to persuade you somehow to be yourself. When you are grounded in the True Self, you won't overvalue or undervalue yourself. The midpoint between these two extremes is a joyful condition indeed. As always, the Cabala is not trying to make you over. It's not telling you to do this or that. It wants to refine your approach to life to such an extent that you won't miss anything. There is a *pressure* on us, in the form of a lurking dissatisfaction, to bring us to the point where we can appreciate the subtle as well as the gross.

▶ The results of spiritual practices are invisible. That's pretty subtle.

The advantage is that you can pass for Joe Doakes any time, no matter how advanced you are in this work. This is highly desirable. It would be terrible if you couldn't move freely in society without somebody making a big fuss. Outwardly, you can look just like anybody else, while inwardly there can be some vast changes.

▶ Is the unrecognized sage "the stone that the builders rejected?"

Not exactly. In *The Book of Tokens*, in his notes on the Tav meditation, Paul Case tells us that the Self is the Stone of the Wise. Everything, including magic, revolves around the Self because there is only One Self and our self is the same as That. When we don't want to be that Self, when we're not interested, that's when the stone is rejected.

▶ I've heard that it is extremely difficult for someone of the grade $10 = 1$ to incarnate on this plane. Is this true?

This grade is a reference to Ipsissimus, at the top of the Tree of Life. I'm not an expert on these grades. The Tree is an *experience,* a living reality. I don't know the answer to your question. All I know is that if you break your neck with the Tarot for x number of years, you finally get to Ipsissimus. Then you know who you are. You discover that you are just what you were before, but there's a lot of work to do!

There's an exact parellel in Zen practice. You go through the whole discipline and when you are done, the mountain is still the mountain. Now you *know exactly* what is happening. From there on you can do anything you want. The *main thing* is to make the proper Self-identification. Once you actually realize that everything you do is immediately connected with the cosmos on a one-to-one basis, your life becomes very expanded, right then and there. Ordinary consciousness interprets everything by reference to the personal ego. In cosmic consciousness, your point of reference is Life Itself.

The Tarot and the Cabala have been teaching us all along that we have a superior Self inside us. We also have a personality, which is inferior. The most magnificent personality in the world is still inferior to the True Self. We *do have* a True, Innermost Self, so that becomes the major consideration. What is *It* trying to do? For an accurate interpretation of *anything,* we have to refer to our highest aspect to find out what is really going on.

The masters of the Ageless Wisdom tell us that our Inner Self wants to give us the *best possible in everything.* It's not trying to put us down or deny us anything. Our *approach* to life is what's important. If we approach it in a haphazard fashion, we don't get the best of it. It's easy to miss the best part. That's why the Adversary fights you when you get in the way of the good that you could have. I assure you that the object of this teaching is that you shall receive the *crème de la crème,* the absolute best that Life has to offer. You couldn't ask for anything more. This is precisely what your Inner Self is asking for.

▶ How do I tell the difference between the resistance that is my medium of expression, and the resistance that means I'm on the wrong track?

If the resistance is expected, as a sculptor expects the marble to be hard—*c'est bon.* If the resistance comes as an unpleasant surprise, then it's a message from on high. At those times we experience friction between the Reality inside us and the personality, which thinks the ego knows best. Never forget that the Inner Self *is yourself*. If it were an outside force, that would make you feel bad, but it isn't. It is the truth of your being.

As time goes on, all of us travelers on the Way of Return will feel more and more at home with ourselves and learn how to take what Life has to offer. We shall become increasingly happier and more successful. So be it.

The procedure in this outstanding Tarot group is that we're going to do it all over again. If it's been working almost forty years, there's no use changing the format. For those of you who have a good, strong stomach, I hope I'll have the pleasure of your company for another round of Tarot meetings, as the Lord allows . . . and that's from the heart.

The Fool epitomizes the entire Tarot. Since we are well versed in symbolism by this time, Key 0 is not going to be the problem it was when I got my first look. I had never seen anything like it in my life. I was more than confused; I was obliterated. It won't be too difficult for us if we remember that the Tarot is not of this world. It deals with inner matters. The Fool represents our Innermost Self, which undertakes the great adventure of life and goes through the whole experience without being shaken. It's the only part of ourselves that can stand the strain.

The Fool is the Key that lifts your spirits more than any other because it shows you the essential freedom of your superconscious Self. The Self is the only sure cure for the blues. Key 0 typifies the Life Breath, the very *inspiration of all life* that enables The Fool to make us happy. We can turn to it with confident expectancy.

I want to thank you for joining me. It is a special joy to come here on Thursdays and be with you. God bless you.

Jason and Arisa on Mt. Tamalpias
Summer 1988

The Taroteers Picnic is held every year on Baker Beach in San Francisco, on the Sunday closest to the Fall Equinox. This was the 1988 invitation.

GLOSSARY

of Words EMPHASIZED on Their First Reference Only

achad (Hebrew) "unity." Has the numerical value of thirteen.
Adytum (Latin) "temple."
Ageless Wisdom Insight into Natural Law, or the Way Things Are, diversely expressed in every culture in the world.
aheba (Hebrew) "love." Has the numerical value of thirteen.
Aima (Hebrew) "Bright Mother." Manifesting power of the mind after insemination by the Paternal *Yod*.
Ain Suph Aur (Hebrew) "Limitless Light." Also called the "Radiant Darkness." Background of the Tree of Life. The source of everything.
Akashic Record (from Sanskrit *Akasha*) "pure space." The memory the cosmos has of itself.
alchemy (from Arabic) A cosmology in which God and Nature are One Thing. Modern science has its roots in alchemy.
Aleph (Hebrew) "ox." First letter of the alphabet. Symbol of the Life Breath. Associated with Key 0, The Fool.
Ama (Hebrew) "Dark Mother." Mind in its latent state.
ankh (ancient Egyptian) "eternal life."
Arcana (Latin) "Secret information known only to initiates."
Atma (Sanskrit) "the *Self*." Corresponds to *Kether* on the Tree of Life.
Ayin (Hebrew) "eye." Letter associated with Key 15, The Devil.
Beth (Hebrew) "house." Letter associated with Key 1, The Magician.
Bhagavad-Gita (Sanskrit) "Song of God." Ancient scripture, often called the Bible of India.
Bhakti (Sanskrit) "love, devotion." The *Yoga* of the Heart.
Binah (Hebrew) "Understanding." Third center on the Tree of Life. Seat of the Divine Mother.
Buddhi (Sanskrit) "discriminating intelligence." Corresponds to *Chokmah* on the Tree of Life.
Cabala (Anglicized Hebrew) "the Reception." The Secret Doctrine of

the West. A body of *Ageless Wisdom* received by sages through divine inspiration.

Chai (Hebrew)   "life."

chakras (Sanskrit)   "wheels." Seven vortexes of spiritual energy aligned with the human spine.

Chesed (Hebrew)   "Mercy, forgiveness, compassion, unconditional love." Fourth center on the Tree of Life.

Cheth (Hebrew)   "fence." Letter associated with Key 7, The Chariot.

Chokmah (Hebrew)   "Wisdom." Second center on the Tree of Life. Seat of the Divine Father.

Coagule (Latin)   "to make solid." An alchemical term for the reconstitution of one's True *Self*, after one's small personal identity has been dissolved in the preceding *Solve* stage.

Cube of Space.   A symbol of the physical universe. An alchemical diagram or three-dimensional model having six faces, eight points, and twelve edges; these add to twenty-six, the number of the *Tetragrammaton*. Meaning: God is immanent in creation; Reality is All That Is.

Da'ath (Hebrew)   "Knowledge." The invisible Sephirah on the Tree of Life, symbolizing the union of *Chokmah* and *Binah*.

Daleth (Hebrew)   "door." Letter associated with Key 3, The Empress.

desire-nature.   The Life Power experienced as motivating energy. Cabalists are trained to recognize its divine source and to trust its guidance.

dharma (Sanskrit)   "That which is permanent and free of change." Universal Law. The Way Things Are. Truth.

El (Hebrew)   "strength, power." The shortest Name of God in the Cabala.

Geburah (Hebrew)   "Severity." The fifth center on the Tree of Life. The resistance necessary for manifestation.

Gematria (Hebrew)   "complete measurement." Study of the hidden meanings and correspondences between numbers and words.

Gimel (Hebrew)   "camel." Letter associated with Key 2, The High Priestess.

golem (Hebrew)   "autonomous materialization."

Great Work.   Self-realization.

gunas (Sanskrit)   "qualities." Described in the *Bhagavad-Gita* as *sattva*, *rajas*, and *tamas*. These correspond to *Kether, Chokmah*, and *Binah* on the Tree of Life, and to mercury, sulfur, and salt in *alchemy*.

Heh (Hebrew)   "window." Letter associated with Key 4, The Emperor.

Hermes Trismegistus (Greek)   "Thrice-great messenger of the gods." The inventor of occult science. The enlightened intellect.

Hod (Hebrew)   "Splendor." Eighth center on the Tree of Life. Refers to the enlightened intellect.

Intelligences.   "The Powers That Be." Various expressions of superconsciousness as symbolized by the 32 paths of wisdom on the Tree of Life.

Ipsissimus (Latin)   "He who is most himself; she who is most herself." Highest of the Rosicrucian grades of initiation. Corresponds to *Kether* on the Tree of Life.

Kaph (Hebrew)   "grasping hand." Letter associated with Key 10, The Wheel of Fortune.

karma (Sanskrit)   "work, action." Action causes reaction, creating a chain of cause and effect.

Kether (Hebrew)   "Crown." First center on the Tree of Life. The Indivisible *Self*. The Primal Will-to-Good.

kundalini (Sanskrit)   "serpent fire." The life force in the *chakras*.

Lamed (Hebrew)   "ox-goad." Letter associated with Key 11, Justice.

lemniscate (Latin)   "infinity." Rhythmic interplay of opposing forces.

lingam-yoni (Sanskrit)   "male/female sex organs." Symbol of the Divine Marriage. Union of opposites. The fire in the water.

Lux Occulta (Latin)   "hidden light." The principle of consciousness. Corresponds to the *Ain Suph Aur*.

magic (from old Persian)   Transmutation of personality into a conscious temple of the Holy Spirit.

Malkuth (Hebrew)   "Kingdom." Tenth and final center on the Tree of Life. The physical universe.

Man (from Sanskrit *manas*)   "Focus of attention in the mind."

Manas (Sanskrit)   "mind." Corresponds to *Binah* on the Tree of Life.

mantram (Sanskrit)   A phrase that an aspirant repeats continually in order to quiet the mind.

Mem (Hebrew)   "water." Letter associated with Key 12, The Hanged Man.

Messiah (Hebrew)   "savior." Through *Gematria*, numerically equivalent to *Nachash*.

Mezla (Hebrew)   "influence." Divine Grace. The conscious energy that flows through all things.

mother letters. The Hebrew letters *Aleph, Mem, and Shin.* An expression of the *Three Supernals.*

Nachash (Hebrew) "serpent, tempter." Through *Gematria*, numerically equivalent to *Messiah.*

namaste (Sanskrit) A gesture that means, "I bow to the *Self* in you."

neti, neti (Sanskrit) "not this, not that." A practice designed to reveal True Identity.

Netzach (Hebrew) "Victory." Seventh center on the Tree of Life. Overcoming ignorance.

Nun (Hebrew) "fish; to sprout." Letter associated with Key 13, Death.

Ouroboros (Latin) A serpent biting its own tail, illustrating how life feeds on itself.

Pachad (Hebrew) "fear." The beginning of wisdom. Attributed to the fifth center on the Tree of Life.

Peh (Hebrew) "mouth." Letter associated with Key 16, The Tower.

Prima Materia (Latin) "first matter." Substance aspect of mind.

Qoph (Hebrew) "back of the head." Letter associated with Key 18, The Moon.

race-thought. An ignorant mind-set that is held in place by social agreement.

rajas (Sanskrit) "fire, passion." Predominating *rajas guna.*

Ramayana (Sanskrit) Rambling epic from ancient India.

Resh (Hebrew) "face." Letter associated with Key 19, The Sun.

samadhi (Sanskrit) A superconscious, formless state in which there is no distinction between subject and object.

Samech (Hebrew) "tent-peg, prop." Letter associated with Key 14, Temperance.

sattva (Sanskrit) "full of light." Predominating *sattva guna.*

Secret Doctrine. The inner teaching, common to all spiritual traditions, that God and the *Self* are One.

Sephiroth (Hebrew) "spheres." The ten centers on the Tree of Life. Singular: *Sephirah.*

Shin (Hebrew) "tooth, fang." Letter associated with Key 20, Judgement.

Solve (Latin) "to dissolve." An alchemical term for release from ego-mind. Followed by *Coagule.*

tamas (Sanskrit) "full of darkness." Predominating *tamas guna.*

Tao (Chinese) "The Way." What is. Reality.

tapas (Sanskrit) Spiritual practice to discipline the mind.

Tav (Hebrew) "signature." Last letter in the alphabet. Associated with Key 21, The World.

temenos (Greek) "a sacred precinct."

Teth (Hebrew) "snake." Letter associated with Key 8, Strength.

Tetragrammaton (Hebrew) "Name of four letters." *Yod-Heh-Vav-Heh.* That which was, is, and shall be. Symbol of the four elements. Formula of divine creation.

Three Supernals. Trinity of consciousness at the top of the Tree of Life: *Kether* = superconsciousness, *Chokmah* = self-consciousness, *Binah* = subconsciousness.

Tiphareth (Hebrew) "Beauty." Sixth center on the Tree of Life.

Tora (Hebrew) "law."

Trimurti (Sanskrit) "threefold pantheon." Brahma the Creator, *Vishnu* the Preserver, and Shiva the Destroyer. Corresponds to the *Three Supernals*.

Tzaddi (Hebrew) "fishhook." Letter attributed to Key 17, The Star.

Upanishads (Sanskrit) "secret teachings." Part of India's most ancient scriptures. The doctrine of the *Self*.

Vav (Hebrew) "hook, link." Letter associated with Key 5, The Hierophant.

Vishnu (Sanskrit) "preserver." Second member of the *Trimurti*. Said to have incarnated as Krishna, Buddha, and Jesus.

yang and *yin* (Chinese) The eternal opposites. Correspond to *Chokmah* and *Binah*.

Yekhidah (Hebrew) "indivisible one." The Supreme *Self* seated in *Kether*.

Yesod (Hebrew) "Foundation." Ninth center on the Tree of Life. Corresponds to the reproductive *chakra*.

Yetzirah (Hebrew) "formation." Third of the Cabalistic Worlds: Atziluth = archetypal, Briah = creative, Yetzirah = formative, Assiah = physical.

Yod (Hebrew) "open hand." A living flame. The Life Essence. Letter associated with Key 9, The Hermit.

Yod-Heh-Vav-Heh (Hebrew) The Cabalistic Name of Names. Worn on the garments of The Fool and the Temperance angel.

Yoga (Sanskrit) "union." The end of dualism. Identification with the Only *Self*."

Zain (Hebrew) "sword." Letter associated with Key 6, The Lovers.

❋✥ HOW TO ORDER ✥❋

✥❋✥❋✥❋✥

THIS BOOK
The Spoken Cabala: Tarot Explorations of the One Self
by Jason Lotterhand
Edited by Arisa Victor

(formerly The Thursday Night Tarot)

Words of truth that go to the heart. - Mary K. Greer

✥❋✥❋✥❋✥

THE COMPANION VOLUME TO THIS BOOK
High School Astrology: A Textbook of Ageless Wisdom
by Arisa Victor

All you need to know to be intelligent about astrology.

✥❋✥❋✥❋✥

OTHER BOOKS BY THIS PUBLISHER
Featuring the early work of Paul Foster Case,
Jason's Teacher
and Arisa's Teacher through written Lessons

✥❋✥❋✥❋✥

Please go to

The Fraternity of the Hidden Light
Fraternitas Lux Occulta

www.lvx.org

The Thursday Night Tarot classes continue to this day.

For information about
The Thursday Night Tarot

Contact Tanya Joyce

(415) 822-8839

Tanya@norcov.com

www.norcov.com/brushworks

www.ingramcontent.com/pod-product-compliance
Lightning Source LLC
Chambersburg PA
CBHW082033230426

43670CB00016B/2640